MW01671008

Global Future
The Next Challenge for Asian Business

Global Future
The Next Challenge for Asian Business

Arnoud De Meyer
Pamela C.M. Mar
Frank Jürgen Richter
Peter Williamson

John Wiley & Sons (Asia) Pte Ltd

Copyright © 2005 by John Wiley & Sons (Asia) Pte Ltd
Published in 2005 by John Wiley & Sons (Asia) Pte Ltd
2 Clementi Loop #02-01, Singapore 129809

All rights reserved.

No part of this publication may be reproduced, stored in a retrieval system or transmitted in any form or by any means, electronic, mechanical, photocopying, recording, scanning or otherwise, except as expressly permitted by law, without either the prior written permission of the Publisher, or authorization through payment of the appropriate photocopy fee to the Copyright Clearance Center. Requests for permission should be addressed to the Publisher, John Wiley & Sons (Asia) Pte Ltd, 2 Clementi Loop, #02-01, Singapore 129809, tel: 65-64632400, fax: 65-64634605, email: enquiry@wiley.com.sg.

This publication is designed to provide accurate and authoritative information in regard to the subject matter covered. It is sold with the understanding that the Publisher is not engaged in rendering professional services. If professional advice or other expert assistance is required, the services of a competent professional person should be sought.

■ Other Wiley Editorial Offices:
John Wiley & Sons, Inc., 111 River Street, Hoboken, NJ 07030, USA
John Wiley & Sons Ltd, The Atrium, Southern Gate, Chichester, PO19 8SQ, England
John Wiley & Sons (Canada) Ltd, 22 Worcester Road, Rexdale, Ontario M9W 1L1, Canada
John Wiley & Sons Australia Ltd, PO Box 174, North Ryde, NSW 2113, Australia
Wiley - VCH, Boschstrasse 12, 69469 Weinheim, Germany

■ Library of Congress Cataloging in Publication Data

ISBN 13 978-0-4708-2130-5
ISBN 10 0-470-82130-2

Typeset in 10.5 points, Times by Paul Lim.
Printed in Singapore by Sail Wah Press Pte Ltd.
10 9 8 7 6 5 4 3

Table of Contents

PART 1

Asian Firms Globalize: The Evidence to Date

CHAPTER

1 The Globalization Imperative

Look through any list of the world's truly global companies – organizations with an integrated network of subsidiaries that span the world – and Asian companies are under-represented compared with their American and European counterparts. This is despite Asia's long trading history and high-profile multinational pioneers from Asia, such as Sony, Samsung and Kikkoman, whose international expansion we explore later in this book.

Today, however, more and more Asian companies are embarking on a transformation that will propel them from national champions into global players. Asia's corporate tigers are taking the global leap.

In this book we examine the new globalization imperative facing Asian companies; what they can learn from the experience of pioneers, builders, and newcomers as they embark on the globalization challenge. We look at the main steps involved as companies "climb the globalization staircase" and what Asian companies can do to improve the chances that they will succeed in building sustainable global organizations – possibly "leap-frogging" older multinationals to create a new breed of global corporations.

Drawing insights from respected Asian chief executives, experts in finance, brand building and people management, and from leading researchers, along with our own experiences, we hope this book will assist Asian companies as they globalize. It should also be of interest to Western multinationals that need to understand the new competitive challenge from Asian companies in global markets.

New pressures to globalize

Historically, most Asian companies pursued some mix of two basic strategies in the face of globalization:

(1) To wall off their home market and become a dominant player locally and
(2) To penetrate overseas markets by exporting from their home base.

Compared with their American and European counterparts, relatively few invested in building extensive networks of subsidiaries with full-fledged sales, manufacturing and service operations, and support functions around the world. Even among those who did, even fewer developed the processes and systems to run them as a single, integrated, global company rather than a portfolio of semi-autonomous businesses scattered around the globe.

Reluctant globalizers

In yesterday's environment, these strategies made a great deal of sense. Until recently, Asia was a collection of highly segregated national markets, separated from each other by a mix of tariff and non-tariff barriers, divergent choices about local standards, and regulatory differences between countries. Within this environment, it made sense for companies to approach each national market pretty much as a separate competitive playing field. This fragmentation was reinforced by various forms of preference given by governments to their local companies through the allocation of licenses, preferential access to finance, and other kinds of direct and indirect support.

Fragmented national markets meant that Asian companies rightly focused on becoming big fish in their local pond. Leveraging their local knowledge and relationships in their protected home-country market, a majority of Asian companies chose to diversify their assets across industries to form sprawling local conglomerates with interests in everything from agricultural products, through manufacturing to property and financial services. Moving into a series of different industries while staying within their national borders allowed Asian firms to exploit their strong relationships with local or national governments, maximize their bargaining power with local distributors and suppliers and access capital from local banks.

When they competed internationally, meanwhile, many Asian companies found their primary weapon was efficient, low-cost manufacturing or service operations – especially while America and Europe were their major markets. Establishing operations overseas would only threaten to undermine this basic advantage. Furthermore, it often made sense to focus on their main source of advantage and to leave local marketing, distribution and service to others with already established networks and existing competence in these areas. Not surprisingly, a popular strategy was to become a subcontract supplier to an original equipment manufacturer (OEM) or to provide outsourced services to established companies overseas, rather than building a multinational. Likewise, many relied on local distributors to perform sales, marketing and service in foreign markets.

The new imperative

Yesterday's environment may have given little incentive for Asian companies to globalize. But the reverse is true today: globalization is now becoming an imperative for more and more Asian firms. The reasons are fivefold.

First, following the Asian financial crisis of 1997, the IMF and other international bodies exerted pressure on the governments of many Asian countries to gradually open up their markets to international competition. Singapore has probably implemented the most far-reaching and rapid changes in this direction, but similar liberalization processes have been initiated in Thailand, Korea, Taiwan and even in Indonesia and Malaysia. These have included the liberalization of restrictions on inward foreign direct investment and cross-border acquisitions as well as moves to reduce intra-Asian trade barriers. Examples of trade liberalization include plans to turn ASEAN into a free-trade area, Singapore's pursuit of bilateral free-trade agreements with its main trading partners, and China's entry into the WTO.

Where trade and cross-border investment barriers had already been removed, multinational companies such as Shell, Toyota, GE Capital or Citibank's card services tended to dominate their respective market segments across Asia. Local companies such as banks in Malaysia, telecommunications companies like SingTel, automobile assemblers such as Astra in Indonesia or Hicom in Malaysia, not to mention the numerous state-owned Enterprises (SOEs) in China, could succeed in the past because they operated in protected sectors and in many cases acted as "national champions". These protective barriers are obviously not being removed overnight. However, gradual liberalization of trade and investment will inevitably result in the incumbent national champions coming under increased competitive pressure from multinational players both through imports and new entry via expansion or acquisition.[1] In response, Asian companies will themselves be forced to globalize in order to remain competitive.

Second, the Asian financial crisis revealed the weakness of the horizontal diversification that had been pursued by many Asian companies. Companies whose core competencies were spread too thinly across a multitude of different businesses were among the most severely impacted, because they lacked the depth of knowledge and managerial capabilities to compete across such a wide variety of businesses in the tough market conditions that have continued ever since the crisis. If diversification into new businesses is no longer viable as the primary way to grow, an obvious alternative is geographic diversification through cross-border expansion of Asian companies' core businesses – those where they enjoy a depth of specialist capabilities.[2] Globalization has therefore become increasingly important as a way to sustain growth.

Third, prior to the late 1990s the profitability of many Asian companies had arguably been heavily underpinned by their ability to leverage the information asymmetries that abounded in an environment characterized by underdeveloped information and communications infrastructure and lack of transparency. Where much of the current investment in information and communications technologies (ICT) in the U.S., Europe and Japan will have an incremental impact, in much of Asia embracing ICT is likely to result in a step-change in transparency and accessibility of information. This will put pressure on the ability of Asian firms to profit from information asymmetries that have underpinned their competitiveness in local markets. One result for them may be to look for opportunities to use the new ICT infrastructure to exploit the cross-border synergies available from globalization to restore margins and open up new profit streams.

Fourth, with the continued emergence of China as "the factory of the world" and India as the world's "back-office" more and more companies from other Asian companies will find that their home base is no longer competitive as the base for the majority of their manufacturing or back-office service operations. To maintain their existing supply-chain advantages they will need to globalize – perhaps relocating some operations to China and India and others closer to their target markets to provide more rapid response and customization.

Finally, many Asian companies now need to broaden their sources of competitive advantage well beyond the low cost of manufacturing or service operations. This means they need to build their own brands, distribution capabilities and service centres in markets around the world. To better differentiate their products and services, they may also need to conduct R&D in global hotbeds of new technology and locations with a deep pool of qualified scientists and engineers, to complement innovation activities at home. This will require the globalization of a new, broader range of activities than in the past.

Together these powerful forces of change are reshaping the competitive environment for Asian companies. For many companies, globalization will be a key to success in this new competitive game.

Challenges of becoming global

Becoming a truly global company means much more than establishing a portfolio of units in different countries around the world. To gain competitive advantage from globalization, the whole must be worth more, in terms of efficiency and/or the capacity to create value for customers, than the sum of its parts. This requires not only global reach, but also the infrastructure, processes and systems that allow the company to gain some or all of the following types of advantages:

- The ability to reap economies of scale in purchasing, manufacturing, capital raising, provision of support services, etc. and from spreading the fixed costs of R&D and product development or brand building over global volume.
- The ability to arbitrage between alternative sources of inputs – sourcing from the most cost-effective locations for everything from raw materials through equipment to support services and talent.
- The ability to co-ordinate across borders so as to provide superior service to multinational customers or those who are mobile (such as international travellers).
- The capability to match the competitive advantages enjoyed by other global competitors and to compete effectively with the same rivals in multiple markets simultaneously.
- The ability to tailor a successful product developed in one market for other markets and to create local variations that respond to different cultures and needs, without losing the distinctive advantages of the original or stretching their brand to breaking point.
- The capability to generate knowledge in different units around the world and both to deploy that new knowledge locally as well as share it with other parts of their global company so as to enhance innovation, reduce costs or improve value to customers.

Clearly, a pure exporter will not be in a position to reap these kinds of advantages of globalization; nor will a company whose global reach is based on establishing a portfolio of largely independent subsidiaries with a low level of mutual interaction.

What then are the key challenges that companies typically face in moving towards this ideal of a global company? Our research suggests these challenges fall into the following categories: laying down the necessary infrastructure (ranging from financial to supply-chain networks); building the necessary capabilities (like brand building or people development); and creating a sustainable global organization that is capable both of learning and of forming viable, long-term relationships with the different stakeholders in the global environment – some of whom may not even be directly connected with the company's operations.

In embarking on these tasks, however, Asian companies need to be particularly mindful of the need to deal with four important handicaps that arise from the kinds of strategies pursued by most Asian companies in the past: strategies that emphasize local presence ("planting the flag") over reaping network economies; under-investment in intangible assets and systems; lack of international experience and capabilities; and a heritage of highly centralized organizations.

Breaking free of the "plant the flag" mindset

Traditional models of internationalization have tended to be based on taking products or services and systems companies perfected at home and replicating these offerings in new, national markets. To achieve sales growth, companies following this approach begin by selling in "nearby" countries (where cultural and economic closeness is more important than geographic distance). This makes it possible to enter new markets without significantly changing either the specifications of the offering or the operations, processes and systems that are used to deliver it. Such firms, therefore, start internationalizing by establishing sales, distribution and service offices overseas. As the local sales grow, they typically add new activities to their offshore subsidiaries, creating mini replicas of their home-base organizations.

Following this internationalization strategy often leads to widely dispersed networks of international subsidiaries linked back to the headquarters, but relatively independent of each other. Internationalization becomes a matter of "planting the flag" in promising new markets.

Asian companies that have adopted this traditional internationalization strategy have frequently suffered from its limitations. Companies like Samsung Automobiles and Daewoo Motors ended up with subsidiaries scattered from Poland to Uzbekistan, each operation isolated from its sisters. In its first phase of internationalization (from 1993-1997), the Filipino fast-food company, Jollibee, established 23 stores, scattered across 10 countries. Lacking the critical mass to gain customers' attention in each of these isolated markets, and with little scope for sharing local fixed costs among stores, each was operating at half the estimated minimum efficient scale.

In order to globalize, Asian companies will need to abandon this "plant-the-flag" model of internationalization. As with leading-edge multinationals from the US and Europe, today the focus will need to shift towards reaping significant network economies by inter-linking their subsidiaries in a tightly connected web. Such a web may be designed to exploit potential cost synergies between subsidiaries, share technologies, systems and best practices, or to unlock new potential for innovation.

Breaking out of this "plant-the-flag" mindset, however, is only one orthodoxy that Asian companies must overcome in order to globalize. A second important change will be an increased willingness to invest in brands, proprietary technologies and systems that they can take with them to compete in overseas markets.

Under-investment in intangible assets

Many Asian companies have prospered based largely on what can be termed "resource-based" advantages: access to low-cost raw materials and labor, preferential access to capital, and government licenses obtained through local relationships. The Salim Group and Asian Pulp and Paper originating in Indonesia or Renong and TRI in Malaysia are good examples. These companies often came to dominate their home markets.

These types of resource-based advantages, however, are largely immobile. A company that thrives because of low raw-material costs or access to a government license can potentially export its product competitively. But a company that relies on resource-based advantages will have little to bring to an overseas market when it establishes a subsidiary there.

The more enlightened of Asian companies, such as Astra of Indonesia or San Miguel of the Philippines, built efficient local assembly plants, powerful distribution networks and sometimes strong local brands to reinforce their underlying resource-based advantages. These types of advantages rest on physical assets that can be replicated in a foreign location. But to the extent that a company is no better than its local or other foreign competitors in building assets like plants, distribution networks and brands in an overseas market, it will lack any competitive advantage as it globalizes.

Foreign direct investors mostly win when they have "system-based" advantages that leverage intangible assets like quality systems, marketing competence, technology and know-how that are proprietary. These are the kinds of competitive advantages that can be transferred to markets which lack these systems. Leading multinationals like Unilever, Procter and Gamble, BP or IBM have prospered by reaping the advantages of their ability to transfer these intangible assets across borders. The problem for most Asian companies is that they generally haven't invested enough in these intangible assets to give themselves a strong platform of systems, brands and technologies that they can use to outcompete the incumbents when they enter an overseas market.

As we will see later in this book, these are Asian companies that have built intangible assets that become a springboard for profitable globalization. Other Asian companies that wish to become global will need to invest in these kinds of assets too.

Gaps in international capabilities

Another important challenge faced by Asian companies seeking to globalize is the significant gap that often exists between their existing capabilities and the skill base necessary for effective expansion across borders. When DBS acquired Thai Danu bank in Thailand (its first significant acquisition overseas), for example, it had only a handful of staff with extensive overseas experience. Its systems for managing overseas units were designed for the relatively simple exchanges between the headquarters and a branch of the bank, not for the complex interaction between Singaporean divisions and a significant overseas entity like Thai Danu, which at the time had over 90 branches of its own. In DBS, a well-oiled Singaporean machine, specialist capabilities were most important. By contrast, in controlling and integrating an overseas subsidiary the skills of an "all-rounder" with entrepreneurial flair were most critical. These capability gaps cost DBS dearly in the initial aftermath of the acquisition as the Asian financial crisis of 1997 worsened. Subsequently the bank recognized that if it were to build and manage an Asian regional bank successfully it would have to systematically fill the capability gaps that were impeding its international expansion through a mix of selective hiring, training and job rotation to build experience.

Likewise, when the Taiwanese computer giant, Acer, set out to build a global position in the branded, personal computer business, its CEO, Stan Shih, observed:

> *"This is the weak point of Taiwanese companies – they are not able to exploit their technical capability to the level where it reaches their market potential... Global expansion and decentralization demand many qualities from managers – business sense, understanding of corporate mission, the ability to control operations, adapt to local conditions and adjust to change. It is difficult to develop such people, especially to meet the needs of overseas operations."*

Clearly, globalization demands that companies invest in building, hiring or acquiring a cadre of management and staff with the necessary experience and skills first to establish or acquire viable operations overseas and then to run the resulting international network.

A heritage of highly centralized organization structures

A final challenge that many Asian companies must overcome before they can globalize successfully is to overcome their organization's centralized decision-making processes. Centralization of decision making – often as a result of control by a powerful founder-patriarch or family clique – has many benefits: it facilitates frequent, face-to-face interaction (the ultimate in "high-bandwith" communication), promotes chance encounters, and helps engender the development of teams where people are both "in-tune" and "in-synch" with each other. But centralization often gets in the way of running a far-flung international network successfully.

Of course, this problem is not unique to Asian companies; many of today's successful Western global companies faced the same challenge. It is particularly acute for Asian companies, however, because they have traditionally relied on close personal ties between individuals, often from the same family group, high levels of shared understanding, and subtle, highly personal interaction where decision factors and criteria are implicit, to manage their companies. Organizations with a much greater reliance on explicit rules, procedures and memos in the management process, by contrast, generally find it easier to cope with the "tyranny of distance" that frequently accompanies the globalization of a company. With more of their management processes explicit and codified, they can make more use of information and communications technologies to bridge distance and time zones. The management processes and style of many Asian companies, by contrast, tend to aggravate the tyranny of distance and limit the scope for effective information and communications technology solutions.

Some Asian companies have addressed this problem by despatching family members, or trusted lieutenants, to manage their overseas subsidiaries, thereby ensuring that key managers have a shared understanding of the organization and management process and are likely to be "in tune" with others in the group. Obviously, however, for most large companies this provides only a limited and temporary solution. Their international expansion is therefore likely to be impeded by the nature of their management processes compared to competitors who have grown up in a different management tradition.

This impediment to internationalization can be observed even among Korean companies like Samsung who have been in the vanguard of recent overseas expansion by Asian companies. When setting up a plant in Berlin, for example, Samsung had at one point more than 200 of its engineers or the engineers of its partners stationed there in order to transfer the knowledge from Korea to Germany. Afterwards it invested heavily in programs to socialize German workers and supervisors into the culture of the company and to integrate them into the tacit knowledge base of Samsung. On the one hand, this could be seen as evidence of an enormous commitment from Samsung to its Berlin plant. But it also demonstrates its inability to transfer culture and know-how in a more cost-effective way.

Taking the leap

Transforming themselves into effective global organizations clearly presents a formidable challenge for Asian companies. But, as we will see in the case studies that follow, they are now tackling this agenda with power and agility. And, paradoxically, the fact that many are latecomers to the globalization game may open up a number of potential advantages they can exploit.

The first, and perhaps most obvious, advantage is Asian companies have examples to learn from and to follow. While the challenges we identified above are typical for Asian companies, they are not unique. Many former "national champions" from Europe, smaller companies in particular, faced similar capability gaps. French companies, for example, often began with more resource-based advantages than system-based advantages when they started down the road to internationalization. Meanwhile, pioneering companies, many from Japan and Korea, have shown that it is possible to overcome the difficulties quite rapidly and emerge as powerful global players.

Asian companies coming late to the globalization game can also benefit from a second advantage: talented and successful Asians have preceded their companies overseas. The best universities of the U.S., Australia, the U.K. and, to some extent, continental Europe are populated with many Asians. Some of these best and brightest have stayed, others have returned home. If cleverly exploited, this group can be an enormous advantage to a budding global corporation. Those who have stayed overseas form a potential network of allies; the ones that have returned bring home potentially a vast wealth of know-how about foreign markets and culture. But a prerequisite to leveraging this potential advantage is an appreciation that today it is knowledge and values, not just resources, that will be decisive in future global competitive battles.

A third advantage that should not be underestimated as a potential contributor to speeding up the internationalization of Asian companies is the underlying power of their local economies, from which these companies can draw strength. China has both massive capacity and market potential and is well managed economically. India is equally big and has the advantage of a reasonably strong infrastructure for business and education. Meanwhile, Southeast Asia should not be underestimated. Together, the major Southeast Asian countries comprise 450 million potential consumers, currently with a higher spending power than in either China or India. As we have already pointed out, successful globalization must be built on company-specific competitive advantage. If and when a company has such an advantage, it is also likely to be strong in its home market. The sheer size and relative robustness of these major home markets consequently provide an advantage for Asian companies to leverage as they build their global positions.

The remainder of this book is devoted to understanding how Asian companies can rise to the challenge of building successful and sustainable global companies, leveraging their unique advantages along the way. Part I analyzes the evidence to date, starting with the lessons offered by early pioneers like Sony, Samsung and Kikkoman. We then examine the experiences of companies well down the path of building global or pan-Asian networks, companies such as Li & Fung, Singapore Telecom and Olam. Finally we turn to the initiatives being adopted by those who have more recently embarked on globalization, including Uni-President, ICBC and China Netcom. We conclude this part with a contribution from George Yip and Ruiming Lin looking at the role of different locations within Asia in companies' globalization efforts.

In Part II, we examine the key steps required to build a global company:

1. Laying down the infrastructure – from the necessary international networks through to a solid financial base that can support the investment necessary to expand globally.
2. Building the necessary capabilities – for brand building through to people development.
3. Achieving sustainability – through continuous learning, the ability to grow in tune with society and the environment, and to maintain long-run competitiveness.

Together these steps form a "globalization staircase" which we believe companies must climb if they are to build sustainable global positions. The choice of this "staircase" analogy is not accidental: it reflects a number of key observations which are elaborated throughout the book. First is the fact that building a global company requires a sustained and determined campaign; you can climb the staircase at the pace you choose, but trying to skip steps is dangerous and risks creating an unstable global edifice. Second is the idea that there is an over-arching sequence to building a global company – foundations come first, followed by the necessary capabilities to push on higher and further. The third message is that climbing each step is an active process that involves corporate and personal learning; the learning loop involved in taking each step will help both to consolidate your position and to prepare you for the next ascent.

Finally, we explore what we see as an exciting opportunity for Asian companies to focus on building sustainable global companies as a guiding objective, rather than an afterthought – as has been the case for many of their Western predecessors. Faced not only with increased competition, but also increasing public disquiet about the impact of globalization and the role of global companies within it, sustainability of global strategies and organizations is now critical because it is far from assured. A key question we pose is whether Asian companies will grasp that opportunity with both hands or let it slip from their grasp.

Endnotes

1 Data on cross-border M&A in Asia, for example, grew strongly from 1997, reaching a peak of over $15 billion in deals in 2001.

2 This argument has been analyzed in more detail in P.J. Williamson, *Winning in Asia: Strategies for the New Millennium*, Harvard Business School Press, 2004.

CHAPTER

2 The Pioneers

There was a time when pundits and business strategists predicted that Asia's fast-growing corporations would dominate major industries across the globe.[1] Sony's takeover of Columbia Pictures and CBS Records, the sale of the Rockefeller Center (and pricey Hawaii properties) to Japanese buyers, and the rise of Korean giants Daewoo, Kia and Hyundai seemed to pressage the coming dominance of Asia's leading companies. The success of the "tiger" economies and its attribution to the "Asian work ethic" or "Asian corporate culture" only underscored the rise of Asia over the West.

Japan's bubble of 1992 and its "lost decade", and the Asian financial crisis of 1997 followed by the unraveling of major Asian conglomerates brought high expectations back down to earth. Certainly there were clear cases of reversals of fortune – such as the acquisition of Nissan by Renault and the splintering of Daewoo – but, in retrospect, the crises have created sieves through which only the toughest Asian companies emerged. Indeed those who have survived used crisis to identify and resolve weaknesses and outplay regional peers. They often did not follow Asia's tradional models of corporate organization such as the *keiretsu*[2] in Japan and the *chaebol*[3] in Korea which gave a clear resource-based advantage. They preferred to build up systems-based advantages such as superior supply-chain management, global branding and a global approach towards human resources. It is hardly coincidental that one common trait in their survival stories is the perceived need to globalize operations or markets, or both. This may seem to recall the heady days of the "expansion-at-all costs" mentality which prevailed before the Asian crisis but, in fact, is of a very different nature.

The three companies featured in this section evolved along the lines of very careful but purposeful globalization. They are true pioneers in that they globalized from the early days of their inception, albeit in varying degrees. Nobuyuki Idei, Chairman and CEO of Sony Corporation, Japan, Yuzaburo Mogi, Chairman and CEO of Kikkoman Corporation, Japan, and Yun Jong Yong, Vice Chairman and CEO of Samsung Electronics Co, Ltd., South Korea, relate their personal journeys towards globalizing their respective companies – experiences of constant learning. Their individual leadership is tightly bound with the success of their respective companies. In addition, they developed the organizations based on long-term commitment and loyalty – a feature now rare in the Western world.

Nobuyuki Idei has spent his whole working life at Sony, and his vision and authority is poised to make as deep an imprint on the company's development as the legendary co-founder Akio Morita. Idei steered Sony through Japan's economic crisis of the 1990s by leading the company's transformation from a maker of electronics into a global leader in entertainment and design. He was one of the first Japanese CEOs to instill so-called Western concepts of corporate governance in a way that allowed harmony across different cultures and economies, bringing the company closer to both customers and shareholders. Sony's success story is well known. With revenues of US$72 billion in the year 2003–2004, Sony is probably the best-known consumer-electronics company in the world. Sony's products include video and audio equipment, television sets, displays, semiconductors, computers and information-storage devices such as micro floppy-disk systems, as well as multi-media products (music and film). As one of the first Japanese companies to go global, Sony has become a household name around the world, thanks to highly innovative products such as the Walkman. Sony's technological achievements in product design, production and marketing helped transform the perception of the "Made in Japan" label from a notion of cheap imitations to one associated with superior quality.

Yuzaburo Mogi is a descendent of one of Kikkoman's founding families which still holds a controlling interest in the company. Kikkoman Corp. is the world's largest producer of soy sauce and one of the oldest Japanese companies. Under Mogi's leadership, the company evolved from being a local producer of a traditional food product into a global powerhouse, with worldwide name recognition and a differentiated product line. The internationalization of Kikkoman started only in the middle of the last century when soy sauce was being sold to Japanese living overseas. Overseas production plants followed in the early 1970s. Kikkoman´s qualification as a true global player came mainly as a result of the company's pioneering investments in the United States, which demonstrated the benefits that foreign direct investment can bring to two and more countries. Kikkoman took a traditional Japanese product – soy sauce – and produced it in the United States. Kikkoman soy sauce is currently relished in almost 100 countries, and the company makes its product in five overseas locations, including Europe and Asia.

Yun Jong Yong has steered Samsung Electronics from a basic manufacturer into a major consumer-products maker that is competing with the established players. He has introduced striking changes that have established the company as a world leader in semiconductor, telecommunication and digital convergence technology. The company was founded in 1969, making cheap TVs under Japan's Sanyo label and generating a high turnover through Original Equipment Manufacturing (OEM) and me-too products. Samsung Electronics flourished for decades, expanding into semiconductors and other high-tech products. In 1993, the company's chairman, Lee Kun Hee, triggered a corporate revolution by introducing an initiative for quality improvement and powerful globalization.[4] He recognized that the company could no longer thrive merely on the basis of its me-too philosophy, and he conveyed the message that Samsung had to accelerate its pace of globalization. Since then, Samsung Electronics has managed to produce more than 70% of its products outside Korea, compared with less than 10% in 1993. In 1997, however, the Asian crisis took its toll. South Korea's companies had become too affluent and its workers too well paid. CEO Yun was determined to give up old ways of doing things in favor of basic business common sense. He slashed production of marginal businesses and sold non-core assets. Most importantly, Samsung Electronics diversified into new high-margin, hi-tech businesses. No longer a copycat producer, Samsung Electronics is now a true innovator on a global scale.

These three companies followed a certain logic of strategic development, focusing on corporate growth based around core advantages and core capabilities, before embarking on the drive to globalization. Early on, they started to network with partners overseas, and tried to tap into international sources of capital. In rapid succession, they also succeeded in integrating capabilities through the establishment of consistent processes in human resources, quality and branding.

The test of any expansion or globalization process is sustainability, or the company's ability to sustain its short-term gains over the long haul. In this regard, Sony, Kikkoman and Samsung Electronics are all poised to carry their gains into the future. Having fulfilled the major steps required for globalization, they stick to good corporate governance, recognizing that pursuing a strict code of ethics that encourages socially responsible activities will promote the development of environments conducive to business and is, therefore, in their best interests. As good corporate citizens, they help by providing basic needs to the underprivileged. As Nobuyuki Idei points out: "We cannot wait for others to take up the mantle of responsibility. It belongs to each and every one of us, and it is up to each of us to contemplate what needs to be done today."[5]

Success is never eternal. Ultimately, the processes of globalization may also take a toll on Sony and other stars from Asia. At the height of its success, Sony is already confronted by competitors that are able to copy its ideas and products and sell them more cheaply and sometimes only months after their release. Undoubtedly, the company has entered a time of crisis, with sales and profits plunging and the company being forced into a major restructuring. Idei has announced the need to slash 20,000 jobs and to trim fixed costs by US$3 billion by 2006. He noted Samsung Electronics' "aggressive restructuring" and concluded that "to survive as a global player, we too have to change". The profit margins of Sony's core electronics division are slim, and the innovation drive is no longer as fast as it once was. Facing mounting financial losses, in the autumn of 2003 Sony and the German media giant Bertelsmann proposed a merger of their music divisions in an attempt to prevent further shrinkage. The merger may lead to further severe job cuts and consolidation of the companies' labels.

One thing is clear: Sony, Kikkoman and Samsung Electronics have to constantly reinvent themselves. Their business prospects are only as good as their next product or initiative. The ability to learn – and unlearn – is a prerequisite even for such successful global pioneers.

▲ SONY

Nobuyuki Idei
Chairman & CEO, Sony Corporation

From its beginnings as an unknown venture amid the postwar ruins of Tokyo over 50 years ago, Sony has expanded into a large multinational corporation, its products and name now recognized across the globe. Since establishing its first sales offices and plants overseas in the 1960s and '70s, Sony's transformation into a global company has been a gradual process, one fraught with difficulties.

It is now relatively easy for companies to build facilities abroad, expand operations, travel, and communicate globally. Through the Internet, businesses are no longer constrained by time and space. But these factors alone do not necessarily guarantee success as a global business. Sony's experience may serve as one example of successful "globalizing". There is no single formula for success: the formula is unique to Sony, as it is for every company. It should be adapted to the distinct characteristics of each country, taking into account the country's specific needs, culture and regulations. The way to do business successfully in one country may be totally different in another.

Underlying these different approaches is a certain corporate philosophy that transcends national boundaries. The founders of Sony wished "to establish an ideal factory that stresses a spirit of freedom and open-mindedness". This notion of "freedom" and a belief in the unlimited potential of human creativity lie at the heart of Sony's corporate philosophy. Together with a venturous spirit, this "Sony DNA" is shared throughout the Sony Group.

Strategically, too, there is a corporate vision that is common throughout Sony's worldwide operations. For many years, the phrase "global localization" (a concept first championed by Sony's co-founder, Akio Morita) became the slogan for Sony's overseas activities. Put simply, "global localization" means "meeting local needs with local operations while pursuing common global concepts and technologies"; in other words, localizing sales, production, research and development (R&D), and management functions under a globally unified strategy. Sony was able to globalize successfully through effective localization.

In this chapter, I would like to present a broad outline of Sony's history: how it entered the global market and expanded its operations abroad. Specifically, I will talk about both operational and management aspects of Sony's global operations. As mentioned earlier, there is no single formula for success, but I hope Sony's experience may provide useful hints for those looking to expand their global presence.

"Global localization": Localizing operations

Establishing the brand name

The breakdown of Sony's sales worldwide is one indication of the global nature of our business. For the fiscal year ended March 31, 2004, the breakdown was as follows: Japan 30%, U.S. 28%, Europe 24%, and the rest of the world 18.5%. We also have a multitude of sales offices, production plants, and R&D centers worldwide.

Sony first began positioning itself overseas through the establishment of several sales offices. Sony Corporation of America (SONAM) in New York, Sony's first legal entity in the U.S., was established in 1960. Other overseas sales offices included one in Switzerland (Sony Overseas S.A.) in 1960 and Sony UK Ltd. in 1968.

A major reason for establishing these direct sales channels was to boost the brand image of Sony outside Japan. When Sony first began selling its transistor radios abroad in the 1950s, it did so by consigning sales to local sales representatives and distributors. Despite our good relationship with many of these representatives, it was soon decided that the best way to communicate Sony's message to the consumer and, hence, enhance its brand image, was through direct sales by Sony salespeople who fully understood, and were enthusiastic about, its products.

Brand image has always been a key element in Sony's business strategy. In 1958, the official company name was changed to "SONY" since "Tokyo Tsushin Kogyo" (the company's original name) was deemed too difficult to pronounce for non-Japanese. From the start, the company focused on establishing its brand name overseas. Rather than sell its transistor radios in the U.S. under the name of a better-established U.S. company (a deal that would have reaped huge profits in the short run), Sony's co-founders insisted on selling the product under its own name. The long-term goal of establishing Sony's name in the U.S. market superseded short-term profits.

The decision to set up showrooms in the prime locations of midtown Fifth Avenue in New York City in 1962, the Ginza district of Tokyo in 1966, and the Champs Elysées in Paris in 1971 was also linked to this idea of establishing the brand name at an early stage.

Thus, the late 1950s and '60s marked the first stage of Sony's entry into the international market, the primary focus being to build its brand image through the promotion of unique products. The goal was to have consumers associate the name "SONY" with unique, high-quality products.

Manufacturing locally

Despite making inroads into overseas markets, Sony, like other Japanese firms, still faced certain restrictions, including volume limitations on the export of industrial goods. In some cases, the government of the host country offered very little support, often pressured by local firms unhappy to see a competitor enter their market. I myself faced such difficulties when I began the task of setting up Sony's sales office in France in the early 1970s. I visited France's Ministry of Finance on many occasions seeking to gain approval to set up our office. But the French government at the time was intent on protecting local industries and sealing its borders to foreign investment.

It took two years of negotiating before we finally established Sony France in 1973. Reflecting on this experience, I realize that these early struggles may have been a necessity. The tough back-and-forth negotiations helped us achieve a certain level of understanding with the government, testing our tenacity and will, ultimately helping us build a firm foundation in that market.

At the time (before I could reflect on these experiences with a certain nostalgia), my experience in France led me to believe that, in order to win acceptance from both the government and people of the host country, we would have to contribute to the community by building plants and manufacturing close to the market. This would also be a way to counter export restrictions and exchange-rate fluctuations.

Sony had actually embarked on building plants overseas as early as 1959, only a few years after its founding. Its first plant abroad was a transistor-radio assembly plant in Hong Kong, followed the same year by another in Shannon, Ireland. The Hong Kong "plant" was actually an apartment with two production lines, a makeshift plant, and management was left in the hands of a local Hong Kong firm. The plant assembled transistor radios for shipment to Europe, Australia and Canada, but was closed after two years following a disagreement between the local management firm and Sony.

The plant in Shannon shared the same fate but for different reasons. Sony initially established the plant in Ireland because this location provided several benefits. First, as part of the British Commonwealth, any products manufactured in Ireland could be shipped to the U.K., Australia, and Canada with relative ease. Secondly, Ireland's scheduled accession to the European Community promised greater access to the European market. The government of Ireland was also actively promoting foreign direct investment, in particular, enticing Japanese firms like Sony. As a result, Sony established its plant in Shannon in 1959, making transistor radios with parts from England and Ireland and transistors from Japan.

The Shannon plant, however, faced several problems. One had to do with the precision and accuracy required in making transistor radios. Production was not efficient because of the inexperience of local employees, and locally available parts were sometimes of substandard quality. The low yield of the plant caused great concern, and communication between the plant's management and Japan was hindered by problems with the telecommunication infrastructure and the exorbitant cost of long-distance calls. It is questionable whether more adequate communication between the local operation and Japan would have improved the situation, since the Sony staff in Tokyo had no experience of manufacturing abroad. Furthermore, recurring labor strikes at the docks delayed delivery of parts from Japan. Sony spent several years trying to resolve these problems but, after repeated failures, the plant closed in 1966. However, these early failures proved to be a good learning experience, paving the way for later success.

One of these early successes was Sony's first plant in the U.S.: its San Diego plant, established in 1972. There had already been talk of building a plant in the U.S. for years; it was simply a question of timing. Akio Morita was a strong believer in establishing solid foundations in a country (that is, understanding the local people, culture and values) before setting up a plant. Rushing into a project before developing such a foundation would only lead to a repeat of the experiences in Hong Kong and Ireland.

By 1972, Sony had already become fairly well established in the U.S. It had been the first Japanese company to issue ADRs (American Depositary Receipts) in the U.S. (1961), it had been listed on the New York Stock Exchange since September 1970, and its name was widely recognized. Furthermore, after years of operating in the country, Sony's management had developed a good understanding of American rules and culture. In essence, Sony had established a solid foundation in the U.S. and was ready to build its first plant.

Of course, there was no manual for "how to run a plant in the U.S.", and the company had to improvise, based on the idea that a unique approach was required for each country. One improvization was to hire local workers who had absolutely no experience in TV manufacturing (the San Diego plant assembled color TVs). Sony's aim in doing this was to infuse standards that were unique to the company. The downside of this plan was that product quality was initially sub-standard. However, after a few months, the quality rose to Sony's standards, which, I believe, were above market standards. Maintaining this common Sony standard globally was not simply a challenge but a necessary one. Another improvization was the salary system which, in the end, was a combination of the Japanese and U.S. systems.

The relative success of the San Diego plant laid the framework for other plants in the U.S., a color TV plant in Barcelona, Spain (1973), a TV plant in Bridgend, U.K. (1974), and other plants worldwide. The Plaza Accord[6] between the U.S. and Japan in 1985 further facilitated an increase in overseas production, leading to an expansion of Sony plants in Asia in the 1980s. The 1970s and '80s thus saw Sony's rapid expansion into the realm of local production.

Localizing R&D

Local sales and production were soon followed by R&D activities overseas. There were several reasons for this. One was the desire to research and develop products locally to meet the needs of the local market. However, if we only developed products with a "European taste" for the European market, for example, we would end up as just another player in the field. In order to distinguish our products, it was critical to balance local needs with something unique to Sony, a need that still holds true today.

Another reason for localizing R&D was to take advantage of local talent and expertise in specific technologies, combining and creating synergies between different regions. For example, the U.K.'s expertise in digital technology may be combined with software and graphics technology in the U.S. One of our first R&D centers abroad was established in the U.K. in 1978 for the development of broadcast equipment. Since then, our R&D operations have expanded globally, utilizing local talent in the U.S, Europe and Asia.

Localizing management

The process of localizing sales and service, production and R&D was all part of the "global localization" strategy mentioned earlier. However, the success or failure of an overseas operation ultimately depends on the people running it. Thus, the fourth (in no particular chronological order) and perhaps most important factor in localizing our global operations was the localization of management. This process began fairly early: an American became president of Sony Corporation of America (SONAM) as early as 1966. In 1972, both the president and vice-president of SONAM were Americans. This was based on the belief that in order to make SONAM a truly U.S. company we would have to implement American management. At times, there were cultural differences leading to clashes in the style of management but, over time, Sony has been able to bridge many of these cultural divides. As a result, the process of localizing management in the U.S., Europe and Asia has been largely successful.

Global management in the network era

So far, I have discussed the globalization of Sony mainly as an electronics company. But the Sony I inherited as president in 1995 was more than just a global electronics manufacturer. Having acquired movie and music businesses – Sony Pictures Entertainment in 1989 and Sony Music Entertainment in 1990 – Sony had become a global electronics and entertainment company.

In addition, the 1990s was the decade in which we saw a sudden explosion of digital/information technology and the rise in new industry players. Thus, my mission has been to manage and lead Sony's electronics and entertainment businesses through the difficult digital and IT competition of the 1990s and into the 21st century.

A web-like corporate structure

One of the first measures I took in 1995 was to introduce the slogans "Regeneration" and "Digital Dream Kids". Through "Regeneration", I emphasized the need for Sony to change. Because the company had experienced many successes in the past, I stressed the dangers of complacency and the necessity to reinvent itself for the future. With the "Digital Dream Kids" slogan, I communicated the direction in which Sony was to change: into a digital company. As a result of everyone's effort, Sony's presence in the digital and IT market grew through the introduction of hit products such as the VAIO notebook computer, the Cybershot digital camera and the AIBO personal companion, to the point where today Sony has become a household name in the digital and IT arena.

In organizational structure, too, I sought a model to take advantage of Sony's unique and valuable assets in both electronics and entertainment, which would be representative of the digital-network era. Rather than the rigid top-down structure of the past, in which all major decisions flowed from the top of the pyramid down to its base, I believed that an organization in the digital-network era should be characterized by a web-like structure in which the parts interconnect with one another and to a central locus point. Based on this understanding, I introduced the "integrated and decentralized management model" in 1999 with the ultimate goal of maximizing the total value of the Sony Group, clearly distinguishing the roles and relationships between business units and headquarters.

Under this model, individual business units are given independence in running day-to-day operations, with due respect given to their unique cultures. The role of headquarters is not to intervene in the daily operations, but to provide a common vision and direction for all business units. In addition, acting as an "active investor", the headquarters will allocate appropriate resources to the business units based on an objective evaluation. The business units are encouraged to work together and complement each other's strengths by forming intra-group alliances, with the aim of maximizing the value and strength of the Group against external competition.

In April 2003, in an effort to advance the integrated and decentralized management structure of our global operations, Sony introduced a system of regional representatives in the U.S., Europe and China. These three regional representatives oversee the appropriate implementation of the group strategy in accordance with local circumstances. They are also responsible for encouraging local collaboration and intra-group alliances between Sony's electronics, game and entertainment units as well as devising new business opportunities with other companies in alliances, mergers and acquisitions. For example, for the New York-based Sony Group Americas Representative, the enhancement of strategic linkages between Sony's entertainment and electronics businesses in the Americas is one aspect of its mission. The Sony Group Europe Representative (based in Berlin) oversees the formulation and implementation of the Sony Group strategy for the European market, in addition to maximizing Sony's business opportunities and coordination between all of Sony's products, services and offerings in the region. The Sony Group East Asia Representative (based in Shanghai) will, among other functions, optimize engineering, manufacturing, sales and marketing operations in East Asia and create new business opportunities in the region. These new assignments are, in short, a way for Sony to strengthen its local presence and match its strategy to local markets, taking into account local culture, tradition, rules and needs.

Differentiation through localizing services

We are currently facing a period of intense global competition. Driven by excess supply, shorter product lifecycles and fierce competition, products these days are quickly becoming commodities. In this age of rapid commoditization, there is greater urgency to differentiate one's products with added value and to promote uniqueness and originality. One critical measure of differentiation is the degree to which the product embodies exclusive intellectual property and knowledge not easily replicable by others. This is an area in which Sony has excelled in the past and must continue to focus on in the future.

However, the introduction of unique products alone does not guarantee market success. Another vital factor is increasing one's responsiveness to the markets by providing products, services and content tailored to local communities that comprise the market. This means understanding that each country, community and individual has unique characteristics and needs; it requires sensitivity that breaks stereotypes. In other words, one of the challenges is to look at markets from both global and local perspectives, avoiding a one-size-fits-all strategy that places too much emphasis on the "global" aspect alone. Even categorizing countries as "developed" or "emerging" is dangerous; upon closer analysis, "emerging" countries are not only vastly different from one another, they also comprise numerous unique individuals and communities. I believe that this approach is important in strengthening our relationship with our customers and in building trust.

The products we create may be "global", but the way we sell the products and the services we offer must be localized. The regional representatives were established in part to foster Sony's strategy of offering localized services.

Global citizenship and corporate governance: A way to build trust

In addition to offering products and services that are appreciated and highly regarded by its customers throughout the world, a global company must also show that its interests are tied to those of communities around the world; in essence, that it is a good corporate citizen of the global community.

When thinking about a company's role, or interest, in being socially responsible, we must recognize the growing interdependence of society and business. At the start of this 21st century, we see that the concept of society itself has changed. Society is no longer confined to a local village, a city, or even a country. Technological advances in communication and travel have made the global community our own society. To be good corporate citizens means, first of all, to understand that each of us, individuals and corporations alike, has a stake in the global community.

There are several dimensions to corporate citizenship. One is the more traditional definition of corporate social responsibility, having to do with basic philanthropy and community activities. This has always been of particular concern for Sony; the idea of working for the good of society was even included in the company's founding prospectus. Sony became a pioneer in corporate citizenship in Japan when it began funding the study of science in Japanese elementary schools in 1959. Sony took the lead among Japanese companies again when, in 1974, it became the first Japanese company to establish a foundation in the U.S. for the promotion of education, health care and community activities. From the beginning, Sony's aim has been to promote the economic, social and cultural development of local communities. This tradition has continued to the present day with community-service activities at the local level, sponsorship of socio-cultural events worldwide, and a particular emphasis on supporting education.

Another dimension to corporate citizenship has to do with being a responsible company and following the rules. It is especially important for corporations to develop and implement a sound corporate governance system in gaining the trust of its stakeholders.

These things may sound rather obvious now, but events of recent years have shown that corporate responsibility is an issue that requires active, rather than passive, attention. One reason for this is that with greater scrutiny from the public and media, corporations must answer to an increasing number of stakeholders worldwide. This requires a coordinated global approach.

Another reason is that business models are changing dramatically, and corporations now have a greater responsibility to actively adjust their internal structures to deal with this changing environment. As we move from a manufacturing to a knowledge-based society, the corporate-governance schemes we adopt must be equipped to handle new business models in IT and knowledge-based industries.

From my own experience of serving on the boards of Sony, General Motors and Nestlé, I have reached the conclusion that there is no single global standard of corporate governance that can be adopted by all. This is because every company must comply with the laws/regulations of its home country in addition to those where they obtain their funds. For example, in Germany, the law requires that a certain number of members of a company's supervisory board are employee representatives who have the ability to appoint and dismiss management board members; certainly a unique system not seen in the U.S. or Japan. In the case of Sony, it must comply with the Japanese Commercial Code as well as the requirements set by the U.S. Securities and Exchange Commission (SEC) because its shares are listed in Japan, the U.S., and other countries. GM and Nestlé have requirements different from Sony and, naturally, this necessitates a different governance system. Moreover, some companies are publicly traded while others are not. Approximately 45% of Sony shareholders are non-Japanese, leading to the question of what governance structure would be widely accepted by such a diversity of shareholders.

Corporate governance schemes have been evolving ever since the founding of the modern corporation and are still in the process of being improved. Japan recently revised its rules and, propelled by the Sarbanes-Oxley Act, the SEC in the U.S. is calling for stricter regulations following some major accounting scandals. Corporations must continue to actively adjust their internal governance structures to deal with the changing environment and legal requirements.

Sony, as a global corporation, has always placed great significance on, and has been in the vanguard of, corporate governance. We have a history of adapting our corporate governance structure to meet local rules and the changing demands of corporate governance, often going beyond minimum requirements. Sony appointed two outside directors in conjunction with its listing on the New York Stock Exchange in 1970. In 1991, a non-Japanese outside director was appointed. In 1997, Sony reorganized the board and established Japan's first corporate executive-officer system, aiming to separate the oversight and operational management functions within the company. The position of chairman of the board was created in 2000, and an international advisory board, composed of expert outside advisors from various industries, was established in 2002 for the purpose of providing insight and advice to the chief officers of Sony and its group company executives.

More recently, Sony decided to adopt the "company with committees" system in June 2003, thus establishing three committees (nomination, audit, compensation) packaged together with the corporate executive-officer system. This change is in line with the revision in the Japanese Commercial Code, and is aimed at delineating the separate oversight and business operation functions of the board. Going beyond these requirements, Sony has also decided to introduce internal standards for the separation of the chairman of the board of directors and representative corporate executive officers. Furthermore, it intends to increase the number of outside directors and, in compliance with U.S. legislation, members of the Audit Committee will all be independent and have no operational responsibilities. Thus, Sony has taken significant steps towards revising its corporate governance structure, merging elements of the Japanese and U.S. systems with its own unique corporate culture.

Conclusion: The challenges ahead

The localization of its operations was vital to Sony's growth in creating a cross-linked chain of global operations. Now that links have been formed worldwide, it is necessary to review the entire picture, to see which links are necessary to keep the web intact, which need to be strengthened or added, and which are redundant. In other words, it is necessary to fine-tune the global mechanism in this recurring cycle of growth and reflection.

It goes without saying that in the face of today's global competition, it is imperative to differentiate oneself from the crowd. Throughout its history, Sony has accomplished this by introducing revolutionary products and penetrating new markets by localizing operations. We must now take this a step further. Although innovation and creativity still form the core of Sony's overall strategy, the success of that strategy ultimately depends on management's implementation at the local level. This requires an accurate understanding of local needs and rules, based on the discovery, transmission and utilization of appropriate knowledge. This is a characteristic of the knowledge-based society towards which we are headed, and Sony will continue to make improvements in this respect, encouraging the process of integration and decentralization of its global operations.

As we approach our 60th anniversary (in 2006), the challenge for Sony is to emerge from today's competition as a leading global technology and entertainment company. Our past success as a consumer-electronics company holds no promises for the future; our future depends on how well we can integrate our electronics and media businesses to create value-added products and services for consumers. Sony, like everyone else, must reinvent itself. Whether or not it can do so will determine if it can thrive, or even survive, in this age of global competition.

TAKEAWAYS

1. **Early moves towards globalization were instilled by the founders' entrepreneurial vision and drive.**
   Despite its somewhat humble beginnings, Sony anticipated that its future would be decided in the international markets rather than at home. Sony's co-founder, Akio Morita, himself moved to New York in 1960 to oversee the U.S. expansion of the company and shaped both products and approach in line with global markets. Only by maintaining this focus was the company able to create the Walkman, which revolutionized the music industry and catapulted Sony into the global leagues. The company has maintained its global focus, even in shareholding.

2. **Sony knew that it could not rely on resource-based advantages like the Japanese *keiretsu*, and thus actively sought to develop systems-based and other advantages.**
   Sony was an anomaly in Japan because it was not member of a *keiretsu* and, while many other companies would have seen this as a major impediment to growth, Sony actively sought to exploit its independence. It was able, for instance, to forge affiliations and cooperative relationships on the basis of business imperatives rather than group relationships, and to grow where it made business sense rather than according to the group's imperatives. In addition, the freedom from *keiretsu* practices enabled Sony to build its own management and operations processes tailored to its global market presence.

3. **In line with its mindset, Sony built a true global corporate culture as a reflection of the company's global presence.**
   Sony's move into the U.S. – the acquisition of CBS Records and Columbia Pictures Entertainment in the late 1980s – strengthened its strategy of becoming an integrated firm which could systemically play out its competitive advantage. Some claimed that in its U.S. foray, Sony became a company of quasi-U.S. identity and, later still, a company displaying a true global corporate culture, with international corporate norms and foreign professionals in a number of senior management positions.

4. **Sony backed its global expansion with a consistent global branding.**
   The name "Sony" itself highlights the founders' intuition and determination to communicate globally. They wanted a name recognizable everywhere, so they chose one that alludes to the Latin word "sonus", meaning "sound". By engaging in marketing that captures the spirit of imagination, entertainment and creativity behind the Sony name, the company has developed the brand to become one of the best known in the world. At the same time, the absence of a specific cultural connotation for the name has also allowed it to fit into local cultures where it produces or sells.

5. **The company has pioneered involvement in corporate social responsibility and accountability within its social community.**
   Sony not only supports numerous grass-roots projects around the world but is also a frontrunner among Japanese companies in establishing a far-reaching corporate governance system. The company has put great emphasis on shareholders' rights, the disclosure of information, responsibility, and accountability in an effort to improve management through transparency. The focus on two important constituencies – social community and

shareholders – makes Sony unusual amongst major Japanese players.

6. **Sony's inroads into global markets have been accompanied by pitfalls and setbacks – and this has become particularly obvious in the series of problems the company faced in 2004. However, whenever the company has faced such problems in the past, it has prevailed through a process of "learning and unlearning".**

   On each rung of the ladder towards globalization, the company has learned from its experiences, good and bad. Sony is currently trying to unlearn past success patterns, as it may have relied too long on its brand name to carry premium pricing. The "It's a Sony" culture is not an iron-clad guarantee of success. The company is currently in the process of reinventing itself to continue its bid to excel globally.

▲ KIKKOMAN

Yuzaburo Mogi
Chairman and CEO, Kikkoman Corporation

Kikkoman Corporation traces its origins back to the early 17th century, to soy-sauce production enterprises located in Noda, Japan. However, the company which would later become Kikkoman, Noda Shoyu Co., Ltd., was established nearly three centuries later, in 1917, as the result of a merger of eight family companies. I am a descendant of one of those families.

The region surrounding Noda, northeast of Tokyo, was ideal for the large-scale production of soy sauce in the 18th and 19th centuries for a number of reasons. Both soybeans and wheat, the main ingredients of soy sauce, were grown in the surrounding area. Moreover, the region was close to the immense and ever-growing market of Edo (now Tokyo), to which it was linked by the easily navigable Edo River, with the trip taking only one day. By the middle of the 18th century, Edo was probably the world's most populous city, with more than one million inhabitants.

Several soy-sauce-making enterprises prospered in the region, with competition leading to higher quality and the need for branding. The Kikkoman brand name was used by one of the founding families, and became the most popular trademark in the early 19th century. Kikkoman soy sauce soon became known as one of the finest in the greater Tokyo region. The name was enshrined in the hexagonal-shaped logo that is still in use today.

In 1868, the Japanese Emperor was restored to power under a constitutional form of government, and Japan began the long process of opening up to the world. The capital was moved from Kyoto to Edo, which was renamed Tokyo ("eastern capital").

During that period, Kikkoman began shipping soy sauce to Japanese who had emigrated to Hawaii. This marked the start of Kikkoman as an international enterprise. In 1879, the Kikkoman brand name was registered in California, U.S.A., and in Germany in 1886. By 1906, it was registered in most states in the U.S.

In 1917, eight soy-sauce producing families in Noda formed the Noda Shoyu Company. After great deliberation, the founders agreed to use the Kikkoman brand name, originated by one of the families, in order to take full advantage of its name value and broad reputation.

Kikkoman was one of the first Japanese enterprises to export products when Japan was opened to trade with the West after 1868. This opening was part of a chain of events which eventually transformed Japan from a feudal society into a capitalist democracy. Another significant result of this opening was the emigration of Japanese people from all walks of society. Most went to Hawaii and the West Coast of North America, to be followed shortly after by the first barrels of Kikkoman soy sauce.

In a sense, this business activity differed from modern Japanese exports in that the consumers were originally from Japan, and that demand for soy sauce in these overseas locations "pulled" the exports from Japan. These Japanese people were already familiar with the Kikkoman brand, so trust in the product already existed. Accordingly, no localization activities were necessary, and consumers purchased and used soy sauce in exactly the same ways as they did in Japan. It would be nearly a century later before Kikkoman took an entirely different approach in order to sell soy sauce throughout the United States. Exports of soy sauce to Hawaii continued, and shipments were also made to North America in line with the increasing number of Japanese moving there.

Modern local-market exporting

It was during the U.S. occupation of Japan after World War II that the idea of selling soy sauce on a large scale in the United States took firm root with Kikkoman management. After the war, not only U.S. military personnel, but also journalists, businessmen, teachers and others came to Japan. Being surrounded by Japanese food, including soy sauce, these Americans had the opportunity to try it. To the surprise of most Japanese people, quite a number of Americans enjoyed many types of Japanese cuisine. Even more surprising was that Americans were seen using soy sauce with their own American foods. In particular, soy sauce nicely complemented the flavor of grilled meats. This gave the management of Kikkoman the idea that it would be possible, in time, to sell soy sauce in the huge U.S. market.

As we have seen, Kikkoman soy sauce was already being sold in the U.S., but mostly to immigrants from Japan and Americans of Japanese descent. In order to sell soy sauce to the vast majority of American people, who were largely unfamiliar with it, it would be necessary to develop ways in which it could be integrated into mainstream American food culture.

It has been comparatively easy for Japanese companies producing popular products, such as cameras and automobiles, to export to the U.S. because markets for these goods have long existed. However, in the case of Kikkoman, the market for soy sauce had first to be created before any level of success could be achieved. This would require more than just exporting the product, and a systematic approach with a development timetable had to be followed. To this end, in 1957 Kikkoman established Kikkoman International, Inc. in San Francisco.

The first task of Kikkoman's U.S. operations was rather simple. It was necessary to expose the average American consumer to soy sauce. Kikkoman believed that most Americans would react favorably to this Japanese condiment if presented to them in a familiar form.

Kikkoman soy sauce was initially demonstrated in supermarkets in the belief that it was always necessary for people to experience the flavor directly before any meaningful relationship could be built. Demonstrators would grill small pieces of tender beef, which had been marinated in the sauce, and offered them to customers. The aroma wafting through the aisles worked well in drawing interest and customers usually reacted favorably.

In fact, while attending Columbia Business School in New York, I spent one summer demonstrating Kikkoman soy sauce in supermarkets and international trade fairs.

Fortunately, this approach worked well, and a year after the establishment of Kikkoman International, Inc., a branch office was opened in Los Angeles in 1958. In 1961, Kikkoman opened a branch in New York, to be followed later by Chicago, in 1965, and Atlanta in 1977.

As it turned out, most American people liked the taste of Kikkoman soy sauce, so the original hunch after World War II turned out to be correct. This led to the company's second task, that of developing ways of incorporating soy sauce in a wide range of popular American foods. Test kitchens were built in Kikkoman International headquarters in San Francisco, and home economists and culinary experts were recruited to come up with recipes which called for soy sauce.

The resulting recipes were condensed and put into little booklets, which were attached to the necks of soy sauce bottles. These gave the average American consumer quite a few ideas on how to use the sauce in a range of dishes.

These recipes were also promoted to food writers, who introduced them in newspaper and magazine articles. As soy sauce became more commonplace in American supermarkets, Kikkoman also published full-sized cookbooks containing recipes for using it.

In parallel with these "localization" activities, Kikkoman also invested in television and print-media advertising. A national campaign was established, and the name Kikkoman literally became a household word synonymous with soy sauce.

All of these activities were part of a long, step-by-step process which ultimately integrated soy sauce into mainstream American cuisine. There is no doubt that other soy-sauce manufacturers also benefited from this promotion. Nevertheless, it was the superior quality of our naturally brewed soy sauce which eventually earned Kikkoman the top share in the U.S. market, a position which it still holds today.

Shifting to U.S. production

Once Kikkoman had firmly established a market that was not limited to Asian restaurants and specific segments of society, demand for its product grew steadily. As sales volume increased, Kikkoman management looked toward the future, and could envision the eventual establishment of a manufacturing presence in the United States.

Initial feasibility studies

This first study to determine the feasibility of Kikkoman building a factory in the United States was undertaken in 1965, well over a decade before there was any question of trade friction between the U.S. and Japan.

For Kikkoman, the question of producing soy sauce in the U.S. was primarily one of good business practice. At the time, the company was importing both wheat and soybeans, the primary ingredients, from the United States to its factories in Japan. Naturally, then, it was only logical to set up production at the source.

After the first feasibility study, Kikkoman found that the sales volume in the United States wasn't sufficient to support efficient production, but the study did provide ideas for alternative approaches.

In December 1967, Kikkoman began exporting soy sauce from Japan in bulk, and had it bottled in the United States by the Leslie Salt Company in Oakland, California. At the same bottling plant, Kikkoman Teriyaki sauce was blended and bottled, and because of this the label indicated "Product of U.S.A.", the first Kikkoman product to carry such a designation.

Sales continued to increase, and it soon became obvious that container shipment of bulk product for bottling in the United States could not be sustained at higher volume levels. In 1970, only five years after the initial study, Kikkoman once again began considering plans for U.S. production. I was head of this project, and assembled a team of five people from Japan and one American consultant. In late 1970, we undertook a second-stage study plan, which highlighted both the merits and the demerits of building a Kikkoman factory in the United States.

The major advantages were that there would be no need to ship product from Japan and the factory would be much closer to the raw materials. Both of these points represented huge savings in freight costs. In addition, the company would not have to pay the 6% import duty on soy sauce.

To be weighed against these advantages were the considerable cost of inland freight and, of course, the cost of building a factory, which would be exceptionally high since all of the equipment would have to be custom made. Soy-sauce production is capital intensive, and a great deal of equipment is necessary.

It became clear that the advantages outweighed the disadvantages, so Kikkoman decided to build a plant in the United States.

Building a factory

After considerable deliberation over some 60 locations, the town of Walworth, Wisconsin, was selected. Close to the Illinois border, Walworth is roughly equidistant from Milwaukee and Chicago (about 90 minutes by car). It is close to wheat and soybean producing areas, and the available water is of good quality. It is a cohesive and peaceful community and is well served by rail and highway connections, facilitating both shipments and deliveries.

When plans for the factory were announced, there was some local opposition from local farming interests who felt that any plant would be incompatible with the farming activities in the area. Kikkoman responded by emphasizing that the production of soy sauce is part of an agribusiness since it represents value added processing of agricultural products. The business would make a positive contribution to the local tax base and the plant would in no way harm the natural environment.

At the time, I and other company representatives addressed several local groups. We gave slide presentations to inform the citizens about our production methods, and to reinforce the message that the factory would bring a series of positive effects to Walworth. We also visited several farming households and even attended county board meetings to explain the company's position in person. After considerable local debate, the plans were approved. Wisconsin State Governor Patrick Lucey held a press conference on December 15, 1971, declaring, "Kikkoman is welcome".

On a site of some 760,000 square meters, construction of the plant began in March 1972, and Kikkoman's first U.S. factory came on line the following year, with an initial annual production capacity of soy sauce and teriyaki of nine million liters.

Kikkoman made every effort to ensure a good, solid relationship with the people of Walworth through its policy of hiring local people for both production jobs and management positions. The company decided early on to adopt American-style management practices for the operation, and make the factory a place where Americans could work easily. An American was hired as the first personnel manager, and the United States flag sits on the flagpole at the factory entrance. Necessary technicians and management personnel from Japan were kept to a minimum, and obtained housing in different parts of Walworth to avoid the creation of a "Japanese village" in the area. Even today, after 30 years of operation, only seven of the 140 employees currently working in the plant are from Japan.

Building brand recognition

From the outset, the company invested heavily in advertising and promotion to increase brand awareness of Kikkoman as a premium, naturally brewed, soy sauce of the highest quality. This approach was soon joined by more concrete advertising and promotion which used existing brand awareness as a stepping stone to show people how to integrate soy sauce into their normal diet.

Advertising

Kikkoman's debut in television advertising in the U.S. set the stage for a bold approach that would be developed in the following decades. During televised broadcasts of the 1956 presidential election, Kikkoman TV commercials were aired in California, exposing consumers to a product of which few had had experience. The product was as new as the commercial, so Kikkoman garnered considerable attention from the public.

More importantly, these commercials gave food brokers throughout the state the impression that Kikkoman was a product so mainstream that it would be advertised during prime viewing hours, and this gave it an even greater degree of legitimacy. Gaining the attention and support of food brokers is essential in getting products into supermarkets and this early television exposure was instrumental in getting bottles of Kikkoman soy sauce on supermarket shelves soon afterward.

Kikkoman also advertised heavily in women's magazines, introducing the product and the concept of using soy sauce as an all-purpose seasoning for everyday American foods, and giving recipes for popular dishes in which soy sauce, even as little as a tablespoon, could be used.

As Kikkoman's market share increased, other soy-sauce manufacturers responded with advertising that represented, in essence, a direct attack on the higher-priced Kikkoman soy sauce. Their products were not naturally brewed and could thus be sold for less than the price of Kikkoman. In turn, Kikkoman released a series of ads emphasizing the difference in quality between naturally brewed and chemically produced soy sauce, enabling consumers to see the difference in the color of the product, not to mention the marked differences in aroma and flavor.

Kikkoman's commitment to the value of advertising continues, with colorful TV and print ads featuring the amusing "Kikko Man" animated character.

Promotional activities

A cornerstone of Kikkoman's promotions from the beginning has been one-on-one product demonstration. Another popular sales promotion was newspaper coupons, which give consumers discounts on bottles of soy sauce.

The company's support for creating and publishing recipes in which soy sauce is used has also been a key factor in the success of Kikkoman products and, indeed, soy sauce in general. Most of these recipes have been developed by Kikkoman's own test kitchens, or by home economists and chefs supported by Kikkoman. The recipes have been the subject of magazine and newspaper articles, which has resulted in soy sauce being integrated into mainstream American food culture.

Kikkoman has also supported food programming on cable television, entered into a sponsorship agreement with Disney World in Florida, and participated in countless public activities as part of being a good corporate citizen. These have indirectly contributed to a more positive image for the company in the U.S. market.

Building market share

Kikkoman recognized the massive potential of the U.S. market and, boldly, took a broad approach for what would conventionally be considered a highly specialized product. Soy sauce has a rich, complex flavor that gives it universal appeal, and for this reason we believed it would appeal to mainstream Americans.

Establishing product identity

Three simple words sum up the Kikkoman approach: “all-purpose seasoning”. These words were displayed prominently on its bottles of soy sauce. Containers were sized for supermarket shelves and kitchen shelves, and it was Kikkoman that brought soy sauce out from its previous Asian food enclave and presented it proudly to American society. This bold product positioning, more than anything else, allowed Kikkoman to gain the attention it would need to capture the hearts and palates of mainstream Americans.

Recognizing early on the potential of Kikkoman and its mainstream approach, the Safeway supermarket chain began displaying soy sauce prominently in some of its San Francisco stores as early as 1956, a year before Kikkoman established its American subsidiary. This was the first time a major Japanese food manufacturer had been taken up by a U.S. supermarket chain, and this led the way for Kikkoman's exposure to non-Asian Americans.

In 1961, the company released a companion product, Kikkoman Teriyaki Marinade and Sauce, which was its first soy-sauce-derivative product in the U.S. The popularity of this product, which was used primarily for barbecuing meats, further strengthened the Kikkoman name as a producer of quality condiments, and prompted some consumers to purchase soy sauce itself.

Commitment to quality for product differentiation

Three more simple words, “Naturally Brewed Kikkoman”, were adopted in advertising and promotion to drive home the fact that Kikkoman tasted markedly different – and significantly better – than other soy sauces.

Naturally brewed soy sauce is made simply from soybeans, wheat, salt and water in a process that takes several months. The result is a rich, complex flavor that has a savory, almost meat-like taste. In addition, there is a delicate aroma with a rich, pleasing character.

In contrast, other major soy sauce products were chemically produced by combining hydrolyzed vegetable protein with salt, water, corn syrup and artificial coloring. This type of soy sauce is much darker and harsher tasting, and lacks the pleasing aroma of the naturally brewed variety. However, this process enables the sauce to be produced quickly and at lower cost.

However, Kikkoman quality was easily recognizable, and this earned it the Good Housekeeping seal of approval in 1964. From May of that year, all product labels bore the seal, which was instrumental in further building consumer confidence.

Use in local dishes

Another three-word phrase, "Delicious On Meat", was key to creating the perception that Kikkoman was more than just an Asian condiment.

While Kikkoman initially promoted soy sauce as a meat marinade for grilling, it wasn't long before Americans were using it to flavor ground meat for hamburgers. Use in casseroles, sauces, vegetable dishes and even salad dressings followed. However, the increasingly diverse uses of soy sauce did not occur by accident. Rather, it was a result of Kikkoman's ongoing promotion campaign in magazines, newspapers and other media.

By the beginning of the 1980s, Japanese food had become popular nationwide as a result of the renewed interest in a healthy diet of natural foods. Sushi, in particular, was all the rage on the U.S. West Coast and in New York, and its popularity soon spread into the American heartland. While this did contribute to some increase in demand for soy sauce, it should be emphasized that most Americans were already familiar with soy sauce. In fact, it could be said that this familiarity helped Americans to become familiar with sushi, particularly since many people had already experienced soy sauce with sushi. The same holds true for other Japanese foods, since on every table of every Japanese restaurant there is invariably the familiar red-topped Kikkoman dispenser bottle.

Expanding beyond the United States

The success of Kikkoman overseas was certain by around 1975, when production levels were steadily increasing in the company's new U.S. factory. Kikkoman management felt that it was time to lay the groundwork for entry into other markets.

In September 1975, Kikkoman established a representative office in Hamburg to research the potential of various European markets. West Germany was selected because countries with a Latin heritage, such as France, Italy and Spain, had a strong pride in their own food cultures, and seemed less receptive to foreign foods. Germans, however, were more receptive to foreign foods if the taste was agreeable.

In 1973, Kikkoman had opened a restaurant in Düsseldorf to serve *teppanyaki*, a cuisine in which meat, seafood and vegetables seasoned with soy sauce are grilled on a hot iron plate. Then, four months before the representative office was established there in 1975, a restaurant was opened in Hamburg. These restaurants used locally procured ingredients seasoned with soy sauce. A major objective was to familiarize more European people with the taste of soy sauce, and to promote awareness of how it could be used with food ingredients they normally ate. These restaurants were popular and, by 1991, a total of seven had been opened, with new locations in Berlin, Cologne, Frankfurt and Munich. In 1979, the company established Kikkoman Trading Europe in a suburb near Düsseldorf for the purpose of further promoting soy sauce.

Recognizing the strong potential of the Australian market, Kikkoman established a representative office in Sydney in July 1980. While Kikkoman soy sauce traditionally had been handled by Japanese trading companies, in 1977 Kikkoman had established an agreement with a locally based distributor, and sales began increasing rapidly.

The primary reason for this popularity is that soy sauce adapted well to the strong "barbecue" culture of Australia. Australians are also big consumers of seafood, with Asian styles of preparation using soy sauce common.

Starting with a campaign in Adelaide in 1978, Kikkoman expanded TV advertising into Sydney, Melbourne and Brisbane in 1979, followed by Perth in 1980. Consumption continued to increase, with exports to Australia nearly tripling between 1979 and 1985. Kikkoman ended its agreement with the local importer in January 1992, with activities being taken over by Kikkoman's Australian subsidiary.

Kikkoman's movement into Asian markets represented a significant difference from its experiences in North America, Europe and Australia. Throughout Asia, soy sauce is an existing culinary tradition, with many establishsed manufacturers. However, Chinese-style soy sauce predominates. Both flavor and color differ greatly from its Japanese counterpart. Nevertheless, with the increasing popularity of Japanese food, there was a small but growing demand for Japanese-style soy sauce, which also goes well with local cuisines.

Kikkoman's obvious potential in Asia made a factory in Southeast Asia feasible. From there, the product could be shipped more economically, too, to Australia and Europe, while local markets could be further cultivated. While the feasibility of a factory in Europe was also studied, it was found that the market there could not support one at that time.

During this time, the early 1980s, Singapore seemed to be the most likely candidate for the establishment of Kikkoman's second overseas soy-sauce production facility. Singapore was selected for several key reasons: both government and economy were stable, and the labor force was well-educated and hard working; regulations on foreign investment were not strict, and it was possible to create a 100%-owned subsidiary; and it was a major financial center and a duty-free port, with a comparatively advanced transport infrastructure. In addition, the government of Singapore was highly receptive to Kikkoman and proved to be of invaluable assistance.

In 1982, the company selected a site in an industrial park, with initial plans calling for a factory with an annual capacity of three million liters of soy sauce and teriyaki sauce. Kikkoman Singapore was established in April the following year and building approval was granted in September. Although Singapore has a very hot climate, Kikkoman was able to adapt its fermentation technology to produce soy sauce with the same flavor as that produced in Japan.

The factory in Singapore was heralded for its automation and, given its central location in Asia, it would play a key role in helping to develop markets throughout the region. Construction was completed in November 1984, and the first products were shipped from 1985. About 10% of production went to the Singapore market, with the remainder exported to Australia, Europe and Southeast Asia. Shipments to Europe continued until Kikkoman's factory in the Netherlands went on line in 1997.

In 1990, Kikkoman established a joint venture in Taiwan with Uni-President Enterprises, the country's largest food-products manufacturer. The new company, President Kikkoman, Inc., would operate Kikkoman's third overseas factory. At that time, some 80% of Taiwan's soy-sauce market (approximately 100 million liters annually) was held by manufacturers of chemically produced soy-sauce products, so it was expected that the Kikkoman brand would be welcomed by consumers. In order to suit local tastes, Kikkoman produced a sauce that was slightly sweeter than that produced in Japan.

Steadily increasing consumption in Europe in the 1980s naturally sparked interest in establishing a Kikkoman factory there. Initial projections indicated it would be feasible with an annual consumption of around three million liters. A number of sites were considered in countries such as Belgium, Denmark, England, France, Germany, the Netherlands and Poland. By 1994, the choice had been narrowed down to Denmark and the Netherlands and, after further surveys and research, the Netherlands was selected in 1995. Among the reasons for this decision was the country's central location and a world-class program in fermentation technology that existed at one of the Dutch universities. The fact that it is easy to function in English in the Netherlands was also a benefit for Kikkoman employees coming from Japan.

Strong and growing demand for soy sauce in the U.S. spurred interest in a second factory there since production could not be increased easily at the existing factory in Wisconsin. The West Coast was a prime location for several reasons. Soy-sauce consumption was strong and growing, helped by a rapidly increasing population and a large and growing population of people of Asian descent. Transport to this market from Wisconsin took four days by truck and eight days by rail. Since a competing soy-sauce producer was apparently supplying the San Francisco area market from its Oregon factory, and commercial deliveries by tanker truck were also possible, Kikkoman redoubled its efforts to build a factory on the West Coast.

Initially, some 150 counties in the states of Washington, Oregon, Nevada and California were considered. After extensive surveys, the choice was narrowed down to sites in Oregon and northern California. While both were excellent choices, California was selected in December 1996 because deliveries to Southern California could be made within one day. While Oregon had the advantage of a cooler climate, the problem of higher temperatures in California was solved by refrigeration.

The northern California site, in the town of Folsom in the foothills of the Sierra Nevada, has a plentiful supply of superb-quality water and excellent highway access. In 1998, a factory with an annual capacity of 10 million liters was completed. Unlike the Wisconsin factory, the new facility placed emphasis on industrial and food-service products.

Kikkoman's factory on the outskirts of Shanghai, China, was completed in May 2002. This facility is a joint venture with Uni-President Enterprises,

Kikkoman's Taiwan partner. Here, the original style of Kikkoman soy sauce is produced, along with a slightly sweeter version to suit the Chinese palate. While there were no major difficulties in site selection and other factors, achieving an appropriate balance of quality and price took considerable time.

Localization in each market

Kikkoman has traditionally focused on its area of core competence, soy sauce, in its overseas operations. In Japan, on the other hand, the company has manufactured a wide variety of products for many years. These include *mirin*, a sweet sake used for cooking, and *sho-chu*, a traditional Japanese distilled alcoholic beverage. Beginning in the 1960s, Kikkoman began to further diversify its businesses in line with the increasing acceptance of Western food and drink in everyday life. Among these were tomato ketchup and tomato juices, sold under the Del Monte brand name, along with wine and soft drinks. It also began introducing a growing variety of soy-sauce-derivative seasonings to make home meal preparation easier.

Initial marketing in the United States, however, created the opportunity to introduce a new type of product derived from soy sauce. In 1961, the company introduced Kikkoman Teriyaki Marinade, a type of meat marinade based on soy sauce. Americans liked its rich, sweet and savory flavors, and teriyaki cooked meats quickly became widely popular throughout the United States. It was not long before the word "teriyaki" entered the English language, and was included in Webster's Dictionary.

The success of Kikkoman's teriyaki marinade in the early 1960s became the pattern for its later successes in the U.S. condiment market. Since then, Kikkoman has introduced a remarkable array of condiments based on soy sauce, including low-sodium soy sauce, low-sodium teriyaki sauce, stir-fry sauce, sweet-and-sour sauce, roasted garlic teriyaki sauce, and marinades in a variety of flavors. In addition, it has also introduced a number of seasonings, sauces and meal-making solutions for the consumer market, as well as products designed for food-service and industrial applications.

In Europe, Kikkoman's product line centers on traditional soy sauce, along with sweet soy sauce, teriyaki marinade and sukiyaki sauce.

The introduction of Kikkoman soy sauce into Asian markets in which soy sauce was already a part of the culinary tradition produced subtle yet significant effects. Since nearly all soy sauce in Asia is produced differently from the traditional Japanese brewing techniques, the taste is somewhat different. Many types of Asian soy sauce are produced using different methods, periods and ingredients. As a result, many are often harsher and less complex than Japanese naturally brewed soy sauce, and do not have the savory, complex aroma that distinguishes Kikkoman from the competition.

Kikkoman soy sauce is more time-consuming and expensive to produce and is, accordingly, priced higher than most local soy sauces in Asian markets. Therefore, Kikkoman does not compete with local soy sauce because it is a premium product in a class of its own.

The presence of Kikkoman in many Asian markets has stimulated efforts toward higher product quality and consistency among local producers. Exposure to Kikkoman's production techniques has led to an improvement in the quality of products manufactured by the company's partner in Taiwan and China.

Effects of globalization on Kikkoman's corporate culture

Its encounters with overseas business practices have led Kikkoman to make slight changes in its approach to corporate governance. In 2000, we introduced a corporate-officer system and stock options, and in 2001 we reduced the number of board members to nine. In 2002, we further reduced the number of inside board members to eight and added two outside directors and one outside auditor. We have also set up nominating and compensation committees.

In addition, Kikkoman has established a compliance committee and is also undertaking activities to promote transparency in its operations, and accountability by its management. These changes have had an invigorating effect on our management environment, while underscoring our commitment to quality and delivering on the expectations of our stakeholders.

When Kikkoman established its first overseas factory in the U.S. in 1973, the company adhered to a policy of hiring local people, giving them on-the-job training and promoting them on the basis of performance and ability. In order to begin its operations on a solid footing, managers were sent from Japan. The personnel manager, however, was an American, since familiarity with local customs and practices was an essential requirement for the position.

In this way, Kikkoman followed a philosophy and policy of hiring, training and promoting local employees. This was, of course, a difficult task given that Japanese traditional natural-brewing methods are complex, requiring intuition as well as technical knowledge in order to produce products of the required quality. However, Kikkoman's active stance toward training has resulted in a strong workforce of highly capable local employees. This philosophy and practice has become a cornerstone of Kikkoman policy in its overseas operations.

Through Kikkoman's globalization efforts, it has taken its tradition of good corporate citizenship to a global level. In January 2001, Kikkoman became the first Japanese company to participate in the UN Global Compact, which specifically defines social responsibility initiatives in three key areas – human rights, labor and the environment. Given its efforts in labor and human rights, it was a logical development for the company to become a participant. Furthermore, Kikkoman has long been sensitive to environmental issues, making its participation even more natural.

Efforts to meet the Compact's initiatives include the drive to have all the Kikkoman Group's major production facilities obtain ISO 14001 certification. Facilities in Japan obtained this between 1997 and 2001, while factories in the United States (Wisconsin), the Netherlands and Singapore received certification in 2002. Kikkoman's California plant has received waste-reduction awards from the State of California Environmental Protection Agency for two years running. Since 2000, the Netherlands plant has provided annual donations to the Water Over Wolfsbarge marshland preservation project.

Kikkoman Corporation is proud of its record of achievements in corporate social responsibility, and will continue to assign top priority to similar activities worldwide in the years to come. Kikkoman agrees with the UN that these initiatives work to create a world in which everyone benefits from globalization.

Future directions

Japan is a mature market for soy sauce, so Kikkoman is attaching increasing importance to high value-added products in this category, while expanding its market share in derivative products. These two areas are considered to be the company's main businesses in Japan for the next decade.

Outside Japan, on the other hand, Kikkoman believes there are still more opportunities for growth. Accordingly, it will continue to strengthen its existing overseas production and marketing, while monitoring potential in new regions.

Worldwide, Kikkoman intends to stay close to its core competence in soy sauce and derivative products and will use this inherent advantage to enter new markets. It will continue to experience strong growth in Europe, North America and Australia, as well as in Asian markets.

In the long term, China is seen as a country with promising growth potential. Other areas which have some potential include Latin America and India, but there is no immediate need for factories in those regions.

The story of Kikkoman's globalization is unique among enterprises producing traditional products. Although various types of soy sauce are produced throughout East Asia, Kikkoman's vision and adept entry into Western markets have established its Japanese-style soy sauce as the world standard. Kikkoman today is the result of a business legacy with over three centuries of tradition; a history matched by very few enterprises in the world.

Another factor unique to Kikkoman's success is that there was only a limited existing market for its product. While companies in other industries entered existing overseas markets, Kikkoman deftly repositioned its traditionally Japanese product – from "soy sauce" to "all-purpose seasoning" – and created demand by integrating it into mainstream American food culture. Kikkoman now enjoys the enviable position of being the clear market leader in soy sauce in the U.S. and elsewhere.

It was also one of the first major Japanese firms to set up production in the United States. This was when the value of the yen vis-à-vis the U.S. dollar was very low, requiring tremendous resources which incurred high risk. Despite initial resistance from within the company, the vision of a U.S. factory eventually won out. This proved to be a wise decision for Kikkoman. While the Japanese market is saturated, placing a natural limit on profitability, overseas business operations have become quite profitable, currently accounting for about 22% of its sales, which represents an astonishing 50% of Kikkoman's consolidated profits.

Kikkoman's experiences in opening factories in the U.S., the Netherlands, Singapore, Taiwan and China have provided a model for other Japanese enterprises to follow and the company looks certain to continue this pattern of success in regions throughout the world.

TAKEAWAYS

1. **The desire to create networks abroad – after 350 years of being "at home".**
   Kikkoman is one of the world's oldest companies, dating back almost 400 years. For most of this time, corporate growth evolved in the company's home market, Japan. Kikkoman's global inroads were made first into the U.S. and later into Europe and Asia. Kikkoman first started as a typical exporter, then decided to build up the permanent structures abroad – plants to brew soy sauce. The company today is a worldwide network of production, R&D and marketing facilities.

2. **Globalization is equal to localization of a very local product.**
   Kikkoman's core strategy has been to diversify soy-sauce-related products in Japan and to expand its international businesses. In doing the latter, the taste of soy sauce has been adapted to each new market. To accommodate local tastes in China, for instance, Kikkoman offers a slightly sweeter product in addition to its regular soy sauce. Moreover, the company has created new markets and brought a new flavor to American and European cooking. The company has found markets for a uniquely Japanese product in unlikely places – the result of a continuous process of discovery and learning.

3. **Delocalizing financing – giving up resource-based advantages.**
The overseas expansion was mainly financed through international banks – an unusual practice around the time of the company's first expansion overseas. Like Sony, Kikkoman has not been part of the all-dominating *keiretsu*, which resulted in disadvantages in the early phase of global expansion when it needed funds. However, in the long run, the independence from *keiretsu* funding was a blessing in disguise as the company had to learn the practice of global financing – a mandatory step to globalize operations.

4. **Quality and branding are Siamese twins.**
Kikkoman's success in overseas markets derives from, among other things, the superior quality of its products. The company established a consistent quality-control system to maintain the same quality standard around the globe. This high quality level easily translated into a good brand awareness. "Kikkoman" is nowadays synonymous with soy sauce, and has almost replaced it as a generic term. The company carefully integrated its capabilities overseas by employing and training locals.

5. **Global compacting guarantees sustainable success.**
In 2001, Kikkoman was the first Japanese corporation to participate in the United Nations Global Compact to help distribute the benefits of globalization to the world. Under the terms of the Compact, Kikkoman has pledged to observe UN principles drawn in the fields of human rights, labor and the environment. Profit-seeking is important but Kikkoman considers it more important to make a contribution to building social well-being. Moreover, the company maintains ancient family codes, dating back to a time when warlords and shoguns ruled Japan, to contribute for the benefit of its customers and employees and for the development of communities and the world.[7]

6. **Future challenges – the impetus for enhanced globalization.**
Kikkoman is still basically a one-product company and its global outreach has mostly evolved from soy souce and its derivatives. Can it survive in this globalized world? Without diversifying further, the company may not be able to reach the level of size and influence of companies such as Nestlé, Kraft and Unilever. The next step in the globalization of Kikkoman may be its most difficult yet.

▲ SAMSUNG ELECTRONICS

Yun Jong Yong
Vice-Chairman & CEO, Samsung Electronics Co., Ltd.

Customer demand continues to grow and diversify with globalization, and the business environment is changing rapidly in the 21st century. Thus, management innovation is an important means for global companies to secure competitiveness amid the uncertainty they face today.

To become a more globalized company, Samsung Electronics has implemented a variety of activities and continued to innovate processes, personnel and products (the 3Ps) and restructure since the Korean foreign-currency crisis in 1997. This effort has enabled Samsung to rapidly emerge as a major global player in the IT industry, despite the global industry slump.

Here, I would like to describe how Samsung Electronics has turned a management crisis into an opportunity to bolster competitiveness in the wake of the 1997 economic turmoil and to become a global company. An analysis is given of the company's philosophy and approach to managerial innovation.

Introduction

Samsung Electronics more than doubled its annual sales in five years, from KRW25 trillion in 1998 to KRW65 trillion in 2003. During the same period, profitability went from break-even to a high margin of at least 16%.

Recently, moreover, Samsung Electronics has been among the few IT companies to continue achieving new income records despite the ongoing slump in the IT industry. In the process, it is quickly emerging as a global IT industry powerhouse.

The most dramatic achievement is related to corporate branding. Through the mid 1990s, Samsung Electronics was seen favorably as a maker of memory chips, but could not shed the stigma of being a producer of low-end finished products. Just five years later, the Samsung name is the world's fastest-growing brand and its brand value has soared.

Samsung Electronics began exporting goods in the late 1970s and established its first offshore production facility, a TV plant in Portugal, in 1982. The company continued to grow as a global operation, with a steady increase in the number of overseas plants and sales offices. Up until the early 1990s, however, offshore production was conducted mainly to avoid charges of dumping or other import restrictions, and the competitiveness of production outside Korea was much lower than that of domestic operations. Moreover, the low-end product image persisted and overseas sales subsidiaries were unable to make major inroads into their respective markets. Most of the profit from the sale of finished products was earned in Korea, while exports and overseas operations suffered chronic losses.

At the end of 1997, Korea was plunged into an economic crisis that required a bailout by the IMF. Samsung Electronics, saddled with such a weak operational structure, was confronted with a serious crisis as well. The massive restructuring and management reform that followed brought great change.

First, a resolute restructuring program was launched in the second half of 1998. A policy called "Concentration on Selective Resources" was adopted, and all units or functions not considered strategically important were sold, discontinued or spun off. Inventories and accounts receivable were reduced, the workforce was downsized by one-third and unprofitable assets were sold.

The sweeping reforms slimmed down the company considerably, including the one-third reduction in employees in less than one year. The force of this restructuring effort greatly increased the consensus among employees that the company was in crisis. This heightened awareness enabled management reform and innovation to be implemented voluntarily throughout the company.

At the same time, a management-reform program known as "3P Innovation" ("Products", "Processes" and "Personnel") was implemented. This was a sweeping reform effort that covered business structure, work methods, and organizational and corporate cultures.

Product innovation enabled the company to reduce its dependency on memory chips and create a balanced product portfolio that includes computers, telecommunications, semiconductors and home appliances. Such a mix is better suited to the era of digital convergence. Heavy investment was made into product lines that were either current world market leaders or had the potential to be so. Samsung has followed a strategy of continuously increasing the number of its leading product categories.

Process innovation greatly accelerated decision-making and supply-chain processes. Inventories and accounts receivable have been reduced and delivery times have been shortened, greatly improving the company's cash flow. At the same time, customer satisfaction has been raised and the chronic practice of getting rid of excessive inventory through discount sales has been discontinued. Moreover, quality improvements achieved through better management of parts and materials have also improved customer satisfaction. The company's overall operation has been restructured into a virtuous cycle of ongoing improvement.

Personnel innovation has transformed the organization's orientation from functions to processes. The organization has been rebuilt to become more market- and customer-oriented. At the same time, each business unit was given greater autonomy through the adoption of a new "Global Business Manager (GBM)" system, which makes each business area more responsible for its activities. Decision-making has become much faster as a result, while lower-level managers are groomed to become the company's future senior executives.

If asked how Samsung Electronics has became a globally known company, I would point to the company's marketing and branding strategy, its overseas operations, its R&D investments and many other factors. However, my personal view is that these factors certainly supported the company's evolution into a competitive global enterprise; in my view, the most important elements were the deployment of the 3P innovations and the successful restructuring during the Asian financial crisis.

Here, I would like to focus on the supply-chain management (SCM) system and IT infrastructure, which have played a pivotal role in process innovation, one of the key elements that helped the company to become a globally competitive enterprise.

These two examples have been selected because they have been decisive in accelerating decision-making and resource management. The improved speed, in turn, has enabled the company to respond quickly to rising uncertainty and operational scale brought on by the digital revolution and globalization.

Tremendous reform has been achieved in the product portfolio and personnel systems, but the process continues. The globalization of Samsung's personnel system still has far to go by comparison with long-established European and North American companies.

Management innovation

Samsung Electronics initiated 3P innovation in early 1997, but little progress was achieved because employees continued to follow old habits and ways of doing things. Moreover, record profits posted in 1995 brought complacency and false security to the organization as a whole.

However, restructuring in the wake of the Asian financial crisis in late 1997 prompted a shared sense of urgency among employees, and prompted a full-scale implementation of 3P innovation. A more competitive and future-oriented business structure was established, while product competitiveness was raised. Processes were also streamlined for simplicity, speed and decentralized decision-making, and the rapidly developing information technology was incorporated into processes to build a highly competitive IT system. At the same time, the organizational and corporate cultures were overhauled to strengthen 3P competitiveness across the board.

Restructuring: A turning point in management innovation

During 1996 and 1997, the market plummeted for major product lines, including semiconductors, IT devices, audio/video products and home appliances. Retail prices for mainstay items continued to fall and financial instability caused payment defaults to soar overseas. The record profits achieved by our semiconductor division in 1995 distorted the perception of the entire company's financial standing. The revenue structure and product portfolio worsened, jeopardizing the very survival of the company as the foreign-exchange crisis hit in 1997.

Samsung Electronics overcame the crisis through a sweeping restructuring effort. The business portfolio was overhauled; the workforce was downsized and the financial structure was improved by reducing inventories, receivables and expenses.

More specifically, the business portfolio was revamped for stronger future competitiveness through the divestiture of non-profitable and non-core business lines. The company reduced staff, directly and indirectly, by 30%. We outsourced simple tasks, lowered overall personnel costs, and improve worker efficiency.

In addition, Samsung Electronics improved its financial structure. Top priority was given to slashing inventories and accounts receivable, while non-profitable assets were sold off and expenses were cut. These measures resulted in lower sales volume, but the company was able to distance itself from its image as a maker of low-end products.

Restructuring brought greater awareness of the crisis to the entire organization and fostered a unified purpose among employees. At the same time, efficiency was raised through process innovation.

The massive workforce reduction forced the company to improve work processes to make up for the shortage in human resources. To this end, enterprise resource planning (ERP) and other IT infrastructure was applied, accelerating innovation.

Meanwhile, innovation in supply-chain processes sped up production, procurement, logistics and sales, and lead times could be shortened. These measures enabled the company to greatly reduce inventories of finished and semi-finished goods, despite the severe economic slowdown. Moreover, the company was better able to supply customers with the products they wanted at the time when they wanted them, laying the foundation for Samsung to receive a fair price for its products in the marketplace. At the same time, process innovation greatly accelerated decision-making, speeding up overall operations.

The implementation of general 3P innovation

The resolute restructuring effort greatly improved the company's revenue base in 1998, and top management decided the time was right to change misguided practices and systems within the organization. Therefore, a sweeping reform of processes, personnel and products – the most important elements of business – was launched.

Process innovation: Improving work methods

For Samsung Electronics, the supply chain involves seven major processes: development, procurement, production, marketing, logistics, sales, and after-sales service. Each of these processes was redesigned to be faster and simpler, reducing overall lead-time and enabling the company to promise faster delivery.

The company invested KRW1.6 trillion over six years to complete this program, which includes the construction of IT infrastructure such as the ERP system.

In addition, the Global Operation Process (GOP) was implemented to expand the process innovation to overseas branches and subsidiaries. The ordering and production cycle was shortened from a monthly to a weekly basis. The development, procurement and production processes were linked and a system was established to carry them out concurrently. At the same time, links between the sales and production processes were strengthened.

The people who participated in the "development" process were drawn from units responsible for product planning, marketing, development, procurement, quality control, logistics and subcontracted parts supply. Cross-functional teams carried out all the processes related to new product design simultaneously. As a result, the company was able to cut new product development time by 30%; from six–nine months to just four–six months.

For procurement, a system of collaborative planning, forecasting and replenishment was adopted with subcontracted suppliers. Management innovation was also put in place at the subcontractors, the starting point in the supply chain, to cut procurement costs. Expanded use of online bidding also lowered procurement costs by reducing inventories and raising the productivity of procurement personnel.

Production output was adjusted to match the volume of orders, shortening the lead-time between receipt of an order and delivery. This new approach also sped up overall processes and improved their flexibility. An advanced planning system (APS) was adopted that raised the efficiency of sales, production, resources and logistics. Delivery dates can now be set in real time and the number of late deliveries has been reduced. Overall, deliveries can be completed faster, greatly reducing inventories.

In addition, activities were launched to cut manufacturing costs in half while doubling manufacturing productivity. These efforts have improved Samsung's competitiveness dramatically, both at home and abroad.

Logistics were rationalized (delivery points were brought together); a direct delivery system was adopted and mixed-product shipments were begun. Ongoing efforts to raise the overall efficiency of logistics management have lowered costs and shortened delivery time.

On the marketing side, employees were given greater power to suggest new product ideas for the future. Demand for each product is forecast and weekly volumes are determined by using point-of-sales data. A global order-management system has also been put into place. Ongoing efforts are made to ensure Samsung products are sold at a sufficiently high price, while price competitiveness is improved and brand power is elevated.

Meanwhile, worldwide after-sales service data have been integrated and the integrated call center functions have been strengthened, raising the company's ability to respond to customers' needs.

Personnel innovation: Revolutionizing the organization and corporate culture

Personnel innovation is a response to process innovation. At the same time, the organization is decentralized with the empowerment of lower-level employees. The organization has been restructured for greater simplicity and speed. The perception of what constitutes an organizational member and an employee at Samsung Electronics has changed, and employees are encouraged to constantly improve their talents and skills. As a result, decision-making has been accelerated.

The Global Product Manager (GPM), a designation that will be changed to "Global Business Manager" in the future, was introduced in January 1998. Individual product lines are handled completely by the GPM and the organization has become more process-oriented.

The old centralized decision-making system has given way to an autonomous system built around the GPM, who bears ultimate responsibility for decisions. At the same time, the orientation of the organization overall has moved from manufacturing to marketing. Decision-making as a whole is faster than it used to be and, rather than being concerned primarily with production, employees now put customers first.

In addition, employee compensation is now assessed fairly and transparently based on performance, and both individual and organizational dynamics have improved as a result. Employees are now paid annual salaries and offered incentives such as stock options and profit sharing. The company can now easily attract top-quality people for core functions such as marketing and new-product development.

Meanwhile, Samsung Electronics has begun to cultivate a "digital corporate culture", with management systems in step with the digital era. In a 1999 address to all employees, I said

> *"Timing and speed will determine life or death of a company in the digital era. Thus, we must take the initiative in eliminating the 'Five Ills' of complacency, habitual practices, formality, authoritarianism and egoism, and equip ourselves with sound management fundamentals represented by speed, simplicity and self-regulation."*

The "Five Ills" refers to factors that cause major, unseen damage to the organization, including delayed decisions, poor interdepartmental cooperation and communications, unnecessary meetings and massive paperwork. Samsung Electronics has engaged in various activities to correct these ills. Working methods have been simplified, and the entire paperwork-approval process is now conducted electronically to speed it up. Laptop computers are now used at all meetings, and a campaign is being conducted to keep all memos to one page or less.

Product innovation: Improving the product portfolio

Product innovation refers to activities aimed at boosting product competitiveness as well as transforming the product portfolio to embrace future-oriented items that will make Samsung Electronics a leader in the digital-convergence revolution. The company is restructuring core competencies for the future. Mainstay business lines such as semiconductors, mobile communications and information appliances (to include digital TVs) are being cultivated into world market leaders. Greater new investment is also being made into the four key value-chain areas of home network, mobile network, office network and core components.

As a result, Samsung Electronics has been able to build a balanced business portfolio since 2000. Sales and profitability are no longer at the mercy of market fluctuations in any single industry.

Successes in process innovation

Global supply-chain-management (SCM) has been at the center of Samsung Electronics' process innovation. The successful establishment of an SCM-based operation and improvements to IT infrastructure have played a decisive role in driving innovation in other areas. At the same time, they represent tangible and concrete examples of successful innovation.

Establishment of the SCM system

Samsung Electronics established SCM to simplify and speed up supply-chain processes. Time-to-market has been improved so that the customer gets the desired product at the right time. SCM innovation is targeted at the seven major processes of development, procurement, production, marketing, logistics, sales and after-sales service across the supply chain.

In establishing SCM, our efforts have been directed at creating supply-chain processes that deliver optimal solutions to customers through market-driven development, production and sales. These same objectives are pursued by many other companies.

Samsung's innovation efforts, however, go beyond simply putting the existing processes online or imitating SCM success stories at leading American or European companies. Instead, Samsung has continued to develop and advance a unique SCM approach.

Firstly, the company redesigned each process in the supply chain to be simpler and faster by making work methods as efficient as possible. Then, new IT systems such as ERP were introduced. At the same time, as part of a comprehensive approach to innovation, the company continued to transform the way employees think.

At the same time, we redesigned work processes to be simpler and faster. The overall supply-chain process was optimized for speed.

In addition, the company removed obstacles in the decision-making process, such as barriers within and between organizational units, bureaucracy, complacency, and fixed notions of how things must be done. These measures improved both the organization and the way employees think about their jobs, resulting in faster decision-making.

The process innovations were incorporated into IT infrastructure innovation, enabling employees to perform their jobs with two goals in mind: to be more responsive to market changes and to raise customer satisfaction. Samsung's approach differs from that taken by many other companies, which have simply applied new IT systems to the old work processes. Much trial and error results when work methods and IT systems do not match.

IT infrastructure innovation

Samsung Electronics has strongly promoted IT infrastructure innovation because the company firmly believes IT infrastructure is the barometer determining process efficiency and function. Samsung also believes faster processes and streamlined decision-making are only possible by improving all processes in the supply chain. Thus, process innovation and IT infrastructure innovation have been consistently and continuously pursued in tandem.

Most Korean companies refrained from spending money in 1997 because of the Asian financial crisis. However, Samsung Electronics continued to invest in IT infrastructure even while downsizing. A total of KRW1.6 trillion won was injected into IT infrastructure between 1996 and 2001, and this figure does not include consulting fees.

Samsung's IT infrastructure innovation began with the implementation of the ERP system. In 1994, the company started an ERP project involving the development, production, purchasing and sales units, and process innovation was pursued along with system implementation.

The next phase began with the restructuring implemented in 1997 and beyond. Management was made painfully aware that financial data was critically important, and the finance division's processes were overhauled while systems were greatly reinforced.

As a result, the time needed to prepare consolidated financial statements was cut by 50% and the company was able to initiate a truly global operational-management system.

In the final phase of the ERP project, Samsung Electronics completed the integration of logistics, finance and personnel operations in overseas markets by the end of 2001. Lead-time from production to sales was greatly reduced.

ERP implementation began at domestic operations in 1994, and the expansion to overseas operations started from 1997. Within about six years, the ERP system was installed and operational at 80 work sites around the world, showcasing the company's advance onto the world stage.

Importantly, Samsung Electronics' IT infrastructure is still evolving. In 1999, the existing system was integrated with the advanced planning system, an SCM solution that allows weekly demand forecasting and production planning for production and sales subsidiaries. As a result, the company can now set delivery dates for customers in real time. In 1997, the product data-management system was also applied globally, enabling product-development units to share information with overseas subsidiaries.

Meanwhile, development of the collaborative product commerce solution is under way, which will allow system-based cooperation with business partners in product and design development. In addition, Samsung Electronics is developing a supplier-relationship management system to establish and implement global procurement strategies with subcontractors and a customer-relationship management system to enhance customer loyalty.

For the past six years, the company has ensured complete success by testing the IT system in specific areas before expanding it consistently to overall operations. Knowledge gained in domestic operations has been applied to the SCM system at more than 60 production and sales subsidiaries overseas. Now, sales, logistics and inventories can be managed globally in real time.

These carefully planned and consistently implemented improvements to IT infrastructure have resulted in a global SCM system that is second to none. This system has become the backbone for the company's global competitiveness.

Major achievements of SCM (1998–2002)

Global SCM has brought strong competitiveness from faster processes and lower costs. From the customer perspective, the on-time delivery rate in Korea improved from 50% in 1997 to 82% in 2002. During that same period, sales increased 2.4 times, while inventories edged up only slightly, from KRW4.2 trillion to KRW4.3 trillion. The average number of days for which inventory is kept has dropped from 108 to just 45.

Trade receivables increased from KRW4.6 trillion at the end of 1997 to KRW5.4 trillion at the end of 2002. However, the average number of days before receivables are paid has plummeted from 75 to 35. Moreover, per-capita productivity in manufacturing operations improved 2.4 times during this five-year period.

Many other hard-to-measure gains were made as well. Improved process flexibility and efficiency has eliminated unnecessary process expenses. Faster time-to-market has prevented lost sales opportunities and customer satisfaction has been raised. Operational transparency has improved and brand value has risen.

Major success factors

Above all else, successful implementation of innovation requires crisis awareness and the ability to forgo existing practices. The top executives must act as "chaos makers" who constantly instill a sense of crisis and lead ongoing improvement by changing the way people work and think.

At Samsung Electronics, organizational reform succeeded through the creation of strong crisis awareness throughout the company in 1997, when Korea was engulfed in the Asian financial crisis.

Second, successful innovation requires a comprehensive approach that encompasses IT infrastructure as well as organizational and corporate culture, products and other areas. The objective of management is to improve performance. However, better performance can only be obtained through a series of steps and processes. Given this, success in innovating in one segment does not automatically bring about overall performance improvement.

Samsung Electronics was able to establish the global SCM by promoting IT infrastructure innovations in tandem with process innovations. That is to say, success was possible because management realized that the key to good performance is balanced and comprehensive innovations in employee awareness and corporate culture as well as along the entire supply chain.

Third, innovation requires gradual and phased implementation; sweeping changes should not be attempted all at once. It is necessary to pursue small changes to showcase successes in order to create consensus for organizational innovation. Successful small changes also boost overall worker confidence. Change should start from a single point and then spread to form lines, then planes and finally three-dimensional space: namely, the all-encompassing system.

Samsung Electronics has thoroughly applied the principals of gradual and phased implementation in the construction of SCM. In addition, the system was first applied in Korea and, once success was achieved, it was expanded in stages to overseas operations. Thus the amount of trial and error was minimized.

Lastly, innovation requires consistent and constant effort. Ongoing management innovation is a must, even if it entails temporary setbacks in business performance, to readily cope with an ever-changing business environment and business targets. Innovation is like a spring. If you stretch a spring, it will be extended, but if you inadvertently loosen your grip, it will suddenly snap back. Likewise, successful innovation requires consistent and constant attention to prevent any tendency to return to the old ways of doing things.

Samsung Electronics reformed its organization to overcome the 1997 Asian financial crisis and consistently pushed for 3P innovation to improve its fundamental responsiveness to a rapidly changing business environment. In the process, significant management benefits, such as higher sales and profits and lower costs, were achieved.

Creating values: Community service and corporate governance

Process, product and personnel innovation cannot be achieved in a vacuum. Samsung Electronics, like any other company, has to monitor its environments supporting the creation of value to the general public. Samsung Electronics contributes to the development of global society in a spirit of coexistence by helping to improve the quality of life in local communities. This effort raises the level of interaction between Samsung Electronics and the world at large.

The "spirit of coexistence" is an ethical and human value very important to all Samsung Electronics employees, from the very highest level down. Social contributions are part of Samsung Electronics' role as a corporate citizen and a basic tenet to which all employees adhere. All employees are asked to pledge social contributions. The following are some of the major contribution programs:

- **Moogoongwha Electronics**
  In 1994, Samsung Electronics established Moogoongwha Electronics to employ disabled persons exclusively and provide them with the means for self-support.
- **Samsung UNESCO Education Fund**
  Samsung Electronics and the Korean National Commission for UNESCO (KNCU) have established a fund for helping needy children in underdeveloped and developing countries, including North Korea. The Samsung UNESCO Education Fund is used to provide educational materials and develop basic education programs for children.
- **Samsung's Four Seasons of Hope**
  Samsung Electronics America launched a children's charity program involving popular figures from baseball (Joe Torre), football (Boomer Esiason), basketball (Magic Johnson) and golf (Arnold Palmer) and charity organizations endorsed by them, as well as major Samsung retail partners (Best Buy, CompUSA, RadioShack and Sears). Samsung donates money and products to the charity organizations, while the retailers have pledged to contribute a percentage of proceeds from the sale of electronics products. The sports figures have also agreed to take part in product promotions to help boost sales, which in turn will increase the amount of money donated to the cause. Everyday customers are also encouraged to get involved through media interviews.
- **Samsung Vietnam Academic Exchange Program**
  Samsung Electronics has been involved in a program to promote academic exchanges between Korea and Vietnam since November 1995, when a US$1 million fund was established. The fund generated US$100,000 in interest that was used to run the program from November 1996. An advisory committee of three Korean

and three Vietnamese members was formed to deliberate on activities and select beneficiaries. Major projects to date include scholarships, invitations to next-generation Vietnamese leaders to Korea and support for academic conferences.

Samsung Electronics received valuable experience in carrying out sweeping restructuring in the wake of the Korean economic crisis of 1997–98. Moreover, the Korean capital market was completely opened to foreign investors in 1998, prompting many to purchase Samsung Electronics stock. Foreign ownership of company stock soon exceeded 50% of the issued shares. In response, we organized our first investor relations roadshow, visiting the U.S. at the end of 1998. Samsung officials, including myself, saw firsthand the strong expectations and demands of U.S. investors, and we realized the difficulty we would have in maintaining the status of a truly global company in capital markets without satisfying those demands.

After that, various initiatives were begun to improve the corporate governance structure. For starters, shareholders' interests were made an important consideration in management policy and performance assessment. The company has worked hard to become a corporation that cares about shareholders and to project that image.

Previously, performance was evaluated on the basis of quantitative results, focusing mainly on total sales and market share. That approach was changed radically to focus on the qualitative aspects of performance. The assessment formula today is 70% EVA, 20% EBITDA and 10% rate of return on stocks.

In addition, major changes were made to the composition and function of the board of directors to strengthen independence. The board, which previously was made up entirely of directors from within the company, was reconfigured so that a majority (seven out of 13) of the members are from outside the company. Importantly, three of the directors are foreign. Moreover, the auditing committee, which is attached directly to the board, consists entirely of outside directors.

These changes have significantly bolstered the control and monitoring of Samsung Electronics management. A nomination committee consisting of 50% Samsung Electronics directors and 50% outside directors has also been formed to heighten the transparency of the process for selecting outside directors.

A new organizational unit dedicated solely to investors relations activities was formed to further enhance operational transparency. This team ensures that the shareholders' right to know about company performance is followed through and acts as an interactive communication channel with top management, providing senior managers with a chance to hear what the investors have to say. Samsung Electronics has established an open-information policy, which includes the public announcement of performance results each quarter and a new web-casting site.

The company accounting system has been revamped in accordance with international accounting practices. In 2000, expenses from the stock option program began to be reflected on the books at the time the stocks were given out to improve the transparency of the company's overall standing.

In addition, Samsung Electronics announced and enacted a new ethical policy in 2001, clarifying the company's determination to operate strictly according to high standards of conduct.

The U.S.-based Institutional Shareholder Services (ISS), the world's leading provider of proxy voting and corporate governance services, recognized Samsung Electronics' efforts with an award for outstanding improvement in corporate governance structure. *Asset* magazine and other leading institutions have also judged Samsung Electronics' corporate governance structure to be among the highest in Asia.

Future tasks for Samsung Electronics

Samsung Electronics is now armed with a global SCM and other customer-oriented processes, as well as improved organizational and corporate cultures. Management now is confident of having the fundamentals to respond more capably to the new business paradigms.

Today, the company is striving to change toward a system that can lead customers. Management innovation since 2002 has been aimed at improving marketing capabilities and processes and building a market-driven culture. Marketing process innovations are transforming Samsung Electronics into a marketing-oriented company, rather than one that is manufacturing-oriented. The company is training employees and hiring marketing specialists to improve market-forecasting capabilities and responsiveness to market changes throughout the entire supply chain, starting from customer contact points.

The philosophy that "management is supervising resources and processes, and is an endless search for innovation" is an inseparable part of the daily business life of the people at Samsung Electronics. The company overcame the 1997 Asian financial crisis through time-consuming yet rigorous management reform, highlighted by restructuring and 3P innovation. This effort brought about new competitiveness that enabled the company to further strengthen its standing in the world market even during an international IT market slump. All these achievements were possible because Samsung Electronics instilled crisis awareness throughout the organization and got employees to participate voluntarily in innovation. The structures of the business portfolio, workforce and finances were changed radically in a short time. They were linked to 3P innovation to complete a successful, sweeping management-reform effort.

Global SCM was the main objective for Samsung's process innovation and served as the catalyst for IT infrastructure innovation as well as innovations in other areas. It showcases the company's tangible achievements in the management innovation drive. Global SCM allowed Samsung Electronics to gain a rare kind of competitiveness and lay a firm foundation for globalization. Successful management innovation required the firm to give up existing practices, to engender crisis awareness and to implement far-reaching rationalization throughout the organization. In addition, innovation must be pursued steadily and in phases. Success can only be guaranteed when management innovation efforts are consistent and continuous.

Samsung Electronics is not complacent about its achievements to date. To take on the new wave of the 21st century, the company is engaged in market-driven change to be reborn as a true market-oriented company.

I did not intend here simply to emphasize successes at Samsung Electronics. Rather, the intention was to highlight the company's philosophy of management innovation: corporate competitiveness can be obtained through continuous innovations as management itself is a constant process of innovation. Samsung Electronics will continue to work hard to achieve its competitiveness in the global market by exercising its strength in innovation and technology.

TAKEAWAYS

1. **Instill a globalization drive from the very top.**
Samsung Electonics began exporting goods in the late 1970s and established its first overseas production plant in the early 1980s. The overseas expansion advanced steadily in the following years. However, the main reason for building overseas plants was to avoid dumping charges and import restrictions. Most of the operating profit was still earned in Korea, while exports and overseas production suffered losses. This changed only in 1993 when chairman Lee Kun Hee announced Samsung's globalization program. From then on, the company embarked on a true global expansion, creating production and R&D centers where it made most sense.

2. **Unlearning I: Leaving behind local cultures and resource-based advantages.**
Realizing that the company's future was at stake during the Asian crisis, CEO Yun decided that the company needed to shed patterns of the past. He started out by cutting a third of its workforce and replacing half of the senior management with younger executives. He also appointed foreign board members. He then redefined Samsung Electronics' corporate culture by defying Korea's tradition of lifetime employment and reverence for authority. He has given his employees a degree of autonomy rare in Korea and in Asia overall, linking pay to their contribution to profits. Moreover, Yun has built Samsung Electronics into a multinational company by consciously shedding elements of the local *chaebol* system. The company is today tapping into international financial markets – domestic financing, subcontracting and staffing play minor roles.

3. **Building a global brand.**
In 2003, Samsung's brand has been rated the "fastest growing" in the world for the second year in a row. In just three years,

Samsung's brand value has more than doubled, from US$5.2 billion in 2001 to its current US$10.8 billion. This dramatic growth reflects the company's continuing record investment in integrated public-relations initiatives.

4. **The deployment of management systems.**
   The strong branding may be primarily attributable to the company's uncompromising quality standards, and continuous innovation processes, personnel and products. Yun calls this combination "the 3Ps", and holds that corporate management should strive towards an ongoing process of innovation. Indeed, Samsung Electronics provides a good example of how a company can excel through building systems. The deployment of the 3Ps is certaintly Samsung Electronics' real strength – the company's abilities as a systems builder has seen its rapid development into a truly global company.

5. **Unlearning II: Discovering ethics.**
   Large Korean companies have not been perceived to have the best record of corporate governance, and most lack effective systems to monitor corporate management and protect the interests of minority shareholders. However, Samsung Electronics has made continuous efforts to introduce good corporate governance practices. Yun devotes considerable time to corporate governance issues and investor relations. Shareholders' interests were made an important consideration in management policy and perfomance assessment. In 2001, the company announced and enacted a new policy of ethics, clarifying its determination to operate strictly according to high standards of conduct. Moreover, Samsung Electronics lives a "spirit of coexistence", supporting grassroots projects worldwide.

Endnotes

1 James P. Womack, Daniel T. Jones and Daniel Roos, *The Machine That Changed the World: The Story of Lean Production*, London: HarperCollins, 1992; Tim Jackson, *Turning Japanese*, London: HarperCollins, 1993.

2 *keiretsu* – the industrial groups such as Mitsui, Mitsubishi, or Sumitomo. *Keiretsu* have been typically organized around a major bank and a trading company which own equity in the other *keiretsu* members and do business with one another. The *keiretsu* system has the virtue of maintaining long-term business relationships and stability in suppliers and customers. The system dominated the Japanese economy until the late 1990s when the major banks merged – leading to the partial dissolution of the *keiretsu*.

3 The term *chaebol* means "financial clique". These large business groups, originally created by Korean entrepreneurs and still partially family-controlled, spread over many different industries. The best known *chaebol* are Samsung, Hyundai, LG, SK and Daewoo. Daewoo went bankrupt in the aftermath of the Asian financial crisis.

4 At around the same time, the then Korean president, Kim Young Sam, made "globalization" one of the major goals of his cabinet. Kim's vision was *segyehwa* (globalization), which had as much to do with effecting change internally as it did with increasing shares in world markets.

5 Nobuyuki Idei, "A Common Responsibility to Promote Stability and Growth", in Frank-Jürgen Richter and Pamela C.M. Mar, *eds., Recreating Asia. Visions for a New Century*, Singapore and New York: Wiley, 2002, pp.305–309.

6 In September 1985, the G-5 (United States, United Kingdom, France, Germany and Japan) met at the Plaza Hotel in New York City to ratify an initiative to use exchange rates and other macro-policy adjustments as the preferred and necessary means to implement a coordinated program to weaken the dollar.

7 The Mogi family mission statement, drafted more than a century ago, has evolved into a constitution with 16 articles outlining a strict code of moral beliefs and acceptable conduct. It also calls for family members to practice peace, politeness, love, diligence and discipline, and address practical concerns, such as the importance of saving, educating and avoiding debt.

CHAPTER

3 The Builders

In the three first case studies we learned about the experience of companies that have been globalizing for more than 20 years. They have built a brand, have experienced and survived crises and been able to establish themselves as well-known international brands. They can be considered established role models for other Asian companies that want to internationalize. They were the pioneers.

The second series of case studies focuses on three companies that embarked on internationalization around 1990 and are to some extent still in the process of building their international management capabilities. They have known success, have developed capabilities and systems, but their position is not yet as well established as that of the first three cases. Li & Fung was a Hong Kong-based trading company that made an impressive evolution towards becoming a supply-chain manager, pioneering the concept of borderless manufacturing. It started this transformation in the late 1980s under the leadership of its current management. At the end of the '80s, Singapore Telecom was also a successful local and government-owned operator. Since then, its competence as a networked company has enabled it to transform itself into a high-performing corporation, a leader in its field in East Asia and Australia. The case of Olam is an impressive account of the transformation of a very old production and trading company in Nigeria into a value-added trader and supply-chain manager for food ingredients operating from Singapore.

While the three companies operate in different markets, and have a very different administrative heritage, there are some commonalities in their experience. All three are in service businesses. All three have a clear strategy, and a clear concept of how to position themselves in the international arena. All three emphasize the absolute imperative to develop the appropriate human resources to manage expansion overseas. Each of them has had to adapt and develop its original management systems in order to be successful.

Both Li & Fung and Olam were originally traders, in textile and food ingredients, respectively. These were highly competitive and quite fragmented sectors, often strongly influenced by governments. Each has been able to take advantage of the liberalization and globalization of the markets, in particular by creating a specific concept to position themselves vis-à-vis their competitors. To a large extent they have attempted to redefine the rules of the game in their industry, thus creating a clear international competitive advantage. Li & Fung defines itself as a supply-chain manager and has developed the concept of dispersed or borderless manufacturing. It has dissected the whole value-added chain of procurement and production of garments, and has allocated each step to the best-performing producer, wherever it is found. The company manages a very complex system of logistics across Asia and beyond, providing a complete service to its customers in Europe or the United States. In order to do so it had to develop an organization that was able to combine local agility and speed in decision-making with centralized control of financial resources, performance indicators and knowledge management. Its information systems, developed in-house, have helped it to gain a true advantage through knowledge management.

Olam moved rapidly from trading cashews between Nigeria and India as a means of gaining foreign exchange to a "one-stop" supply-chain solution for its customers directly from the farm gate in the producing countries to the factory gate in the consuming markets, and this for a variety of products. They are integrated along this physical supply chain and engaged in sourcing, processing, storing, transporting, distributing and managing the risks at each link of the supply chain. The company's source of profit is therefore a logistics or value-chain margin and not a traditional positional margin. In order to achieve success Olam needed not only to position itself carefully, expanding into selected adjacent fields of food ingredients and raw materials for the food industry, but also to develop an effective organizational system. The company argues that its greatest strength has come from creating an environment that has helped it to secure the highest possible *independent initiative* from its staff. This includes the ability to attract talented people to live and work in difficult, emerging-market conditions; the capacity to develop "global" managers by requiring that everybody go through the same "rite of passage" of living and working in similar conditions; its policy of promoting from within; and the policy of aligning owners' and managers' interests by giving the latter substantial ownership stakes in the business. Every time it sets up a new business or starts operations in a new area, it will, without exception, deploy a core of senior managers who are tried, tested and proven, who understand Olam's culture, risk systems and business model, and who can serve as role models in the new operation. This emphasis on building organizational systems is critical to success in new markets.

Singapore Telecom is a very different company. It started as a government-owned monopoly, in a protected market and with no specific advantages in telecommunications compared to its competitors from the U.S., Europe or Japan. But willpower and vision to internationalize, combined with operational competence and good business acumen, have led it to become a strongly networked player in South and East Asia, with a second node in Australia. This is a case study of learning and unlearning, trial and error and organizational growth. "Pragmatism" is the term Lee Hsien Yang uses to describe this learning process. He also puts great emphasis on the challenge of HR development for international operations. He argues that one of the most significant challenges for Singapore Telecom was to get the appropriate personnel for international assignments. In the late 1980s and early 1990s, the company had great difficulty in persuading staff to take up international assignments. They were reluctant to be uprooted from the comfort and security of life in Singapore. And to make matters worse, international assignments were not always glamorous; they had to be carried out in difficult circumstances without support such as cost-of-living allowances, accommodation, schooling, and other elements that are taken for granted today.

Singapore Telecom is also to a large extent dependent on its partners. The case study gives some interesting insights into its choice of partners in developing its international network. Lee Hsien Yang argues that Singapore Telecom chooses its partners on the basis of local knowledge, financial capability and, most important of all, for their values. While strong partners inevitably have to work at accommodating each other's views and interests, the choice of partners and the success in making partnerships work are two good reasons why Singapore Telecom has succeeded where others have failed. In short, this case shows how a company turned its heritage, local strengths and international vision into advantages, and in doing so learned to operate globally and effectively.

These three case studies are about builders and building the capabilities that enable a company to roll out a well-defined business concept. Their stories are about building concepts, building systems, building people, building organizations in highly competitive service sectors. It is their ability to build appropriate capabilities that has enabled them to be successful.

▲ LI & FUNG GROUP

Victor Fung
Chairman, Li & Fung Group

The Li & Fung Group is a Hong Kong-based multinational with three distinct core businesses: export trading, distribution and retailing. Founded in Guangzhou in 1906, Li & Fung Group today has an annual turnover (2003) of over US$5.4 billion, operations in over 40 countries and regions, and over 10,000 employees worldwide. Our core competency is supply-chain management.

The export trading business is operated by Li & Fung Limited (hereafter referred to as Li & Fung) and contributes the majority of the group's revenues. Through a network of 68 offices in 40 countries, Li & Fung sources high-volume, time-sensitive consumer goods – such as garments, fashion accessories, furnishings, gifts, handicrafts, home products, promotional merchandise, toys, sporting goods, and travel goods – on behalf of customers worldwide. Li & Fung provides its customers with the convenience of a one-stop shop with a value-added package starting from product design and development, through raw material and factory sourcing, production planning and management, quality assurance and export documentation, to shipping consolidation. And, instead of owning production facilities, Li & Fung manages over 7,500 quality-conscious, cost-effective producers who deliver on short deadlines for its customers.

The privately held Li & Fung (Distribution) Limited ("Li & Fung Distribution") operates a distribution network covering nine ASEAN countries as well as Greater China. It distributes fast-moving consumer and healthcare products on behalf of 300 multinational principals. Li & Fung Distribution specializes in manufacturing, marketing and logistics, which are integrated to create optimized supply chains for its principals.

The final business of the group – Li & Fung (Retailing) ("Li & Fung Retailing") – operates two specialty chain stores in the ASEAN region and Greater China; namely, Circle K Convenience Stores and Toys 'R' Us. The two chains – which comprise over 190 outlets with an average of 400,000 customers per day, per chain – offer product diversity in a friendly and appealing environment.

Li & Fung's evolution

Li & Fung started doing business in Guangzhou during the Qing Dynasty as a trade intermediary, charging a fee to bring buyers and sellers together. As a broker able to communicate with both buyer and seller – the Chinese factory operators spoke no English and American buyers spoke no Chinese – Li & Fung's commission was 15%.

As the need for trading companies diminished, Li & Fung became a regional sourcing agent for Pacific Rim production, with offices in Taiwan, Korea and Singapore. Li & Fung brought enormous knowledge of the region to its customers. Most big buyers could manage their own buying if they dealt only with Hong Kong, which had a limited number of factories. However, more demanding customers had wider needs which needed a wider sourcing base. Li & Fung's coordinated regional sourcing network and dedicated customer-oriented teams served to provide manufacturing information around the region to customers, match customers' production needs with factories' capabilities, and supervise production and quality control. Finally, we were able to help customers navigate a complex quota system for textiles entering emerging markets. In short, we could provide a package sourced from across the whole region rather than just a single product from Hong Kong.

Supply-chain manager – adding value along the way

In the 1980s, Li & Fung moved one step further to become a manager and deliverer of manufacturing programs. Under the old model, customers would identify a specific item and ask us to find the best place to buy it for them. Under the new model, customers identified, for instance, a "look" for a season, with desired colors and quantities. Based on the design concept from customers, we searched for the right type of yarn and dye swatches to match the colors, realizing a prototype to be approved. We would create an entire production program for the season. Although we contracted out all manufacturing, we ensured quality and on-time delivery through close work with factories to monitor the production process.

In the 1990s, the emergence of the Asian Tigers, and the increasing expenses of Hong Kong as a production base, propelled Li & Fung to the next level of development. We witnessed the mass migration of entire manufacturing lines in Hong Kong to lower-cost areas such as the Chinese mainland, which was just launching its open-door policy. Hong Kong's manufacturers were able to reduce costs by moving the labor-intensive portion of their production across the border, particularly into the special economic zones in the south. Riding on this opportunity, manufacturers created little kits such as plastic bags filled with all the components needed to make, for instance, a transistor radio and shipped them to the mainland for assembly. After the labor-intensive work had been completed, the finished goods came back to Hong Kong for testing and inspection. In this case, the labor-intensive middle portion of the value chain was done in southern China whereas Hong Kong was responsible for front-end and back-end support.

Using this model, Li & Fung was able to take apart the value chain and disperse manufacturing functions to the most effective places. For instance, low-skilled, labor-intensive tasks might be performed in one country, testing and packaging in another, and distribution in a third, all according to the respective strengths of each jurisdiction.

Holistic supply-chain management

Managing dispersed manufacturing was a big challenge, but also a huge breakthrough for Li & Fung. Once we mastered it, it was clear that our reach should extend beyond southern China. We therefore began to search for new and better sources of supply and extended our geographical scope globally, thus further developing our model of "borderless manufacturing". Under this model, Li & Fung analyzed the value chain, and looked for the best solution at each step. Thus we maximized the cost, quality and other advantages presented by different points along the global supply chain.

Regional coordination is key to this model. Say we received an order from a European retailer to produce 10,000 garments. For this customer, we might decide to buy yarn from a Korean producer but have it woven and dyed in Taiwan. Since the Japanese have the best zippers and buttons, we would go to YKK, a big Japanese zipper manufacturer, and order the right zippers from their Chinese plants. Having considered the factors of quota and labor, we might decide after all that the best place to make the garments was Thailand. To meet delivery deadlines, we might divide the order between five different factories. Five weeks after we receive the order, 10,000 garments arrive on the shelves in Europe, all looking as if they came from one location. Basically, we would pull apart the value chain, optimize at each step, and reassemble for the customer.

In addition to acting as an agent, Li & Fung also works with customers as a principal. We handle all the work along the supply chain, including research on consumer demand, product development, raw material sourcing, production planning, factory sourcing, quality assurance, export documentation, shipping consolidation, distribution and logistic management and marketing, sales and customer service. We orchestrate global supply chains, managing each customer's production programs. The challenge for us is to break down the supply chain into smaller components, hone logistics, and run things in parallel rather than in sequence. With efficient supply-chain management, Li & Fung succeeds in lowering the overall cost, even after paying freight and handling for moving raw materials and goods.

Li & Fung's strategic innovation – Supply-chain management

Today it is impossible to satisfy consumers with a single product. Rather, different products have to be designed and produced to meet multiple tastes across many consumer niches. Such fragmentation of consumer demand means that retailers now order more frequently, in smaller quantities. In response, Li & Fung divides the consumer market into niches or market segments, thereby enabling us to respond promptly to changing consumer preferences. Effective supply-chain management – and ensuring our focus on our core businesses – plays a critical role here.

Prior to the late 1990s, the environment for competition was characterized by information asymmetries arising from underdeveloped telecommunications infrastructure. The advancement in information and communications technologies (ICT) has shrunk the ability of firms to profit from information asymmetries. For us, it means that we can no longer cling to business as a mere "trading agent". Rather, we must use new IT infrastructure to enhance the efficiency of supply-chain management and open up new profit streams.

The principles of Li & Fung's supply-chain management

Our core competency is built around our ability to manage supply chains in a flexible, agile, cost-effective and responsive manner. We must also marry this ability with skill in collaboration. As companies increasingly focus on their core competency and outsource the rest, their success will depend on how well they can mobilize different aspects of their business through outsourcing, while maintaining the ability to satisfy customer needs quickly and precisely.

Li & Fung's evolution from a sourcing agent into a global supply-chain manager has been based on seven key principles:

- Be customer-centric and respond to the market demand
- Focus on the company's core competency, outsource non-core activities, and develop a positioning in the supply chain
- Develop a close risk- and profit-sharing relationship with business partners

- Design, implement, evaluate and adjust the flow of work, physical activity, information and cash in the supply chain
- Adopt information technology to optimize supply-chain operation
- Shorten product lead-time and delivery cycles
- Reduce costs in sourcing, warehousing and transportation.

Extracting value in the supply chain

Li & Fung has traditionally been in the trading business – matching buyer and seller for consumer products exported from Asia to major markets around the world. We have now extended our scope to manage the entire supply chain, integrating the whole process from the earliest stages of production all the way to the consumer. The ultimate goal is to find the best place to produce the required product in the most cost-effective manner and deliver it to the retailer and consumer in the shortest time possible.

In my view, success today requires that we carve out and focus on a niche that can be extended globally. For instance, for an order of trousers for a major American clothing brand, we would have the fabric woven in mainland China because the factories there can dye it the dark green indigo the client wants, while choosing fastenings in Hong Kong and Korea because they are the most durable. The materials will be shipped to Guatemala for sewing, since workers there can finish the job quickly, while being close to the U.S.A. If production problems arise there, we could always relocate the order to other countries within our global supplier network to avoid delay.

This example shows that our role is to deliver a product both cost-effectively and quickly, adding value throughout the whole production process. It is not a question of chasing the latest low-cost supplier but, rather, of turning the whole production process into a concept of supply-chain management. In short, Li & Fung becomes the *orchestrator* of the whole chain; from yarn to fabric to garments, to warehousing and shipping the finished goods.

Capital-light/leveraged-growth business model

Today, Li & Fung buys from around 7,500 suppliers and manufacturers in some 40 countries with specialized product and manufacturing capabilities.

However, we own none of the processing facilities, nor any of the equipment used in the various stages of production. If we did, we would have to invest huge amounts to acquire a supplier network, not to mention the trucks, ships and warehouses for transportation and storage. Early on we decided that this was not viable for us. Instead, we pursue a "capital-light" strategy which leverages the assets of other companies and mobilizes them to reach our growth initiatives. In other words, we are process managers, developing deep relationships with suppliers and manufacturers at each stage of the production process and leveraging their expertise to carry out the production. The role of Li & Fung, therefore, is to broker our knowledge across different production streams, to facilitate collaboration between different parties. We tap into partners' assets, rather than own them, and thus reduce our risk. This capital-light strategy also allows us to enter a market more quickly, and be more responsive to potential market shifts and technological changes.

Li & Fung's capital-light strategy is particularly suitable for Asia, where debt is denominated in U.S. dollars but revenues are in local currency. Fluctuations in currency values can cause shifts in asset values and local-currency interest payments. Holding too many assets would pose considerable threats. A recent study by McKinsey in Asia[1] found that to produce $1 of sales, the average Western company needed only $1 of assets, compared with $4 for an average Asian company. Our capital-light strategy keeps our balance sheet relatively free of debt, and also helps us to deliver a return on equity of more than 20%. Employee productivity is also high. With 5,300 employees worldwide, the company generated over US$4.7 billion revenue in 2002, close to $1 million in sales per employee.

Despite initial successes, we did not become complacent. During the 1980s, Li & Fung extended its sourcing offices beyond China, to elsewhere within the Asia Pacific region and into Africa, the Mediterranean and Latin America. Following our capital-light strategy, our supplier network will continue to expand and move in accordance with customers' needs and the cost structures of different countries.

Managing the supplier network

The real challenge facing Li & Fung is not finding the supplier or manufacturer, but maintaining the ability to grow to meet more fragmented consumer demands and drastically reduced turnaround times.

There are considerable challenges to be faced. For instance, for the past five years the garment business has been faced with declining margins in spite of increased sales, and a traditional focus on product marketing has been insufficient to arrest this trend. Inefficient supply-chain management is especially onerous in the apparel industry since the demand and price of a garment product are largely time-dependent. The price of a garment will start declining as soon as the season begins, decreasing the margin at each step. In addition, the manufacturing of apparel involves numerous steps, with variations from season to season, from style to style and even within the same style for the same season. Even if the components of a supply chain are the same, the grouping and order of manufacturing steps can be different, depending on the capability and capacity of individual suppliers as well as quota considerations of different countries. We need to help retailers – our customers – avoid product obsolescence and inventory markdowns while meeting this complex market demand.

In order to shorten the delivery cycle, we have to adapt the production process for flexibility and agility. We have a deep understanding of the respective capabilities of each of our suppliers and manufacturers, and we allocate the job according to their respective strengths. For example, we would know which apparel cutters can handle coarse wool but are less able to handle high quantities of finer forms of wool such as angora or cashmere. It goes beyond mere knowledge – we need to work with them so that we are able to stitch together a network of suppliers to satisfy our orders.

Of course, knowing our suppliers is crucial, as is monitoring the production process. But this does not mean taking control at the factory level, which would not be practical for us nor good for the supplier. We do not specify in great detail how factories should complete their jobs, but rather specify production milestones to ensure that the final product meets customers' requirements. For example, we would instruct the Taiwanese dyer on the specifications for the final product, including color and quality, and the date on which the fabric should be shipped to the sewer. However, we do not tell the manufacturer how to do his job.

Aside from streamlining the process, we also share responsibilities with suppliers. We have, for instance, reached out to help suppliers solve sourcing and manufacturing problems. For instance, during the Asian financial crisis in 1997, many factories could not obtain credit to buy raw materials, and the typical sourcing agent would simply pass the buck back to their customers. This meant that the retailers could not gain access to some production markets unless they financed the purchase of the raw materials themselves. In such cases, Li & Fung would step in to help finance the production of the order, extending such help mostly to its best and most loyal customers and the most capable factories.

In other cases, where a manufacturer has relatively limited purchasing clout with its suppliers, Li & Fung will leverage its supplier network to secure materials for that manufacturer at a better price and faster delivery date than would be possible if the manufacturer were left to depend on his own resources. We also provide economic incentives for suppliers. For each supplier, we take 30–70% of his production capacity over the long run. We try not to go beyond this upper limit because we do not want our partners to become too dependent on us. We believe our partners can grow their capabilities and absorb new techniques by working with other customers as well. We try not to go below 30% because we want to maintain our bargaining power and obtain priority attention from the partner.

Aside from ensuring revenues, Li & Fung also provides another important incentive to suppliers – the opportunity to improve their performance and technology standards. Each of our product teams has established detailed and measurable benchmarks for suppliers, and our staff closely monitor the performance level and the quality of products. The product teams provide suppliers with in-depth feedback on their performance, strengths and weaknesses. The suppliers can work with the product teams to improve their shortcomings and both parties will work toward bridging any performance gaps. This kind of collaboration has created a powerful platform for continuous performance improvement.

In a nutshell, Li & Fung provides intellectual and technical leadership and incentives that hold all the suppliers and manufacturers in the network. We manage information flow in the entire network, as well as relationships with customers and suppliers, to achieve reductions in cycle time, cost and risk. This supplier and manufacturer infrastructure matches a wide variety of customers to create a virtual supply chain.

What we do is more important than where we do it

The effects of globalization on consumer markets are not confined simply to an increase in the variety of products from around the world. Competition at the international level also means that a product's lifecycle is becoming shorter, requiring suppliers and retailers to practice timely manufacturing to respond to the ever-changing consumer markets. Li & Fung's customers demand either a quick turnaround production schedule, as in the case of clothing products where time-sensitivity is crucial, or a low-cost production plan that isn't concerned too much about production time. Whether customers are looking for quick turnaround, low cost or both, we are able to fulfill their needs because we believe that what we do – manage the supply chain – gives us unlimited freedom and flexibility as to where we do it.

Two examples illustrate my point. Following the terrorist attacks on New York and Washington D.C. on September 11, 2001, Li & Fung quickly shifted production from high-risk countries to low-risk locations. We reallocated hundreds of millions of dollars' worth of merchandise within the space of a week. We were able to do this because we have always had a very large sourcing base so that we can easily divert production orders from countries or regions beset by economic or political crises to others that are more stable. We are quick to adapt to different circumstances because we enjoy the benefit of having a flexible supplier network, a deep knowledge of suppliers' capabilities around the world, a high level of supplier collaboration and extensive experience in managing distributed manufacturing.

Another example to show Li & Fung's flexibility in managing its business is its timely and professional approach in dealing with the outbreak of severe acute respiratory syndrome (Sars) in Hong Kong in March 2003. When the World Health Organization issued a warning against travel to Hong Kong and South China on April 2, some of our overseas customers cancelled their trips to China for the following two months, a busy procurement season. To prevent a possible loss of business, Li & Fung arranged video conferences with our customers, and, as part of the contingency planning, we moved half of the top management team to the U.S. and Europe offices. In response to our customers' requests, we allocated their manufacturing orders to several mainland factories to ensure that production would continue even if one or more of the factories was forced to shut down because of Sars.

Li & Fung also offers its customers a range of choices as to where to make their products. For customers located in the U.S. and who value a quick-response service, we would seek a manufacturer in a neighboring region such as Mexico or the Caribbean Basin. For customers who are looking for low price, we would source from Asia. To support its growth in the U.S. and European markets, Li & Fung has taken several steps to expand its sourcing network over the years. Before 1996, sourcing was undertaken mainly in Asia. The acquisition of Inchcape Buying Service (IBS) that year served to support our growth in the European market. Li & Fung realized that customers of IBS, who were located mainly in western Europe, were willing to pay extra to have quick turnaround from nearby countries, such as Turkey and Portugal, rather than ordering six to nine months in advance from China. In order to better serve the needs of our European customers, we began to set up more offices and expand our supplier network in Europe. In 1996–1997, we opened sourcing offices in Egypt and Tunisia to support our expansion into the European market.

In 2000, Li & Fung acquired Colby Group Holdings, which further strengthened our sourcing capabilities and expanded our customer base in the U.S. department-store sector. The acquisition of Janco Overseas Limited in 2002 was in line with the strategy of expanding our hard-goods business, which enabled us to penetrate the supermarket and hypermarket sector, where there is significant growth in private label and non-food business.

Regardless of where Li & Fung's sourcing network is heading in the future, it is set to provide the same high level of contract manufacturing services to its customers. What might be changing is the more extensive use of information technology to increase transparency and enhance the connectivity of the supply chain between all participants.

Business drives information technology

Li & Fung is a company that makes garments without owning factories, cloth or sewing machines, and whose employees do not stitch. We rely on a wide network of suppliers to do the work; our task is to intermediate the process, and while there are little secrets as to how the goods are made, we are able to leverage information and technology to facilitate the entire process, from order to delivery.

Back in 1997 when B2B exchanges and other forms of B2B websites started to appear, people were wondering whether we would lose our middleman role. Our answer to this question is that the Internet is simply another communication tool that allows us to provide more value-added services and bridge communication gaps with our customers. In the same way as the emergence of the fax machine did not harm our business in any way, the Internet poses no threats to us and will only further secure our role.

Li & Fung has established a sophisticated, hybrid Internet-based system to communicate with its customers. For large customers, we have created an extranet called *Export Trading System* (or XTS, version 5) that allows them to browse through product lists and place orders online.

For example, as a garment moves through the production process, clients can make last-minute changes to their orders via Import Direct (a software interface that links to XTS-5), which tracks the entire production process. Back in the days when Li & Fung was solely run by phone and fax, an order of, say, 60,000 polo shirts, would take no less than four months to deliver because of numerous back-and-forth readjustments. Now, up until the fabric is dyed, the customer can change the color online; until it is cut, the customer can change the size and design online; and until the material is woven, the customer can cancel the order online. With faster communication, we are able to minimize mistakes and better fulfill customers' needs and adjustments.

The XTS-5 system is largely designed and written in-house by Li & Fung, but it also uses Hewlett-Packard and Compaq computers and Oracle database software to manage information and store data. Altogether, the XTS-5 system currently holds a remarkable 1.5 terabytes of data, which is equivalent to 1.5 million books. The system is linked to the offices where staff can supervise the manufacturing of customer products.

The level of communication between country offices and the Hong Kong headquarters varies, depending on the sophistication of the country's telecommunication system. For instance, in more advanced markets, the local branch offices can be linked directly to Hong Kong. Staff at those offices can link up with the central databases and send digital photos of fabrics or products back and forth. Staff at Li & Fung call this "thick connection". In countries where telecommunication systems are relatively primitive, the branch offices will use Lotus Notes to communicate via email and email attachments. This is called "thin connection".

In the old days when most staff at Li & Fung still relied on paperwork, much of the information received from customers would be input manually into the central database. For instance, when staff received a purchase order from a customer via EDI, email or fax, the information would be typed into the central database and transmitted to the respective suppliers. The suppliers would then have to retype that information and forward it to their own suppliers. This made the mechanism both time-consuming and prone to mistakes. The use of EDI was a big step in more effective data transmission between business partners. However, EDI is not only costly but a lot of its programming codes for an order cannot be reused for other customers.

Li & Fung is also fully alert to the need to improve the transparency of the supply chain. Take our traditional supply chain for a garment as an example. Without knowing the shipment dates, the parts supplier may not be able to secure sufficient supplies, and without knowing what the final product looks like and the complete picture of the customer's order, the supplier cannot offer the best choice and make any cross-selling for the order. Communication gaps are likely to impede the flow of products along the supply chain, causing delays in delivery.

In March 2002, Li & Fung worked with Microsoft's Biztalk to improve the efficiency of its supply chain by better connecting front-end orders from its customers with the back-end order-processing system. There are two major components to the improved system: the Li & Fung Trade Gateway, which is the central document-exchange hub, and the Supplier SCMTalk solution that ensures smooth and efficient data transmission between Li & Fung and its suppliers' systems. Customers can submit purchase orders, requisitions and other trade documents in any number of formats, such as fax, EDI, Microsoft Excel or Word files, to Li & Fung. The Gateway will convert the documents into XML format and integrate the data into Li & Fung's order-processing system.

This does not mean that with this new technology every step in the supply chain will become mechanical. We still retain and depend on human expertise at every crucial point in the supply chain, such as the designing of products and allocating big orders to different factories. Staff are also essential for ensuring the arrival of materials to suppliers and that production and shipment arrangements are properly scheduled. We have to make sure that manufacturers comply with the customer's requirements and we have to know how they treat local labor. These things require human judgment and experience and cannot be left to a computer. For these reasons, the Internet is unlikely to take control of the whole supply chain, nor can it orchestrate the supply chain. Rather it should be looked upon as an enabler to help us make the supply chain more effective and improve communication with participants. Our view on information technology is always "business drives IT", and not vice versa, which means that we have to be very clear on what we want to achieve with technology.

Since our customers are increasingly demanding more customized services, we have started to design and build customized extranet sites for customers to manage their ordering and tracking online. For example, a few years ago, Coca-Cola and its many independent bottlers around the world were increasingly relying on premium merchandise tied to sporting events to promote the brand. But Coca-Cola, being a beverage company and not a manufacturer of premium products, found it expensive to manage all the manufacturing activities and the process too slow to keep up to date with sporting and other entertainment events.

In March 2001, Coca-Cola commissioned Li & Fung to design and build an extranet site which allowed Coke executives and bottlers to co-design and order products, or to review what other bottlers had ordered. If one of Coke's branch offices selects a product that is useful in its market, it can piggyback on other existing orders to achieve economies of scale and a lower cost. We have now extended this aspect of our business, moving from six to 15 such sites for various customers in 2001–2002.

Organizational innovation

Owing to advances in manufacturing and distribution, the cost of developing new products and services is dropping and delivery lead-time is decreasing. This has resulted in an increase in customer demands as well as local and global competition, which in turn put pressure on the supply chain. In order to stay competitive, Li & Fung has structured its organization in such a way as to create a tightly integrated network of business units.

Customer-centric divisions

The organizational framework of Li & Fung is designed around its customers. We have about 120 customer-centric divisions, each focusing on one customer or a related group of customers. For instance, there is a "theme-store" division that services only theme-store customers, such as Rainforest Café and Warner Brothers. We keep each of these divisions small and entrepreneurial so that it can create a customized value chain for each of the customer's orders. Each division does between US$20 million and US$50 million of business a year, and is led by an entrepreneur that we like to refer to as a "little John Wayne", implying that they are like John Wayne standing in the middle of a wagon train, shooting at the bad guys (that is, working with customers rather than sitting in the office all the time). Managers at Li & Fung consider independence as essential to their own and their colleagues' satisfaction with the company.

Take one of Li & Fung's largest garment divisions, Gymboree, as an example. The division serves only Gymboree and has its own separate office space within the Li & Fung Building in Hong Kong. The division consists of around 40 staff, each of whom has a computer that is linked directly to Gymboree and Li & Fung's IT system. The staff are organized into functional teams, such as raw-material sourcing, merchandising, quality assurance, shipping and technical support. There are also sourcing teams in the Philippines, Indonesia and China to handle the large-volume sourcing required by Gymboree. Whenever there is a need to source products in a particular country, Li & Fung has a team dedicated to serve Gymboree.

For many traditional trading companies, their organizations are structured geographically, with branch offices in each country serving as profit centers and competing against each other. Li & Fung does not calculate the profit and loss of its individual branch offices, nor that of the managers who supervise the branch offices. As a result, branch office managers are therefore more likely to decide impartially which is the best branch office to handle a particular order. We believe this single-country, customer-centric organization structure can optimize the supply chain by better fulfilling customers' needs, maximize performance and maintain high levels of quality.

The "little John Wayne" in each division runs the division like he/she would his/her own company. Li & Fung supports the division leaders in every way in running their own business unit. We provide each division with the financial resources and the administrative support of a big corporation, but we also give them a great deal of autonomy in meeting the needs of their customers. We have been nurturing entrepreneurial behavior in the divisions so that division staff can be creative in meeting customers' needs and attracting new customers.

We will continue to nurture a smaller number of deep and lasting relationships. Our approach is: *Think like a big company, act like a small one*. We believe that it is only by maintaining small divisions that we can grow rapidly without becoming bureaucratic. As the market continues to change, our organization can adjust immediately.

Operation support group

The organizational structure of Li & Fung provides employees and customers with the efficiency of a small company and the support of a large one. We centralize and manage tight financial control and operating procedures. We have set up an operation support group (OSG) to serve as the back-office hub. OSG is the nucleus of Li & Fung and administers three functions: information technology, finance and human resources. OSG maintains Li & Fung's IT system that keeps a database of about 7,500 factories around the world (about 2,000 of which are producing for our customers at any given time). OSG also supplies each business unit with personal computers and a network connection. The charges for this are taken from the business unit's revenue, all of which goes to OSG's centralized treasury.

In financial control, OSG is very conservative, acting as the "central bank" that keeps track of all revenues. All cash flows are managed centrally through Hong Kong and all letters of credit will come to Hong Kong for approval and are then re-issued by the central office. This means that Li & Fung is guaranteed payment before it executes an order. OSG also offers cash-lending options to business units, charging a rate that is cheaper than if they go outside. Depending on the type of consumers, OSG also provides trade financing to customers.

Aside from IT and financial control, OSG also acts as an in-house human resources provider, offering recruitment services and internal matching of staff and training.

As indicated, through taking care of all the back-end needs, OSG allows business units to focus on their core objectives. We regard OSG not as a cost-based back-office exercise, but rather as a flexible operation and a competitive tool designed to address today's challenges effectively. Li & Fung's small, customer-centric business units can respond quickly to customers' needs while, at the back-end, they are supported with the resources and network of a large company.

Corporate social responsibility

Companies with global operations are increasingly called upon to address issues of sustainability, environmental protection and social responsibility.

In line with market expectations, Li & Fung is actively committed to the principles of corporate governance that are consistent with the prudent enhancement and management of shareholder value. We have a high regard for the interests of our stakeholders, including employees, customers, suppliers and communities associated with our operations around the world.

Commitments to shareholders

Li & Fung strives for full compliance with all local laws and practices in the places in which it operates. The management of Li & Fung endorses the principles of good corporate governance that emphasize transparency, accountability and independence in its management philosophy and public reporting.

With a trading tradition of nearly 100 years, Li & Fung has developed a corporate culture in which ethics and values are fully embedded in its business practices. Li & Fung's culture encourages employees to perform their duties with an entrepreneurial spirit and with honesty and integrity. They are required to avoid conflicts between their personal interests and their responsibility to Li & Fung. We do not tolerate corruption, nor do we condone employees' activities involving bribery or anti-competitive pricing. We also prohibit employees with access to unpublished price-sensitive information from trading in securities.

The management of Li & Fung has also put in place high standards for formulating a strategic and control environment that monitors and manages material risks effectively and safeguards material assets from unauthorized disposition.

Commitments to employees

Li & Fung is committed to treating employees at all levels with respect and consideration and to providing training for their advancement and development to maximize their contribution within our global network. Our culture also promotes workplace equality and a healthy working environment (our headquarters building is a non-smoking office, for example) and prohibits the use of child labor and forced labor.

Commitments to customers and suppliers

As a global supply-chain "orchestrator", Li & Fung strives to meet customer and market expectations by promoting and protecting the rights of workers especially in countries with low-cost production.

To meet this goal, Li & Fung has developed a code of conduct to be observed by all its approved suppliers around the globe. The code is a set of rigorous labor, health and environmental standards based on national labor laws, the conventions and treaties of the International Labor Organization (ILO), and international best practices. For example, suppliers are prohibited from hiring child or involuntary labor and from practicing corporal punishment or any form of discrimination. The importance of environmental protection, occupational health and safety standards and compliance with the law is also highlighted in the code.

Li & Fung monitors compliance with the above by undertaking factory inspections and interviewing the management to understand the factory culture and practices. It also reviews workers' wages and working hours, and other health and safety records, and interviews workers to ensure that factory policies and practices are being complied with. For each new supplier, our local compliance officer will conduct a comprehensive inspection before a contract is signed. Suppliers are required to provide details of the operation and working conditions inside the factory. The quality audit and compliance auditors, usually located in the supplier's country, will visit the supplier to ensure that the production operation and working environment fulfill the requirements under the code. They make recommendations for any changes that may be necessary and ensure that the procedures are followed. Each supplier is subject to an annual audit check. Conscious or repeated violation of the code will result in the cancellation of orders. In addition, Li & Fung provides structured training or guidance, both internally to its employees and externally to its suppliers to equip them with awareness, knowledge and the necessary skills to meet compliance requirements.

Li & Fung is a member of Business for Social Responsibility (BSR), an international organization based in the U.S. that promotes the respect for ethical values, people, community and the environment. For example, in conjunction with a BSR labor-rights project in 2002, Li & Fung, together with several other U.S.-branded companies, created a "labor-rights pocket guide" along with a labor law protection and aid poster specifically targeted for migrant factory workers in Guangdong, China. At the 2002 BSR Annual Conference held in the U.S., Li & Fung was the corporate sponsor of the welcoming reception.

Our company is also a participant of the United Nations' Global Compact initiative that forms a platform for the promotion of human rights, labor welfare and the environment through the promotion of good practices. Li & Fung is also a constituent of the Dow Jones Sustainability World Index, the world's first global index tracking the performance of companies worldwide that lead their industry in corporate sustainability, taking into consideration social, economic and environmental responsibilities.

Commitments to communities

Li & Fung and its offices, as an integral part of the communities in which they operate, contribute consciously to the well-being of those communities and provide support to people in need. The management of Li & Fung endorses the appointments of its senior executives to public offices, which currently include various government and non-government advisory boards and professional associations promoting Hong Kong's exports, international trade, quality-housing solutions and best corporate governance practices.

Li & Fung also provides institutional support in the form of sponsorships for universities, as well as charitable support through direct donation or direct employee involvement in fundraising activities organized by leading charitable organizations. These efforts and contributions towards a better society were duly recognized in 2002, when the company won the "Caring Company Award" organized by The Hong Kong Council of Social Service for its caring culture and good corporate citizenship.

Most of the commitments outlined above are under the direct supervision and management of our chief compliance officer. Through our corporate governance division we conduct regular meetings with staff in Hong Kong and overseas to ensure that our group governance culture and business practices are understood by our employees, and reinforced and embedded in the group's operations.

With the active involvement of its chief compliance officer who reports directly to the audit committee, Li & Fung will continue to embrace a high level of corporate social responsibility and harmonize its culture and appropriate business standards and practices throughout its global supply-chain operations.

Three-year plan – the tradition of innovation

Li & Fung develops its business strategies around a three-year plan. In the course of our evolution, we have realized that reactive responses are not enough to ensure survival in a rapidly changing business environment. Enterprises have to anticipate change and re-invent themselves to keep up with new challenges. We have always believed that having a strategic plan is necessary to guide the organization in making changes and re-inventing ourselves. We would paint a scenario of where we wanted to be and then would look back to find the gaps that needed to be filled. To institutionalize the process, we started formulating three-year plans in 1992.

While most companies come up with rolling five-year plans, Li & Fung's three-year plans are zero-based; that is, they start from scratch. During the planning process, the management has to think about the fundamentals of the business to help determine whether the current business model can be sustained over the next three years. A zero-based plan takes more time and effort to formulate but it allows management to analyze the environment and assess the company's potential, regardless of previous results.

The three-year plan allows Li & Fung to strike a balance between changes in the business environment and the stability required for implementation. During the first year, we adopt and begin implementing the plan. In the second year, the whole company concentrates on executing the plan. The plan is then completed and reviewed in the third year. Even within this three-year plan, divisions have the discretion to seek out new opportunities in response to changing business conditions.

Environmental-scenario painting

Plans must be based upon the current and future environment. The first step in formulating the three-year plan is to imagine the situation three years down the road. By analyzing trends, the management can build a scenario for the business environment. The analysis incorporates the macroeconomic situation, the market for suppliers and customers and the impact of technology in a business context.

In our three-year plan for 1999–2001, for example, the environment analysis took into account the respective trends in our customers' markets (the U.S., Europe and Japan) and those in the sourcing markets (mainland China and Asia after the financial crisis); and the impact of currency fluctuations (such as those arising from the introduction of the euro), new international trade rules, new technology, and rivalry within the industry. Every factor that could affect business was considered.

Li & Fung's mission is to be the premier global consumer-products trading company, delivering the right product at the right price at the right time. The vision is a general guideline for long-term growth and articulates the values that an orchestrator of the supply chain can provide for its clients.

Stretched objectives

An effective way to achieve a sustainable competitive advantage and continuous innovation is to set challenging yet attainable objectives. The company's objectives should be based on current conditions augmented by additional challenges.

In many cases, established companies are prone to staying within their current comfort zone. A challenging objective can encourage a company to break out and explore new markets and new ways of doing business. In our three-year plans during the 1990s, we invariably set a goal of doubling both revenue and profits. This goal was attained in the period 1996–1998. In the following three-year period, while our revenue doubled, our profit was slightly below the target because of exceptional losses in certain overseas businesses. Nevertheless, these "stretched objectives" have encouraged management and staff to strive to achieve more than expected.

Backward planning and identifying gaps

If "stretched objectives" point to the destination on a map, then "backward planning" is a method of identifying the gaps between the point of origin and the destination. Performing a SWOT (strengths, weaknesses, opportunities and threats) analysis can help identify such gaps, while demonstrating the strengths and opportunities that are available for achieving the goals. At the same time, the analysis identifies the weaknesses that the company should tackle, and the potential threats that it has to anticipate if it is to achieve its planned goals.

By analyzing the gaps, Li & Fung has been able to identify ways to improve its operations. For example, to create added value for customers, the company has extended the supply chain by engaging in the product-development process. It also leverages its financial strength by providing trade financing to selected suppliers in difficult times.

Developing strategies to bridge gaps

After we have assessed the operating environment, we begin formulating a strategy and action plan. Innovation is important in this regard because a previously successful model may not work for new targets. For example, in the early 1990s we found that we could not easily double our profits through organic growth as we had done in the past. We had to explore alternatives. For instance, in the plan for 1996–1998, we grew rapidly by acquiring and integrating Dodwell into the organization. Such acquisitions fuelled our growth throughout the second half of the 1990s.

Developing organizational structure to achieve stretched objectives

A targeted and structured implementation plan is crucial to the success of a business plan. The management of a company must detail the resources to be deployed, the implementation schedule and milestones for measuring progress and achievements. It is important to assign senior managers to supervise the progress of each step of the implementation process and coordinate cross-departmental efforts. In our plan for 1999–2001, our executive directors were each in charge of a specific strategy, in addition to their daily responsibilities.

The process of formulating the three-year plan not only paints a roadmap for the company to follow but also encourages communication throughout the company.

Looking ahead

The major directions for Li & Fung Trading include continued investment in information technology for greater efficiency; leveraging the vast China market, both as a sourcing base and a consumption base; fostering collaboration between different business units within the group; and continuing to identify viable acquisition opportunities.

The combined effects of the widespread global slowdown, the Middle East conflict and threats of terrorist attacks have reduced people's propensity to spend in Li & Fung's two largest export markets, the U.S. and Europe. In spite of this, we were able to maintain growth in turnover and profit in 2002, when our profit rose 38%, reaching HK$1 billion (US$128.2 million). This growth was in line with our expectations as worldwide demand for supply-chain management services continued to increase across the board. Li & Fung's leadership status in supply-chain management has enabled us to capture a significant portion of that rising demand and ensured its sustainable growth year after year.

The China market

Much of Li & Fung's growth in 2002 was attributable to the surging exports from China's Pearl River Delta. Currently, about 35% of Li & Fung's goods are sourced on the Chinese mainland, where we currently have 16 offices, of which five are in the Pearl River Delta. The opening up of China's manufacturing, distribution channels and logistics operations to foreign participation is likely to have a profound effect on the further development of the economy. China will continue to be a major manufacturing powerhouse and one of the world's centers of excellence in industrial production. The completion of major highways in the eastern and central regions by 2005 will further contribute to the sophistication and efficiency of China's supply-chain network, as well as its integration into the global supply chain. I believe that the Chinese economy has already gathered a critical mass for explosive growth and fundamental change.

While Li & Fung has traditionally focused on the export supply-chain business from China, we also see tremendous opportunities in the import supply-chain business to that market. We believe that the skills we have acquired and brought to bear in the former can be equally applied in selling to Chinese consumers.

Collaboration between business units

We have been trying to leverage the Li & Fung Group's trading and distribution capabilities to drive more business opportunities. We have incorporated the distribution and trading groups to jointly offer services to customers. In October 2002, Li & Fung Trading and Li & Fung Distribution jointly managed a discount-store project for a supermarket chain in Hong Kong. The trading arm manages the entire sourcing process, while the distribution arm manages the distribution of goods to stores, merchandising, category management, marketing and promotion, logistics and staff training. This collaboration demonstrates how an organization of independent entities can work seamlessly to manage the entire supply-chain process, leveraging each other's capabilities to maximize value for customers.

In 2002, the Trading Group and IDS International (a subsidiary of Li & Fung Distribution) jointly signed a contract with Business Products Group International (BPGI), a purchasing consortium of office-supply companies covering the U.S., Canada and Europe. Li & Fung Trading is responsible for sourcing products while iSCM Asia coordinates the delivery of goods to the respective members. The above models show how companies can collaborate across industries and geographical boundaries. Within the supply chain, companies can build a collaborative environment that is flexible and adaptable to changing customer needs. They must break down the traditional boundaries established to protect the company and form partnerships within the supply chain. Participants should work as a team to eliminate non value-added processes, while leveraging the capabilities and technologies of each team member to maximize value. We expect the trading and distribution arms of the Group to engage in similar projects in the future.

Innovative IT

In today's highly competitive global market, companies are forced to re-evaluate the way they do business. Customers are no longer making their buying decisions based solely on price and product quality, but are also demanding speed, a high level of service quality and added value. One way to meet these challenges is by turning the traditional supply chain that is focused on product and efficiency into one that is innovative and customer-focused. At Li & Fung, embracing information technology is seen as a critical link in the company's extensive supply-chain network and as instrumental in providing customized, high-quality support for customers and their time-sensitive needs. We will, therefore, continue to invest in new technologies for greater efficiencies across all aspects of the supply chain and improve our product-design capabilities in order to further strengthen our leadership position in global supply-chain management.

Growing sourcing base and acquisition opportunities

Li & Fung's target is to increase the company's value to shareholders. In the midst of a global economic downturn and the continuing economic effects of the war in the Middle East, we believe that the key lies in adding more high-value sourcing markets to our list and in our ability to identify good acquisition opportunities.

The ability to manufacture and distribute products quickly and at a low cost on a worldwide basis is increasingly important. Li & Fung will continue to find new sourcing markets where the customers' needs for high-value, low-cost goods are fulfilled. One such market is Vietnam, where, in 2002, we sourced goods worth US$180 million, compared with US$28 million the year before.

On the acquisition front, Li & Fung has steadily boosted volume through a series of buyouts. During 1999–2000, we bought Colby Group, Camberley and Swire & Maclaine. These three acquisitions together contributed a total of 21% to the growth of Li & Fung's turnover. The outsourcing trend in the U.S. market is expected to grow stronger in the current weak economy as retailers tend to rely more on the type of services Li & Fung offers, instead of running their own buying organizations that incur fixed expenses.

Li & Fung has remained on course with its diversification strategy. In October 2001, we formed an alliance with Japanese trading firm Nichimen Corporation, which focuses on importing and exporting products such as textile goods, lumber, metals, machinery, fuel, chemical products and food. With this new alliance, we now enjoy a stronger presence, especially in the apparel and home-improvement products sectors, in the Japanese market, which is conducive to our long-term growth prospects.

Matching our diversification into hard goods, in 2002 we acquired Janco Overseas Limited, a buying agent headquartered in Hong Kong. The acquisition allows us to further strengthen our penetration into the supermarket and hypermarket sector, where there is significant growth in the private label, non-food business.

With these successful acquisitions, today's enlarged Li & Fung is more diversified in terms of product mix, geographical coverage and customer base, and enjoying sustainable economies of scale. We are confident that acquisition opportunities in the future will help to meet the goals set out in our plans. Major opportunities continue to exist in the U.S. and European markets, and our growing presence in Asia and Australia also means new opportunities. We have been consciously stepping up activities in East Asia and the Southern hemisphere to open up additional possibilities and to maximize the company's potential.

The globalization trend and its resulting competitive pressures, along with China's increasing economic importance in the global market, will underpin the practice of supply-chain management. As consumers and suppliers demand quality and efficiency across the entire manufacturing value chain, Li & Fung's track record as a global supply-chain management leader will certainly help to generate confidence and reassurance.

TAKEAWAYS

1. **Li & Fung has developed and honed processes to ensure organizational learning and upgrading.**
   These include the three-year, zero-based planning system, and SWOT analysis. Fundamentally, the businesses of trading and supply-chain management are based on the ability to exploit

generally available information and capitalize on information asymmetries. Li & Fung's ability to rapidly exploit information asymmetries is driven in large part by the in-house development of information management and knowledge-sharing systems. Each is tailored according to prevailing market circumstances and is constructed so as to ingrain organizational learning in a way that is useful to the customer.

2. **Li & Fung has learned to evolve with the market shifts and changes in the macroeconomic environment, to develop a creative concept and appropriate strategy.**
The company's development from a traditional trader into a supply-chain manager, integrating concepts such as dispersed or borderless manufacturing, has provided a strong sense of purpose to the internationalization process, while allowing the company to respond to changing client demands and market expectations. The group's response to the global changes in textile quotas at the end of 2004 will mark the next stage of its evolution.

3. **Li & Fung has grown into a global company, both organically and through acquisition.**
Central to its successful internationalization is the combination of entrepreneurial independence (both in company operation and the operations of subsidiaries or operating divisions) with the strong central management of resources such as finance or information. The company's success in absorbing other companies has been built on its deep knowledge and understanding of its core business as well as clear aims about the purpose of the acquisition. The company, through its in-built organizational learning processes, has also ensured that the expertise of the acquired business and its markets is also fed back into the rest of the organization, a process which helps build trust and increases the chances that the acquisition will be successful.

4. **The company's capital-light strategy and the emphasis on entrepreneurship.**
These have helped it to rapidly scale up to take advantage of opportunities that arise, without keeping too many capital assets or long-term debts on its books. Many Asian companies would do well to learn from this example, and grow through leveraging or extending capabilities rather than through resource expenditure. The group has been prescient in choosing its strategy: investments in suppliers could become liabilities given market shifts arising from changes in global textile and tariff regulations.

▲ SINGTEL

Lee Hsien Yang
President & CEO, Singapore Telecommunications Limited

Background

With little fanfare, SingTel began to expand into overseas markets in 1988. At that time, we were still the Telecommunication Authority of Singapore (TAS), a statutory body providing telecommunications for our small island-nation. The monopoly operated in a relatively vibrant economy, with revenues growing steadily at 7–8% a year. There were enough business opportunities at home without having to look elsewhere.

In that situation it would have been easy for the TAS management to rest content, satisfying domestic demand, maintaining margins, and making sure subscribers were happy with the quality of the services offered.

Koh Boon Hwee, who became TAS Chairman in 1986, saw it differently. He was the managing director of Hewlett Packard in Singapore and the first Singaporean to head the local operations of the American firm. For him, dealing with competition was part and parcel of everyday business. In the private sector where he worked, one of the major criteria for the success of a company was its ability to grow. While the TAS was still a monopoly on the island, Boon Hwee and the TAS board of directors were convinced that growth, in the long term, had to come from abroad. So they decided to pursue an international expansion strategy.

To insulate the government from the risks and liabilities of entering the global market, TAS incorporated in 1988 Singapore Telecom International (STI), a limited-liability company to act as an investment vehicle. A year later, STI took its first tentative steps, buying a 5% stake in Infonet, a value-added network company based in the U.S. The US$7 million purchase involved us taking an Infonet franchise in Singapore to offer electronic mail and data interchange facilities. This was followed by the US$10 million purchase of a 5% stake in Mtel, a U.S. company that planned to set up a global paging network.

At that time, few Singapore companies had the vision or interest to venture abroad. For a government authority to do so was, to say the least, uncharacteristic. The safe and simple course would have been to concentrate on the domestic business, and milk the monopoly status for cash. This was well before the Singapore government began encouraging its people and businesses to go overseas and grow a "third wing" for the Singapore economy.

Like us, other telcos in Asia and most parts of Europe were still viewed as natural monopolies. There was virtually no competition in domestic markets. New and cross-border services were introduced to customers only after rounds of cosy bilateral negotiations. Regulation was based on preventing the telcos from making monopolistic profits.

At that time, our main revenues and profits came from international direct dialling (IDD) services and providing international leased lines to corporate customers. Returns from the small domestic telephony market, on the other hand, were low. There were very few data services, cellular had not taken off and there was no Internet or broadband.

By the late 1980s, TAS was an efficient and well-run statutory board in Singapore. It had fully satisfied the domestic demand for telephones generated by a population of 2.8 million (now four million) and it had built an advanced telecommunications infrastructure on the island. TAS introduced fiber optics in the network in 1982, moved to 100% push-button telephony in 1983 and introduced ISDN service in 1989. TAS was always among the first to introduce new technologies, making it a leader in the industry with small but very high-quality operations.

With little left to tackle on the domestic front, management took up the challenge set by the board to look for overseas opportunities, just as the markets in the U.S. and U.K. were being deregulated.

Being pragmatic

The TAS approach to globalization was pragmatic. Because it was still an arm of the government, the limited-liability company, STI, was used as a vehicle through which we could form alliances with other telcos and hold equity investments that could lead to an operating role. STI's corporate status also meant it could be more dynamic and move with fewer constraints than TAS, a statutory entity.

Our overseas business was initially confined to consultancy work. This included training telephone engineers in China, the Philippines and Saudi Arabia; installing telephone exchanges in Colombia; and helping Mauritius set up a radio paging service.

As an early adopter of new technologies, we were well placed to offer expertise and knowledge to partners and were careful not to present ourselves as a threat to incumbent players. We had no manufacturing business and therefore had no conflict of interest in equipment sales. As a result, STI had no problem finding operators keen to work with us.

The big drawback in consultancy projects is that they are labor-intensive and low-return. After a year or two, we realized that if we were serious about becoming a player in the international arena, we would have to get involved in joint ventures and put our capital at risk.

Since we could not control the pace of market deregulation, we tended to look at projects as and when an opportunity arose. This resulted in a varied and diverse portfolio that included a paging and data company in Thailand; cable TV operations in Sweden and the U.K.; and mobile telephony in China, Sri Lanka, Vietnam and Norway. During those times, there were few opportunities in Southeast Asia; deregulation started here after Europe. If we had waited for deregulation to come, we would have sat around and done nothing.

We also had to be content with small minority stakes of between 10–25%, often with no control over the investment. This situation has not altered much in Asia today, despite deeper deregulation worldwide. While we would like to have controlling stakes – to be able to consolidate the accounts and direct the business the way we think best – limited deregulation in Asia continues to impose constraints on us. The reality is, if we didn't take minority stakes, we would be out of the game altogether.

By the mid 1990s, STI faced a new challenge as the pace of deregulation quickened. There was greater competition for licenses as more global operators started scouting for new opportunities, especially in Asia – "where the future lies" according to many of them. Many European and US companies, with much larger operations than ours, became interested in investing in Asia and competed aggressively for licenses and opportunities in the region. License conditions and procedures set by the host countries in Asia also became tougher.

Defining our strategy

STI, by then, had a sharper focus on the type of investments it wanted – core telecommunications businesses with particular emphasis on mobile telephony such as paging and cellular. The latter is a fast way of entering a new market as the infrastructure can be set up quickly. Fixed telephone lines, on the other hand, are capital-intensive, require high investment up front, and have a long payback period. The charges for fixed telephony service are also heavily regulated and driven by domestic politics. Fixed telephony was seen as a basic utility operating in a monopoly market; mobile phones were seen as something only the wealthy could afford and, in any case, were usually in a competitive market.

Besides mobile telephony, we were interested in large infrastructure projects. In the U.K., we had a license to provide cable TV and telephony for over 1.2 million homes. In the Philippines, we invested in Globe Telecom which had the license to be a full-service provider.

We also went into data communications in a small way, but this was not an easy business. Unlike cellular, data is a specialized service that appeals only to big business users. It was not an easy product to sell in markets like Sri Lanka and Thailand, where we set up data communications companies.

In terms of spread, 35% of our investments were in Asia, 44% in Europe and the rest in the U.S. Eventually we rationalized our investments, gradually exiting from Europe and the U.S. as more opportunities in Asia Pacific beckoned. With its vast population, relatively low telephone penetration and growing economies, Asia Pacific offered us the best opportunities for growth. It was a region where we had comparative advantages. Not only was it closer to home, we had employees familiar with Asian languages and cultures.

By 1992, SingTel had set a target of achieving 15% of its earnings from overseas operations within five years. In 1995, when I was appointed CEO of SingTel, we revised those targets to 20% by 1998. Today, more than 60% of our proportionate EBITDA comes from outside Singapore. Optus, which we acquired in 2001, is a major contributor. We achieved this feat without any additional equity from shareholders, using funds generated from our operations. And we have paid a steady dividend every year.

Globalizing is not a piece of cake

Government-run monopolies are often poorly equipped to succeed in fiercely competitive overseas markets and we were no different. Our mission to establish ourselves as an international telco was ambitious and ahead of its time. With nothing in our standard operating procedures on how to operate in a foreign country or how to foster entrepreneurial spirit, the pioneers behind our global expansion plan had to overcome many challenges.

One of the most significant challenges was to get the personnel. In the late 1980s and early 1990s, we had great difficulty in persuading staff to take up international assignments. They were reluctant to be uprooted from the comfort and security of life in Singapore. And we did not have the necessary expatriation procedures in place to cater for the cost-of-living allowances, schooling and so on – all the things we take for granted today.

Some of the projects that we undertook in the earlier years were not at all glamorous. We would have a 10–15% stake, no control, and we were sending people there and making them responsible for the investment.

Many of our staff at that time were good specialists, but had not had opportunities to develop broad management skills. We had to find people who were flexible enough to adapt to a foreign culture. While they went with the blessing of HQ, once they were out there on their own they had to fend for themselves. Thrown into a competitive environment for the first time, they had to understand the local dynamics, learn to take the initiative and be resourceful.

The lack of human resources was one of STI's major weaknesses and we tried to overcome it by hiring and training local people. The aim was to minimize the number of Singaporeans in our overseas operations. Our paging operations in Thailand, for instance, had more than 1,400 staff but only one Singaporean to head the team.

We also had to weigh the risk of political instability. While business prospects in war-torn areas may offer high profits, they carry high risks for both staff and investment. In Cambodia, Indonesia and Sri Lanka, for example, our staff came face to face with civil unrest.

Anticipating risks

There is bound to be financial risk when investing overseas. Telecommunications projects are expensive and it can be five to 10 years before you see any return on some of them. There is a huge investment to be made up front. If you do a good job, you will win customers and eventually turn a profit, as long as circumstances beyond your control do not derail your plans along the way.

During the last Asian economic crisis, our investments in Globe Telecom in the Philippines and Bukaka SingTel International (BSI), in eastern Indonesia both took a beating from heavy forex losses from U.S.-dollar denominated liabilities. It was not possible to anticipate nor adequately hedge for these kinds of risks.

When the rupiah fell to record lows, we took a conservative view and wrote down our Indonesian investments completely. The foreign-exchange losses on loans in the Philippines were provided for up front instead of capitalizing them. Analysts applauded these moves saying that our conservative accounting would help if things turned around later. Today both Globe and BSI are solvent, have strong balance sheets, and have started paying cash dividends to their shareholders. We remain committed to these investments.

We ceased to be a statutory board and became a corporation in 1992, and a listed company in 1993. The new SingTel had to manage shareholders' expectations and strike a balance between short-term earnings and long-term investments.

Our losses from overseas ventures hit S$88 million in 1995–96 – the worst result we have had. In 1998, when companies were hit by the regional economic crisis, many analysts were convinced that it would be difficult to make good returns in Asia and we should lift our foot from the overseas accelerator. Instead, we took advantage of the situation to look for new acquisitions.

Having the money to invest overseas is one thing; spotting the right investments demands skill. Sung Sio Ma, who was appointed chairman and CEO of STI in 1989, recalled that they had to go through a learning curve. In the early days of globalization, we had no systematic way to ferret out good investments. While the chairman of STI would speak to investment bankers who provided leads and recommendations, he also sent a few of our people around the world to scout for opportunities. Some of our most successful ventures today are the result of such meetings.

For instance, in 1989, Thaksin Shinawatra, a former Thai police officer, met with STI and proposed forming a partnership to provide telecommunications services in Thailand. He had a small company leasing IBM computers and his only big customer was the Thai police force. Sio Ma told him to first get hold of a telecommunications license and then STI would consider his proposal. In 1990, we started our first Build, Transfer and Operate project, Shinawatra DataCom.

The relationship that we have nurtured with the Shinawatra Group over the years has led us to Thai investments in paging, directory publishing, and in AIS, Shinawatra's cellular company. AIS is now the largest mobile company in our group in terms of number of customers. It is also one of the most profitable companies in Thailand.

While we had internal criteria, such as rate of return, to evaluate a potential deal, there was a real need for good judgment and gut feeling. Are the partners trustworthy? Can we make money out of this? While it is always easy to tweak a model to deliver the required IRR, it is hard to make the judgment call on whether the model is realistic, whether it represents a reasonable guess at the future potential of the deal.

Lessons learned

Over the years STI built a credible portfolio of investments – and these early endeavors overseas provided valuable experience. We learned how to evaluate an investment, how to structure a joint-venture agreement and how to work with partners. We set up systems and processes for our people to go overseas and, more importantly, we learned how to integrate them within the organization when they returned.

By starting small and learning from our mistakes, we had more confidence when making larger investments later on when opportunities came along for us to invest in AIS in Thailand, Bharti in India, and Optus in Australia, for example.

We learned to deal with personality issues, both within our organization and in our dealings with our partners. After 15 years of venturing overseas, SingTel has emerged with a different corporate mindset. While we have not totally erased resistance among staff to take on overseas assignments, our people are generally more global in outlook and the organization as a whole is more open to taking calculated risks.

Our people have learned to work in cultures where the approach to management is different. They operate in markets where customers behave very differently and where they have no "home court" advantage. Holding minority stakes in our ventures also requires different skills. Instead of command and control, we need to work with and convince partners that we add value.

SingTel employees seconded to senior management posts in overseas joint ventures learn that they must quickly understand the local systems and produce results as quickly as feasible. On the plus side, they return from overseas with new ideas and a wider perspective on how things should be done back in HQ. Change has been very positive for the organization as a whole.

Our early exposure to the competitive environment overseas stood us in good stead when the telecommunications market was liberalized in Singapore. The mobile market was opened in 1997 and on April 1, 2000, the whole telecommunications market in Singapore was liberalized.

Right from the start, STI had chosen to invest in certain ventures so that it could learn new technologies. Through our early U.S. investment in Mtel, we were able to bring "sky paging" technology to Shinawatra Paging. And when paging services in Singapore were open to competition, we were able to replicate some of our Thai successes in the local market. Today, we continue to move information and expertise among the various mobile operations we have in Asia.

Roadmap for success

With 20/20 hindsight, it is easy to know which were the correct decisions and what we could have done better. Going overseas is not without risks, but the SingTel board and our management have always been prepared to take a long-term view of all investments.

While there is no secret formula for a successful globalization strategy, we have maintained a coherent and consistent approach. Our strategy has been to stick to the business we know best – providing telecommunications services. That is our core business and our forte. We choose our business partners carefully to complement our own skills and strengths, and we seek to maximize their contribution for the success of the venture.

We choose our partners on the basis of local knowledge, financial capability and, most important of all, for their values. While strong partners inevitably have to work at accommodating each other's views and interests, our choice of partners and our success in making partnerships work are two good reasons why we have succeeded where others have failed.

Geographically, our focus remains on Asia, the environment with which we are most familiar. In contrast to earlier years, we have developed a clear profile of the type of partners and investments we want. A balanced portfolio of developed and developing markets provides us with the ability to grow our business and with opportunities to add value. But now, instead of starting a greenfield project, we prefer to invest in an existing profitable operator that can add immediate returns to our bottom line.

We believe that every transaction has to be win-win and we will only do a deal if it creates value for our shareholders. We establish how much we are prepared to pay based on our view of the potential market, and we use that as the basis for our bid. If a deal does not make financial sense, we walk away – even if it means that the media and the analysts view our decision as a negative outcome for the company.

In January 2000, we announced that we were in negotiations to merge with Cable and Wireless HKT, the former Hong Kong Telecom. The merger would have created a US$60 billion company but the project was aborted a month later. The company was acquired the following month by Pacific Century Cyberworks, a Hong Kong Internet start-up which was established less than a year before. The events leading to and after this acquisition were fodder for many news reports and the subject of much speculation.

Within a matter of weeks, SingTel was again in the news for having "lost out" in a bid for Time Engineering of Malaysia, an affiliate of the Renong Group. Critics again pointed to government and political intervention and our inability to play in the big leagues.

We wanted to do both those deals but only if the terms were right. It is easy in a merger or acquisition to be driven to a point where you try to win at all costs. Then you can be saddled with the winner's curse: overpayment. No matter how much pressure we faced from shareholders, financial analysts and the media, we needed to do what was right, and not what was expedient.

The lessons we have learned from our overseas ventures are exemplified by these three case studies:

Case I: Globe Telecom in the Philippines

In March 1993, we made a relatively small investment of S$24 million for a 29.6% stake in Globe Telecom, a joint venture with the Ayala Corporation in the Philippines. Over the years, we increased our investment to S$757 million and the market value of our stake is today almost double our cost.

Although it is a full telecommunications service provider, more than 80% of Globe's revenue in 2002 was derived from mobile operations. At the end of December 2002, it had 6.6 million mobile customers and another 223,000 fixed-line subscribers. In the course of the year, Globe increased its profits by more than 50% and added another 2.3 million mobile subscribers – more than the total number of customers in our Singapore business.

But the story at Globe was not always rosy. As a greenfield project, the investment had a difficult start. Between 1993 and 1998, losses from Globe Telecom made the headlines and drew much criticism from the media and financial community.

From the beginning, Globe was a full telecommunications service provider licensed to provide fixed, mobile and data services. This put it in direct competition with an established incumbent, the Philippine Long Distance Telephone Company.

At that time, mobile phones were still a new technology that few could afford. However, while Globe was signing up new subscribers, it was unable to track their usage on its billing system or get the bills out on time. Globe was also saddled with the burden of heavy capital expenditure from its commitment to roll out a fixed-line network.

In 1997, Globe's share price fell by more than half and losses shot up to S$50 million, mainly from foreign-exchange losses. Doomsayers were saying SingTel had "lost its pants" in the Philippines and would be making a quick exit.

However, SingTel and its partner, Ayala, made a strategic review of the business and decided that we could fix the managerial, operational and process problems – and make it work. We wrote off the forex losses, brought in a new management team, and pulled in expertise from Singapore to overhaul the billing systems, expedite network expansion and revamp the marketing strategy.

Globe was a clear example of how we add value by pulling resources from SingTel to turn a situation around. Staff who had worked in other overseas ventures were dispatched to the Philippines to advise our partners on the roll-out of both fixed and mobile infrastructure and improve the IT and billing procedures. Within three months, we managed to clear the backlog of bills and set up the operations and procedures to cater for future growth.

To ensure that mobile services took off, SingTel and our partner put in more money to expand the infrastructure and improve coverage, a basic need in the mobile business. The Asian economic crisis actually worked to our advantage. Saddled with financial problems, our competitors were not able to roll out their networks as quickly as we did.

To compete more effectively, we knew that we had to offer customers a unique proposition. Globe became the first operator in the Philippines to offer free SMS and prepaid mobile services. The first measure propelled the growth of mobile usage while the second reduced the risk of fraud.

By the end of 2003, Globe had 8.9 million mobile subscribers, up more than 30% from the previous year. As one of the fastest-growing companies in the Philippines, it stood out as the only one able to raise international equity in the face of negative sentiment among global telecommunications investors from 2000.

Case II: AIS in Thailand

In February 1999, at the tail-end of the last Asian economic crisis, we bought an 18.63% stake in AIS, a subsidiary of the Shinawatra Group and a major cellular operator in Thailand. We have since increased our stake to 21.5%.

AIS was our first major investment in Asia after we decided to refocus on the region. We paid over 11 billion baht (S$550 million) for our initial stake, at 230 baht per share, a premium over the prevailing share price. There was no guarantee that the shares or the business would turn around shortly afterwards.

AIS had just under a million mobile subscribers and we thought its first year's contribution to our bottom line would be negligible. We could not have been more wrong. In 2000, AIS contributed S$34 million to our net income and doubled that to S$69 million the following year. In 2003, AIS added about S$180 million to our bottom line.

Despite the economic situation in Thailand and the slowdown in the region in general, the number of Thai mobile subscribers continued to increase rapidly, month on month. Between 2000 and 2001, the number of new mobile subscribers jumped from 108,000 to as high as 350,000 per month.

When the prepaid segment of the market was unlocked in 2002, the number of new mobile subscribers in Thailand rose to an average of 788,000 per month, with AIS adding the lion's share of around 455,000 new subscribers every month. Today, AIS commands approximately 60% of the market, despite increased competition from three new mobile operators since 2000.

In September 2001, AIS acquired Digital Phone Company, the third-largest mobile operator in Thailand. The acquisition increased AIS's market share and provided it with additional frequency and base stations to cope with the ever-increasing growth in subscribers.

In December 2003, AIS had 13.2 million mobile subscribers, an increase of more than 20% over the course of one year. Today, it is one of the largest companies in Thailand and an unmitigated success story in our globalization strategy.

Case III: Optus in Australia

From 1993, when we went public, to 2000, we had steadily grown our revenues and net profits, and increased our proportionate revenues from international investments from zero to 24%.

We had set ourselves the goal to be a truly pan-regional player. The target was to have half our revenues coming from markets outside Singapore. And Optus provided us with the unique opportunity to realize this goal.

Australia is an important market – attractive not just for its vibrant telecommunications sector, but for its political and economic stability, availability of skilled manpower and government support for such initiatives.

Optus has established a strong market position in the Australian market, and there is a strategic fit between our portfolio and Optus's assets. The key strengths of the Optus business include a strong and competitive mobile operation that has managed to capture one-third of the mobile market, a strong brand name and attractive growth prospects for its mobile and data services.

Optus controls an extensive, high-capacity next-generation network that provides connectivity to key international markets. We were also impressed by the experience and expertise of the management team that has been responsible for many of the accomplishments in this business.

There were obvious benefits in combining SingTel and Optus. The transaction would immediately enhance the size and scale of SingTel's regional presence and expand its international reach. SingTel would be the region's number-one multi-market mobile operator in, at that time, five key Asia Pacific markets and we would have the most extensive data network in Asia, with significant infrastructure assets.

There were synergies that we could achieve from pooling together our wireless content and providing mobile customers with enhanced services through joint product development. For the data business, SingTel and Optus could benefit from more efficient traffic pooling and improved selling power to multinationals. Across all divisions, we would be able to achieve procurement savings through increased purchasing power. Also, our combined financial strength would result in lower financing costs for Optus's funding needs.

Now, in retrospect, the acquisition has realized many of these synergies. Optus has capitalized on SingTel's ownership to transform its profitability and cash-generation capabilities. The combination of Optus's proven challenger approach and its new status as part of a powerful pan-Asian telco with sound financial stability has positioned the company very well for continued growth in the Australian telecom market. In 2003, Optus delivered its first profit under Singapore GAAP and was strongly cash-flow positive for the first time in its history.

Challenges in closing the transaction

SingTel indicated its interest in acquiring Optus to Cable & Wireless in February 2001. It would take another eight months before we succeeded in getting 100% ownership of the company in October 2001. The road to acquiring Optus was, at times, arduous. There were other serious and strong contenders for Optus and we won the transaction against stiff competition.

There were many occasions when we thought that we might have to discontinue discussions and walk away. However, the extended negotiations that we had with Cable & Wireless were only the first steps in this journey.

Immediately after our announcement in March, both analysts and the media raised concerns that the price for Optus was too high; that there would be a share overhang given that SingTel was paying for the offer mainly with its shares; that the price of SingTel shares had fallen following the announcement of our bid; and that SingTel was a government-owned company.

In the ensuing months, this last point was to become the rallying cry of those who were opposed to the deal. Taking advantage of the elections in Australia and wanting to put pressure on its government, certain business leaders led a campaign in the media to oppose Singapore-linked companies such as SingTel and Singapore Airlines from taking stakes in Australian companies.

There was even talk that military secrets could be compromised if Optus were to "fall into" SingTel's hands. Some radio talk shows claimed that "spies" for Singapore and other Asian nations had been operating

Down Under for 20 years and that the Australian government should be wary about giving SingTel access to its defense satellites.

Criticism of SingTel as a government-owned company is not new. In the Hong Kong Telecom transaction, we saw all kinds of stories in the press. The Singapore government may have a majority share in SingTel but the company is accountable to all its shareholders and its board for delivering results.

We look at all our transactions on a purely commercial basis and we have always said that we will do transactions only if they create value for our shareholders. We decided that we would not be drawn into the political debate that was obviously fuelled by a fairly narrow segment of the Australian community.

Instead, we took proactive steps in explaining and reiterating the benefits of the transaction to both the media and the investment community in Australia. Through meetings with key Australian media and discussions with analysts, we were fairly successful in getting our messages across; that is, that we have no political agenda; we have a business in Australia and we want to make it successful and value-creating for shareholders. The acquisition of Optus was in line with the international expansion strategy set by SingTel to achieve its growth objectives.

Once SingTel obtained all regulatory approvals on August 27, 2001, Optus shareholders moved quickly to accept SingTel's bid. Within three days, we managed to obtain more than 90% acceptance from Optus shareholders, paving the way for us to acquire 100% of Optus by October 23 that year. It is notable that SingTel managed this without an aggressive advertising campaign to win shareholders' approval. With proper positioning of our messages, we were able to garner support from both the media and analysts.

Our conclusions

The pace and manner of deregulation remain a contentious issue in many markets. Full liberalization is still a distant dream. In markets like India, the Philippines and Taiwan, foreign-ownership regulations have prevented us from acquiring more control over our investments. Such regulations are the rules of the game in Asia and we have learned to work within them. In fact, the domestic conditions in some countries have led us to prefer working with a local partner who understands them.

Minority stakes have never prevented us from contributing to the success of our joint ventures, as illustrated in the first two case studies. Sharing our experience and expertise with partners leads them to value and respect us as shareholders.

We take a pragmatic view towards issues like branding and control. When we started paging and mobile services in Sri Lanka, Cambodia and Vietnam from scratch, we tried to create a common regional brand. But AIS, Telkomsel and Optus are brand leaders in their markets and it may not make sense to create a new, albeit unified, brand. We would rather take advantage of expertise and experience in each market to create common services that benefit customers across all networks.

SingTel's overseas investments have radically reshaped the company by transforming its business and geographical mix. The acquisition of Optus was a significant milestone in our corporate history. Unlike our earlier ventures, this was a unique opportunity for SingTel to gain 100% control of a leading competitive carrier in a very large and attractive market.

With Optus, SingTel is no longer a local company. We now operate from two hubs, with the bulk of our staff and customers in Singapore and Australia. There are cross-cultural and cross-country issues that we continue to address. Our immediate challenge is how we can fully integrate Optus successfully into the group's operations.

There are obvious strengths that both SingTel and Optus can draw from each other to form a winning combination – and these synergies can benefit from our earlier participation in other overseas ventures. This, I believe will be our competitive advantage in the years ahead.

When I joined SingTel in 1994, close to 50% of our revenues were from one business: international telephony, or IDD. We had just over 200,000 mobile customers in the Singapore market. Today, we have 44 million mobile subscribers in Asia, 220 times as many, and IDD is just 10% of our consolidated group revenue.

Despite the difficult economic environment and market conditions in Asia in recent years, SingTel has become a more resilient and diversified business – well placed to continue to grow, prosper and be an industry leader in the region

TAKEAWAYS

1. **Having clear ambitions, but not losing sight of the need to experiment, learn and consolidate experiences.**
   An early internationalizer in its industry, SingTel went through different growth phases based on its geographic concentration, culminating in its 100% acquisition of Optus. In this process, SingTel has developed its understanding of what it needs to operate internationally, has learned from its ventures, and is now able to withdraw from those that do not fit the strategy.

2. **Recognizing the importance of human resources.**
   SingTel's CEO is clearly well aware of the human resources challenges of managing a global organization. He leads the organization as it deals with issues such as the initial reluctance of personnel to leave the comfort of Singapore, grooming international managers, reintegrating the international managers, or working with strong partners. By addressing the issues, Lee constructs a more robust and world-ready organization.

3. **Managing government networks in a highly regulated industry.**
   The telecommunication industry in Asia is still highly regulated by governments and in many cases SingTel can operate only as a junior partner. Successful internationalization in this environment requires astute management of networks and relationships with partners and governments. With its two hubs in Singapore and Australia and its many partnerships throughout Asia, SingTel manages the network flows of information and technology, rather than controlling the many nodes in the network. Moreover, it has a rigorous process for choosing potential partners. Lee Hsien Yang emphasizes that partners are chosen not only for straightforward commercial reasons, but also for the values and local knowledge they bring to the

partnership. In these ways, SingTel has honed its network-building abilities into a competitive advantage that supports the company as it extends its reach.

4. **Spreading knowledge from outposts to the rest of the organization.**
   The internationalization of SingTel has broadened the horizons of the employees who have spent time abroad in partnerships or foreign markets. Managers abroad are forced to deal with new situations, different political environments, and working with foreigners, while still delivering results. Realizing that their knowledge is valuable, the company has ensured that managers returning from overseas assignments bring the learning back to Singapore. Their flexible and results-oriented approach has helped the company to become more agile in dealing with the home market and SingTel's overall development.

5. **Knowing when to persevere and when to pull back.**
   The path to globalization will have challenges; the successful must know when to persevere. The first attempts by SingTel to internationalize were not easy. It took vision and a strong will to proceed. The vision created and the role played by Koh Boon Hwee with his experience from HP seems to have been crucial in these early stages.

▲ OLAM

Murli Kewalram Chanrai
Chairman, Kewalram Chanrai Group
Sunny George Verghese
Group Managing Director & CEO, Olam[2]

Olam's heritage and history

Anchored in the KC Group

Olam was established in 1989 by the Kewalram Chanrai (KC) family (main sponsors) in Nigeria and is part of the KC Group, which has a long and successful business tradition that can be traced back to 1860. The Group, currently headquartered in Singapore, is a conglomerate with diverse business interests that include textile manufacturing, agribusiness, distribution of office-automation products (IT), distribution of automobile and automotive parts, property development and supply-chain management for agricultural raw materials. The Group today operates in over 45 countries and employs over 12,000 people worldwide.

The Kewalram Chanrai has always adhered strongly to the core values of honoring commitments, being fair to all stakeholders, and being a good employer. The family has also taken many progressive and proactive steps to professionalize all aspects of the business, having concluded early on that it was in its best interests as activist shareholders to allow the best management talent to guide the business, whether that talent be a family member or a professional manager.

To create an alignment between the managers' goals and those of the family, the family offers shares in the business to these managers. Thus, in Olam's case, the management team was given a 28% stake-holding in the company to help secure the maximum possible effort from them. This governance model was also particularly effective in driving accountability. In the earlier dispensation, the family found it difficult to evaluate their brothers, cousins, uncles or nephews and found it impossible to ask a particular family member heading a business to be accountable for a business failure and to sack or remove him from that position as they all had equal ownership rights. However, now with professional managers heading the businesses, the standard of accountability is much higher and the ability to enforce that accountability is also easier.

Another feature of this changed mindset is the family's willingness to dilute its ownership in circumstances where the business has potential to grow but needs access to external capital markets or private equity to fund that growth. This shift in stance stemmed from their realization that it is better to be a smaller shareholder in a business that is a growing than a major shareholder in a business that is not able to grow because it does not have the capital or other resources to support that growth. A lot of family businesses struggle to grow because the family finds it difficult to cede control. The KC family has been able to transcend the confines of this restrictive mindset with its progressive approach to building and creating value for its businesses. All family shareholders subscribe to a written family constitution that governs their action as shareholders This includes, for example, provisions/rules for a family member leaving the business and the orderly way in which such an exit is managed. It is this progressive governance model that is at the heart of the continued growth and success of the KC family business.

The KC Group has developed particular expertise in managing the risks and doing business in emerging markets. The Group has had over 120 years' experience of operating in Nigeria and has been present in Ghana for over 80 years. From the very beginning, we at Olam have benefited from the Group's 140 years of business experience in various parts of the world, with a particular emphasis on emerging markets

This heritage has provided a strong foundation for Olam's growth into a dynamic multinational based in Singapore.

The start in Nigeria

When we were first set up the Olam Company in 1989 in Nigeria, our mandate was to develop an export market for products manufactured by the KC Group out of Nigeria. The Group had, and continues to have, extensive trading (automobile and automotive parts distribution, electronics distribution) and manufacturing (textile milling, oil milling, cotton ginning) interests in Nigeria. To support these operations, the Group needed to raise foreign currency to fund the import of machinery, raw materials, spare parts, and so on. Since the availability of foreign currency was a problem in Nigeria, Olam was tasked to export Group company-manufactured products with a view to generating foreign-exchange earnings required to support the Group's activities in the country. Over the course of the next two years (1989–1991), we developed an export market for the various products manufactured in Nigeria, including cotton lint, open-end and ring-spun cotton yarns, gray fabric and de-oiled cakes. At the end of this period, we handed over the customer relationships and the franchise that we had developed for these products to our associate companies and received a revised mandate from the Group to develop non-Group-related and third-party export activities out of Nigeria. That was the genesis of Olam as it is known today.

Expanding horizons

To execute this revised mandate, our first step was to scan the Nigerian environment to establish the principal items that comprised the bulk of non-oil exports out of the country. This proved to be agricultural commodities and, given the KC Group's experience in sourcing and trading cotton and other oil seeds in Nigeria, we felt that we had the basic competence and skills to develop the exports of agricultural commodities.

The first product that we chose to export was cashew. Most Nigerian cashew exports were to India and Vietnam, and we felt that we understood the Indian market well.

From that initial activity where we sourced and exported cashews from Nigeria, we have grown into a global company with a strong presence in many of the world's emerging economies and a leading global position in all our chosen businesses. Thus, in the span of little over a decade, we have transformed ourselves into one of the major global players in the supply of food ingredients and industrial raw materials, with an excellent understanding of these product markets.

From a start-up operation in a single country with a single product, Olam has grown into a large and successful business, with sales revenues of US$1.2 billion in financial year (FY) 2003, supplying 12 products, with operations in 35 countries and employing over 2,000 people worldwide. Sales and profits have grown at 54% and 50%, respectively, between 1990–91 and FY 2002–03. In the last six years alone, our sales revenues have grown) at 28% and after-tax earnings by 31%, and consistently earned a return in excess of our cost of capital (average equity spreads of 20% earned throughout this period).

This growth record is even more impressive as it has come entirely from de novo expansion or organic growth and without acquisitions.

We have also grown sales at a rate (28% CAGR over the last 6 years) that is significantly above industry growth rates (estimated at 3–4% CAGR), signifying that we have taken share from existing industry incumbents. The agricultural-commodity sector is a low-growth industry. As a rule of thumb, aggregate increase in demand for agricultural raw materials grows at half the world GDP growth rates. Thus, for example, if the global GDP growth rate is 5%, then aggregate growth in demand for agricultural raw materials will be 2.5%.

Strategic clarity

Defining the playing field and our position in it

The speed and directions in which we have grown over the years are anchored around a rather tight, rigorous and clear definition of what we believe our core business is. We are supply-chain managers of agricultural raw materials from/to emerging markets.

This clear definition immediately limits the scope of our activities. We are not speculative commodity traders. We are not positional, proprietary or directional commodity traders. We do not allocate risk capital to take positions based on our knowledge or insight in which way these commodity markets are likely to evolve and bet along those trends. Instead, we see our role as supply-chain managers by acting as the bridge between the farm gate in the producing countries and the factory gate of our customers in the consuming markets. We are integrated along this physical supply chain and engaged in sourcing, processing, storing, transporting, distributing and managing the risks at each step of the process. Our source of profit is therefore a logistics or value-chain margin and not a positional margin. Our earnings, as a consequence, are more stable and less volatile. A good example of this focus is illustrated by the role we play in the cocoa business. Nearly 72% of world cocoa production takes place in four West African countries; Cote d'Ivoire, Ghana, Nigeria and Cameroon, in that order. However, most chocolate consumption takes place in the developed countries. Our role is to source cocoa beans in the producing countries, process these into cocoa butter, powder, liquor and cake and supply the cocoa beans and products to the chocolate industry (including Mars, Hershey, Nestlé and Cadbury). We link and leverage our presence in the producing countries and consuming markets and capture the value present in the supply chain.

Secondly, by defining ourselves as supply-chain managers of agricultural raw materials, we also clearly define the product scope for participation. We do not trade all commodity asset classes but restrict ourselves to trading a single commodity asset class – agricultural raw materials. Within that scope, we trade multiple commodities (12 in all, currently). This provides us with great focus and dramatically reduces our execution risk as we grow. There are common underlying themes that bind the various products in this space together, including the way we look at and manage risk for the various agricultural raw materials, the way we draw up crop balance sheets, the way we understand quality, and the way we look at processing out-turns and controls. This commonality provides accelerated learning-curve benefits.

Thirdly, one leg of our transaction is always placed in an emerging market. This part of our core business definition limits our geographical scope. We are either sourcing from or selling into an emerging market. The KC Group and Olam over the years have developed a familiarity with and expertise in managing risks and doing business in emerging markets. Most of the agricultural raw materials that Olam has chosen to supply are grown mainly in these developing economies and Olam leverages its expertise in operating very effectively in such environments.

Based on our experience, over the years we have continuously tightened and defined our core business more rigorously. This focus has helped us to continue to invest in the core and considerably reduce our execution risk as we accelerate growth and expansion around our core business.

Industry analysis

Most of the agricultural raw materials that we have chosen to deal in are grown in developing countries/emerging markets, while most of the consumption of these raw materials takes place in the developed markets. At the time we entered this business in 1989, most trade in agricultural raw materials in the producing countries was controlled by government monopolies or commodity boards such as the Bulogs in Indonesia, the Coffee Board in India, the Caistab in Cote d'Ivoire, and the Cocoa Board in Nigeria. Over time, these government monopolies grew into large bureaucracies, with burgeoning costs, attendant inefficiencies, leakages and, in many cases, endemic corruption, resulting in opaque decision-making processes. Under the dispensation of the commodity boards, the farmer received only a fraction (estimated at between 30–35%) of the realizable FOB value of the produce exported. This was also a period when a large number of these producing countries were facing serious economic difficulties. Most turned to the IMF and World Bank for economic support. One of the many reforms that the IMF insisted on in providing the much-needed financial support was for the recipient countries to deregulate and liberalize their commodity boards and state agricultural monopolies. The late 1980s and early '90s saw a rapid wave of deregulation and liberalization of commodity markets in most of these producing countries. The early success of these liberalization efforts enabled farmers to secure almost 70% of the realizable FOB value of the foods exported by them. We did not enter this business because we foresaw these changes. Instead, it was fortuitous that these substantive changes and the consequent new rules of the game that emerged came about around the time we started off in this business.

During the days of the commodity boards, the large global trade houses (GTHs) could sit in the international trading centers (New York, London, Geneva, Paris, Amsterdam) and source their raw-material requirements from these state monopolies and could enter into six-month, one-year, and, in some cases, even two-year forward contracts to buy cocoa or coffee, and had a sovereign guarantee backing that performance. The GTHs could then comfortably sell the commodity to their end-buyers on a similar forward basis without having to be too concerned about the threat of a default. It was the boards in the producing countries that collected the produce from the farms, cleaned, sorted, processed, stored and transported it and bore all the risks till it was eventually shipped to the customer.

This entire dynamic changed quite dramatically after the liberalization of the commodity boards. With the dissolution of the boards, the players who emerged as exporters from the producing countries were the former licensed buying agents (LBAs) of the boards, who were commissioned by the boards to collect the produce from the farmers and deliver it to a designated warehouse. These LBAs were poorly capitalized and relatively unsophisticated as they did not understand the complexity of the futures markets or have adequate knowledge of derivative tools to hedge their price and currency risks. So while they sold forward to their overseas customers, as the boards had before them, they were unable to manage the risk effectively if the prices at the time of covering against those contracts were out-of-the-money. In such scenarios, their usual posture was to simply default on their shipments. Indeed they could not absorb the consequent losses and claims. In any event, the end-users – the chocolate manufacturers or the coffee roasters, for example – were really not interested in receiving a financial settlement as they couldn't "roast" or "crush" dollars. On the other hand, they were very particular about receiving the specific quality/grade of cocoa or coffee from a particular origin that imparted the characteristic flavor and aroma of their brand, the integrity of which had taken several years to build and cultivate with consumers.

At Olam, we were quick to recognize the significant opportunity that this change in the market structure presented to us. We developed extensive procurement, processing and logistics infrastructure in the producing countries and approached our customers and convinced them to limit the risk that came with contracting directly with suppliers in the producing countries by contracting with us in Singapore instead. In the process, they were replacing the emerging-market supply risk with a developed-market supply risk, and in a jurisdiction where the rule of law worked quickly and efficiently and they could enforce their contractual obligations more effectively.

Through our direct presence in the producing countries, we were able to demonstrate a superior delivery and fulfillment capability, a critical factor in the customer's choice of a supplier, given the dynamic and volatile nature of prices in our industry. By consistently executing well on this strategy, we today enjoy unparalleled counter-party credibility with our customers who consider us good enough to enter into long-dated supply arrangements that are as far forward as 18 to 24 months in some cases.

Competitive strategy

The agricultural commodity industry has mainly two kinds of participants. Firstly, there are the GTHs, which have significant market strengths, including long-standing customer relationships, trading skills, risk-arbitrage and risk-management skills, market research and analysis skills, and which are supported by robust capital structures. Examples of successful global trade houses include Cargill, Bunge, Glencor, Noble, and Louis Dreyfus. Then there the origin trade houses (OTHs), local, indigenous players based in the producing or origin countries. The OTHs have solid origin strengths, including sourcing, primary processing, inland logistics, contextual familiarity, low-cost procurement infrastructures, relationships with local farmers/suppliers and government contacts.

OTHs are usually weak in market skills. GTHs, on the other hand, while they have a presence in the producing countries, are generally weak in "origin-management" skills. There are few industry players that combine both of these skills. Olam's competitive strategy is to "out-origin" (achieve better relationships in supplying countries and accumulate more knowledge) than our competitors (both OTHs and GTHs) while concurrently matching the marketing, trading and risk-management skills of the GTHs. The phrase "out origin" is a reference to our ability to buy from the lowest level of aggregation in the producing countries, to manage the integrity of cash, stock and debtors on a real-time basis across distributed sourcing or warehousing points, and to develop an extensive network of supplier relationships as close to the farm gate as possible.

We are currently the only industry player that integrates origin and market skills to that high a degree across 12 businesses and 35 countries.

Building and assembling a platform of capabilities

Our growth over the years has been attributable to series of small, measured steps. Each step has helped us assemble a suite of skills/capabilities/competencies/relationships/assets that helped us execute our strategy. Successful execution resulted in an accelerated building of scale, which helped us to compound our skills and the broader platform of capabilities that we had acquired. These in turn opened up adjacent opportunity pipelines that we could exploit by leveraging the assembled and compounded skills and competencies.

This capability platform includes three different competencies, namely:

- origin-management advantage
- trading/marketing/risk-management advantage, and
- organizational advantage.

It takes a lot to be able to secure a sustainable competitive advantage by assembling, combining and then institutionalizing such a set of constituent skills and capabilities. To do this successfully requires a lot of focus and discipline. We have tried to identify some of the key elements that went into building and embedding these capabilities in the company that gives us a sustainable competitive advantage.

Origin-management advantage

This is built on such things as an in-depth knowledge of each country/place of origin and its catchment areas; crop patterns; identifying and developing relationships with suppliers and opinion leaders; setting up procurement infrastructure; developing and implementing robust field operating systems to control the integrity of cash, stock, debtors and quality on a real-time basis across distributed sourcing points; developing processing knowledge and controls; and sharing resources by cross-sourcing products to better amortize standing-still costs (over multiple products and a larger volume).

Trading/marketing/risk-management advantage

To acquire this competency, the constituent skills that Olam had to assemble include developing direct end-customer relationships to get better demand visibility and eschewing second-hand trade with brokers and dealers; developing the ability to manage the various trading risks (price, basis, counter-party, credit, currency), the operational risks (quality, weight claims, asset integrity), and the legal, compliance and political risks; and aligning systems and controls to facilitate the effective management of these risks. At Olam, we have developed a proprietary system to capture and measure risk at a transactional level. This helps us monitor and manage our risks better. We have chosen business-performance measures that are risk-adjusted (Risk-Adjusted Profit After Tax (RAPAT) and Risk-Adjusted Return on Capital (RAROC)). We are not seduced by nominal profits but are more concerned with residual income generated net of the risks taken to generate it. Incentive systems are aligned to these risk-adjusted performance measures, further reinforcing the control and governance systems and thereby directly influencing a manager's behavior.

Organizational advantage

Our greatest strength as a company has come from creating an environment that has helped us secure the highest possible discretionary effort from our managers and staff. This includes our ability to attract good-quality talent to live and work in difficult, emerging-market conditions; our capacity to develop "global" managers by requiring that everybody go through the same "rite of passage" of living and working in similar conditions; our policy of promoting from within; and our policy to align owners' and managers' interests by giving the latter substantial ownership stakes in the business. Every time we want to set up a new business or start operations in a new area, we will, without exception, deploy a core of senior managers who are tried, tested and proven, who understand our culture, our risk systems, and business model, and who can serve as role models in the new operation. This method has proved extremely valuable in reducing the execution risk of the various growth initiatives that we have launched over the years.

How this works in practice

Our ability to grow at a rate that is several times higher than the industry growth rate is testament to the competitive advantage that these three capabilities have given us. Being able to crack the code on the myriad challenges involved in securing an origin-management advantage, and then leveraging this across similar geographies in Africa and Asia, has created a unique competitive advantage for us and is the heart of our repeatable growth formula. This then is our core capability and the ultimate source of our value-creation logic.

Rules of the game and portfolio selection

Having defined our core business as "supply-chain managers of agricultural raw materials from/to emerging markets", we still needed to clarify in which lines of business we wanted to be present. Over the years we have crystallized the following five rules:

- **Rule 1:** ***High absolute market share***
  We target a global market share of 10%. In a fragmented industry like ours, this is a meaningful market share. We would also like to be amongst the top three global players in each business. The logic behind this rule is not to grow bigger for the sake of size, to plant flags or build an empire, but because we believe that by achieving that kind of leadership position we develop some customer control and pricing control, which are drivers to our profitability.
- **Rule 2:** ***Strong presence in key origins***
  We want to be in all the key producing countries for each product. In dynamic and volatile commodity markets, the only way we can

have a reliable and consistent delivery and fulfillment capability against our contracts with our customers is to be directly present in the origins and be in control of the origination and other aspects of the supply chain. We would not have the confidence to enter into forward contracts if we had to source these raw materials from third-party exporters/suppliers.

Thus, cashew is grown in 18 countries around the world and we are the only industry player present in every one of these 18 countries. We are present in every producing country in sheanuts, all the producing countries of sesame with the exception of Sudan, all the cocoa-producing countries with the exception of Venezuela (a minor producer), and all the key robusta-coffee-producing countries. This principle runs across all other products in our portfolio as well. In addition to dramatically strengthening our delivery and fulfillment capability, strong presence in the origins also gives us access to proprietary market intelligence on the size, the timing and the quality of the crop, all of which helps us both trade and manage our risks better.

- **Rule 3:** ***Strong end-market presence***

  In order to be closer to our customers and provide customized supply-chain services, we are actively creating regional marketing hubs to service customers in those regions. Thus, in the recent past, we have set up a Moscow office for marketing our products in the Russia and CIS region, an office in Warsaw for Eastern Europe, an office in Marseille for France and North Africa, an office in Rotterdam for Holland, Belgium and Germany, an office in the United Kingdom, an office in the United States for North America and another office in Dubai for the Middle East market.
- **Rule 4:** ***Direct end-customer relationships***

  We only want to sell directly to the end-users (the coffee roasters, the chocolate manufacturers, the edible-nut roasters, the spice manufacturers), rather than sell to the second-hand trade (other dealers) or through brokers. This helps us get closer to the customer and provides demand visibility and helps us understand their needs better. It is this kind of relationship that has helped us provide value-added services to our customers. Thus, one large chocolate manufacturer wanted us to guarantee that the African cocoa and cocoa products we are supplying to him came from plantations where child and slave labor are not employed. Since we buy directly from the farm gate in the producing countries and have a clear line of sight from there to the customer, we were able to certify this for him. In turn, he was willing to pay us a premium for offering such guarantees. Another large coffee roaster who has distributed coffee-roasting facilities in Europe and the United States, and sources 40 different grades of coffee from 15 different countries, wants us to provide vendor-managed inventory services (VMI) for him. He informs us that he wants certain quantities of specific grades of coffee to be delivered to his factory in Hamburg on a Friday morning, six months forward. He wants us to then manage his inventory for him and is willing to offer a value well in excess of the costs that we would incur in providing that kind of customized service to him. Yet another chocolate manufacturer wants us to ensure that the label shows clearly that the cocoa beans used in the manufacture were procured through fair-trade practices (FTP). Given our supply-chain strengths, we were in a position to do that. For a lot of our customers, we offer risk-management solutions along with the supply of the physical product, for which we can get a premium. Thus, by customizing and integrating products, solutions and services based on the need of each individual customer, we are de-commoditizing our business and securing higher value.

- **Rule 5: *Differential value-chain integration***
  As supply-chain managers, we are integrated along the entire physical-supply value-chain. However, we do not have any strategic orthodoxy that we would be similarly integrated in each business. Thus, for example, we source, process and export coffee from 12 countries. While we do toll-processing in India and Indonesia, where we believe the service providers do that very efficiently, we own our own coffee-processing facilities in Cote d'Ivoire and Cameroon, where we believe that we can capture significant value by owning the bricks and mortar ourselves.

Financial criteria

In addition to these rules, we have a set of financial standards that each business or geographical area should meet to justify its continued inclusion in our portfolio. All products and areas receive investment and resource support based on their capacity to grow and create value. All managers are aware that profitable growth in Olam means achieving both volume and earnings growth, and generating a positive equity spread (return on equity less the cost of equity capital) concurrently and simultaneously. This clarity makes capital-allocation decisions and the evaluation of business performance much more effective.

Growth and globalization: Exploiting adjacent opportunities

Olam's growth rate has been a function of moving into various adjacent possibilities or opportunities by leveraging its competencies into these adjacent areas. Growing by expanding into related areas reduced the execution risk of these moves.

In determining which areas to move into, the company rigorously applied four criteria:

Was there customer sharing?
Was there cost sharing?
Was there capability sharing?
Was there channel sharing?

If all, or at least two, of these conditions applied, we felt more confident about exploiting the opportunity.

As explained earlier, we started our operations by supplying one product from one country to one market. This trade flow proved to be very successful. Within a matter of two cropping seasons, we had already achieved a 45% market share of total Nigerian cashew exports. If we had continued to view ourselves as a Nigerian-cashew supplier to the Indian market, then we would have had very little headroom for further growth. We subsequently chose to develop the Vietnamese market and our customers in India and Vietnam requested that we try to source cashew from other West and East African countries. By this time we had acquired a reputation for having superior delivery and fulfillment capability for agricultural raw materials in dynamic and volatile commodity markets from difficult developing countries. Having secured a common customer base in India and Vietnam and having developed good product and channel knowledge, we gradually expanded into other areas where cashews were grown. We repeated this model across various cashew-producing countries. Today, cashew is grown in 18 countries around the world and we are the only industry player to be present in each one of them. We are, in fact, the world's largest supplier of cashews, with over 25% global market share.

We then replicated this model by moving similarly into other products, starting with cotton, then sheanuts, cocoa, coffee and sesame, to the point where we now supply a total of 12 products. Thus, for example, we started supplying sesame seed from Nigeria to the oil crushers in Japan (namely Kadoya, Kuki and Nishin). These customers then asked us if we could also supply them with sesame from other producing countries and we now supply their needs from Burkina Faso, Senegal, Tanzania, Uganda, Mozambique, Myanmar and India. We are amongst the top three suppliers of sesame seed globally. Similarly, we started supplying coffee from one origin, India, to one market in Europe. Today we supply coffee from 12 different countries and sell these into over 20 different markets and have become the world's largest shipper of robusta coffee.

We have repeated these adjacency moves from one product and one country, to 12 products and 35 geographical areas over the course of the last 13 years. In each case or in each move, the pattern of repeatability only changed one variable at a time; a new area or a new business.

A third adjacency vector that the company exploited was vertical integration in the value chain. For example, when we first started in the cashew business, we were only trading the raw cashew but soon we began to process cashew by shelling and blanching them into cashew kernels. We then began processing cocoa beans, sheanuts, sesame seed, coffee and a range of other products. In all these cases, we were engaged in the primary processing of these raw materials into intermediate products, thereby adding value to them.

We sold the blanched cashew kernels to edible-nut roasters and salters, who enquired whether we could also supply peanuts. This customer sharing opportunity provided us with an opportunity to move into the edible-nut business. In the future, our plans envisage supplying the full complement of nuts, including almonds, pistachios, hazelnuts, brazil nuts and macadamia nuts, to these cashew customers.

We have not always been this successful, however. We have exited some businesses and areas because they did not meet some of the rules that we identified earlier.

Conclusion

We have recently been asking ourselves whether we have reached the limits of this economic growth engine. Are our growth initiatives becoming too reflexive and too routine so that this engine is likely to start sputtering?

We strongly believe that this growth model still has significant room to grow and create value for us. In addition, we are currently engaged in opening up a new growth vector by trying to tap into the unarticulated needs of our customers and integrating and customizing products, solutions and services to meet those needs.

The journey so far has been exciting and there is nothing to suggest that the future will be any less inspiring. We see a clear pathway to grow similarly across the various adjacent areas and do not have any particular worries about where our next US$1 billion-worth of growth in revenues is going to come from.

TAKEAWAYS

1. **Understanding the market and defining a value proposition.**
   Olam has a clear strategic understanding of a fast-changing market and has been able to define a real value proposition. Its clear understanding of what it means to be a supply-chain manager for agricultural raw materials from and to emerging markets helps it to focus, to determine its scope and to develop clear rules about its growth and development. This focus also allows it to develop rapidly while avoiding uncontrolled growth.

2. **Realizing the benefits of company heritage.**
   The KC Group is an international group and the Olam management benefits from its experience in operating in diverse markets. Olam adopts a step-by-step approach to developing its international know-how. It started in markets (Nigeria and India) that it knew well and moved outward by adjacent expansion, while building knowledge of international markets.

3. **Making the transition from resource-based advantage to strategic competitive advantage.**
   Olam recognizes that it owes its beginnings to some very concrete resource-based advantages, such as its knowledge of Nigeria and India, and the need to help the KC Group to earn foreign currency. However, the company has learned to transcend these origins and build a competitive position on system-based advantages such as a presence in each step of the value-added chain and an understanding of risk management in agricultural trade.

4. **Boosting knowledge management to further support competitiveness.**
   Olam is able to fully exploit its presence in, and control of, the entire value chain by building a good knowledge-management system. As a result, it is able to "go the extra mile" for its customers through, for example, helping European firms to find products from socially acceptable sources. As it moves ahead, it is clear that this customer-centric, knowledge-based approach will serve it well.

5. **Accelerating learning through clear thinking about activities and operations.**
   A step-by-step approach and the strategy of adjacent expansion enables the company to learn quickly. This rapid learning goes hand-in-hand with great flexibility, as is illustrated by the way Olam was able to take advantage of the rapid liberalization in the supply of raw materials.

Endnotes

1 *McKinsey Quarterly*, 2002, Number 1

2 Olam is today a global leader in the supply of agricultural raw materials. Its distinctive position in the industry is based on the strength of its origination capability (through its direct presence in the key producing countries) and the superior value-chain economics that it enjoys (through being integrated along the entire physical-supply value chain). Olam offers a one-stop supply-chain solution to its customers directly from the farmgate in the producing countries to the factory gate in the consuming markets. As supply-chain managers, Olam is engaged in the sourcing, processing, storing, transporting (inland transits), shipping (marine transits), distributing, trading and marketing of a range of agricultural raw materials.

Olam's product portfolio currently includes the supply of 12 raw materials, 10 of which are food ingredients (cocoa, coffee, cashew, peanuts, sheanuts, sesame, beans and pulses, spices, rice and sugar) and two industrial raw materials (cotton and timber).

Olam's customers today include some of the world's largest packaged-food multinationals, including Nestlé, Sara Lee, Philip Morris (Kraft), Mars, Cadbury, Hershey, Lavazza, Tchibo, ADM, Blommer, Planters, Sanfilipo, Nut Company, etc.

CHAPTER

4 The Newcomers

The companies which have only recently (within the last five years) begun to pursue their globalization strategies are what we call "the newcomers". While the term "newcomers" seems to connote beginners or somehow imply a lightweight status, these companies are certainly not lightweights. They are already dominant players in their home markets, and may have achieved a similar status in neighboring or regional markets. Of the three companies featured in this section – Uni-President Taiwan, China Netcom Corporation, and Industrial and Commercial Bank of China (ICBC) – two are from a developing market and one is from a developed market.

The three companies in this section are from what is traditionally called "Greater China": Uni-President Enterprises Corporation (UPEC) from Taiwan, and China Netcom and ICBC from the mainland. Though this is purely coincidental on our part, it may nevertheless serve to underline the rapid rise of the region within the global economic context. These companies and, in many senses, the entire Chinese economy have burst onto the global scene and, despite their late entrance, are now seen by some as rising powers. The size of the domestic economy and the fact that only a fraction of potential consumption and production have been reached have given Chinese companies a presence beyond their years. They build their portfolios and competencies in a sizeable home market before reaching out as huge global players. The raft of recent Chinese entrants – from Huawei in telecommunications, TCL and Haier in electronics and white goods, Sinopec and Petrochina in oil, to name just a few – is more than coincidental. It is the start of a much bigger trend. China is not only the world's new growth engine and consumer market, it is also the source of the leading contenders to become industry's dominant global players.

The three budding global giants in this section represent the wide spectrum of market tendencies and corporate instincts that are at play in the grooming of tomorrow's world-class companies. Consumer-products companies are frequently faulted for entering China only with 1.2 billion people in their sights. They are, in a sense, blinded by volume, and thus more easily commit the errors of overreaching, over-investment, or failing to approach the market in the right way. As a result, the consumer-products industry is one of the most tightly contested and strewn with heavy casualties. Because it has long been one of the more open sectors in China, the food and beverage category displays all of these traits and frequently in a heightened way.

From amidst this competition, Uni-President Enterprises Corporation (UPEC) has emerged as a leader, triumphing over its Taiwan heritage (which could have been a political burden) to carve for itself a significant presence in this fast-growing sector of the economy. Despite its achievements, the company maintains a humble approach, knowing that the China market is a "must" for gaining global prominence among multinationals. Perhaps unique for a company which had built such a dominant presence at home, UPEC has approached its foreign markets with a great deal of humility, seeking to learn even from the most contentious or troubled situations. The company continues to exhibit great use of organizational learning, to look within and to analyze its experiences to discover the critical factors for building an organization fit for the 21st century. If the 19th century was about industrialization and the 20th century was about productivity and efficiency, the mantra of the 21st century is centered on the customer and innovation. And as this story unfolds, UPEC has already seen that the customer, wherever and whenever, will respond to branding. Thus, in addition to developing its presence in China, UPEC as an organization has set itself the task of building brand equity and thus ensuring that its name is carried into the future.

Attention to brand is one of the common threads in this section and has already begun to set China Netcom apart from its state-owned cousins, China Telecom and China Mobile. Several years ago, when China Netcom Corp (CNC) first started, visitors to CEO Edward Tian's office might, on any given day, be shown one of the latest installments in the company's new advertising campaign. The CNC campaign was at that time unique in the telecommunications and wider market, showing vistas and mountains as in a Chinese painting, rather than the famous personalities who were then more commonly used for advertising the latest products. The reason, explained Dr. Tian, was that CNC needed to build a "brand" that would withstand the test of time and place. In the China market this strategy is distinct. Although telecommunications is one of the most highly regulated industries in China – with the government keeping a firm grip on competition amongst companies and services – this far-sighted approach has enabled CNC to emerge as a major player despite its humble origins and narrower market space. CNC is also unique in that it has already taken the leap to internationalization long before any of its older and more established cousins, with its acquisition of Asia Global Crossing.

One of the factors working in CNC's favor is that it has had to compete from its inception, amongst multinational players. It did not grow up as a monopoly, but has always had to face competition from corporate network providers on the international markets. At the same time, CNC's services were not "must-have" services such as mobile phones or normal fixed-line telephones. Rather, the company actually had to engage in marketing and adapt its products to the market's needs. These competition and customer orientations will serve CNC well as it develops its product scope and its regional strategies.

As one of China's "big four" banks,[1] ICBC also operates in a tightly controlled sector, but with the threat of international competition looming clearly on the horizon. Ever since China committed itself to joining the WTO to open up the domestic banking sector to foreign and private-sector competition, observers have been writing obituaries for China's big four banks. They are beset by high levels of non-performing loans (NPLs), thousands of employees in a wide and loosely controlled branch network, continuing instances of corruption, uneven levels of information-sharing and use of IT in operations, amongst other challenges. The injection of over US$40 billion into two of the four banks (not including ICBC) in January 2004 only seemed to confirm that the big four may eventually need to be bailed out.

In this situation – and with the urgent need to build competitiveness in its home market – ICBC has launched an ambitious internationalization strategy. Starting by growing a subsidiary, ICBC Asia, from Hong Kong and seeking opportunities in the rest of Southeast Asia, the bank seems to be gambling that the first steps of Chinese companies overseas will be into the same region. The bet is probably a sound one, given the initial moves already made by state-owned giants such as Petrochina and Sinopec. In a short space of time, ICBC Asia has made a name for itself in Hong Kong not only because of its clear mandate to expand into Southeast Asia, but also by forming a team that looks more like its peers in Hong Kong's equity and investment banking community than its parent in Beijing. At the same time, ICBC continues to inject elements of reform into its domestic operations – through selling NPLs, integrating technology into operations, and rationalizing the organizational structure – and with the same humility, pragmatism and willingness to learn from setbacks which have helped the company to survive the potentially crushing effects of NPLs.

The very public international forays of Chinese companies such as Haier, TCL or Petrochina may lead some to assume that ICBC is something of a latecomer on the path of a well-trodden strategy. However, the truth will become clear in the longer term. First, ICBC has taken a prudent approach to internationalization by building foundations, rationalizing its internal structures and organization, and building its financial sustainability – all of which will carry the bank from its heritage as a traditional state-owned enterprise to its future as a focused commercial bank built around its core home market. In the same way, Uni-President is also finding itself in transition organizationally, as it moves from being a company structured around manufacturing to one focused on brands. In this process, it can be expected that its market-entry methods, which in the past have been more akin to those of a family-run business, will start to gel around standardized global best practices. In addition, Chinese companies are just starting to think about going global. The "winning strategy" is therefore far from clear and those who, with the right assets and resources, are able to win small victories on their journey may in the end reap the greater rewards.

The last element which is only just beginning to affect newcomers' strategies is social responsibility. In essence, despite being new globalizers, newcomers are expected to uphold the same respect for community and society as more established multinationals. In a sense, the financial markets may give more slack to young companies in judging whether they operate according to best practices, but the *social* markets – society – do not make such distinctions. Thus, newcomers will need to incorporate social responsibility into their business models from the beginning. Whether this early adaptation to society's expectations creates different corporate growth patterns remains to be seen.

In this section we have three different models to examine – one entering the mainland market from the periphery as a step towards greater global standing, and the other two starting from positions of strength at home and reaching outwards into Asia. All three have been able to benefit from lessons of their peers in their respective sectors. Indeed, in China Netcom's case, it could be argued that it was precisely the failure of one of its global peers that enabled this once-small company to make the jump into the global standings. In any case, these latecomers have the benefit of hindsight and the springboard of China – as one of the dominant engines of Asian and global growth – to support their quests abroad.

▲ UNI-PRESIDENT ENTERPRISES CORPORATION

C.Y. Kao
Chairman, Uni-President Enterprises Corporation
Alex C. Lo
Group Executive Vice-President, Uni-President Enterprises Corporation

In October 1992, we were interviewed by *Asian Money & Finance*. Asked whether the Uni-President Group aspired to become the world's largest food company by 2017, which would mark the company's 50th anniversary, our only response was to laugh loudly. Of course, it's something that we would always aim for, but it would take a huge amount of hard work, determination and good fortune to achieve it.

Though I, C.Y. Kao, am semi-retired today, I still hold a keen interest in shaping the future of Uni-President Enterprises Corporation (UPEC) in the coming decade. "Going international", as I have always said, has been the paramount guiding principle for the Group's development and future.

Company background

UPEC started its business in 1967 when Taiwan's government relaxed a moratorium on the ownership of flourmills by private enterprises. That year, our company began to produce animal feeds using by-products from flourmill operations and, in 1969, we began manufacturing instant noodles. Since then, the company has pursued a strategy of product diversification and vertical integration to take advantage of the many opportunities presented by the growing Taiwan economy. In the two decades from 1970 to 1990, the Taiwan economy expanded at an average annual rate, in real terms, of 9.5%, so the opportunities were real indeed.

It took only five years for the company to grow into Taiwan's largest food conglomerate; however, we did not stop there. Mainland China's Open Door policy, which reduced political tension across the Taiwan Straits, and the Taiwan government's lifting of restrictions for Taiwan-based companies to invest in China, have enabled us to grow our business on the mainland. Today we have roughly 46 different operations in the PRC. As we were entering and expanding on the mainland, we also headed into Southeast Asian markets – in Thailand, Indonesia, Vietnam and the Philippines. In 2002, the company achieved US$2 billion in sales in the food sector alone.

As a diversified Taiwan-based conglomerate, the group dominates the local retail sector as its largest player. UPEC operates 3,304 *7-Eleven* stores in Taiwan and 173 in the Philippines; 75 gas stations in Taiwan; 107 Starbucks Coffee shops in Taiwan and another 25 in Shanghai; 90 personal-care products stores in Taiwan; 29 hypermarket outlets in Taiwan and six in mainland China in collaboration with the French-based Carrefour organization. In addition, the company has substantial interests in financial services and real-estate development. Total group sales for 2003 were about US$1.9 billion.

Strategic intent and moves

We intend to spend the next 15 years creating a global food empire by adapting a formula that has proven successful in Taiwan over the past 36 years. As we go forward, the market on the Chinese mainland will undoubtedly play a major role in shaping the company's overall resource deployment. We already have 125 sales offices in China, in addition to the

46 operations mentioned above. Our sales in mainland China passed the US$1 billion mark in 2004.

However, we realize that our group's current resources alone will not be sufficient to achieve our expansion objective and, thus, we are actively seeking and forming strategic alliances with other global concerns for mutual development and exploitation of favorable opportunities. Many of the operations already mentioned benefit from partnerships. These include Carrefour to operate hypermarket outlets; Nissin for edible oil and instant noodles; Kikkoman in soy sauce; Cargill in grain-based commodities; and Starbucks for coffee outlets, in addition to many others already operating or being developed.

Key strategies in mainland China

We realize that only a company which achieves number-one status on the mainland will have the power and mass to become a global leader in the foods industry in the future. The mainland market – due partly to its sheer size but also to the fact that it is just starting to develop – is a key determinant of a global food company's future success. We recognize this reality and are therefore shaping our company's short-, medium- and long-term strategies for the next decade in order to achieve that goal.

These strategies can be grouped into four areas:

- building brands;
- improving business portfolios;
- reducing costs; and
- leveraging scale and capitalizing on geographic expansion.

All are important, but we view the first, building brands, as the most challenging task because of the level of planning and execution involved, and also because it has great impacts on the company's structure and organization. An enduring brand is the ultimate manifestation of the company's overall organizational capabilities and its specific ability to implement goals.

The route to globalization

Our strategy of going international is built around a much more elaborate plan to build worldwide manufacturing bases, supported by a strong distribution network. Going international will also help us to take advantage of changing consumption patterns and new market opportunities. In 1990, UPEC was the sixth-largest conglomerate and the ninth-largest publicly owned manufacturing company in Taiwan in terms of market capitalization. In the food industry, UPEC had about three times the annual sales of its largest competitor and had no serious competitors in the increasingly saturated market at home. Because of this, we were anxious for the ROC government to lift restrictions banning private companies in Taiwan from investing in mainland China. The mainland market had already demonstrated a lot of economic momentum, especially in the wake of its Open Door policy, and it became clear that we needed to invest there in order to grow in the ways that we envisioned.

We began our quest to go international in 1990 by undertaking the largest acquisition by a Taiwan company in the U.S., in buying Wyndham Baking Company, Inc., which at that time was the third-largest cookie company in the United States. In the fall of 1992, to build on this position, UPEC acquired the San Francisco-based Famous Amos Chocolate Chip Cookie Corporation. The consolidated sales for the American operations exceeded US$600 million.

In addition to building a base in the U.S., UPEC also utilized its American operations to invest in mainland China with two plants in Tianjin and Shanghai, respectively. In 1991, the Taiwan government eventually removed its ban and allowed companies in Taiwan to invest indirectly in China. This changing scenario prompted UPEC to carefully consider its resource allocations. In 1998, UPEC took advantage of economic prosperity in the U.S. and sold its American operations to another cookie company. Loaded with handsome returns from this sale, UPEC was in a better financial position for developing markets in Asia. In retrospect, we were fortunate to have been able to enter and exit the U.S. with such positive results.

Moving into mainland China

In 1991, UPEC set up its first operation for producing tomato products in Urumqi, Xinjiang, the most northwesterly province in China. That operation – a joint venture with the local government – formally marked the first step in our ambitious plans for the vast mainland market. Since then, UPEC has established its plants and operations in coastal provinces and developed its bases along the Yangtze River. Today, most of our 46 operations on the mainland, with another four projects currently in development, are in the food sector.

In the first phase, UPEC's entry into the Chinese market was achieved by forming joint-venture companies with local government agencies or with local state-owned enterprises (SOEs). The reasons for this were our relative lack of knowledge and connections necessary for doing business on the mainland. Thus, in addition to the tomato venture in Urumqi with the local government, and along the same principles, we started instant-noodle operations in Beijing and livestock operations in Shanghai. Over time, these ventures have presented mixed results. We have found that government companies or SOEs have had different motives and philosophies which may or may not match our own attitudes. Thus while we take a long-term and grand development plan for the mainland market, and would like to reinvest any profits back into our operations to enhance market standing, in our experience, government agencies or SOEs have been eager for a quick return from these operations to pay off debt. This divergence in beliefs tends to create tensions between the companies and management, and these have become roadblocks to our broader expansion plans. Of course, we have tried to learn from these lessons, which have given us a valuable understanding of the local market. We have also more diligently cultivated good relationships with different levels of government agencies.

Our second phase of expansion on the mainland is marked by starting to establish fully owned plants across the country. Meanwhile, in our existing joint ventures, UPEC plans to mitigate influence from SOEs, either by offering an attractive premium to buy back shares or increasing capital to dilute the partner's stake.

In Taiwan, UPEC developed its successful business model starting from grain-based products, and then moving to consumer-packaged goods and then retailing products. The hope was that, eventually, each business would become a leader in its respective market space. Ideally, we wanted to replicate this model for success on the mainland, and thus tried it from the very beginning. With the benefit of hindsight, using our Taiwan market model for the mainland turned out to be somewhat costly in terms of resource deployment.

Although UPEC is one of the largest grain-based concerns, on the mainland we do not yet have the latitude to fully exert the expertise and skills which have been acquired in Taiwan. We had missed a sensitive and subtle aspect in doing business in this sector on the mainland, which is that grain-based businesses are still highly regulated by the government. The state regulates supply and demand, as well as pricing, in order to provide a stable environment for consumers, which we agree is critical and necessary in an emerging economy such as that on the mainland. As a result, UPEC's grain business is still struggling to survive, despite having been in the market for 10 years already. On the other hand, we can look with pride at our operations in instant noodles and beverages, market sectors in which we have a leading position. Overall, we are fortunate that, taken as a whole, our mainland operations are profitable.

Partnership with multinational companies

Collaboration with international concerns to develop joint businesses in China or Southeast Asia is another of our critical factors for success as we globalize our operations. Even with 10 years' experience and knowledge in developing business in mainland China, UPEC recognizes very well that there is no company in the world today that has enough resources to reach and fully tap a market as large as that on the mainland. The country is endowed with vast geographic size, a huge population and tremendous potential. Working with multinational companies to share costs and develop businesses thus seems a logical approach and we are working to refine that as part of our business model. Our rationale is that many issues that we have faced on the mainland are common to many foreign businesses operating there. Many of these issues, though not all, relate to the problem of how to establish effective and efficient distribution channels. If UPEC is willing to share its infrastructure and platform with other players, all parties involved could benefit by sharing costs, reaching a larger market, and enhancing their respective positions. Indeed, our idea of serving as a gateway for multinational companies to enter China has proven to be quite persuasive and welcomed by potential partners.

To date, UPEC has formed a number of alliances with global companies. Our main approach is to be very flexible in designing organizational structures to accommodate the specific conditions of each partnership. For example, UPEC has formed joint ventures with six out of Carrefour's 32 outlets in mainland China; with Nissin Oil in edible oil; with Kikkoman in soy sauce; with Kirin in beer; and with Cargill in grain. On May 15, 2003, UPEC announced a strategic alliance with Nissin Foods, a Japan-based concern and the world's largest instant-noodle producer, to jointly develop instant noodles on the mainland and in Taiwan. Under that agreement, Nissin eventually has the right to invest for a 10% holding of UPEC's subsidiary in Kunshan, outside of Shanghai. The equity participation in this subsidiary by Nissin Foods has turned a new page for UPEC to apply in its strategies for working with international partners.

The lessons learned

Since Deng Xiaoping's Open Door policy in the early 1980s, the country's economy has grown to seven times larger than it was 20 years ago, and it continues to enjoy what may be the greatest economic expansion ever witnessed, any time, anywhere. Today, foods and beverages is one of the largest industry sectors on the mainland, and consumer-packaged food and beverage sectors are among the least strictly regulated. This enormous opportunity has driven companies from across the globe to enthusiastically build their presences on the mainland. Perhaps because this has created an intensely competitive market, most foreign food-and-beverage companies still find it difficult to attain even modest profitability in the mainland market.

As a case in point, UPEC entered mainland China as early as 1991, but we did not start making money until 1999, many years later than we had initially anticipated or hoped. Through more than 13 years' experience in doing business in mainland China, UPEC has learned that other foreign companies have encountered similar adversities. Many problems have been due to our flawed understanding of market demand and the level of competition that we would face, which leads companies to commit mistakes such as excess investment, improper resource allocation, or inaccurate reading of consumer expectations (for example, assuming that China is an extremely underdeveloped market that would absorb outdated products). Moreover, foreign companies usually severely underestimate competition from local companies, which is often much fiercer than expected.

Though many factors have proved workable in mainland China, UPEC has drawn up its own recipes for building a successful business there. In fact, most successful companies in mainland China recognize some of these success factors.

No amount of excellence in execution can compensate for a bad decision about where and how to invest. Like leaders in combat, business leaders must first decide which battle to fight, the optimal configuration of forces to use, and how best to deploy the forces to break through competitive positions. According to research released by a Chinese government agency, for the second half of 2002, 90% of 600 major merchandisers suffered from oversupply; an increasing pressure compared with that of the first half of the year. This oversupply results from severe duplication of investments and market deflation in the short term. Clearly, selecting structurally advantaged categories in which to invest becomes the first agenda to consider. Categories with an advantage have three defining attributes: (a) immediate acceptance by a large base of consumers; (b) high affordability; and (c) sufficiently robust economics for market leaders, even in the face of rising competitive intensity.

As already emphasized, affordability is critical to widespread consumer adoption. Selecting an appropriate price band is thus the second critical strategic choice. The power of value-pricing and scale lies in their integrated nature and the ways in which they complement one another. In general, value-pricing could generate the demand required to build scale. In turn, that scale would translate into a low-cost operation that would further support value-pricing. For pricing strategies, mass-market pricing, value-for-money pricing, high-end pricing and premium pricing are most often adopted. A tiered portfolio approach to pricing can usually raise overall category profitability.

The third key choice is the breadth and pace of volume growth and geographic expansion. Scale is all-important in a large emerging market like that on mainland China. Mergers, acquisitions and alliances, together with effective integration plans, are critical to building scale and capabilities.

Where to focus resource investments plays a critical role in making decisions. Experience shows that hybrid approaches to people and asset use might yield surprisingly similar market results. The mainland China market is still evolving and transforming fast in consumption patterns, tastes, behavior and style. UPEC suggests that the companies doing business in mainland China had better invest their limited resources in softer aspects such as local marketing, sales skills and organizations, rather than in hard ones such as physical assets.

Ultimately, food-and-beverage companies operating in mainland China will earn most of the value created by their industry if they build strong brands. This is common to many consumer markets. Therefore, building enduring brand equity will be the ultimate task for any food-and-beverage company. A strategy built around brand equity has also been applied to developing our operations in Southeast Asia.

Moving into Southeast Asia

UPEC's very clear corporate objective is to build our presence into a leading market player in mainland China, but we never let ourselves be overwhelmed by that market's potential. We know that we could not put our entire company's future into one market, even one as large as that on the mainland. This understanding has led us to focus on other markets within Asia, especially those in Southeast Asia, even though these markets are totally different in mode and background from that in China. To execute our parallel entry into both regions, we needed a very clear understanding of our company's relative strengths and potential in these markets. These market developments have followed a completely varied track and presented mixed results, thus shedding light on our management of international operations.

UPEC's entry into the Hong Kong market is rooted back in the 1980s. A Hong Kong native who was also a good friend of the chairman of UPEC was granted rights as the exclusive agent to import our products from Taiwan for distribution in Hong Kong. In mid 1990, to integrate operations between its Hong Kong business and that of the Pearl River Delta in China's Guangdong province, UPEC decided to try to regain control of the distribution rights. However, the company was surprised to find out that the CEO's good friend had already registered all trademarks for the distributed products in Hong Kong under his own name. It took UPEC about two years to settle suits and retrieve all of its trademarks. Then, it set up a branch office in Hong Kong. The business mainly operates in trade by integrating operations from Hong Kong and the Pearl River Delta.

In 1992, an overseas Chinese businessman who lived in Jakarta approached UPEC's chairman for possible collaboration to set up a company in Indonesia. Intent on going international, the chairman immediately decided to form a joint-venture company with the Chinese-Indonesian to produce instant noodles. In Indonesia, the market for instant noodles was vast and was monopolized at the time by Indofoods, a local conglomerate. Equipped with differentiated products, knowledge of the local market and marketing skills, the joint venture took little time to develop into a successful and stable organization with a 10% market share. Except during the period of the Asian financial crisis, the business was profitable. We strongly believe that it will continue to bear fruit well into the future. At present, UPEC's top management is evaluating more opportunities by expanding operations into beverages. After market analysis, the company has decided to go ahead with a market test by working with another local producer.

Thailand was the second market in Southeast Asia that UPEC entered. However, this move was far from being a product of sound analysis and background research. In 1994, an overseas Chinese who lived in Thailand approached the chairman of UPEC and invited UPEC to invest in the country. Without too much thinking and evaluation, the chairman assigned the project to his vice-president for the beverage division to proceed. Coincidentally, the VP at that time was very intoxicated by the unprecedented success achieved by his division in the domestic market and thus perhaps too eager to set up an overseas base regardless of location. In a sense, he wanted to earn credit as a pioneer who developed overseas markets. His aspirations might have been commendable, but his process was definitely out of order, since it was based on emotional and almost personal concerns. Thus the joint venture was established in Thailand without a well-formulated strategy backed up by information and good execution.

As could have been expected with such a move, the venture did not see even a minimum level of success until recently. During the past nine years, the Thailand business burned three times its initial capital and had to buy back all of its shares from its Thai partner. It never established even one winning and sustained business, and executive-level management at the head office received only endless bad news. After review, head office attributed the repeated disappointments over the first five years to a string of bad decisions made at the initial stage, while bad management was to blame for the rest.

Actually, the move into Thailand attracted little attention from UPEC's management, which at that time was just starting to direct most resources towards the growing business in China. With that distraction, the head office left all decision-making regarding the Thai operations to the division, which was operating the business in a very laissez-faire style. In 1997, our top management deemed the "black hole" to be out of control and immediately removed the divisional management team, both at home and abroad. In 2000, the cleaning process continued by changing the managing director for the Thailand office and returning the governance of that unit to the newly established strategic business unit (SBU) for beverage products. Since then, after launching several appealing products which were well received by the market, the Thai operation has developed into a much more stable organization. The company turned its losses around and, starting the final quarter of 2002, the division was fully back in the black.

We visited Vietnam's central government with a Taiwan government-led trade mission in 1993. During the visit, the Vietnamese government warmly welcomed UPEC to invest in their emerging market and generously granted an exclusive permit for producing flour, animal feed and instant noodles. Motivated by those incentives, UPEC established a 100%-owned subsidiary and poured a total of US$40 million into the initial phase. It formally launched products in early 1999 and, by the first quarter of 2003, UPEC had already posted profit from its Vietnamese operations, mainly because of successful products in animal feeds. Simultaneously, instant noodles have demonstrated an upward momentum as well.

UPEC's entry into the Philippines has been very rough. The original plan was to form a joint-venture marketing company with East Asiatic Company (EAC), a Danish-based international trading company. That collaboration was aborted because EAC decided to withdraw from the Southeast Asian markets, which were badly battered by the East Asia financial disaster of 1997. With frustration, UPEC's representative in the Philippines had to take another two years to pursue another option. By

2001, it finally reached an agreement with RFM, a locally based food concern, to form a joint-venture company to produce instant noodles. UPEC owns a 51% stake in the joint venture. In late 2002, the joint venture started to roll out its first offerings to the market. Encountering strong counterattacks by local competitors, the joint venture has learned a strong lesson from its initial results and will be taking a very long road to attaining even a modest footing in the market.

Challenges

Comparing experiences in China and Southeast Asia

Despite the fact that markets in mainland China and Southeast Asia share certain similarities, such as a young consumer profile, strong market momentum and increasing opportunities, we have found that we need different approaches to tap these. To succeed in business on the mainland requires a collective business model, with different strategic components working together in a closely coordinated fashion. For example, conventional wisdom asserts that the key to success in China is a combination of low costs and low prices. However, reality proves that a more dynamic and sophisticated model is needed to achieve this goal.

The markets in Southeast Asia are very varied in culture, religion and ethnic composition. For UPEC to be successful in the region, it has to devote its efforts to not only traditional strategies such as scale, cost, and price, but also to local market insights and creative thinking regarding resource deployment. Usually, working with a good local partner will assure some success.

Challenges vs. opportunities in building a brand business

Like many other consumer-oriented companies in the world, food-and-beverage companies such as ours realize that we will earn the most value from the industry by building strong brands. Therefore, building enduring brand equity is the ultimate goal guiding the company's development. However, companies that recognize and appreciate brand value may find it difficult at times to translate this concept into reality. In Taiwan, the traditional export-driven economy has long shaped the island's industrial structure, which in turn has encouraged Taiwan-based companies to acquire greater capabilities in manufacturing than in marketing. Moreover, Taiwan's domestic market is not very big and thus companies find it particularly costly and difficult, if not impossible, to build their own brands. As a result, Taiwan has long been known worldwide for its manufacturing capabilities and it is good at supplying a wide variety of products under the umbrellas of international clients, but rarely does anyone recognize Taiwan brands.

The opportunity to enter into mainland China has potentially changed this scenario. Driven by visions of the country's one billion consumers and the belief that early movers will reap a permanently disproportionate share of one of the 21st century's biggest markets, consumer-goods companies have long poured investments into mainland China. Nobody can deny that the greatest attraction for Taiwan-based food-and-beverage companies entering mainland China is the huge domestic market that can support any committed company that consistently builds enduring brands for competing around the world.

Change of organizational structure to accommodate strategies

To implement the newly formulated strategies successfully, starting in 2000, UPEC has publicly vowed to transform its business from one rooted in and oriented towards manufacturing, towards one driven by marketing and consumer orientation. We realize that one of the most steep challenges in this task is the transformation of our institutional culture. UPEC has started to restructure its command and report relationships by embracing the conventional organization wisdom that "form should follow function" and "roles should follow function". The company established SBUs in 2002, and it has been retrieving final jurisdiction for branding management, which operating divisions used to own. Then, it has been handing the brand management back over to the function-enhanced Corporate Marketing and Planning Division.

Challenges to building brands across borders

Although management at the head office has set up the organizational framework to transfer brand-building skills across borders, there are still internal conflicts and thus a great need for coordination among diversified business units operating in multiple and sometimes distant locations.

While reviewing its portfolio, management has been astonished to see that the top 200 out of the company's 2,400-odd Stock Keeping Units (SKUs) contribute 70% to 85% of company-wide sales and profit, respectively. With that in mind, we realize that we need to speed up the process of brand consolidation to better deploy and focus the resources necessary to boosting overall performance.

Prior to the formal establishment of SBUs in 2000, UPEC had already built a substantial presence on the mainland. In turn, that operation has evolved many specific local operational modes and even created some expedient realities. Although, ideally, we may want to break or change these realities in order to consolidate the brands across the Straits of Taiwan, this may not always be very easy, and in some cases could be quite sensitive. During this process, head office has identified some common and recurrent problems. Some of these are due to the development of our business on the mainland, which UPEC has found to be much thornier than initially expected. Under the assumption that Taiwan and the mainland shared the same culture and language, initially – and with great optimism – UPEC launched products that had proven successful in Taiwan into the mainland market. This confidence immediately turned into a string of nightmares as all the successful products from Taiwan proved to be either failures or merely survivors. It took us around six years to become acquainted with the tastes on the mainland and to be able to develop products tailored for consumers in that market. Because we had to change the attributes and texture in those products for the mainland market many times, our goal of consolidating our brand has not yet been achieved.

Language stands as another interesting, but tricky, subject for the consolidation of brands. At first glance, Taiwan and mainland China appear to share the same language; the only difference is that the mainland uses simplified characters, while the Taiwanese use the traditional characters, which are unrecognizable to most people on the mainland, particularly the younger generation born after 1949. However, the difference in characters has more significance. The same Chinese characters or phrases may carry different connotations and some phrases may exist in one language but not the other. Thus one cannot simply transfer an existing brand directly from Taiwan to the mainland. Moreover, in many cases on the mainland, a specific brand name has already been registered by someone else. A similar set of issues awaits us in trying to create products for Southeast Asian markets where English is not a native language. In Taiwan, English is spoken and written widely. Therefore, naming products in English to serve needed markets is frustrating and often impossible for staff at head office.

Apparently, head office staff still need to establish the necessary credibility to transfer the knowledge and skills of brand management to other markets. This reality often legitimizes parochialism. Operational managers at local markets usually lack an appreciation of the significance of consistency of brand value that has been built successfully in the home country. They tend to apply their discretion to the local preference for naming those products, which even share the same attributes with those already distributed in the home country. They can always find hundreds of reasons to defend their adoption of locally preferred brands instead of those already established and offered by head office. How to achieve a balance between centralization and decentralization remains a frequent question for management locally and abroad.

UPEC's need to protect its copyrights in foreign markets is another daunting task, particularly in mainland China, where intellectual-property protection is notoriously weak. Unfortunately, copycats emerge from every corner of the country and immediately imitate a successful product that has been achieved through hard work. While we should be happy that our products are so successful as to offer incentives for copycats, in reality the violation threatens the survival and success of the original product. Thus we need to work effectively with different levels of government agencies to crack down on those counterfeits; indeed, in some parts of the organization, this is part of our daily agenda. In Taiwan, we have established a comprehensive procedure to tackle these imitations. On the mainland, though, local management in some cases has not yet determined the rules of the game.

Managing challenges and dealing with conflicts

Building consensus around brand value is the most important criterion for communicating with all management and operations teams at different levels. In achieving this consensus, there are several types of minds to convince. Some people lack the marketing sense necessary to appreciate the value created with brands; some do acquire the concept of branding, but do not have the know-how to build it up; some have the sense and know-how, but are not sufficiently equipped to implement what they may know they must do. Management needs to apply different kinds of education or resource support to accommodate all of these types.

Our corporation has intensive and regular brand-management education and training, which is widely delivered at all executive levels. In order to instill the concept and value of brand-building, the CEO personally monitors and announces the progress of selected leading brands in a monthly management meeting, and SBU managers have to carefully preserve and sustain these brands. By doing so for about two consecutive years, all managers have gradually acquired a notion that, like each individual, each product has its own name, but that very few can be successfully built into a preferred and valuable brand.

Responding to the increased complexity in brand management, UPEC has started to seek advice from internationally known brand image-development firms such as Landor and Interbrand, in addition to advertising agencies that have long been working with the company. These third parties can provide insights and valuable advice to our executive team to enable us to better steer or manage our brand.

Some of these efforts are beginning to bear fruit. Over the past two years, UPEC has already established seven mega-brands, each with at least NT$1 billion (approximately US$35 million) in annual sales in the Taiwan market. This performance is unrivalled by any other competitor. Furthermore, UPEC has added another six mega-brands that are generated from the mainland portfolio. The company has vowed to sustain the value of these great brands and is committed to building up at least 10 more in the coming years.

Objectively, building a mega-brand in the mainland market should be relatively easy compared to doing the same task in Taiwan. In Taiwan, UPEC's best product took only four years to build a brand and pass the NT$1 billion mark in annual sales. Most others require at least 10 years. However, given its market size, with hundreds of millions of potential consumers, mainland China offers UPEC a much better chance at developing mega-brands by sheer numbers alone. If the company positions its products with sound marketing and good execution, we should be able to reach this goal. The six mega-brands that have already been established in the mainland market have all been built from scratch, among them a juice product carrying the brand name "More", which will hit US$300 million by the end of 2003. For that product, UPEC took only two years to reach that level, which fully demonstrates the beauty of that continent-style economy.

Social responsibility: Realizing another dimension to business

It would be tempting to think that we can enter and expand within markets with only business issues such as market share, sales and profits as our primary goals. However, we have become very aware that we exist within a complex society, and that we as a major business have a social responsibility to fulfill.

In October 1987, Uni-President encountered an unprecedented crisis within the food industry. A blackmailer known as "Man of a Thousand Faces" sent an aseptic carton filled with a poison-contaminated drink and a letter to extort NT$15 million (US$530,000) from the company. He threatened to inject poison into the company's products everywhere if his demand was ignored or rejected. Enraged by such intimidation and surrounded by mixed proposals from his management team, Dr. Kao, the CEO and president at that time, was determined not to yield to this blackmail. He made an open announcement advising the general public to stop buying the company's products until the felon could be identified and caught. In the meantime, he made a recall of all the company's products from every retailer's shelf, and destroyed these in front of a government agency as a witness.

That decision put the public's anxiety to rest; furthermore the villain never took additional steps against the company. Though the company lost billions of dollars in this incident, it earned invaluable trust and confidence from the community. More significantly, the company set a model example to the industry on how to manage similar crises. Since then, a blackmail attempt of this nature has never succeeded in Taiwan's food industry.

At the start, when Uni-President set up shop with only 82 employees in a small southern Taiwanese city, it felt indebted to the community for the confidence it had in the company. The blackmail crisis engendered in Uni-President a deeper sense of its social responsibility. Uni-President recognizes that building a credible company alone is not enough; but as a high-profile enterprise, it seeks to influence or even guide society through its exemplary organizational behavior. Today, the company has a significant presence in many markets, and it employs as many as 60,000 people across the Asia Pacific region. We certainly sense our ever-expanding responsibilities towards the communities in which we operate.

As part of its commitment to being an exemplary enterprise, Uni-President constantly reminds all its employees that they need to adhere to the law in helping the company to maximize shareholder value. This adherence is a basic yardstick of a responsible corporate citizen. We believe that a greater company should set an even higher standard by always taking action to better our social behavior and value system, to protect our community's ecological environment, to utilize and allocate social resources more efficiently, and to contribute to our society in more meaningful ways.

Corporate social responsibility must not be embraced merely as a publicity slogan. Rather it is an endless process and a determination to show persistent and continued commitment. Uni-President pursues its vision of being a brand-driven entity; however, it understands that it can never achieve this goal without being perceived by the general public as a responsible corporate citizen. The management entrusted with this responsibility is as important as the brand portfolio. Corporate social responsibility is an indispensable pillar that complements the company's efforts in building its brand. As society increasingly associates a specific brand with the company it represents, the company can enjoy perpetual economic prosperity from a brand perceived as the ultimate choice.

Uni-President is fortunate to have acquired abundant opportunities to demonstrate its social responsibility. In Taiwan, the company has already established numerous foundations and has actively participated in a wide range of activities for various social causes. Since 2000, the company has promised to provide even healthier foods by using only natural ingredients in all its products. In 2002, to reinforce these commitments, Uni-President established a foundation named "Love for the Millennium", which is dedicated to carrying out the company's ongoing commitment to healthier and better living standards. In addition, the company's retailing subsidiaries such as *7-Eleven* are positioning themselves as the best neighbors to their respective commercial communities and are leveraging their pervasive presence by providing customers with both tangible merchandise and virtual services.

Always ranked as one of the most admired companies in Taiwan, Uni-President continues to improve itself. We realize that our success lies in continuing to have meaningful interactions with our diverse stakeholders. If Uni-President does the job well, then society will reward the company. The company has established itself as a good corporate citizen in its home market and will strive to replicate that reputation in other areas as it expands its markets geographically and culturally.

Conclusion

Motivated by strategic drive, UPEC must establish a new, highly complex managing role, which coordinates relationships between SBUs and does so in a highly flexible way. The key is to focus less on managing activities directly and more on creating an organizational context that is conducive to the coordination and resolution of differences. Creating the right organizational context involves establishing clear objectives, developing managers with broadly based perspectives and relationships, and fostering supportive organizational norms and values. Having built flexible central and local management capabilities, the next challenge is to link them in an organization that allows UPEC to do what it must to survive in an international environment – to think globally and act locally.

We cherish the hope that our company can continue to improve itself as it engages in different markets and in different societies. Though we are already a multi-billion dollar organization, UPEC will continue to experience a series of growing pains in its transformation from a local company into a global entity. We realize that in the future UPEC will enter a completely new battlefield with global rivals such as Nestlé, Unilever and Danone. Our response must be to upgrade overall competitiveness to survive and prosper. In our journey to become a world-class player, brand building is just a starting point, just as the mainland China market is only one market on the international map. UPEC realizes that there are still many organizational challenges like this that lie ahead.

TAKEAWAYS

1. **Growing from family-run to strategy-run.**
   Uni-President entered several markets in ways that are commonly associated with a family-run or founder-led company; that is, by emotion or instinct rather than according to coherent strategy backed by market research and business development plans. In retrospect, the company acknowledged this approach as "misdirected" and made tangible plans to rectify the investment. In addition, by accepting and identifying the causes of the error, they have been able to learn from the episode and, through new systems of checks and balances, ensure that their future investments are made on much sounder ground.

2. **Aligning business plans with realities of markets and culture.**
   Uni-President has been flexible in developing strategies which are tailored to meet the specific cultural, historal and industrial situations of various Asian countries. For instance, because of the structure of the industry and the cultural aspects of food products, they chose to enter several Southeast Asian markets with local industry leaders, such as with RFM in the Philippines. On the other hand, in Vietnam, where the government takes a stronger hand in industrial development, Uni-President accepted the government's recommendation to invest in a wholly owned venture. In mainland China, the company has used a combination of entry strategies – including partnership with the government and franchising – to meet the specific needs of each market.

3. **Rationalizing business structures as the organization grows across borders.**
   The company has created new structures to meet the demands of a growing organization, and today has the SBU (strategic business unit) as an integral part of its strategy to extend brands across borders. The company realized that it needed to maintain certain functions (core administration, long-term strategy) at

headquarters but that it also needed to evolve an organization that could give limited autonomy to business units. Today, this structure allows new business units to be created as needed, whilst the central office manages activities and brands in an integrated manner.

4. **Assuming the mantle of industry and business leadership.**
The company has not been slow to assume the mantle of social responsibility that comes with being an industry leader and an organization with a growing global impact. As a part of this, they consider their employees as extensions of the company and thus try to instill civic values amongst employees across the company as a whole. This step sets UPEC apart from others in its industry group and in Taiwan.

▲ INDUSTRIAL AND COMMERCIAL BANK OF CHINA

Jiang Jianqing
Chairman & President, Industrial and Commercial Bank of China

The past two decades have been marked by a very visible trend towards globalization in international economic and financial sectors, especially since the 1990s. This trend is being driven by increased international trade and capital flows, widespread application of modern information and communication technologies, and stronger and more frequent economic and financial links between major economies. China, as the largest developing country, gained accession into the World Trade Organization (WTO) in 2001, which symbolized its active participation in the course of economic globalization in all dimensions. As China accelerates its pace of globalization, Industrial and Commercial Bank of China (ICBC) and its commercial banks in China, has entered a critical phase of restructuring. It is confronted with severe challenges and intensified competition, not only from other domestic players but notably from large multinational banks from developed countries.

In the face of these external challenges, ICBC has stepped up its own momentum to restructure and be innovative in tackling reforms. We wish to convert the challenges of economic globalization into opportunities to take part in global economic integration and the international market. We aim not only to excel in the domestic market, where we see more and more competition from international peers, but also to build a presence in the international financial arena, with a new global outlook.

ICBC: The backbone of China's financial industry and a new international player

ICBC was created from the People's Bank of China in January 1984 and has grown continuously alongside the opening of China's economy and the deepening of the country's financial sector. Today we are the largest commercial bank in China, with the most extensive network of outlets in major cities throughout the country. Internationally we are ranked 16th in tier-one capital among international banks, and we have also started to build our presence in major international financial centers in the world at large.

ICBC prides itself on being the most competent commercial bank in China, in the scale of our operations and the wide coverage of our network. By the end of June 2003, ICBC's total assets stood at RMB5.1 trillion, with deposits outstanding of RMB4.4 trillion and loans outstanding of RMB3.3 trillion, accounting for more than 20% of the total value for all China's banks. We estimate that this will double every five years.

ICBC has the most extensive network of business outlets in China, covering all major cities, including 37 tier-one branches, more than 380 tier-two branches and 25,000 banking offices. It boasts abundant customer resources, with 8.1 million corporate accounts and 420 million personal accounts. The bank offers a full array of financial products and services that enjoy favorable prospects for development as the market grows. We have the largest market share among our peers in deposits, loans and remittance business, and have also carved out a leading position in innovating new products such as personal mortgages, consumer credit, bills finance, credit cards, fund custody and distribution, bullion trading, wealth management and e-banking. Through the balanced development of corporate, institutional and personal banking businesses and the interaction of commercial and investment banking businesses, we have tried to nurture creativity and comprehensive competitive advantages. In 2003 the American market research company AC Nielson identified ICBC as "the bank most used by consumers in China", and its Peony card as "the banking card most used by consumers".

ICBC aims to preserve its strong profit position amongst commercial banks in China, and we eliminate risks resulting from transformation the most rapidly. Like many banks in emerging economies, ICBC experienced a period of accumulating many non-performing loans and assets (NPLs) during economic restructuring. In recent years, with the support of the government and the fast and healthy development of the economy, ICBC has given priority to managing these NPLs, which has boosted the bank's comprehensive reform. This all-around reform includes adjusting our operational structure, strengthening risk management, and speeding up business innovation, resulting in eventual improvement in the quality of assets and a significant increase in operational profits.

The NPL ratio of ICBC began to decrease significantly in 2000 and, from 2001, both this and the outstanding amount of NPLs have continued to decrease. By the end of September 2003 the NPL ratio for the bank as a whole had decreased to 21%, 26 percentage points lower than in June 1999, representing the most rapid recovery and disposal of NPLs among state-owned commercial banks. In recent years, the NPL ratio for new loans extended to corporations has been 1.82%; for individual mortgage loans offered to the public the figure is 0.2%; and for other individual consumption loans it is 0.6%, all of which are maintained at a good level of quality.

With the constant improvement of asset quality, ICBC has improved its profitability remarkably. For the bank as a whole, operational profits increased from RMB9.6 billion (US$1.16 billion) in 2000 to RMB43.9 billion (US$5.30 billion) in 2002, with an annual growth rate at 119%. The bank is expected to make operational profits of RMB60 billion (US$7.25 billion) and become the most profitable commercial bank in China. As ICBC has maintained a steady growth of book profit in recent years, we still use 80% of operational profits to cover historical burdens to maintain a good pace in eliminating risks.

Information technology is another driving force behind our transformation, and we would like to be the commercial bank which integrates IT must fully into its operations. We have thus studied the latest research developments in modern information and network technology and actively adopted state-of-the-art practices in our international banking sector. In recent years various information projects such as large-scale data centers of internationally advanced standards, data pools for analyzing information, and a comprehensive, customer-oriented, computer application system have been put into effect. The e-banking system, with Internet-banking, call-center and self-banking facilities as its major components, has been improved and completed. ICBC will continue to maintain its competitive edge in technological standards in line with industry developments, and will extend these to other parts of its operations.

Relying on its advanced computer platform, ICBC has taken the lead in launching a full array of information products and managerial software every year. ICBC's Internet-banking business has achieved international standards, winning an number of awards, including "Best Banking Website 2002" from the Britain-based *Banker* magazine, "Best Corporate Internet Bank China 2002" and "Best Individual Internet Bank China 2003" from the U.S.-based *Global Finance* magazine.

We realize that in the context of economic globalization, we will be judged on global standards, and not merely in comparison to our domestic peers. Thus, we are making significant efforts to align our operations with international practice and standards. We began our international operations in 1991 and by the end of June 2003 total assets in foreign exchange amounted to US$51.4 billion. ICBC's market share in China for foreign-exchange deposits, international settlements, the purchase and sale of foreign exchange, and foreign-exchange dealing for the customers' accounts ranks as either No. 1 or No. 2 among its peers.

ICBC continues to follow the trend of economic globalization and in recent years has steadily implemented a strategy for regional expansion. At present it has 66 overseas offices, among which there are eight overseas branches, three wholly owned subsidiaries and three representative offices. In addition, ICBC is the controlling shareholder of three financial companies in Hong Kong. To supplement this network, ICBC maintains correspondent banking relationships with 1,020 banks in 105 countries and regions on six continents.

In July 2000, ICBC acquired Union Bank, a publicly listed bank in Hong Kong, and transformed it into ICBC Asia. The deal made ICBC the first Chinese commercial bank to own an internationally listed bank. ICBC Asia absorbed the business that was conducted under the bank's Hong Kong branch, which gave it a significant base on which to grow. We are positioning ICBC Asia as the group's flagship company for our overseas expansion. ICBC Asia has already taken a stake in Tai Ping Insurance (24%) and has completed the acquisition of Fortis Bank Asia HK in 2004. When this merger is complete, ICBC Asia will be one of the strongest banks in Hong Kong, with over US$12 billion in assets and over US$7 billion in customer deposits. In short, it will be well positioned for a round of accelerated expansion of its business.

ICBC continuously strives to improve its international reputation and recognition. In recent years, it has been given various international awards including being named "Best Bank in China", "Best Commercial Bank in China", and "Best Retail Bank in China" by *Euromoney* and the *Banker* (U.K.), *Global Finance* (U.S.A.), the *Asian Banker* (Singapore), and *Asiamoney* and *Finance Asia* (Hong Kong). ICBC was named "2002 Most Respected Chinese Company" by domestic media. In 2003, the British *Emerging Markets* magazine in the U.K. gave ICBC the "Best International Relationship" award. These achievements give us more confidence that our current program of reform and restructuring is the right one.

Developing management and operations to suit the development of the Chinese economy

From its incorporation until 1993, ICBC had functioned as a specialized state bank in three areas: extending credit to state-owned industrial and commercial enterprises; taking savings deposits from Chinese residents; and conducting settlements.

From 1993 onwards, in line with the government's decision to reform the financial system, ICBC began to transform itself from the specialized state bank into a wholly state-owned commercial bank. After the incorporation of three policy banks by the Chinese government in 1994, ICBC moved out of this market space and focused on commercial business. The Commercial Banking Law of the People's Republic of China in 1995 gave ICBC legal status as a state-owned commercial bank. After that, ICBC accelerated its steps to become a fully fledged commercial bank, despite its 100% state-owned status. Gradually a new operation and management mechanism was set up within the bank under which the bank will conduct the business solely on its own decisions and take the associated risks, be responsible for its own profits and losses and practice self-restraint.

In recent years, and particularly after China's entry into the WTO, the Chinese government stepped up the pace of its economic and financial reforms and more accurately defined the direction and goals for reforming state-owned commercial banks. In light of this, ICBC deepened its own comprehensive reforms, sparing no efforts to learn and adopt international standards and practices, to transform itself into a modern financial enterprise. This 20-year evolution has not been easy, but the pace of advances in recent years has given us a strong base for moving forward. We realize that the particular conditions of China's developing market economy demand multiple tasks from its commercial banks, and we are working hard to transform our institution to meet these. With our constant efforts to properly control the risks involved in commercial banking and implement the wide-ranging changes needed to compete in a changing market, we are confident we will be able to compete vigorously in the years ahead.

The features of our evolving competitive framework include management, risk management, internal control, corporate governance, human resources, and an international outlook. Each of these is described below.

A new management system

The bank now has a management system under a unified entity, and is simultaneously implementing a multi-tier authorization system. Since 1994, in order to achieve commercialization and to comply with financial regulatory requirements, ICBC has adopted measures to enhance the "single legal person" system under which funds are mobilized and appropriated within the bank by the head office. Payments and expenditures are also managed bank-wide to ensure payment to customers, and to consolidate accounting and tax payment. Asset and liability management and equity management are carried out based on the needs of the operation of the whole bank.

In 1996, ICBC was the first bank in China to implement the legal-person authorization mechanism based on the "single legal person" system.

Under this system, the head office, under the bank's overall strategic planning, granted branches varied power to make operational decisions according to their autonomy, market resources, business performance, management level, and business prospects. Branch office decisions are subject to checks and balances within the head office to ensure that there is quality control and that these decisions are appropriate to the actual market conditions. Currently, all business activities benefit from this system of stringent control.

Continuing to deepen reform

In line with requirements for building a modern commercial bank, ICBC borrowed from the international standards and practices to reorganize its structure and streamline business processes. ICBC is now redeploying its network. On the one hand, we are closing redundant branches and withdrawing from non-profitable business areas. On the other hand, we renew and expand profitable branches to support business growth more actively. In the past five years, ICBC has closed 14,000 redundant outlets, which is approximately one-third of the total number of outlets at any one time. Simultaneously, we have renewed some large branches to enable them to provide comprehensive business services. Injecting additional resources into these branches has had a positive impact on their competitiveness and enabled them to broaden the portfolio of services that they offer. Meanwhile, measures designed to tackle the bank's overall reorganization are under way, with the goal of setting up a new internal structure and business process that highlights risk control internally while being externally oriented to the customer. We have decreased the layers between management and operations and shortened reporting lines so as to improve management quality and ensure an efficient, quick response to all issues. The cards business and bills-discounting business have been centralized to achieve specialization and economies of scale and to sharpen our competitive edge.

Internal control and risk management

Relying on modern information technology, ICBC established a new management mechanism under which the head office directly controls all the operations of the provincial branches and supervises the operations on the city-branch level and sub-branch level. Our internal warning system registers an alert if a branch violates some internal control requirements, and the operation will be suspended until necessary rectifications are made. At present, ICBC is focusing on extending the scope of its supervision to each branch and each major business transaction. The goal is to realize full oversight of branches on every level within the whole bank, on the major businesses, on risks associated with each business, on business costs, and on the efforts made by the heads of branches to fulfill their responsibilities.

Moreover, after an objective overview of the bank's risk profile, we discovered that risks are highly concentrated on credit business. We thus established a risk-management committee charged with deepening reforms in this area and with consolidating the bank's risk control of its credit business. Centers for industry analysis, credit approval and credit supervision have been set up within the head office. Other departments designed to deal with NPLs have also been set up.

Meanwhile, ICBC also established a complete risk-management system under which non-credit asset risks, off-balance-sheet risks, market risks and operational risks are managed appropriately. We also adopted a very prudent accounting system, which brought ICBC's risk-management capability up to a new level.

ICBC has always laid emphasis on internal auditing and we are now continuing to implement further innovations in this area. Bank-wide we put in place an independent internal-auditing department which is charged with producing regular evaluations and reinforcing internal controls backed by a veto mechanism. Meantime, ICBC is continuing to introduce external auditing practices. The bank employs major international accounting firms to conduct external auditing on the whole bank. In information disclosure, the bank complies with international standards and remains a very transparent bank among China's domestic non-public banks.

Reforming management of human resources and incentives

In recent years, ICBC has attracted qualified staff while successfully cutting its surplus labor thanks to a standardized labor contract. Our focus on quality has enabled us to reduce the total number of employees from

570,000 to 390,000. A corporate culture oriented toward modern commercial banking was established in accordance with the bank's new strategic objective, and the use of incentives in managing the bank's key personnel contributed to its vibrant management and operation.

ICBC embarks on a new course

A new era has come in China's economic development, marked by the sustained progress towards a market economy and all-round efforts to improve people's living standards. ICBC, for its part, grasps every opportunity and endeavors to overcome all challenges in dealing with the historical legacies of China's economic transition. Our objective is to become a modern commercial bank with a sound corporate structure, good financial conditions and the ability to compete in international markets.

We are also aware that China is both a transitional and an emerging economy. Thus, ICBC has adopted a new strategic focus on absorbing the trends of globalization, both broadly and in the international banking industry. Financial disintermediation and market-determined interest rates have reshaped China's financial industry, just as they have transformed those of other developed economies. In addition to innovations in balance-sheet businesses, the bank taps into intermediary and even investment banking markets. In this way, it is able to meet market demand, to diversify risks and broaden its sources of income. Among the primary focuses for income generation are:

- Special features: While delivering across-the-board services, the bank strives to enhance its core competitiveness and builds its brand via financial innovation.
- City orientation: There are more business opportunities and higher returns in China than in developed nations arising from its rapid industrialization and urbanization. Therefore, local markets will be the focus of ICBC's future development. We will grasp opportunities to optimize operations in urban areas across the country.
- Globalized operations: Globalization is an irreversible trend and thus ICBC will continue to develop international businesses and increase its presence abroad. Furthermore, we need to go

international on all levels, from operations to customers, businesses, profits, shareholders and management.

- Adopting IT for efficiency: ICBC is as strongly committed to IT as it is to reform. Its ambition is to build powerful information management and electronic banking systems on the basis of its advanced IT infrastructure.

In this way, it hopes to reach its objective of becoming a modern commercial bank. In its international operations, ICBC is moving actively to accommodate itself to different legal frameworks on universal banking. It is aiming to grow into a corporate group that provides diversified services but with commercial banking at the core.

As we move ahead to the next stage of reform and development, ICBC will start to intensify reforms and improve corporate governance with the aim of attracting new shareholders in line with government policy. ICBC aims to reach a healthy capital adequacy ratio (ratio of capital to loans outstanding), lowering its non-performing loans (NPL) ratio, properly allocating provisions and, finally, going public abroad by the end of 2006. Thus, it can not only have new sources of capital but also a scientific organizational structure comprising a board of directors, properly constituted management and board of supervisors, and shareholders' meetings.

The current organizational structure still needs to be streamlined. While closing less-efficient outlets, it is imperative to empower key branches to provide diversified services.

In accordance with the new requirements in Basel II, the bank is endeavoring to put in place effective internal control at every stage of its operation and management in order to strengthen the head office's monitoring of all branches and businesses. An independent internal-auditing system will be established and will gradually shift its focus from compliance to risk management.

The bank conducts comprehensive analysis of its credit, market and operational risks for early warning and risk control. An IRB project will be carried forward to establish uniform risk-weighted assets and capital-control mechanisms. Credit application and loan approval are to be separated for credit-risk management purposes. In addition, a risk-compensation mechanism will help prevent mismatches between returns and the risks involved.

A uniform performance-evaluation system will provide the basis for improved performance by employees, and an incentive mechanism built on this will motivate people and create value. In addition to economic incentives, more training opportunities will be offered to attract high-quality staff.

In line with changes in China's financial market, the bank is becoming more customer-oriented in its management. In addition, it is playing a more active role in guiding customers' choices, and paying more attention to market segmentation. All business procedures are customer-centered with a view to creating value for customers. Packaged services are being provided through combining frontline services and back-office support. Data-warehousing technologies are being used to identify and lead target markets. It is the bank's goal to optimize its client base through differentiated services and pricing.

Economic and financial globalization is an irreversible trend. After two decades of reform and development, ICBC now boasts a big market share, solid strength and a modern organization. It is therefore well equipped to take advantage of China's economic reform and sustained growth, to commercialize, to expand its domestic market and to participate in international competition and cooperation. China is an emerging economy. ICBC is an emerging bank, marching forward toward the world financial market.

TAKEAWAYS

1. **ICBC as a microcosm of the Chinese economy: The transition from a planned economy to a market mindset.**

   ICBC is an anomaly when compared with the other companies featured in this book. Although its history is short in years, its heritage of lending based on state directives weighed heavily on the bank from the very beginning. The company has had to overcome the burdens of its history whilst learning the ways of the market. In a sense, one task is political, the other is market-based. Its development is thus a microcosm of China's own transition from the planned economy to one based on the market. As this is in many ways a once-in-history shift, and within that shift the banking sector also carries a degree of specificity when compared to other sectors in China, the lessons of ICBC are likely to be adaptable only in the broadest sense.

2. **First survive the present, then ensure survival in the future.**
   When ICBC declared its ambitions to become a first-tier, fully fledged commercial bank, many industry observers may have been sanguine: not only did the bank suffer from a myriad of issues over organizational control, risk, credit and management, but its high rate of NPLs also threatened its viability in the short term. Jiang knew that before he could create the structures of a "great" bank, he needed to ensure its short-term stability, which meant addressing the NPL issues. He thus made NPLs his first priority, whilst implementing the organizational or structural changes necessary for the NPL issue to be resolved. Today, with NPLs under control, the bank is implementing structural and operational changes with a more decisive hand, as it knows that these will be crucial to surviving in the future. The approach of dealing with the most immediate concerns first and foremost, whilst delaying other reforms that are needed only in the long-term, can also be seen in the Chinese government's managing of the economy.

3. **Ensure independence, accountability and checks across operations.**
   Among the first organizational changes that Jiang instituted at ICBC are those which ensure independence, transparency and accountability across business operations and regional offices, while reinforcing the bank's internal system of checks and balances. The importance of these in Chinese financial institutions is particularly evident given the history of state-directed lending and corruption, but will be essential to most other businesses as well. Many may argue that ICBC should recruit new capital more aggressively in order to bring down its

NPL ratio. Yet, astutely, the bank realizes that without reinforcing its internal structures, such new drives would only be creating more problems for the future. It thus keeps its priorities in line.

4. **Merge or acquire only when complementarities are clear.**
   Like other budding globalizers, ICBC knew that it could either buy or build its assets overseas. Both models have been tried in the Chinese banking industry through the Bank of China, which both "built" its own proprietary operation in Hong Kong, whilst acquiring several smaller indigenous banks, which it continued to operate under their original names. ICBC carved its own route, based on its internal abilities and market availability by taking over ICEA and transforming it into a core operation of ICBC Asia. In 2003, it undertook to purchase the Asian operations of Fortis Bank, one of the first occasions that a Chinese bank has taken over a so-called foreign (Western) financial operation. ICBC's open approach to mergers, which enabled it to "discover" available assets, assess their quality and potential synergies, and then implement it in a relatively short amount of time, served it well. One would hope that ICBC Asia, with a mandate to build up a regional bank serving the entire Asian region, would undertake future expansions with an equal degree of rigor.

▲ CHINA NETCOM CORPORATION LTD

Dr. Edward Tian (Tian Suning)
CEO, China Netcom Corporation Ltd

Introduction

Incorporated in June 1999 with the mission to build "e-frastructure" for China's economic development, China Netcom Corporation Ltd. (China Netcom or CNC) is today a leading player in China's telecom sector. It has grown against the backdrop of China's sustained rapid economic growth and accelerating integration into the pan-Asia region. CNC now moves in sync with this economic integration, to support the regionalization of the Chinese telecommunications industry.

The continued rapid growth of the Chinese economy in recent years has injected a new dynamic into the economic integration of the East Asia region. China is a key player and driver behind the region's transformation, and we should note several significant trends. First, China's economic status in Asia and in the world has been improving, and an economic and trade mega-zone has emerged, built around China and its neighboring countries. Second, world-class multinational companies have entered the Chinese market. Manufacturers, in particular, have established multiple bases in China, helping to create the "world's factory" in a real sense. Increasingly, this is being complemented by the shift of business services, research and development to China. These trends will deepen as China becomes more integrated into the Asian and world economies, and as more and more overseas companies become embedded in the Chinese market. The telecom sector is responding to these developments by speeding up its own reform, strengthening the network in China, and starting to regionalize operations into the greater East Asia area. These will enable it to capture the new emerging opportunities for business expansion.

Fundamentally, the telecom industry is at the core of the information-based economy. Even in the aftermath of the bursting of the technology bubble in 2000, its central role in the information society has not been questioned. In the foreseeable future the development of the information industry, with the telecom sector at its center, will be the major driving force of economic growth, as it has always been. In contrast to Europe and America, where the industry has experienced serious setbacks and competitive weakening, in China the industry's growth has continued at speed. This has been a good opportunity to shore up its rational structure and competitiveness. Today, China's telecom industry embraces a greater international market and an unprecedented opportunity for regionalization and, further into the future, globalization.

In this strategic context, I would like to offer my own observations on the industry's development and also compare the practices in China with those of other Asian counterparts such as Singapore Telecom (SingTel). I also offer my views on the implications of regionalization for China's telecom sector, of China's participation in and promotion of the global telecom industry, as well as the strategic options and strategies for CNC's own growth into the region and beyond.

Background: Emergence of the China–pan-Asia economic circle

An economic mega-zone around China is now taking shape. Statistics from the Ministry of Commerce indicate that China's imports totaled US$412.8 billion for 2003, marking an increase of 39% over the previous year. Many of China's foremost trading partners are in Asia and the relation is growing stronger as the partners discover new complementarities. China's trade with Asean grew 42% in 2003, hitting a record of US$78 billion. Premier Wen Jiabao forecasts that trade between the Asean nations and China will be over US$100 billion by 2005. In addition to Asean, trade between China and neighboring regions of Hong Kong, Japan, Korea, Taiwan and Singapore alone contribute over half of China's yearly trade.

Investment into China is similarly driven from Asia. As revealed by the 2001 World Investment Report released by UNCTAD, in 2000, 45% of overall investment in Asian countries other than Japan flows to China, with 25% going to Hong Kong. Moreover, more than half of the inflows in Hong Kong have been put into the mainland. Since China became a full member of the WTO, there has been a great surge in the number of foreign companies flowing into the country. On the other hand, a large number of Chinese businesses, such as Lenovo and Haier, have begun to seek opportunities overseas or have grabbed a niche in the global market.

Business inflows and outflows alike bespeak economic liberalization in Asia and have created new spaces for expansion and extended the value chain for China's telecom industry. These developmental trends require that the industry adopt a new development framework built on the regional market, in addition to the domestic one. With economic growth there is a skyrocketing increase in the information flow and telecom flow and the emerging Asian economic region is a good example of this. Telecom inflows and outflows will thus increase exponentially in the years to come. This is a logical requirement in the context of the modern information-oriented economy. This marks a significant transition of the business modes from the traditional local telephony and data services to regional and global entities offering end-to-end solutions.

Asia, and the Greater China region in particular, will become a fast-growing area with regard to the telecom sector. Current development trends in the global telecom industry, industry deregulation and stronger economic strength in Asia will all feed the shift of the bulk of global telecom flows from America to Asia. Internal flows within Asia, formerly in transit from the U.S., will be converted to direct internal transfers. In 2000, statistics show, 77% of the flows in mainland China, 70% in Taiwan, 69% in Hong Kong, 53% in Japan and 48% in Korea terminated within the region. Asia, and the Greater China region in particular, will become the fastest-growing region for telecom service volume.

Regionalization efforts of our counterparts in Asia

Forward-looking counterparts in the telecom industry in other Asian countries have already begun to reach out beyond their borders to ensure their own competitiveness as the industry goes regional and global.

SingTel's experience provides us with a valuable reference in our efforts to promote regionalization in telecom operations. Since 1990, Singapore has witnessed burgeoning derivative telecom flows as a result of the strengthened economic and trade ties between Singapore and its neighboring countries. As there was a well-established telecom market within the country and greater external competition, SingTel increased its investment and acquisition efforts in neighboring countries so as to make a quick debut into the regional market, and found itself an advantageous position. Among its new acquisitions are AIS of Thailand, Globe of the Philippines, Bharti of India, NCIC of Taiwan, Telkomsel of Indonesia and Optus of Australia. These efforts have resulted in a more convenient telecom and increased flows and subsequent accumulation of telecom assets and revenue. The total turnover of SingTel reached US$5.73 billion in 2003. One-third of the revenue will come from the overseas business. Through external investment and acquisition, SingTel has gradually become one of the major telecom operators in the Asia Pacific region.

Another similar acquisition related to Asia is that of the sea-cable assets of American Level 3 last December by Reach, which is a joint venture of Hong Kong PCCW and Telstra. Level 3 is the builder of the first long-distance comprehensive IP backbone network in the U.S. and has always been a well-favored player on the U.S. market. Therefore, it was considering building a sea cable all the way through East Asia in an attempt to rival AX and replicate its success story in Asia. But the prospects appeared to be meager, as the sea cable has a large excess capacity and dropping prices, thwarting Level 3's efforts and forcing it to sell off its unfinished project. During this period, Reach kept a wait-and-see attitude towards market changes. When the timing was right, Reach offered to relieve Level 3 of its burdens at unduly low cost and with heavy concessions. In the process, Reach had converted itself from an enterprise with a core business in leasing backbone network to an independent facilities-based operator and greatly enhanced its competitive advantage.

Defining our regionalization strategy

The emergence of the pan-Asia economic region is transforming the telecom industry's focus from one based on nations to one based on the entire region. China in particular is growing exceptionally fast, and is starting to have an impact on the region in demand and communications flows. Meanwhile, the increasing number of big enterprises that invest and operate in China are giving Chinese service providers the opportunity to operate more networks featuring seamless connection between China and other parts of Asia and the world. In fact, this is today a necessity for high-quality service. It provides decision-makers and production bases with end-to-end broadband telecom service to other parts of Asia. We have developed CNC's regional strategy around this phenomenon. We aim to provide large enterprises with an integrated solution through a regional network centered in China and connected up with other parts of Asia. We aim to become the leading operator in the pan-Asia region and to embody the "going global" strategy of major Chinese telecom operators.

As a matter of fact, many forward-looking operators have heeded the existence of such opportunities and invested significant sums so as to gain an inroad into this market. Globe Telecom and Level 3 are two examples. Yet their cases show the difficulties in investing astutely into this market. Undoubtedly, there are enormous potential opportunities in this market, but if operators cannot provide integrated end-to-end service, their investments will not be well rewarded. They also need connections with local markets. In a word, the gorgeous sea-cable broadband assets are optimized through penetrating the local markets and, when this is not achieved, their market value depreciates significantly. Excessive investment schemes and a lack of local connection will eventually lead down a path of false growth.

However, as a sound and well-managed telecom operator with a market niche and competitive advantage, CNC sees strategic opportunities in the current industrial restructuring for speedy advance towards regionalized operation. CNC can become a part of other expansions in the pan-Asia economic circle quickly and at low cost. In addition, it delivers integrated services of long-distance calls, data, web-hosting and IP products. This marks a great extension and expansion in CNC's business capacity towards big corporate customers and a turning point in its regionalization conversion.

Given the present transnational data-business model, it will take two to three operators' joint efforts to provide an end-to-end private connection service for multinational clients. The coordination process can be very slow and costly. However, by establishing seamless connection between the LANs in major cities of Asia and major backbone networks in China, CNC has been able to extend the enhanced networks in China to other cities and parts in Asia, thereby offering to large corporate clients metropolitan and end-to-end one-stop telecom solutions.

On the basis of the natural extension of regional networks, CNC will establish extensive strategic alliances so as to have quicker access to local markets and local end-users. For instance, through its cooperation with its strategic partner Equant, CNC acquired a large share in the data localization market among large corporate customers. The strategic alliance provides CNC with valuable experience in regionalized operation. In addition, by taking advantage of the current industrial restructuring together with low-cost M&A, CNC may make its presence known in the target market and establish a sound client base. In this regard, SingTel's acquisition of Optus sets a very good model for us to follow.

Leapfrogging development through M&A and industrial restructuring

In the past year the world telecom industry experienced a decline in its industrial readjustment cycle. The emerging telecom business model once much favored by the capital market was suddenly queried. Since the very existence and expansion of such a business depends on support from the capital market, changes in the capital market cut off the lifeblood of these enterprises, leading to many business breakdowns.

Although the structure of the global telecom industry continues to evolve, I am confident that the extensive replication of regionalization technologies and further deregulation will spur the growth of the industry. This is despite the global malaise surrounding the industry and capital markets. Amid this apparently gloomy context, CNC decided to avail itself of the industrial restructuring taking place all round the world. We have expanded through acquisitions and implemented our regional strategy: to provide enterprise clients in the pan-Asia region with end-to-end telecommunication services through seamless network connection built around major metropolises. This strategy can serve many needs at the same time and set in place many synergies, including lower operation and R&D costs, business transition, and exclusion of rivals. Reach bought the unfinished East Asia sea-cable project at about 30% of the book value of the construction cost, thus enabling it to overcome competition from Level 3. French Telecom advanced itself to the leading position of the data service to multinationals through its acquisition of Equant, extending the market penetration scope of French Telecom to the whole world.

It goes without saying that there will be more competition as a result of the quickening economic integration in the Asia Pacific region. Under the present market situation, a company must either expand and develop or it will fall behind. Despite their burgeoning domestic market, Chinese telecom companies cannot adopt a complacent and conservative approach or let internal strife delay their regional strategies. Instead, the industry should pick out assets and businesses with very strong driving forces, adopt the most appropriate operational and financial frameworks, effectively merge and acquire such assets, form strategic alliances with business partners and keep in step with the most up-to-date players. In this way, the industry's major players will establish themselves soundly in the region's market and avert situations in which they find themselves beset by competitors on all sides, or unable to respond appropriately to the competitive advantages of others. I believe that the reshuffling of telecom assets all around the world will root out many incompetent enterprises and, at the same time, enable the strong to reinforce their positions. There are risks, but the opportunities are too great to ignore, both in terms of the market and for China and the region's overall development.

The first step towards regionalization: Acquisition of Asia Global Crossing

Asia Global Crossing Ltd. is the only operator in Asia that had pan-Asian sea cables committed to the provision of city-to-city connection and data services. In early 2002 the parent company went bankrupt and was not able to honor its investment commitment of US$400 million. This greatly weakened the financial strength of Asia Global Crossing. To enhance the financial capacity and sustain its operation, Asia Global Crossing began to seek new investments and undertake corporate reorganization. In consideration of the potential synergies in network, clients and flows, and with a regard for the CNC management team's international outlook and business plans, Asia Global targeted CNC as the best option for its investment expansion. Other companies interested in Asia Global were also willing to join CNC in its efforts to acquire the corporation's quality assets.

In November 2000, CNC signed a formal asset-acquisition agreement with Asia Global Crossing, capturing US$1.9 billion of assets, or 17,900 kms of sea cable. This has been our first step towards achieving our regionalization strategy. In effect, we were catapulted into the fast-growing Asian regional market and were able to compete for a share of one of the world's fastest-growing markets for telecom flows and services.

The acquisition of Asia Global Crossing's network assets will be an important driving force for our strategic transition from a domestic company, operating only in China, to a regional operator. We will be able to explore overseas markets, as the acquisition expands our network in one step to major areas in Asia Pacific, including Australia, New Zealand, Korea, Japan, Taiwan, Hong Kong, the Philippines and Singapore. It will allow us to fulfill our mission to provide "enterprise clients in the pan-Asia region with end-to-end telecommunication services through metropolitan seamless network connection". In a narrower sense, this acquisition is also the first step in our regionalization strategy. We look at this deal from several vantage points.

Asia Global Crossing has an integrated, fully operating network, with which CNC enters directly into the fast-growing Asian telecom industry. We piggyback on this and expand business in major countries of the region without having to undergo a long network-construction period with high investment costs and unpredictable risks. Most importantly, Asia Global

Crossing has business operating licenses in all major Asian countries, a high-profile client group, a competent sales team, a well-famed brand and well-established sales channels. Thus before entering the Asian market, CNC has in its possession very competitive assets with proven market value, which all serve as solid foundations for the expansion of its businesses.

As a result of the doldrums in the telecom market, we were able to acquire Asia Global Crossing's quality assets at a price far below book value or the construction cost of the networks, through debt and equity reorganization. In a word, we paid US$80 million for assets worth upwards of US$1.9 billion, including 17,900 km of quality sea cable, landing stations and land extensions of the sea cables in major countries of the pan-Asia area. This acquisition price will boost the competitiveness of our operational costs which would otherwise have had to absorb the amortized investment costs, had we built from scratch or acquired at book value.

Another "plus" is that the Asia Global Crossing network is the only one with a multi-layered function, which makes it possible for the company to independently provide a wide range of businesses to operator clients and corporate customers. The sole proprietorship gives Asia Global Crossing a competitive advantage in decision-making, cost control, business extension and network management. We are considering relocating the Australia-based operation center and the Singapore-based client center to mainland China, which could further reduce operating costs by around 70%.

Once this pan-Asian network is seamlessly linked to our backbone network and other resources in China, a unique network will emerge with a huge geographical and demographic coverage. This is an advantage unmatched by other telecom operators in the region. All these elements will add to CNC's capacity to provide end-to-end international telecom service to the clients and to have access to high-profile corporate customers within the region.

At present CNC has used the client-oriented "CNC Connected" framework to extend our service to major commercial buildings in leading Chinese cities, putting us within reach of a significant number of high-profile corporate customers. The acquisition will enable CNC to use the client resources of Asia Global Crossing better, and to offer cross-agency and tie-in sales, thus improving the operation capacity of end-to-end services. Overall, the synergies between our existing service platform and the newly acquired resources will be profound. They will boost our market-expansion efforts and increase our overall competitiveness in major countries in the region.

Our company is also being looked on by the market as a test case of a Chinese operator undertaking a regional expansion to be at the forefront of the Asian telecom industry. It also, in a wider sense, will support China's economy, by laying a sound basis for information infrastructure development, which in turn will enable China to be an industry leader and a propeller of growth in the Asia Pacific region.

Conclusion

After four years' arduous operation and through the acquisition of the major operational assets of Asia Global Crossing, CNC made a successful first step towards regional expansion on behalf of the Chinese telecom sector. As part of the sector's globalization efforts, CNC has initiated a strategic regionalization operation by offering large corporate clients integrated telecom services on the China-based regional network that penetrates major cities of the pan-Asia area.

Certainly, there are great challenges ahead for CNC as we try to extend our leadership in telecom operations in this part of the world. However, the initial steps in the implementation of our strategy are under way and we have covered significant ground already. I am confident that with the emergence of an Asian economic region, with China as a key player, CNC will be able to deliver high-quality end-to-end services to ever more major corporate clients both regionally and in China, and undertake more and more fast-growing derivative services within the region. In a word, CNC will become an established regional business, providing the "e-frastructure" for the economic development of Asia.

TAKEAWAYS

1. **Growing according to strategy but maintaining flexibility for new market opportunities.**

CNC has faced challenges in that it operates within a heavily regulated sector, since telecommunications is viewed as a crucial instrument of national development. Thus, its strategy has had to adapt to mergers, acquisitions and market spaces that have not always been determined by normal market development. Nevertheless, the company has been able to capitalize on opportunities such as the Asia Global Crossing purchase because of its flexibility and quick turnaround time for action. At the same time, it has been able to make good use of the global market downturn to build up its assets at a cheap cost.

2. **Consciously learning from other players.**
   Industry knowledge is by no means static and a company's development must always take into account the vagaries of local market conditions and regulations, especially in a closed market such as China. Even within this framework, China Netcom has tried to learn from the actions and strategies of its peers, both in Asia and globally, and tried consciously to apply these lessons to its own development strategies.

3. **Thinking broadly about the market's growth – China and beyond.**
   CNC began as a domestic operator of broadband-based services primarily to corporate customers in China's main cities. It had the fastest infrastructure growth in the industry, in terms of the amount of cable laid in a short period of time. Even by these standards, the acquisition of the vast network of Asia Global Crossing was a big leap in expanding the network. The company was able to do so only by realizing the regional nature of its customers' operations and its own need to compete with international telecommunications providers. Thus, it uses its strong base in China to imagine a larger pie – stretching across the pan-Asia region – and thus move beyond the restrictions that plague many state-owned enterprises seeking to go global.

Endnotes

1 China's "big four" banks are the state-owned banks which until recently controlled most of the commercial lending in China: Agricultural Bank of China, Bank of China, China Construction Bank and ICBC.

CHAPTER

5 Reflection: The Role of Geography

■ George S. Yip
Professor of Strategic and International Management,
London Business School, and
Lead Fellow, Advanced Institute of Management Research (ESRC)

■ Ruiming Lin
PhD Student, London Business School

In the 1960s through the 1980s, a first wave of Asian companies internationalized successfully. Many even achieved global status.[1] These firms came from the early industrializing nations of Japan and South Korea, and from the two special cases of Hong Kong and Singapore. From the 1990s onward, a second wave of Asian companies from emerging Asian economies has begun to internationalize. This chapter focuses on the challenges facing companies from these "follower" or "late" Asian economies – especially China and India, but also the Philippines, Malaysia, Thailand, Indonesia and Taiwan – and specifically questions the role of geography in determining a company's globalization success potential. Put another way, does a company's home-base economy shape the nature of its globalization project, and if so, how?

The experiences of companies from "latecomer" economies are distinct from those of what we call "Early Asian" economies such as Japan, Korea, Singapore and Hong Kong. Japan, for instance, was already an industrialized economy before World War II, with a high per-capita income and sizeable domestic market by the 1960s. Japan already possessed successful multinational companies, which benefited from their pioneering strategies of combining industrial competence, technical expertise and comparatively low labor costs (compared to American and European companies). So, Japan's rise following the war was almost like a return to a previous growth path. The initial Japanese model of internationalization can be summarized as follows:

Industrial Competence + Technical Expertise + Large Domestic
Market + Low Labor Costs
= Internationalization as Direct Challenger

To a lesser extent, Korean companies followed a similar model in their internationalization. Hong Kong and Singapore also developed rapidly economically, and should be seen as special cases due to their unique home environments and natural-resource endowments. This has meant that most of their international companies are in exporting and trading and have followed the internationalization model:

Pro-Business Government + Highly Educated and Entrepreneurial
Population + Access to Low Cost Labor + Entrepot Status
+ Strategic Location
= Internationalization as Go-Between

Companies from the follower Asian economies cannot employ either the Japan/Korea model or the Hong Kong/Singapore model of internationalization since their economies have fundamentally different structures and advantages. The difference between Japan and Korea and the other Asian economies is highlighted by the fact that in 1996 only they had significant numbers of firms in the Fortune Global 500 list of the world's largest companies, as shown in Table 5.1. Even though by 2002 the number of mainland Chinese companies on the list had grown from two to 11, most of these were operating in resources, domestic utilities or banking, rather than manufacturing or non-financial services. The differences in sectors should be carefully noted, for internationalization of resource-based companies does not prove international capability but merely the good fortunes of natural endowment. In the same way, large domestic utility or financial-services companies are driven by domestic population rather than by the competitive or international capabilities of the company. The real test of international competitiveness is whether an economy has companies which internationalize by selling to foreigners. On this basis, one can say that success in the internationalization of manufacturing or non-financial services is the real test of international competitiveness.

Table 5.1 Asian companies in Fortune Global 500 (ranked by annual revenues)

	1996	2002
Japan	126	88
South Korea	10	13
China	2	11
Taiwan	0	1
Hong Kong	1	0
Singapore	0	1
Malaysia	1	1
India	1	1
Indonesia	0	0
Thailand	0	0
Philippines	0	0

Source: *Fortune*, August 4, 1997 and July 28, 2003.

Framework for internationalization

We identified for Japan/Korea and Hong Kong/Singapore some specific reasons for the successful internationalization of their companies, and many economists have also investigated similar sets of conditions.[2] We propose here an alternative model of internationalization for companies from follower economies in Asia. This model combines country conditions and company characteristics but focuses specifically on international business:

Country Globalization Drivers + Industry Globalization Potential
+ Transferable Bases of Competitive Advantage + Use of Global Strategy
= Internationalization of Companies

In our discussion below, we will draw distinctions between the internationalization strategies used by companies from the United States and Europe (i.e., the first internationalizers) from "Early Asia" (primarily Japan, South Korea, Hong Kong and Singapore) and from "Late Asia" (all others).

Some Late Asia companies going international

In the rest of this chapter we describe the successful internationalization experiences of eight companies (seven different industries) from six countries/economies we consider to be "Late Asia".

• Acer (Taiwan)

Established in 1976, Acer is among the world's top 10 personal computer vendors, offering a broad range of PC products from high-end PC servers and multimedia desktop computers to notebooks, computer peripherals and components. Acer is also a major Internet-enabler, providing Internet component technologies, devices and services, including end-to-end solutions, mobile phones, plasma displays, TFT LCDs, projectors and wireless communications. The Acer Group employs nearly 35,000 people in 232 enterprises spanning 41 countries worldwide, supporting dealers and distributors in over 100 nations across Asia Pacific, Europe, the Middle East and the Americas. Acer Group revenues were US$4.64 billion in 2003.

- **Bajaj (India)**

The Bajaj group is one of India's largest companies, specializing in the automotive business, with revenues of over US$1 billion. Bajaj has used its dominance of the Indian markets for two- and three-wheeler vehicles to expand all over the world. Bajaj has built a distribution network in over 60 countries worldwide and multiplied its exports from 1% of total revenues in 1990 to over 5% today.

- **Charoen Pokphand (CP) (Thailand)**

Founded in 1921, Charoen Pokphand Group is today a diversified agro-industrial conglomerate with 10 business areas, including agrifood, retailing and telecommunications. Agrifood alone accounts for over 70% of total revenue. Although based in Thailand, CP Group operates in more than 20 countries including China, India, Mexico, the Netherlands and the U.S., as well as in Southeast Asian countries. In 1995, it was estimated that 60% of CP's revenues came from China, the first time that non-Thai earnings had made up a majority of sales. In 2002, CP Group had assets of US$12.6 billion and an annual turnover in excess of US$13 billion.[3]

- **Haier (China)**

Haier Group was incorporated in 1984 and today produces a wide range of household electrical appliances and white goods. In its first 18 years, Haier averaged an annual sales increase of 78%, and today has 18 design institutes, 10 industrial complexes (including one each in the U.S. and Pakistan), 58,800 sales agents and 11,976 after-sales service employees throughout the world. Haier products are exported to 160 countries. Sales in 2002 reached $8.6 billion.

- **Indah Kiat Pulp & Paper, IKPP (Indonesia)**

IKPP is the largest pulp-and-paper producing company in Southeast Asia. In 1994 it produced 790 thousand tons of pulp and 624 thousand tons of paper. Two-thirds of its paper production is eventually exported, but it does not have any overseas operations.[4] Revenues in 2002 were US$1.4 billion.

• Lenovo (China)

Lenovo (formerly Legend Computer) is a diversified technology company providing IT products and services. Established in 1984, Legend is already a legend of sorts in China. Its PCs have been the best-selling brand for six consecutive years in China since 1997 (with a 27.7% market share in 2002) and the best seller in the Asia Pacific region (excluding Japan) for three consecutive years since 2000. In 2002, sales volume of Legend desktops ranked fifth in the world. Now employing over 10,000 staff, Lenovo has prepared for internationalization not only by changing its name ("Legend" was already patented outside of China) but has also established sales subsidiaries in Europe and the United States. The company aims for sales of 20% from overseas by 2008, compared to less than 5% in 2003. Lenovo aims to become, in the vision of its founder Liu Chuanzhi, China's IBM or HP and "a member of the world's largest 500 enterprises...with an image of high technology...before 2010".[5]

• VIP Luggage (India)

VIP Luggage is India's largest luggage company and the world's second-largest producer (after Samsonite) of molded luggage by volume. [6] Its plant at Nasik is one of the world's largest luggage plants, and the state-of-the-art VIP Design Lab at Nasik has helped VIP to maintain the highest standards. Indeed, it is the only Indian local luggage producer to export even to top-of-the-line stores in Europe and the U.S.

• YTL (Malaysia)

YTL Corporation Berhad is one of Malaysia's leading integrated infrastructure conglomerates. Under the leadership of managing director Francis Yeoh, YTL has transformed itself from a modest construction business in the late 1970s into an infrastructure-and-power conglomerate with a market capitalization of US$1.3 billion by 2003 and revenues for 2002 of over US$680 million. Over the last 15 years, YTL has experienced a compound pre-tax profit annual growth rate of 55%. In 2002, YTLPI (YTL Power International) acquired Wessex Water, the U.K.'s most efficient water and sewerage utility, as the firm's first major foray into Europe. By 2003, about 57% of revenues were derived from overseas operations, mostly from Wessex Water and YTL's power transmission arm in Australia.

Country globalization drivers

We believe that in examining the internationalization of companies, a focus on the readiness of countries for international business is instructive. There is a two-way effect: the more foreign companies participate in the domestic economy, the more likely an economy's own companies will be able to internationalize. One critical mechanism is that open economies encourage the entry of foreign firms, who then transfer skills to local managers and companies. Among the Early Asia economies, Hong Kong and Singapore exemplify this argument. Within the relatively open economies, companies in those two cities have had to become internationally competitive from early on. In Late Asia, Taiwanese and Malaysian companies have also benefited from the participation of foreign companies in their home markets.

We use the concept of "country globalization drivers": market, cost, government and competition. These were developed in a book, *Asian Advantage*, to explain the attractiveness of Asian economies to foreign multinational corporations (MNCs). [7] We have adapted these drivers to also explain how they might help domestic companies to internationalize from Asian economies. Table 5.2 summarizes the differences in country globalization drivers faced by economies from the United States and Western Europe, Early Asia and Late Asia.

Table 5.2 Country globalization drivers

Country Globalization Drivers	U.S. & W. Europe	Early Asia	Late Asia
Market	Set global tastes and standards	Some ability to set tastes and standards	May have to follow pre-set tastes and standards

Table 5.2 (cont'd)

Cost	Initial scale economies from large home markets	Combination of home-based scale and initially low labor costs	Initially low labor costs, to be followed by home-based scale
Government	Initial protection withdrawn early on	Protection maintained for long period	Some protection, but also need to promote FDI
Competitive	Starting from strategic countries	Made themselves strategic, especially Japan	Only China enjoys strategic status, with India coming up

Country market globalization drivers

Country market globalization drivers – common customer needs, global customers, global channels, transferable marketing and lead countries – particularly affect whether and how foreign MNCs should participate in Asian markets, the types of products and services they should offer, and the marketing approaches they should use; and conversely the ease for Asian companies to break into global markets. In general, Late Asia does not enjoy strong country market globalization drivers. Its countries do not lead global customer tastes and trends.

Country cost globalization drivers

Country cost globalization drivers – global scale economies, favorable logistics, favorable country costs and the role played by technology – affect the global cost advantages of companies, whether domestic or foreign, operating from that country. In general, Late Asia has to rely on low labor costs but must quickly develop other advantages such as infrastructure and technology.

Country government globalization drivers

Country government globalization drivers – trade policies, FDI rules, compatible technical standards, common marketing regulations, government-owned competitors and customers, and host-government concerns – affect the openness of an economy to international business. As argued earlier, the more open the economy, the more globally competitive domestic companies can become.[8] Although governments in Late Asia may be pressured to protect so-called strategic domestic industries, we believe there are significant long-term and competitive benefits to opening their countries to foreign investors and participants.

Country competitive globalization drivers

Country competitive globalization drivers – global and regional strategic importance of a country, globalized domestic competitors, and the presence of foreign competitors – indicate the potential competitive leverage of domestic companies. Domestic companies in countries with strong competitive globalization drivers benefit from the know-how and resources brought by foreign companies. In addition, local companies can more easily find overseas partners as they seek to internationalize. In Early Asia, Japan rapidly established itself as a globally strategic country. In Late Asia, only China has done the same, although India has potential to do so.

Unfortunately, companies have limited leverage over countries' globalization drivers, though they can try to influence government policies. Hence, we focus the rest of this chapter on the determinants of globalization success over which they have more control.

Industry globalization potential

Companies from developed economies have in the past created global industries through their own globalization; for instance, IBM for the computer industry or Ford for the automobile industry. In contrast, companies from follower emerging economies usually do not have this transformative effect; instead, they have a greater chance of internationalizing if they operate in industries that are already global or have high globalization potential. Such companies can ride the industry slipstream. Even better would be if emerging-economy companies could identify industries with increasing globalization potential, but in which developed-economy companies have mostly not yet globalized. In these industries, emerging-economy companies will suffer less of a latecomer disadvantage. Table 5.3 summarizes the differences in this regard between companies from the United States and Western Europe, Early Asia and Late Asia.

Table 5.3 Comparison of industry globalization potential

Companies from U.S. and W. Europe	Companies from Early Asia	Companies from Late Asia
Did the initial globalizing of most industries.	Completed the globalizing of some industries (e.g., Japan and Korea for automobiles and consumer electronics)	Must enter already-globalized industries (e.g., Taiwan's Acer and China's Legend into personal computers; Malaysia's Proton and India's Tata Motors into automobiles); or in a few cases industries with potential but relatively ignored (e.g., YTL in utilities).

An existing framework for industry globalization potential identifies four sets of industry globalization drivers: market, cost, government and competitive.[9] These industry drivers are related to, but different from, the country globalization drivers discussed in the previous section. The drivers are as follows:

- ***Market Globalization Drivers***
  Common customer needs and tastes
  Global customers
  Global channels
  Transferable marketing
  Lead countries

- ***Cost Globalization Drivers***
  Global scale economies
  Steep experience curve effect
  Sourcing efficiencies
  Favorable logistics
  Differences in country costs (including exchange rates)
  High product development
  Fast-changing technology
- ***Government Globalization Drivers***
  Favorable trade policies
  Compatible technical standards
  Common marketing regulations
  Government-owned competitors and customers
  Host-government concerns
- ***Competitive Globalization Drivers***
  High exports and imports
  Competitors from different continents
  Interdependence of countries
  Competitors globalized
  Transferable competitive advantage.

These drivers determine the potential of an industry for its companies to become international. For instance, despite its already global nature, the automobile industry may have additional potential, and is allowing Late Asia companies to go international even under their own brands, as in the case of Malaysia's Proton or India's Tata Motors. By 2002 overseas sales accounted for about 9% of Proton's revenues and about 5% of those of Tata Motors. In this way, various Late Asia companies are exploiting their industries' globalization potentials.

Many of the eight companies introduced above operate in industries with high globalization potential. For example, Malaysia's YTL internationalized in the utility industry, which has some increasingly favorable globalization drivers. In terms of market globalization drivers, there are common customer needs and tastes, in that people everywhere need water and electricity. In terms of cost globalization drivers, there are strong opportunities for global scale economies by exporting power from domestic plants, the ability to exploit differences in country costs (YTL has one of the most competitive prices, selling power at US$0.038 per kilowatt/hour) and compatible technical standards. Government globalization drivers are mixed but becoming more favorable: regulatory differences are localized; there is now relatively low regulation of utilities in developed markets (for example, U.K. and Australia) and more attention to cost, which facilitates entry of foreign producers like YTL. In other jurisdictions, there are new pushes for deregulation (for example, in Singapore, Thailand and the Philippines), which may indicate future opportunities. Competitive globalization drivers are also favorable: U.S. power and water companies are withdrawing from Asia and Europe while there are a limited number of truly internationalized competitors, which decreases the latecomers' disadvantage.

In such an industry environment, YTL can pursue an international strategy of providing "world-class products at third-world prices". To date YTL's main strategy for internationalization has been through acquisition. By 2002, about 57% of its revenues came from overseas operations. On the other hand, YTL exports only a very small portion of the electricity it generates in Malaysia.

Thailand's CP Group internationalized in the food industry. CP has exploited favorable globalization drivers not by exporting goods but by moving a highly sophisticated production and sourcing system overseas. The food industry has high market globalization potential: the emergence of a middle class in Asian economies exemplifies common customer needs and tastes, allowing the measured use of transferable marketing (for example, market knowledge skills and government relationship skills) across neighboring countries. Thailand also has a leading country position in agrifood, enabling CP to more easily transfer its knowledge of food marketing in Thailand to other Asian economies. Cost globalization drivers are favorable: a large labor component in agribusiness production and similar wage levels in CP's Asian country production sites enable the company to apply common production technology. Government globalization drivers are favorable: agriculture accounts for roughly 22% of Asia's GDP and remains the driving economic force and a major source of employment in many countries. So agribusiness investments are generally welcomed in those countries, even if operating regulations vary by country.[10] Even variations in regulatory conditions have not posed large barriers for CP.

China's Haier and Lenovo and Taiwan's Acer internationalized in consumer durables or electronics industries, which are somewhat globalized already, but continue to bear strong globalization potential. They have, for instance, strong market globalization drivers: global channels (for example, Haier's customers such as Wal-Mart are global players); lead countries (Japan and the United States are trendsetters, but latecomer companies can quickly exploit these trends); and common customer needs allowing for global products. This last driver often has an asymmetric effect that favors emerging-economy companies because emerging markets often retain local preferences in consumer durables.

The durables and electronics industries also have strong cost globalization drivers: high product-development costs and fast-changing technology; great potential for global scale economies in both R&D and manufacturing; large sourcing efficiencies; and big differences between countries in production costs. Government globalization drivers are quite strong: these industries are not heavily protected or regulated; home government support as China and Taiwan view these industries as strategically important; and compatible technical standards. Competitive globalization drivers are mixed, in that the industry has many major global players from developed countries already. However, the other industry globalization drivers, combined with the territorial advantages of China and Taiwan, have allowed Acer, Lenovo and Haier to quickly catch up.

Transferable bases of competitive advantage

Companies can internationalize only if they have bases of competitive advantage that are transferable across borders. For example, technology advantages can often be transferred, whereas relationships with local customers or governments are less easily transferred. There are six major bases of competitive advantage that might be used for internationalization:[11] customer market; products and services; business systems; assets and resources; partners; and economies of scale and scope. Table 5.4 summarizes how companies from the United States and Western Europe, from Early Asia, and from Late Asia differ in their ability to exploit bases of competitive advantage for internationalization.

We take Singapore Airlines as an example of how a company used one base of advantage to expand into others. Its first source of competitive advantage was low labor costs, which allowed system. So initially,

Singapore Airlines was able to offer lower prices. It was also able to deliver very high levels of service, due both to cultural factors and management attention, so it rapidly added product/service advantage. The Singapore government, which owns Singapore Airlines, contributed significantly to building up a collateral asset, Changi airport, as an asset-based source of competitive advantage. Moreover, the company has developed its fleet of planes as a competitive advantage, constantly upgrading them and maintaining the fleet's newness. The company has also assiduously built up a network of partners through alliances, which adds to its customer base by feeding passengers into its network.

But despite this success, Singapore Airlines remains relatively small, and without high economies of scale and scope relative to its competitors. It has never enjoyed competitive advantage from its home market or customer base. Not only is the population of Singapore small, its geographic position is convenient, but not inevitably more so than neighboring airports such as Kuala Lumpur. As neighbors upgrade their airport facilities and the quality of service of their national carriers, Singapore Airlines will face increased competition.

Table 5.4 Comparison of bases of competitive advantage for globalization

	Companies from U.S. and W. Europe	**Companies from Early Asia**	**Companies from Late Asia**
Customer Market	Exploited wealthy home markets and followed domestic multinational customers	Exploited home markets and followed domestic multinational customers	Home markets often a weak base → often have to start with foreign customer markets
Products/ Services	Started with highest quality	Started behind in quality but caught up in many cases	Will be behind in quality for many years
Business Systems	Built complete business systems at home, then spread around world	Also built complete business systems and quicker to relocate	May need to operate as part of others' business systems

Table 5.4 (cont'd)

Assets and Resources	Brands, technology, money and management	Caught up in assets and resources	Few initial assets aside from workforce and natural resources
Partners	Partnered with local companies to get access	Gain know-how and access through Western partners	Need to gain know-how, credibility and access through partners
Economies of scale	Early-mover advantage supports economies of scale	Caught up in many cases	Most a long way from achieving global scale advantages
Economies of scope	Early movers built broad product portfolios	Gradually increasing product scope	Disadvantage of starting with limited product scope

Customer market

Internationalizing companies can build on their existing customer markets in a number of ways: they can follow the internationalization of their domestic customers, they can use them as a reference, or they can use the standards set by domestic customers as a springboard to develop the capabilities needed for foreign markets. In general, this requires that the customers are either multinational companies (for example, Japanese automobile companies as customers for Japanese component suppliers) or that the customers have a lifestyle or standards to which other nations aspire. Companies from Late Asia mostly lack these advantages. One special case is that of emigrant populations. The relative poverty of many Late Asia countries has encouraged large amounts of emigration. Some companies have successfully internationalized by following emigrants. For example, Jollibee, the Philippines fast-food company, initially went international by following the diaspora of Filipino workers to other Asian countries.

But if there is one commonality among most successful Late Asia globalizers in terms of their customer market characteristics, it is that they dominate their domestic markets. Moreover, because many Late Asia countries have a relatively large domestic market in population terms, market dominance gives the companies a solid customer base at home before internationalizing. For instance, YTL was Malaysia's first independent power producer, winning its first license in 1992 under Malaysia's privatization policy. This pioneer status gave it a first-mover advantage over domestic followers.[12] Similarly VIP Luggage created the modern luggage industry in India, beginning in 1971 when the company introduced hard suitcases molded from high-density polyethylene (HDPE).[13] It then grew to dominate the industry in India. CP Group also dominates its domestic market as the country's largest integrated agrifood entity, with significant market shares in poultry and swine production as well as livestock and shrimp feed production.[14] In China, Haier is the largest domestic producer of electrical appliances. It enjoys a 29% market share in refrigerators and 26% in washing machines, and is also one of China's leading exporters, selling $1.4 billion of products abroad annually.[15] Lenovo enjoys a similar weighty market presence in China and increasingly in non-Japan Asia. Lastly, Acer was one of the first Taiwanese companies to market PCs under its own name, as well as to manufacture complex and powerful DRAM (Dynamic Random Access Memory) chips. It was also a pioneer in making components such as plasma displays and handsets.

Products and services

Having a superior product or service is, of course, a very common basis of competitive advantage. Thailand's CP Group distinguishes itself from most other emerging-economy food companies by its world-standard products, allowing it to compete head-to-head with established Western companies. CP has achieved this partly by seeking out international certification and awards. Its factories have been awarded the HALAL (an international food certification under Islamic regulations), EST/TH, ISO 9002 and ISO 14001 certification for their environmental management practices. CP's attention to quality control helped Thailand create one of the best food-safety records in the world. In the European market, which strongly emphasizes animal welfare, CP was the only chicken producer from outside the European Union that was able to sell to Tesco, the U.K.'s biggest supermarket.[16]

Acer competes by continuous innovation in products. For example, in 1986, it beat IBM in launching 32-bit PCs; in 1991, Acer introduced ChipUp technology – the world's first 386–486 single-chip CPU upgrade solution; in 1992, it created the world's first 386SX-33 chips; in 1994, it introduced the world's first dual Intel Pentium PC; in 2001, it launched the Acer S10, the world's first Chinese Palm OS handheld computer.

Some other Late Asia companies are still striving hard to achieve world-standard products or services. India's VIP Luggage sets international standards as its yardstick and rejects ruthlessly anything that falls short of these. Indonesia's IKPP invests heavily in advanced machinery to move toward the productivity, quality and service levels of its competitors from North America and Sweden. China's Haier also engages itself in a "high-quality, high value for money, high after-sale service" strategy.

Unfortunately most companies from Late Asia do not have products that are unquestioned global leaders. Instead, they succeed at a different tactic: selling to countries that are not touched or not desired by the market leaders (for example, Chinese construction firms in many parts of Africa), or offering products that cater to the conditions of developing countries (for example, Bajaj motorcycles are designed for India's rough conditions and perform well in other countries with poor roads). Haier provides another example of an adapted product strategy. Although Haier has U.S. sales of over US$200 million, its penetration mainly remains in specialized market niches, such as in the compact refrigerator or portable electric wine-cellar categories. Meanwhile, mainstream items such as air conditioners, family-sized refrigerators, and washing machines remain dominated by the American leaders, Whirlpool, General Electric and Maytag.[17]

Business systems

Companies may have a superior business system or value chain as the basis for internationalization. For example, Toyota has created the world's best-performing business system for building mass-production cars, as have many other Japanese and Korean companies in their various industries. Companies from developed countries also increasingly relocate some of their business system, especially the labor-intensive parts, to developing economies with lower wage scales. Companies from Late Asia are already in those low-cost places, which is a definite advantage. But latecomers typically cannot build a worldwide, world-class business system quickly. They usually have to start with just the factory or production part and in one location only. To grow that advantage into a world-class business system, they may need first to become part of a larger multinational's business system. For example, India's Sundaram Fasteners has become a leading supplier of radiator caps to General Motors' North American division. Sundaram has used this relationship to improve its capabilities to the point where it can supply customers all over the world.[18]

But some companies from Late Asia are building globally competitive business systems on their own. Acer's CEO, Stan Shih, pioneered his famous "smiling curve" theory of value chain – navigating Acer along the PC industry's value curve to higher value-added activities. Originally, Acer focused on the assembly business, which is the least profitable segment. However, it learned from the exposure to global technology and best manufacturing practices, which helped it move upstream into manufacturing motherboards, peripherals and central processing units. Acer also expanded downstream by taking over local assembly, by starting to source locally, opening new channels and building a global brand needed to free the company from the low-margin OEM business. By 2000 Acer had moved into software and Internet businesses, which will support the next stage of its global expansion.[19] Geographically, Acer also relocated quickly to China, its strategic market, as both a low-cost production site and a market for the Acer brand. At the same time, assembly work in western Europe is being shifted to cheaper plants in the east.[20]

Like Acer, Thailand's CP Group aggressively followed a strategy of vertical integration to build competitiveness, essentially creating the pieces of the production chain needed to supply an end product to the consumer. For instance, if CP wanted to produce shrimp but was concerned about the quality and availability of feed, it would develop feed mills. If it had state-of-the-art chicken farms but little opportunity to create value-added chicken products, it would build a processing plant. This strategy was particularly effective in developing economies where the commercial infrastructure did not yet exist. CP actually created markets that allowed for the growth of the economy and the logistics, storage and grading systems that supported it.[21]

Other companies also invest heavily in rationalizing the efficiencies of business systems, globally or locally. In 1998 Haier started a management-restructuring program that focused on improving information management for purchasing and supply, as well as after-sales services, inventory and the reduction of operation costs. From 1999 to 2001, it established well-equipped physical-distribution centers in Qingdao Hi-tech Industrial Area and Qingdao Economic and Technological Development Zone, which have greatly improved the efficiency of its product-distribution process.[22]

To optimize production, Lenovo combined material-resource planning and just-in-time manufacturing methods to minimize deficiency and production costs. After adopting these measures, costs were reduced to 8%, 4% less than in 1995, and saving US$3.6 million in annual interest.[23]

Assets and resources

Companies from the developed West typically have a variety of assets or resources, such as brand names, technology, money and management skills. Japanese and Korean companies started with few such assets but quickly caught up. They leveraged low-cost and dedicated labor into high-quality products, which in turn built their reputations or other assets. The Toyota brand used to stand for low quality, but now commands premiums of up to 15% in the U.S. market. The same holds true of many other Japanese and, increasingly, Korean brands, in differing categories. Taiwan's Acer stands as a branding exception from Late Asia. It is one of the very few non-Japanese companies to have built a globally recognized brand. In 2001, *Reader's Digest* subscribers confirmed it as Asia's No.1 computer "SuperBrand", for the third consecutive year.

Companies from Late Asia find it much harder to build internationally competitive assets, and thus have to resort to acquiring these. For example, Malaysia's Proton acquired Britain's Lotus Cars as a way to build its own technology capabilities. YTL's acquisition of Wessex Water provides a rare example of a Late Asia company having the management skills to acquire and actively manage a company in a developed country. YTL won the bid against rivals that included the Royal Bank of Scotland, Li Ka-shing's Cheung Kong Infrastructure, and Italian utility Enel.[24]

Indonesia's IKPP represents those Late Asia companies who succeed in international competition by leveraging plentiful natural resources. IKPP has moved aggressively into export markets by drawing on steady supplies of timber, low harvesting costs and government-guaranteed concessions. It thus enjoys production costs that are nearly half those of its North

American and Swedish competitors, giving it a huge competitive advantage globally.[25] On the other hand, IKPP's dependence on its local resource base will prevent it from becoming a true multinational unless it can add other sources of competitive advantage.

Partners

Partners play a key role in internationalization. Companies can follow their partners as they internationalize, they can have their partners follow them, or they can find local partners. For example, U.S. and European companies typically partnered with local companies in emerging economies as a way to gain market access, often partly because of government regulations. In their early internationalization efforts, Japanese and Korean companies often partnered with Western companies to gain know-how and access. Companies from Late Asia need partners for these things, too, as well as for credibility. For example, India's Tata Motors has become the sixth-largest manufacturer of trucks in the world, mostly through exports but also with help from technical collaboration with Daimler-Benz. Tata is now entering European markets via a partnership with Britain's MG Rover Group, through which it will custom-manufacture a Rover-branded car in India for the U.K. and European market.[26]

As another example, Acer entered a joint venture with Texas Instruments in 1989 to develop new products.[27] Haier's partnership in the 1980s with Liebherr, a German appliance maker, became a key source of technology. Haier also set up distribution access swaps in 2002 with Sanyo of Japan and SAMPO of Taiwan. Thailand's CP Group has over 100 strategic partnerships. Typically, CP provides operational expertise (local market knowledge and execution skills) while the partner provides technological know-how.[28]

In its case, India's VIP Luggage formed a marketing partnership with a local distributor that promised access to Britain's largest retailers. A breakthrough came when the distributor, with VIP's help, won the franchise to establish a specialty luggage department in each of Debenham's stores nationwide. VIP invested heavily in staff training for the specialty department, gaining as a result a 60% share of Debenham's hard-luggage sales.[29]

Economies of scale and scope

Large home markets can provide the starting basis for economies of scale in production and other aspects of the business system. U.S. and many European companies benefited from such initial and continuing advantages, as did many Japanese and Korean companies. But most companies from Late Asia are a long way from scaling up their businesses in this fashion, unless they do so by focusing on a narrow product line, as in the case of Sundaram Fasteners. But such a strategy then works against economies of scope gained through a broad product range. Furthermore, going international from Late Asia usually requires new, more advanced products, as Bajaj has had to do with its motorcycles for the European market.

But some successful Late Asia companies do succeed in achieving international economies of scale or scope. By 2002, Lenovo had the world's fifth-largest sales volume in desktop computers, although over 95% of revenues were domestic. Haier's activities in a wide range of household electrical appliances in 86 categories and 13,000 specifications make economies of scope possible. CP Group has an extremely broad product scope in the agri-industry business, including milk processing and the production of feed-mill machinery. The individual businesses are related as part of an integrated food-delivery system, which is ultimately the product that CP provides to some of its customers.

Using global strategies

Companies are more successful in internationalization the more they can use global rather than national strategies. Indeed, a major reason for the success of Japanese companies was that they jumped more quickly to global strategy than did American and European companies who had globalized in an earlier era of greater differences between countries and other barriers to global integration.[30] There are five major dimensions of global strategy:[31]

- ***global market participation*** – involves the choice of country-markets in which to conduct business, and the level of activity, particularly in market share.
- ***global products/services*** – involves the extent to which a worldwide business offers the same or different products in different countries.

- ***global activity location*** – involves the choice of where to locate each of the activities that comprises the entire value-added chain – from research to production to after-sales service.
- ***global marketing*** – involves the extent to which a worldwide business uses the same brand names, advertising and other marketing elements in different countries.
- ***global competitive moves*** – involves the extent to which a worldwide business makes competitive moves in individual countries as part of a global competitive strategy.

Table 5.5 compares how companies from the United States and Western Europe, Early Asia, and Late Asia use global strategy.

Table 5.5 Comparison of use of global strategy

Home Base of Company	U.S. and W. Europe	Early Asia	Late Asia
Global Market Participation	Initially selective markets, but eventually reached all key countries	More discriminating in selection of strategic countries	Careful thinking about viable, similar, or strategic markets
Global Products/ Services	Begin with multi-local products, eventually replaced by global products	Start with global products	Must adapt or upgrade local products for other markets
Global Activity Location	Activities started in home country and slowly spread globally, often with too much dispersion	Activities started in home country and rapidly spread globally, but concentrated	Must be very selective about global spread of activities

Table 5.5 (cont'd)

Global Marketing	Often from countries with globally transferable cultures and lifestyles	Initial imitation of Western styles eventually augmented with own styles	Own cultures and styles seldom transferable, especially outside Asia. Have to quickly adapt brand names and marketing.
Global Competitive Moves	Extensive global networks allow companies to make global competitive moves	From the start focused on playing a global competitive game	As latecomers, hard to make global competitive moves on own; probably need to partner.

Global market participation

The globalization of Japanese companies provides many examples of a global-strategy approach to market participation. One study found three typical paths of expansion, each exhibiting a clear global plan.[32] The most common was to move from Japan to developing countries to developed countries. Typically, the United States was then the first developed country to be penetrated, because of its large size, its relative closeness to Japan and the lower levels of tariff, cultural and language barriers than in Europe. The second expansion path – going straight to developed countries, particularly the United States – occurred in hi-tech industries such as computers and semi-conductors. A third expansion path was to skip the home market and start directly with developed countries. This happened with products for which the Japanese home market was still not developed or too small – videotape recorders, color televisions and sewing machines.

Each of these three paths is more difficult for Late Asia internationalizers, given that Japanese and Korean companies have gone before them. Bajaj initially sold its motorcycles to countries even less developed than India. Only later did it expand to the developed countries in Western Europe and the United States. Furthermore, Bajaj used developing markets primarily to generate volume and developed markets primarily to learn.

The first path, going first to developing countries, is the most common for Late Asia companies. This path is easier in that Late Asia companies can sell to countries at similar or lower levels of economic development and sophistication (in terms of the products they demand). CP Group initially internationalized its agrifood business into China and other neighboring nations, then exported its quality products to developed countries such as the United States and Europe. Lenovo entered Asia Pacific markets, but not Japan. Haier has gone a little further in competing in developed markets, perhaps as a result of its vision that "the battlefields of competing with global rivals such as Whirlpool, GE and Electrolux should directly involve their domestic markets".[33] Malaysia's YTL is one of the very rare Late Asia examples who went from the home market directly to compete in developed markets. To date, its overseas utility and power business mainly involves two major acquisitions, both in developed countries: Wessex Water in Britain and a 33% stake in a power-distribution company in Australia.[34] Lastly, few significant Late Asia companies have used the third path of skipping the home market and going straight to developed markets. Exceptions include Creative Technology from Singapore and Li Ka Shing's telecom ventures from Hong Kong to Europe and Australia.

Global products and services

Japanese companies have done even better than Western comapnies at developing globally standardized products that sell all over the world. Early efforts in cars and consumer electronics focused on low price, simple design and high quality. Later efforts included innovations such as the Sony Walkman. Recent efforts include sophisticated products that are global, yet allow for local adaptation. To solve the car platform problem, in the late 1990s Honda developed the world's first adjustable-width automobile platform. [35] The platform, developed over a three-year period by Honda's engineers, allowed three distinct Accords that cost 20% less to bring to market than the single Accord developed in 1994.

Generally speaking, Late Asia companies find that their home-country products are seldom saleable overseas without extensive adaptation or upgrade. Hence they find it difficult to create global products. But some successful companies, like Acer, have managed to succeed in this respect.

Acer now produces only about six different models of desktop PCs and three or four notebook PCs globally. What is more, standard components are reused across the range. So, for example, all Acer desktop PCs are built using one of just three different main circuit boards.[36] Other Late Asia companies are also beginning to catch up – China's Huawei in telecom equipment, Taiwan Semiconductor, Haier in appliances, and CP in food.

Global activity location

Late Asia countries have increased their participation in global supply chains, especially as Western and Early Asia companies relocate parts of their operations to gain cost advantages. This has built up local capabilities, as know-how is gradually transferred to local companies. Haier got parts of its initial key technology from its joint-venture partners Liebherr, and Marconi.[37] Similarly, Lenovo was primarily a distributor for Hewlett-Packard and AST until 1991, and these partnerships gave the company both managerial expertise and technological skills for its move to manufacturing and design.[38]

As yet, most Late Asia companies are keeping their production activities within their own countries. So their internationalization is limited in nature. But those from the higher-cost countries, such as Malaysia, now face huge pressures from the lower-cost countries, especially China. So they themselves are starting to relocate activities. Examples include Thailand's CP Group and Taiwan's Acer, both of which have relocated significant production operations to China.

A few Late Asia countries, especially India, are also becoming favored locations for R&D activities. In the late 1980s, Texas Instruments set up a software-design subsidiary in Bangalore, India, in order to access the low-cost but highly skilled technical workers available there. This subsidiary communicated with Texas Instruments' R&D center in the United States via satellite each day, thus operating very much as part of a global network. This location strategy and the resulting benefit of high-quality design work at low cost is made possible by the strength of the differences in country costs. In the 1990s and early 2000s, many more companies followed TI's example as India developed as a major R&D sourcing center. Motorola has set up a corporate research center, also in Bangalore, to develop software for all Motorola companies worldwide. Matsushita is developing an R&D base in India, not only to adapt existing products but also to develop new products from scratch. Its South Asia regional office in New Delhi will play a key role in the company's activities.[39] These investments by developed-economy companies will train local engineers and managers who will eventually migrate to local companies and help their internationalization. Even Chinese companies are setting up R&D in India. In 2001, China's Huawei Technologies, a major telecom company, chose Bangalore for its largest software-development center outside China.

Global marketing

Companies that can use global marketing can leverage global brand names, global advertising and global positioning. But doing so usually depends on coming from a home country that has a globally attractive and transferable culture and lifestyles. No countries in Late Asia are in that fortunate position, nor will they be for at least the next 10 years. So Late Asia companies will probably have to play the global marketing game by hiding their national origin, rather than stressing it. Many Asian brand names, even when translated into English, tend to sound strange to Westerners. For example, Korea's Lucky Goldstar took decades to realize that its company name signaled an Asian origin out of touch with Western tastes. Only in recent years has it changed its name to the neutral (but boring) "LG". Its local competitor, Samsung, has over the last few years poured millions of dollars into building what is becoming a powerful brand (rated the 25th-most valuable in the world in 2003, and the only Late Asia brand in the world's top 100).[40] Similarly, China's Haier will find it hard to penetrate Western markets with a name that is so hard for Westerners to pronounce. In contrast, Taiwan's Acer chose a name with Western connotations of strength (steel, etc.), and it is likely that the word "legend" would have been favorable for the Chinese computer maker had the name not already been taken in some target markets.

Since China comprises more than 60% of its total revenue, CP Group chose a name to suit. CP founded its Chinese subsidiaries under the name Chia Tai, which was CP's original Chinese name and translates literally as "big and upright", a very positive image in Chinese.[41]

Global competitive moves

At one time, Japanese companies were adept at outflanking their often larger Western rivals with global competitive moves. In the videocassette-recorder industry, Japanese manufacturers like Sony and Matsushita combined rapid coverage of all key markets, offering the first global products, and an efficient production network, to secure adequate volume and a strong competitive position, including in the U.S. market. American competitors such as RCA, Zenith or General Electric were unable to compete, least of all in Japan. By the time these companies had set up their activity network with production and component purchasing in the Far East, the Japanese products were established and competing no longer on price, but on recognized quality.[42]

Companies from Late Asia are less able to make global competitive moves by themselves, and thus may need global partners. For example, in 2001, Taiwan's Acer developed a new strategy of transforming itself from a manufacturing to a service company. It also adopted a new corporate identity to symbolize Acer's commitment to enhancing people's lives through technology. It supported this new objective through a strategic alliance with the U.S. firm Palm (now called PalmOne), enabling it to license the Palm OS operating system through 2005. Acer used this platform to deliver its first Acer Mobile Device, in late 2003, as part of Acer's Mobile Data Strategy – a vision aimed at providing easy wireless access and exchange of enterprise and personal information via a handheld computer.[43]

Conclusions

In reviewing the evidence on the globalization of Asian firms, it is clear that geography *does* play a role primarily by shaping a company's resources and competitive advantages because success in globalization is driven by a complex mix of factors – including customer market, products and services, business systems, assets and resources, partners, and economies of scale and scope – most of which are impacted by their native-country environments. The dominant domestic market positions of potential globalizers accentuates the degree to which they may be bound by various conditions in their home markets. As a result, companies in what we have called "Late Asia" have a much steeper hill to climb in the process of internationalization, when compared to those from the U.S., Western Europe or Early Asia.

We suggest four critical competitive strengths that companies from Late Asia need to build in order to succeed in globalizing. These are: their own countries' globalization drivers; selecting industries that are already globalized; building competitive strengths that can be transferred internationally; and making clever use of global strategy. We have shown examples of Late Asia companies that are succeeding by combining two or more of these approaches. The experiences of these companies should serve as a lesson to all would-be internationalizers from Late Asia that they should approach these four key factors in setting global strategies proactively and systematically. Although global markets are increasingly competitive and predatory, these and other case studies show that it is still possible for Asian companies to play a significant part in the globalization of industries.

Endnotes

1 We define "internationalization" as companies extending their activities (selling, producing or other) beyond their home country. We define "globalization" as companies achieving broad geographic spread in their activities. There is no agreed definition. But a minimum should be activities in two continents. Lovelock and Yip (1996) give a more stringent definition, requiring a global company to be present in both the northern and southern hemispheres and both the eastern and western ones. See Christopher H. Lovelock and George S. Yip, "Developing Global Strategies for Service Businesses", *California Management Review*, *37*, 3, pp.64–86, Winter°1996.

2 Michael E. Porter, *The Competitive Advantage of Nations*, New York: The Free Press, 1990.

3 Ray A. Goldberg, Thomas N. Urban III, and Jane L. Weitz, *Charoen Pokphand: The New Conglomerate*, Boston: Harvard Business School Publishing, No. 9-596-033, 1996; and Ray A. Goldberg and Cate Reavis, *Charoen Pokphand Group: A Renewed Focus*, Boston: Harvard Business School Publishing, No. 9-903-415, 1990.

4 Niraj Dawar and Tony Frost, "Competing with Giants: Survival Strategies for Local Companies in Emerging Markets", *Harvard Business Review*, March–April 1999.

5 Source: www.legend.com.

6 See Sumantra Ghoshal and Meeta Sengupta, "VIP Luggage: It Takes a Lot to be a VIP", case study, London Business School, 1998.

7 See George S. Yip, *Asian Advantage*: *Key Strategies for Winning in the Asia-Pacific Region (Updated Edition–After the Crisis)*, Cambridge, MA: Perseus Publishing 2001, chapter 1.

8 See David B. Yoffie and Helen V. Milner, "An Alternative to Free Trade or Protectionism: Why Corporations Seek Strategic Trade Policy", *California Management Review*, Summer 1989, pp.111–131.

9 George S. Yip, *Total Global Strategy: Managing for Worldwide Competitive Advantage*, Upper Saddle River, NJ: Prentice Hall, 1992; and *Total Global Strategy II: Updated for the Internet and Service Era*, 2003.

10 Goldberg et al. 1996.

11 For a full description of bases of competitive advantage, see George S. Yip, "Bases of Competitive Advantage", in Stuart Crainer and Des Dearlove, eds., *Financial Times Handbook of Management*, London: Financial Times/Prentice Hall, 2nd edition, 2001, pp.253–263.

12 "Power Grab: Malaysia's Electricity Tycoon Snaps Up Assets Worldwide", *Far Eastern Economic Review*, February 20, 2003, pp.40–43.

13 Ghoshal and Sengupta, 1998.

14 Goldberg and Reavis, 1990.

15 See "Haier Reaches Higher", *Fortune*, September 5, 2002.

16 Goldberg and Reavis, 1990.

17 *Fortune*, 2002.

18 Dawar and Frost, 1999.

19 Christopher Bartlett and Sumantra Ghoshal, "Going Global: Lessons from Late Movers", *Harvard Business Review*, March–April 2000.

20 Source: HYPERLINK "http://www.acer.com" global.acer.com.

21 Goldberg et al., 1996.

22 Source: www.haier.com.

23 Bettina Büchel and Steffen Raub, "Legend Group and the Chinese Computer Industry", in Kulwant Singh, Nitin Pangarkar and Gaik Eng Lim, eds., *Business Strategy in Asia: A Casebook*, Singapore: Thomson Learning, 2001, pp.55–66.

24 See "YTL in Hot Water", *Fortune*, September 19, 2002.

25 Dawar and Frost, 1999.

26 Neeraj Bhardwaj, Cheng Hwa Chua, Giorgio Delpiano, Srinivas Krishna, Ben Lee, Barbara Pozdorovkina, and Joe Schorge, "Tata Engineering Limited – Assessment of Global Strategy", London Business School course report, March 19, 2003.

27 Source: HYPERLINK "http://www.acer.com" global.acer.com.

28 Goldberg et al., 1990.

29 Bartlett and Ghoshal, 2000.

30 George S. Yip, "Global Strategy as a Factor in Japanese Success", *The International Executive*, *38*, 1, pp.145–167, special issue on Japan, January/February 1996.

31 Yip, 1992 and 2003.

32 This paragraph is based on Philip Kotler, Liam Fahey and S. Jatusripitak, *The New Competition*, Englewood Cliffs, NJ: Prentice-Hall, 1985, p.174.

33 *Fortune*, 2002.

34 Source: www.YTL.com.my.

35 This example is adapted from *Business Week*, "Can Honda Build a World Car?" September 8, 1997, pp.100–108.

36 See "Reinventing Acer: Computer Giant Acer is Taking Drastic Action", *Far Eastern Economic Review*, May 24, 2001.

37 See "CEO pushes China's Haier as global brand", *USA Today*, February 1, 2003.

38 Buchel and Roub, 2000.

39 K. Ramachandran and George S. Yip, "It's Time to Glocalise Now", *General Management Review* (*Economic Times*, India, Vol. 2, No. 1, 2000, pp.40–47).

40 Valued at $10.85 billion in brand value by Interbrand Corp./*BusinessWeek* (although the methodology can be questioned in that it tends to overstate the value of brands). See "The Top 100 Brands", *BusinessWeek*, August 4, 2003, pp.48–50.

41 Goldberg et al., 1996.

42 This example is adapted from Herbert Henzler and Wilhelm Rall, "Facing up to the Globalization Challenge", *The McKinsey Quarterly,* Winter 1986, pp.52–68.

43 Source: HYPERLINK "http://www.acer.com" global.acer.com.

PART II

Climbing the Globalization Staircase

CHAPTER

6 Enacting Global Strategy

Introduction

We started the first chapter with a rather bleak view about the internationalization of Asian companies. But we hope that the nine company cases presented by their CEOs in the first part of this book have convinced you that there are some interesting examples of Asian companies that have broken free of the "plant the flag" mindset and have grasped the opportunity offered by the forces of globalization. These case studies were more than a set of interesting examples. They are also an opportunity to learn more about how these companies have gone through internationalization and what some of the key success factors can be to become a significant international business player.

Each case is, of course, different. And the longstanding experience of a Sony or the drastic managerial reorganization of Samsung Electronics are difficult to compare with the careful first steps to internationalization of ICBC or China Netcom. But, like us, you will also have observed some interesting similarities.

All of the companies that were presented may not have had a clear internationalization strategy from the start, but they had a clear strategic intent. And they developed fairly quickly a unique concept that helped them in their quest. Whether it is the creative supply-chain management in Li & Fung or Olam, or the "3P Innovation" of Samsung Electronics, they all have a concept that helped them to roll out their strategy.

They also seem to have built carefully a defendable portfolio of intangible and tangible assets and capabilities that helped them in the expansion. Li & Fung's electronic information network is an example of how a company created a strong tool to exploit information in order to create value for the customer. Kikkoman, Sony and Samsung did a remarkable job in building a brand, sometimes even a different brand from that which exists in the home market, as was the case with Kikkoman.

All the cases also show to some extent that the management of each company strives to consolidate its successes and to learn from each step in the internationalization. SingTel's gradual construction of its network of partnerships in which it had only a minority interest, leading in the end to a full acquisition of Optus, is an example of the learning process. The same is true for its learning in its human-resources policies , or in Olam's concept of adjacent diversification.

Can we make some sense out of these common factors of success? Can we develop a conceptual tool that may help other Asian companies to think about their own internationalization? We will argue here, and in the following chapters, that there is indeed such a concept and we will compare it to a staircase to be climbed. Success with internationalization for an Asian company will depend on whether the company can climb the globalization staircase.

Why a staircase

In the next chapter Orit Gadiesh and Charles Ormiston will argue their belief that

> "*...many firms expand too quickly internationally, chasing 'global scale' with a limited understanding of how scale translates into competitive advantage ... many firms misunderstand the structure of their industries, believing that international expansion is a logical step when a company reaches a certain size.*"

This quote, while taken a bit out of context, indicates two potential traps for an Asian firm wishing to internationalize. First, it suggests that there may be a common assumption that internationalization is a logical step, implying that it is simply an extension of doing what one is good at in the domestic environment, except on a higher scale and in a different country. It is, perhaps, the mistake that Acer made in its first attempts to penetrate the European market, misunderstanding the complexity and diversity of the European customer, even for a quite standardized product such as a notebook. It is also one of the flawed judgments made by Jollibee, the Filipino fast-food company, when it assumed that the food choices made by Filipinos would meet great success in neighboring countries. Or it is the mistake made by the Hong Kong-based fashion chain Giordano when it failed in its first attempts to establish itself in the German market: Germany was more than simply a bigger version of Hong Kong, and had very different traditions in retailing, branding, fashion preferences, and so on. Kikkoman provides an interesting example of a company that realized relatively quickly that the positioning of soy-based sauces in Australia or the United States needed to be totally different from those they used in Japan. Internationalization is not a "logical" extension but needs a clear understanding of which system-based advantages the company can exploit.

Second, Gadiesh and Ormiston point out that many companies may try to go too fast. Perhaps it is not the speed that is the real threat, but the risks inherent in trying to bypass a few essential steps. While SingTel or Olam have moved relatively quickly in their internationalization, their stories also reveal a fairly gradual process whereby they ensure that each forward step is firmly grounded before they move on to the next. The attraction for Asian firms is understandable, perhaps, because they are keen to catch up with the industrial leaders from the U.S., Japan or Europe. And they may believe that the concepts of international management developed in the U.S. can be transferred without adaptation to the Asian environment. While there are lessons that are transferable, some of which have been hinted at in Part I, we are convinced that they have to be conditioned to the Asian environment.

In our analogy of the staircase, each step is not simply a step forward, it is also a step higher. (See Figure 6.1.)

Building the staircase on solid ground

In order to climb the staircase safely you need to be sure that it is built on solid ground. You cannot build an ambitious internationalization on marshland. You need to drain the ground in order to have solid foundations. This solidity requires that two conditions be fulfilled: that a relevant and focused strategy is developed, and that the management system at home is cleaned up appropriately.

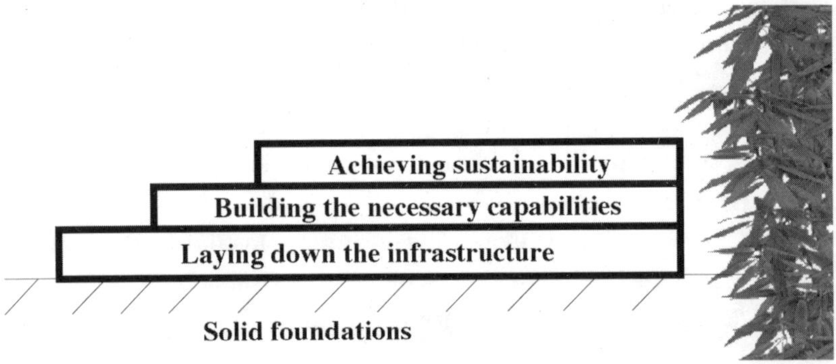

Fig 6.1 The globalization staircase

In each of the nine case studies in Part I, the companies had a focused and successful strategy for international development. We are not suggesting that this strategy was developed at the start and implemented without hiccups. Far from it. But, time and again, what is clear is the incremental but logical emergence of a concept that offers value to the international customer. Olam has developed a form of value-added supply-chain management and carefully expands this into adjacent markets. Li & Fung developed the concept of virtual manufacturing and rapid supply-chain management. SingTel sees itself as a networked company with two main hubs in Australasia. Kikkoman offers an ideal barbecue sauce for meat lovers in the U.S. and Asutralia. In the next chapter, Gadiesh and Ormiston will expand on the need for a careful industrial analysis that will enable your company to choose where and how to expand.

But rolling out such a strategy will only be feasible when you have covered your back: your domestic market has to be properly managed.

The case of Samsung Electronics is an interesting illustration of this. The company had been successful before with the expansion of its manufacturing network abroad, starting with its first TV plant in Portugal in 1982. Yun Jong Yong described how the financial crisis of 1997 revealed the weakness of the company's operational structure in Korea. This sudden collapse in the domestic market put Samsung's internationalization on shaky grounds. The company pulled itself through this crisis by implementing a drastic restructuring in conjunction with a management-reform program. The demise of Daewoo Motors after the 1997 crisis is an illustration of how an internationalization strategy can collapse if the domestic back office is not clean and well managed.

Taking the first step: Laying down the infrastructure

A first step in climbing the globalization staircase is the creation of a solid infrastructure. You may remember that the word "infrastructure" (literally, in the original French, "the underlying foundations") had its roots in the development of railway systems in Europe in the early 19th century. To create value by moving passengers and freight with rolling stock, it was first necessary to build tracks, stations and management systems. The international architecture necessary for globalization needs the equivalent of the tracks, stations and management systems.

The architecture of the infrastructure is about entry strategies, the organizational choices – the acquisitions, partnerships, or the make-or-buy decision described by Gadiesh and Ormiston. The development of the information systems described by Victor Fung is an interesting example of the development of a keystone for Li & Fung's infrastructure.

Having a design is not sufficient. It also has to be laid down, which requires the mobilization of the appropriate resources. In many of the case studies there were hints of the difficulty of finding people capable of implementing the international architecture. This requires more than adventurous flag planting. Success is often dependent on the exceptional skills of the international pioneers who can build and maintain a bridge between the domestic market and international activities.

It goes without saying that the construction of the tracks also requires financial resources. Establishing a presence abroad, investing in brand building, acquiring companies, all require a lot of money. The cost of financial resources can be prohibitive for international expansion plans, or the difference in the cost of money between Asia and the rest of the world is potentially a strong competitive disadvantage for Asian companies. Kwong Ki Chi describes in his chapter how Hong Kong is developing as an important source of financial resources for Chinese companies who want to expand internationally.

Moving up the staircase: Building the necessary capabilities

The second step on the staircase begins with the identification of the capability gaps that may hinder the company in operating effectively outside the domestic environment, be they in people, management style, systems, brands or intellectual property. The goal must then be to build the capabilities to fill these gaps through a systematic process that also maximizes the learning relative to the resources and time expended, as well as augmenting the capability base with external resources such as new staff or through alliances.

Throughout the Olam and SingTel cases it is evident that the development of the appropriate human resources is a challenge to maintain the momentum for internationalization. Brand building seems to be less important for SingTel, at least at this stage of its international development, but proved to be crucial for the three pioneers; Sony, Samsung Electronics and Kikkoman. For Sony and Samsung, who both position themselves as strong innovators, the development and protection of their intellectual capital is of the utmost importance.

The chapter on "Managing People", by Kevin Kelly, and "Building Brands", by Miles Young, provides examples of how to build two key capabilities in Asia. This is by no means an exhaustive set. Other capabilities, such as intellectual property, may well be equally important, particularly in Asia where there is little tradition of respect for intellectual ownership. People and brands may well be the most important capabilities in the early phases of the internationalization. Others, such as the management capability to implement sophisticated M&A or invest in the protection and exploitation of IPR, may come at a later stage of the process.

In particular, the development of people creates a challenge for Asian companies. Their HR practices are often very local and influenced by family connections, the importance of the group over the individual or outdated employment practices which reflect earlier stages of their development or the conditions that prevail in their country of origin. As will be argued in the later chapters, it has become apparent that Asian-style lifetime employment is a liability in the internationalization process. The group of builders (Olam, SingTel and Li & Fung) are all heavily investing in state-of-the-art employment systems, including the replacement of home-grown managers by foreigners.

The next step: Achieving sustainability

It may be argued that draining the marshlands, building the infrastructure and developing the necessary capabilities is no different for Asian companies than for a U.S.-based or European company. Perhaps the environment is somewhat different in Asia and the boundary conditions impose different practices, but the principle is the same. We believe that the third step on our globalization staircase is quite special for Asian companies. Beyond developing and implementing the architecture of the infrastructure, beyond the development of capabilities, we also need to achieve sustainability through continuous learning and our ability to grow in tune with society and environment.

Let's face it; Western companies have often been able to consolidate their international positions by virtue of their control over essential resources (natural or otherwise), their sheer market power or, in many cases, through the absence of real competition (who in Asia can compete with Boeing or Airbus, for example?). For virtually all Asian companies these advantages do not exist. Where the resources are not controlled by Western companies, they are in the hands of governments, and most Asian companies enter a crowded competitive field when they internationalize. The only way to sustain an internationally competitive position is to adopt the strategy of the underdog: learn fast from successes and failures alike and consolidate this learning. Kikkoman and SingTel are impressive examples of companies that have enjoyed success, but have also learned from their less-successful ventures.

Once established, foreign subsidiaries have to switch their roles from being receivers and "learners" to teach the rest of the network as well. The flow of knowledge between home and overseas must become a two-way (or multiple-way) flow. This requires changes in mindset and attitude in both the headquarters and domestic facilities and the overseas operations. Too often the sheer difference in size between the domestic and the overseas operations leads to a sort of benign neglect: there is pride at home in the success of the overseas ventures, but there may be little understanding of what is actually happening there. The headquarters needs to develop a mindset and channels that are open to ideas from its overseas operations, which can be powerful sources of technical probes, tests and innovations about how customers in a different environment may experience the product. This in turn may lead to great opportunities to improve the value offered to the market. It also requires that a new set of capabilities be built around mobilizing and melding knowledge scattered around the international operations and leveraging this for international competitive advantage. It requires equally a change in mindset of the overseas ventures, which often cherish their independence and guard it carefully, up to the point of being unwilling to share with headquarters or other subsidiaries. They need to understand that it is their responsibility and obligation to teach the rest of the organization.

Exploiting the advantages of an underdog requires that an organization adapt to the local customs. We don't mean this in a purely cultural sense (though that may be important, too) but in the sense of adapting to the social framework and the environmental priorities in the countries in which the company is seeking to do business. Sustaining the internationalization advantage will require a heavy investment in the ability of the Asian firm to adjust to and grow with the societies in which it operates. SingTel needed to adjust to the fact that outside Singapore it was not a national jewel but simply another operator. It did so competently, though it suffered in some of the deals where it may have been perceived as being too close to the government. Careful management of public perceptions of and investment in the appropriate lobbying has helped SingTel to overcome the initial defensive reaction from some parties in Australia during the early stages of the acquisition of Optus.

Taking two steps at a time

While the three steps are broadly self-contained and in sequence, the reality will never be as clean and neat as suggested by our model. The three steps will probably overlap to some extent and preparations for the next step may run in parallel with the implementation of the previous step. But internationalization will be resource-intensive over a prolonged period of time. Prioritization and focus on which steps to take will be required and understanding that one step lays the foundation for future steps is essential.

Each step represents a quantum change that must be consolidated before moving on. Significant internationalization is seldom achieved from incremental linear change. You cannot go halfway into internationalization, adopting a half-hearted approach. A toe in the water is not sufficient. You have to take the full plunge, to develop both the infrastructure and the capabilities.

In the next three chapters we illustrate how to climb the three steps of the globalization staircase. They give some personal but interesting insights. In Chapter 7, we get the views of two partners (Orit Gadiesh and Charles Ormiston) from Bain and Co. on the preparation of the foundations and the implementation of the infrastructure. Through the description by Kwong Ki Chi, the former chief executive of Hong Kong Exchanges and Clearing Limited, of Hong Kong as a source of finance for Chinese enterprises we get an example of how to mobilize the resources to implement the infrastructure.

As mentioned earlier, Chapter 8 gives two illustrations of how to develop critical capabilities: people and brands. The points of view come from two privileged observers; Kevin Kelly, managing partner of Heidrick and Struggles, Asia, and Miles Young, chairman of Ogilvy and Mather in Asia.

Chapter 9 presents some ideas about the third step, how to achieve sustainability.

These three chapters will give you the opportunity to form your own opinions. You may want to compare these insights with some of the learning from Europe as described by Geoffrey Owen in Chapter 10, as well as with our own conclusions in Part III.

CHAPTER

7 Establishing Infrastructure

The globalization of any organization must be underpinned by a solid infrastructure if the effort is to be profitable and sustainable. The first element of this infrastructure is a sound strategy that defines the boundaries of the business and pinpoints the sources of advantage that the company can leverage globally.

The second element that must be put in place is the set of networks on which global operations rely. This may include an international network of distributors, of sales offices, of manufacturing plants and of operations centers. This network can be built through investments to establish subsidiaries, can make acquisitions or form joint ventures and alliances.

The third element of global infrastructure that must be put in place is the set of relationship networks that is necessary to give access to critical resources ranging from capital to supply of materials, components, technologies and people with the right experience and skills.

Companies that seek globalization for the "wrong reasons" or without a clear grasp of what they are trying to achieve often run the risk of believing that money can buy most, if not all, of the infrastructure required for the task. They may correctly identify the factors laid out above, with a spending plan to acquire these, without realizing that "infrastructure" in fact goes beyond tangible instruments. In our view, assets that are not backed by a sound expansion strategy are not real assets, but rather potential cost-centers. The case studies in Part I of this book have identified a number of instances in which companies have expanded their tangible infrastructure through investments overseas, but without the necessary strategy to deliver competitive advantage in the new markets they have entered. Where a company lacks sources of advantage over the competitors they meet overseas, the tangible international infrastructure will become a drag on the company. Restructuring such failed expansion can cost even more to resolve or turn around than the original investment.

Of course, once an organization has outlined a sound strategy and vision for globalization, it can choose to pursue this either through mergers, acquisitions, joint ventures or partnerships, or internally, under its own organization. Often what begins with the former, eventually must become "internal"; that is, embedded in a seamless organization without clear boundaries but with a culture that permeates across the network.

This chapter includes two contributions that examine different aspects of what it takes to lay down the infrastructure for globalization. The first, by Orit Gadiesh and Charles Ormiston of Bain & Co., looks at the fundamental question of what kind of international network a company should try to create. Gadiesh and Ormiston approach the task with the advantage of having advised many companies on the globalization process and seen some of the most brilliant successes, as well as trouble-shooting some well-known failures. They begin by pointing out that globalization is by no means a guaranteed route to higher profits, and that a clear understanding of the competitive advantages to be gained from globalization is the first building block that must be put in place. (This includes a judgment on whether the advantages are available to regional players or only to global players.) They then go on to discuss options for building the infrastructure of an international network, including the potential role of acquisitions, joint ventures and alliances. They then examine some of the "softer" – but no less important – aspects of global infrastructure, such as corporate values and culture. Finally, they point out that a company's network of infrastructure and related capabilities must continue to expand as it develops through different stages of internationalization towards what they note is often described as the "holy grail": the "global entity" – a company with effectively no center.

Why is a company with no center an appropriate defining image of a global organization? Essentially, this reflects our definition of a globalized company as one which is effectively operating and creating value regardless of its geographical location. Thus, a company which merely sells its product throughout the world but generates all its long-term value, strategy and vision at its headquarters, would not qualify as being truly globalized, despite perhaps having a strong global brand. In a truly globalized company, the headquarters may move (despite sentimental attachment) without greatly altering the company's outlook, prospects or strategy because it is the international network that forms the core of a global company.

The second contribution, by Kwong Ki Chi, former chief executive of Hong Kong Exchanges and Clearing Ltd, which runs the Stock and Futures Exchanges of Hong Kong, sheds light on how companies can build a solid financial infrastructure for globalization. It goes without saying that most companies undergoing the globalization process will at some point need to raise money. But, as this contribution shows, building the financial infrastructure to underpin successful globalization is much more than a matter of having access to cash. It includes bringing the company's accounting, financial reporting, incentive systems and governance processes up to international standards.

Using the case of Chinese enterprises listing on the Hong Kong exchange to open up a new source of capital, Kwong's analysis examines the role that listing on an internationally recognized exchange can play in helping a company globalize and reveals that this goes far beyond simply a one-off injection of capital.

Since the first Chinese red-chips and H or N shares listed in Hong Kong or New York over a decade ago, over 100 Chinese companies have listed abroad and many more are seeking listings, often in preference to local markets. Indeed, often China's best and most promising companies have listed abroad before listing domestically as a part of a clear internationalization strategy. A great deal of this may be prestige. But as Kwong clearly demonstrates, the listing process delivers many other benefits that can play a critical role in globalization. Specifically, the listing process forces a clearer articulation of the company's strategy. Repeated contact with international investors helps build a global outlook and experience within the management team. It opens up new incentives for management (such as options) that can help drive the value-creation process in the company, while the need to conform to international accounting standards can help improve financial control and give management a clearer view of how the business is performing.

Many have claimed that the cleaning up of China's domestic stock markets and the education of Chinese investors will greatly decrease the attractiveness of an international listing. However, the jury is still out on this. In the meantime, the story of risk and reward for Chinese companies gaining access to international capital markets remains an excellent example of how companies can use a capital-raising strategy as a substantive builder of international capability.

Creating the right infrastructure may not be the most obvious, or even the most exciting, part of the globalization process. But, as these contributions demonstrate, it is essential. Globalization built on sand is ultimately doomed to collapse. By contrast, a sound infrastructure acts like the roots of tree, not only providing stability but also acting as a network through which a company can go on drawing in the new resources it needs to grow internationally.

▲ CREATING NETWORKS

Orit Gadiesh and Charles M. Ormiston[1]
Bain & Company

Like the famous British mountaineer George Leigh Mallory, who answered the question "Why do you want to climb Mount Everest?" with the words "Because it's there", many executives commit their firms to international expansion without fully understanding why. Sometimes they seek a challenge. Sometimes they believe that success at home should translate into success abroad. Often, they strike out overseas because growth has slowed in the domestic market. But, like climbing Mount Everest, global expansion carries enormous potential risk. And misguided or overly aggressive international expansion has claimed its share of victims, as a leading cause of corporate failure and turnover at the top.

Bain analyzed the financial results of 7,500 publicly traded companies from seven developed economies between 1996 and 2000, and came to a surprising conclusion: only one company in six achieves sustained, profitable international growth, even when the hurdle is relatively modest – growing foreign revenues and profits at least at the rate of GDP plus inflation for a five-year period.[2] The mix of international and domestic revenues for major companies in the G-7 barely changed over the five-year period. In addition, our research showed that margins earned by companies outside their home country were often below, and almost never above, margins earned at home.

The rewards for getting it right, however, can be very attractive. Companies that achieved sustained, profitable international growth delivered extraordinary financial results. Over the five-year period, their total revenues, as well as their foreign revenues, grew at more than three times the rate of average firms trying to expand internationally. The operating margins of profitable international-growth companies were more than 60% higher than the average, with share prices appreciating 1.7 times faster than the major stock indices in the U.S., the U.K. and Japan. Global scale can also have a major strategic impact when used by smaller domestic players to gain advantage over their larger domestic rivals – as Japanese data-storage CD-players learned to their chagrin when Hitachi Maxell and Olympus Optical leapfrogged into international brands. This paper highlights a number of examples of successful international expansions.

Why is profitable international growth within reach for certain companies but elusive for the majority? Successful global-growth companies excel at defining the boundaries of their businesses. They clearly understand whether the cost structures and customer profiles for their industries compel them to expand overseas, or whether they are better off viewing global expansion simply as one growth option among many. They base their global expansion strategies on a rigorous understanding of how money is made in their industries, which guides their decisions to acquire foreign assets, build organically from a strong domestic base, or pursue joint ventures and strategic alliances. Finally, a number of successful international companies have *decades* of accumulated experience, institutionalizing the lessons learned from both successes and failures.

This paper is divided into two sections. The first section frames the critical decision by executive teams on whether and how to expand internationally, posing three questions:

- How does industry structure (factors such as government regulation, number and relative size of competitors, value-chain structure, and the relative power of distributors, suppliers and customers) affect the desirability of international expansion as well as the nature of competition?
- How do strategic considerations such as cost competitiveness and product differentiation color international expansion strategies?
- How does relative competitive position affect the appropriate strategy for expansion?

In the second section, we consider the network required to grow successfully overseas, and how companies can set priorities based on industry structure, strategy requirements and relative competitive position. This includes perspectives on:

- Making a network and market positions rather than buying them
- Short-cuts to accelerating international expansion (joint ventures, alliances, franchising…)
- The centralization/decentralization trade-off for an internationalizing company
- The importance of values, culture and leadership
- Functional capability requirements at discrete stages of expansion.

Guidelines on international expansion strategy

Industry structure and its impact on the desirability and nature of international expansion

Companies seeking to expand abroad first need to understand clearly why they are making such a move. In addition, they need to delineate whether their expansion strategy should be based on cost advantage or differentiation, since each of those characteristics carries different implications for local, regional and global organization and tactics.

We believe many firms expand too quickly internationally, chasing "global scale" with a limited understanding of how scale translates into competitive advantage, squandering cash flow and management talent from their home markets. Similarly, many firms misunderstand the structure of their industries, believing that international expansion is a logical step when a company reaches a certain size. In fact, while some industries are "naturally global", many are not.

Defining the competitive landscape is the first step in a process we refer to as "business definition". To understand how "global" or "local" a business is, companies must first evaluate the extent to which costs and customers (or at least common customer needs) can be shared between markets. Some businesses have significant customer (or customer needs) overlap between countries, and also benefit significantly from cost or technology sharing between countries. These tend to be "naturally global" businesses. Other industries have relatively little cost or customer sharing between countries, and are therefore more "naturally local". Business definition thus becomes a strategy tool that guides the development of required capabilities. The interaction between these two factors – cost structure and customer profile – in determining the potential for profitable globalization in an industry is illustrated in Figure 7.1.

In a few industries, firms have to be global if they are to achieve leadership. As the example above shows, computer makers such as Dell in PCs or Hewlett-Packard in printers have cost structures that keep improving with the increased scale of going global. Once Intel turns on a fabrication facility, scaling up to increase production adds only incremental cost. Pharmaceutical companies like Pfizer or software companies like Oracle must sell globally to amortize their enormous product-development costs. Investment banks are driven to expand globally because their core clients operate in all major financial markets around the world. The profit economics of these industries are global: in some cases, their customers respond to a single, global value proposition; in others, the companies can capture benefits of world scale facilities.

Figure 7.1 The potential for profitable globalization

Cost structure	Locally distinct	Globally uniform
Global economies of scale	**Compelled by costs** • International expansion required to capture scale benefits, e.g. – personal computers – passenger cars • Continued cost scale and scope benefits from growth outside domestic market. • Regional or global market share emphasis to leverage capex • "Splitting" of "global" and "local" value-chain activities may occur, e.g. contract manufacturing	**Naturally Global** • International expansion is core to profitable growth, e.g. – airline leasing – semiconductors • Single, global value proposition – global brand with uniform product features/benefits – global marketing theme • Global market share emphasis – exploit scale in central, global facilities
Local economies of scale	**Naturally Local** • International expansion is an optional growth adjacency, e.g.: – mobile-phone operators – food retailing • Distinct and tailored value proposition in each market: brand may be local or global • Locally specific marketing campaigns. • Local market share emphasis	**Compelled by Customers** • International expansion required to serve global customers or a growth option for homogeneous customers, e.g. – investment banking – oil extraction • Similiar customer value proposition replicated globally • Separate but coordinated marketing campaigns across local markets • Local market share emphasis

Customer profile

Yet, even in an era of liberalizing trade regulation and, some argue, converging consumer tastes, international expansion is more often a choice than a necessity. Winning in food retailing or beer, for instance, is the result of building market power and influence at the national or regional level, not globally. In this book, the case study on Kikkoman illustrates wonderfully the value of a steady expansion overseas, the need to develop local brewing capability in each major market (including two breweries in the U.S.), the need to systematically understand and tailor to local tastes, and to train users in how to incorporate Kikkoman's product into established dietary habits. Kikkoman deployed key global capabilities, a common brand and well-defined corporate values in each market, but a reading of the study leaves the distinct impression that soy sauce is a local business. With 30% of sales and 50% of profits overseas, Kikkoman's success is a clear demonstration of "thinking global and acting local".

Companies in industries that are not "naturally global" stumble badly when they try to use their home-country cost structures as the basis for international expansion. This mistake led to the humbling of multi-billion-dollar telecommunications Goliaths (NTT-Communications, British Telecom and Deutsche Telekom, for example) by the local Asian Davids in their expansion into the Philippines, Malaysia and Indonesia. The larger players failed to recognize that the advantages of global scale do not apply to an industry primarily driven by local scale and performance – as the fixed-line telecommunications service is. A more frequent pattern among Asian companies is failure to recognize that the scale of their local operations is uncompetitive when global scale is the critical driver of success. Such misunderstanding led to tremendous losses borne by the government-sponsored semiconductor fabrication facilities in Singapore, and also led Malaysian auto executives to overlook the unlikely prospects for Proton in a globally competitive passenger-car industry.

Regional leadership – stuck in the middle or a source of competitive advantage?

Businesses with high transport costs, but with few barriers to trade other than distance, often evolve into regional businesses. Examples include grocery retail, perishable food products, bulk liquid products (beer, soft drinks and condiments), air transport, third-party logistics, and so on. In these cases the "business boundaries" are often how far a truck can travel in a day, not national boundaries.

Great businesses have been built up understanding the primacy of regional share – Singapore Airlines in Southeast Asia air transport, Uni-President (discussed in Chapter 4) in food and retailing, and Evergreen in container shipping. Regional businesses should be particularly interesting to expanding Asian companies, as the benefits of strong local-scale positions may create defensible positions against global players seeking to leverage their global scale and customer positions.

In this book, we observe several honest assessments of business leaders experimenting to get business definition right. Lee Hsien Yang's contribution on SingTel's initial international expansion provides a number of lessons on how the unique regulatory environment in each country hampered SingTel's plans to regionalize key activities and approaches; the success stories in Thailand, the Philippines and Australia have been driven by the quality of strategy, government relations, local management and partners in individual businesses rather then regional scale.

Other firms have seen their regional positions threatened by "global giants" seizing the most attractive market segments, leaving regional and local players to fight over the scraps. Examples of global businesses defeating regional businesses include investment banking and trading activities, affluent consumer banking, personal computers, tobacco and liquor products, air freight and legal services.

Key strategic levers: Cost leadership and/or differentiation?

For most companies, international expansion begins with a clear understanding of their strategic advantages. The most successful global-growth companies have no confusion about whether their products and services compete primarily on a cost advantage or through differentiation. In general, firms or divisions that compete primarily on the basis of cost are more successful when a strong center maintains control over global operations and strategy, ensuring a standardized approach across markets and emphasizing the capture of cost-reduction innovations wherever they occur.

A firm relying on differentiation must be able to discern local market practices and preferences, and then respond accordingly. Differentiation typically requires a company to develop sophisticated customer-segmentation strategies, as well as the ability to feed local preferences into the firm's global value chain in an efficient manner (for example, convert the local requirement for Japanese-language software into a global decision on handling multi-byte characters in the software code). Generally, companies that compete primarily on differentiation are more decentralized and look more to local innovation and coordination among different parts of the value chain. This of course adds overhead costs and slows decision-making.

Dell and Compaq starkly illustrate the difference in these approaches as they built up their Asia Pacific personal computer businesses. Personal computers do not lend themselves to product differentiation, since the primary value added by the manufacturer is to assemble widely available standardized components into products, configured to the needs of either business or consumers. The core designs can have a high degree of standardization for any market around the globe. Successful PC manufacturers focus on *reliability* (which can raise average selling price as well as lower cost structures), *low inventories* (which save obsolescence and carrying costs), *low manufacturing costs*, *low distribution costs* and *low after-sales costs*. Global or regional account management has also become increasingly important.

Dell entered the region in 1995, with limited sales driven by pre-existing distribution arrangements. They were the number 32 in market share. Over the next two years Dell entered eight countries with the direct model, initially sourcing all finished product from a manufacturing site in Penang, and serving the vast majority of service calls from a single call center. During the 1995–1999 period, Compaq operated several factories and country-based service centers. Dell's overhead costs where less then half of Compaq's. By 1999, Dell had US$2 billion in sales, achieved acceptable profitability, opened its second Asian factory (in China), and was on its way to regional market leadership (ex-China). Meanwhile, Compaq was losing cash and experiencing flat growth. Compaq was sold to HP in 2002.

Dell's regional head during the growth period was Phil Kelly, who ran a tight ship. Monthly operations reviews of hundreds of line items for each country were models in speed, efficiency and standardization. Success in any one market was quickly rewarded and replicated in other markets. Failure was quickly stemmed or penalized. This was a company focused on execution. The global strategy, with minor modifications, was the standard.

Merrill Lynch's painful experience in Japan brokerage is a good example of how a highly successful global bank could fail in a business (securities brokerage) that is driven by local scale and local custom. In 1998 Merrill Lynch took over selected employees, assets and branches from the failed Yamaichi Securities Company. Recognizing the tough task at hand, Merrill Lynch committed to a significant program of sales training, branch overhaul, technology investment and advertising. Numerous "best practices" were transferred from abroad, including a focus of the account managers on portfolio planning, caution in handling cash (to combat concerns about money laundering), and compensation systems based on assets under management rather than transactions-linked fee generation. Despite significant commitment, investment, soul-searching, and trial and error, Merrill Lynch failed to hit targets for assets under management, and significantly downsized the operation in 2002.

Many firms succeed at home with broad market participation and cost leadership, only to stumble overseas because they fail to adjust their international market strategies and execution to the need to focus and differentiate. This failure can take several forms – imposing overhead burdens from home markets formulaically to nascent markets with sub-scale positions; building broad value-chain participation in markets where only selective participation was affordable; and entering market segments where the lack of cost advantage militated against success. Consider, for example, the consistently low profitability of U.S. auto manufacturers overseas, or the failure of firms like Sony, NEC and Panasonic to build a major presence in personal computers in the United States.

Cost leadership and differentiation strategies are not black and white. Most firms can manage both, but one strategy usually winds up being dominant.

Leader or follower?

Most business leaders understand that market leadership is a major source of competitive advantage. We have yet to encounter a market leader who had strategies in place in which the ultimate goal was not to maintain leadership.

In Chapter 5, George Yip and Ruiming Lin delicately introduce a fact of life for many companies in Asia: they usually start out as followers, not leaders, from sub-scale markets with relatively unsophisticated requirements. Companies with weak starting positions need to adjust their expansion strategies accordingly:

- Avoid globally competitive industries or sectors unless you have a protected technology.

- Understand your relative cost position and the factors behind cost advantage. Have a bias towards businesses where local or regional scale confers advantage (or you may have patented technologies, a business model, or low-cost labor pools that allow your firm to sustain an advantage for a significant period).
- Avoid direct battle with the market leaders until your cost position, product or service acceptance, and financial position would allow you to win.

The success of Olam International, described in Chapter 3, is one of our favorite examples of a fast-growing follower. Recall its clear strategy of selecting food and industrial product categories where local presence is important to ensuring the quality and reliability of supply, where the market size is attractive but not "must-win" for existing majors, and where there is value added to high-quality supply-chain management. Olam was also clear about its advantages, including the ability to draw on very high-quality management talent from the Subcontinent, to ensure all of its top management has spent time in some rather "challenging" market conditions, and a culture of managing costs to the penny.

A second example is the extraordinary growth of several Indian software firms in the software-development and outsourcing sectors. India had a unique set of circumstances that paved the way for a globally competitive software business. When socialistic government policies caused IBM and others to leave the market in the mid 1970s, a number of entrepreneurial Indian companies were established to maintain and improve existing equipment. Over time, this base of engineers began to undertake mundane "outsourced" projects for software firms and large end-customers with proprietary systems, taking advantage of their proprietary knowledge and very low-cost labor. When panic ensued in the late 1990s over the "Millennium Bug", India had a large base of experienced and low-cost software engineers familiar with the legacy systems that had become unfamiliar to engineers in the markets in which they were developed.

Combined with new data-transmission technologies and strong project-management capabilities, the Indian software community has emerged as a world-class, low-cost player, in the top right of the industry structure framework. At this stage, firms like Infosys, Tata and Wipro are beginning to compete directly with their former customers such as Accenture, IBM

Global Services and EDS. However, the chessboard is far from fully played out, as these global firms migrate significant activity to India to capture some of the key sources of Indian firms' advantage (low-cost, high-quality labor).

Implications for network development

Make or buy?

Firms expanding internationally constantly face choices of whether to make or buy. In general, acquisitions for international expansion are more effective when local scale is the critical differentiator – when it is hard to leverage the global-scale position into a local-market position. In addition, properly integrated acquisitions can provide companies with a boost to global scale in an industry undergoing rapid consolidation.

Four key principles can help guide acquisition strategy:

- Acquiring and successfully integrating is a skill that requires captive experience. "Serial acquirers" – those firms that systematically, in good times and bad, make acquisitions, will generally win out over those who only occasionally make acquisitions.[3]
- The complexity of gaining control of and integrating acquisitions in multiple countries means that fewer acquisitions, spaced over multiple years, generally win over rapid acquisitions.
- Given a choice between gaining greater scale in an existing market, or building a series of sub-scale positions in multiple markets, a firm will almost always benefit from greater scale in fewer markets.
- Many firms are surprisingly willing to take much higher risks with an acquisition then they are for a major organic expansion – which is frequently a mistake. As an example, several global and regional banks (for example, Standard Chartered, ABN Amro, DBS Bank, United Overseas Bank) spent heavily to evaluate acquisition opportunities in Indonesia in the years immediately following the Asian crisis. None was able to close a significant deal. Citibank, meanwhile, concentrated its efforts in Indonesia on expanding the number of branches and ATMs serving the market directly. As

BusinessWeek noted, "Taking advantage of liberal new bank rules, [Citibank] signed leases for 61 branches, most the size of a public rest room – enough to accommodate an ATM and an attendant. Smart move. The number of accounts rose 300% from 1998 to 1999; most were opened by upscale Indonesians leery of local banks. Citi earned a 100% return on its $10 million investment in the new branches in their first 12 months of operation."[4] Citibank has emerged as the clear market leader in Indonesia's retail consumer segment, with a relatively low-risk organic approach.

Shortcuts to market access and network development.

In between organic growth and acquisitions are "short-cuts" – strategic moves that promise some of the benefits of acquisitions or partnerships. These include equity joint ventures, strategic alliances and non-equity partnerships across the supply chain. In all situations, it is important to distinguish alliances between "two giants" and those alliances that involve a "global" with a "local" player.

Joint ventures are like Siamese twins: on paper four eyes, four hands and four legs might appear to be an advantage; in fact, most twins prefer to live separately. Joint ventures tend to slow decision-making, raise overhead costs, and fail to attract the best management of either company because they carry the potential of being "stranded". If cost advantage or differentiation are the twin poles that guide international expansion strategy, then joint ventures tend to be "stuck in the middle" against a focused, 100%-controlled entity.

Joint ventures have the potential to work in "naturally local businesses", and should almost always be avoided in "naturally global" businesses. Joint ventures are generally appropriate as a means to gain preferred local-market access, to share the financing costs of a local venture, or as temporary structures for a specific project (for example, a real-estate development).

To facilitate market access and speed entry into the Chinese market, for instance, Volkswagen successfully partnered with Shanghai Automotive Industry Corporation (SAIC). SingTel's savvy leverage of joint ventures with the Ayala family (Globe Telecom) and the Shinawatra Group (Thailand) demonstrated a respect for "local rules" as well as an ability to share some of the risks and benefits of local-market participation. As the case studies in this book help to explain, success depends in part on control by the multinational partner of key operating and finance positions. However, don't believe the press releases; most foreign partners would prefer to buy out their local partners if regulation permitted and the price was fair.

Coca-Cola's bottling franchises, Starbucks' local joint ventures to access real estate, and the hotel industry's leasing model are good examples of a long-term approach deploying joint ventures to spread the financing costs of market expansion (as well as to improve the quality of market access). One cautionary note is that the legal safeguards taken for granted in OECD countries are often lacking in emerging Asian markets.

Many companies enter into unfavorable joint ventures because they overestimate the benefits of being "first mover", or are simply out-negotiated by savvy local entrepreneurs. All too often, joint ventures become disadvantageous once markets open up to competition, and better-capitalized, lower-cost competitors move in to disrupt the cosy market structure which existed prior to deregulation. Examples include several Pepsi joint ventures in China, Deutsche Telecom's investments in Celcom and Satelindo, and unsuccessful joint ventures in India such as HP/HCL and Fiat/Premier Automobiles.

Most companies are better off forming formal, long-term "buyer-supplier" relationships with key partners based on contracts rather than shared equity. For example, HP's long-term relationship with Venture Manufacturing has given HP significant cost benefits and supply flexibility while helping to build a major new company in Singapore. Long-term purchasing relationships have numerous advantages, including keeping the goals of the relationship visible, maintaining flexibility so partners can change commercial terms and commitment as market circumstances and regulation evolve, and maintaining market discipline in the relationship.

Crafting values and culture for global growth – the role of leaders

Words like "values" and "culture" are often used interchangeably, when the relationship between them is critical for prescribing the setting for leadership of international companies. The values of a firm are a set of shared beliefs about how the firm should serve its major stakeholders –

customers, employees and shareholders. Culture is how shared values and beliefs are translated into how things are done and how people behave. A cohesive culture is more responsive to direction from the center, and is less likely to stumble as a result of miscommunication. Yet, the same efficiency reduces the potential to attract diverse talent and tailor business approaches to the local market. Managing these trade-offs is the role of a leader in a multinational, who must make explicit the implicit values of the company, integrate the values into the culture and practices of the company, and recognize which changes in the business environment (often created by internationalization, changes in industry structure, or maturation of the industry lifecycle) mandate shifts in the firm's culture.

How can leadership encourage and reinforce a culture that is both cohesive and outwardly focused? We find this is a topic that captures significant mindshare from the chief executives of the world's leading multinationals.

The first step of international leadership is to make explicit the implicit values of the company, values that are relevant to your customers, employees and shareholders regardless of nationality. In Bain & Company, we focus on a set of values embodied in the concept of "True North" – a willingness to confront the conventional wisdom (magnetic north), whatever the consequences, when our understanding of the situation dictates a more appropriate direction (true north). While key cultural elements of Bain are adapted to local market conditions (including how "true north" recommendations are communicated to our clients and employees), the core value is constant and perpetual.

The values of a firm are generally established by the firm's founders, and are shaped by successive leaders. One reason founder-entrepreneurs are so interesting is that they are generally outspoken about their values, and there is generally a clear linkage between these values and their personal behavior. It is hard to imagine Microsoft without a "techie" chief executive, Oracle without a flamboyant chief executive, or Apple without an innovative chief executive (even though they tried twice). Subsequent leaders should make a commitment to articulating the values that guided the founders, guide them, and guide the company.

Even at the early stages of internationalization, the culture of a firm is far more complex than a mirror of the "home country" national culture. Thus, although U.S. retailers Wal-Mart and Neiman Marcus are both from the South, their cultures are hardly "southern" and are very different from each other. Similar differences can be found between automakers Toyota and Honda, hotel dynasties formed by overseas Chinese like the Kweks, the Kuoks and the Ongs, and Thai banks like Thai Farmers Bank and Bangkok Bank.

Indeed, the best-run international companies don't reflect the home country at all. They have a firm culture, which has evolved to be highly adaptable without losing sight of the shared values that inform any strong culture. Nestlé, which has factories or operations in almost every country in the world, has built such a culture. When the company expands to new overseas markets, local businesspeople are hired and trained in the values of Nestlé, including its selling strategies and operating systems, adjusted for each market. The company invests millions to educate local employees, tailoring programs by country. Field training for an account specialist in the Philippines, for example, includes selling Maggi bouillon cubes to street-stall vendors. But the strong sense of shared values means Nestlé employees transfer readily from country to country without becoming disoriented or losing focus. Indeed, strong values keep Nestlé's culture intact while the company continues to refine necessary local adoptions.

Failure to address cultural issues can lead to crisis – often on an accelerated basis in a merger, but also in a "slow death" when a firm is unable to respond to changes in the business or social environment. The poor financial performance and unacceptable safety records of several Asian passenger airlines dominated by military cultures, the clear disregard for the law and the rights of minority shareholders by several now-bankrupt Korean *chaebols*, and the lack of inclusiveness of women in a number of Asian enterprises are examples of the importance of values and culture in an Asian enterprise. Multinational Asian companies need to address this issue directly at a level of commitment far above a debate on "Asian values versus Western values".

Returning to a key paradigm, businesses that compete primarily on costs tend to require more uniform and cohesive cultures, while firms competing on product or service differentiation need to develop an organization that embraces and capitalizes on diversity. The examples provided by Sony, Kikkoman and others in Chapters 2 and 3 of this book aptly illustrate the importance of a strong – and adaptable – culture in successful global expansion.

Network development at different stages of internationalization

Export stage: At the first stage of market development, a firm generally exports from its home base. Representative offices may be established to provide a legal structure for exports. When Sony branched out overseas in the 1950s, for instance, it began selling transistor radios through local sales representatives and distributors. The key success factors include:

- Recruiting and managing an overseas sales force (which is generally interacting with wholesalers and distributors, not end-customers)
- Responding to customer feedback to innovate products and services
- Supply-chain management
- Financial control and treasury
- Pricing and hedging strategies
- After-sales service.

Companies generally set up an international division that manages virtually all interfaces with the international customers.

First country operations: At this stage, a company sets up an overseas entity with a broader set of value-chain activities overseas – potentially direct distribution, overseas manufacturing or simply a local customization capability. Picking the right country is critical. Companies that compete on cost should view overseas expansion as a means to improve the global cost position, by providing a base for low-cost manufacture or potentially greater purchasing scale. An example of this would be Sony's initial emphasis on the U.S. market for its electronics products. If differentiation is the basis for a company's competitive position, then the criteria for selecting a country would be weighted more heavily towards establishing presence in markets viewed as innovative or "leading-edge". An example of the latter would be Starbucks' foray into Japan as a precursor to a broader Asian expansion, or Kikkoman's first moves into the U.S.

Where customer needs are relatively similar, companies will find markets that exhibit characteristics common to the home market easier to penetrate. Consider Osim, the Singaporean health-products company, which systematically expanded in Asia with a consistent brand and market positioning. In industries where cost is the primary basis of competition, companies do better to look for markets that are nearer to the home market, to take advantage of the home-country cost base in the new country – as Li & Fung did with its initial focus on China (see Chapter 3).

At this stage, companies must develop new capabilities for the new markets:

- Overseas manufacturing and supply-chain management
- Recruiting suppliers and distributors to replicate the relevant portions of the home-market value chain
- More significant financial and legal control infrastructure
- Human-resource policies that can adapt to local market conditions, as well as attract, develop and motivate local talent
- Transfer-pricing mechanisms.

Unless global-scale requirements compel a company to move very quickly through this expansion stage, most companies benefit from staying at "two countries" for several years, until the ability to run an overseas operation profitably is demonstrated. Companies often make the mistake of expanding too quickly at this stage, developing a series of sub-scale positions, or entering the "wrong markets", because the experience of the first expansion has not been fully captured.

Multinational: At this stage a company begins expanding into multiple countries. Depending on the nature of competition, the firm should either look to markets that improve its global scale and cost position, or markets that share similar customer needs and requirements to its successful home market.

Key capabilities that need to be developed at this stage include:

- Management of a multi-divisional structure, organized by geography or product division, or some form of hybrid (for example, a product-based back-end, geographically segmented front-end matrix)
- Sophisticated financial management (accounting, corporate finance, M&A, treasury)
- Strategic-planning capability
- Multi-plant operations.

At this stage, most firms face a decision about whether to organize by region or by product line. In our experience, most firms operate more effectively with a regional structure. If product lines are large enough, then the regional structure can be replicated for multiple products. Firms that try to manage through "global product lines" generally end up too far from end-customers to effectively tailor their products, with high, duplicative overhead structures, and very poor coordination across product groups.

Companies often stumble by entering too many small markets that do not have a material impact on financial potential, but unnecessarily complicate management and introduce significant risks into the business. Ahold's simultaneous international expansion into Latin America, Eastern Europe and Southeast Asia illustrates the eventual costs of such an approach. In the end, Ahold was unable to invest to create "leadership economics" in any individual market.

Global entity: A "global entity" is viewed as a "holy grail" by many firms – and is just about as rare. Global entities effectively have no "center". They operate in many countries, with separate country-specific value chains that undergo continuous improvement; top managers are drawn from multiple countries; innovation occurs in multiple markets; and end-consumers are indifferent to the company's origins.

Becoming a global entity in some ways represents a by-product of success as a multinational – how to simultaneously become a low-cost player while responding to the diverse requirements of the customer base. With the exception of a few industries at the extremes of Bain's internationalization framework, most companies are forced to manage the inevitable tensions by managing diversity.

The most important "capability" for a global company is to explicitly articulate values, which guides decision-making across the diversity of the value chain, management, product line and end-customers. In this book, Sony's success in participating in every major market, across a broad set of product lines, with highly distributed research, product development and operations is one of the best examples of a global company. However, Sony's current financial challenges also serve to illustrate the complexities and risks of a global company – at what point is a smaller, more focused, low-cost player able to whittle away at their dominant global position, as Dell did with Compaq, or Nintendo with Sega?

Advantages of the right network

The infrastructure a company will need to globalize, then, is directly related to the industry structure, the key strategic levers for the business, the relative competitive position of the company, and the stage of international expansion. When companies design and build an international network that addresses these needs, and sustain it with appropriate levels of investment, overseas growth becomes real. What's more, their domestic businesses frequently develop new momentum, as well. The profitable foreign-growth companies in our survey tended to outperform their domestic competitors and build even stronger core businesses in their primary markets. It seems that the words of the German writer Goethe apply to companies as well as travellers: "Go to foreign countries and you will know the good things you possess at home."

▲ LEVERAGING FINANCE: THE CASE OF CHINESE ENTERPRISES

Kwong Ki Chi
Former Chief Executive, Hong Kong Exchanges and Clearing Limited

Listing in Hong Kong has provided an important conduit for Chinese enterprises to gain access to the global capital markets and, in many cases, to create international exposure and improved reputation. But listing also assists, and sometimes forces, many other changes, ranging from a clearer articulation of strategy through to improved accounting and governance standards. Making these changes to their business strategies, structures and processes in order to meet the requirements of a Hong Kong listing, therefore, has an important by-product: it means these companies begin to build an international financial, reporting and governance infrastructure. Building this infrastructure represents an important step on the road to becoming a truly global company.

Introduction

When mainland China announced its "Open Door" policy in 1978, it embarked on a gradual process of liberalizing successive sectors of the economy. The market-opening process has gathered pace in recent years, supported by China's accession to the World Trade Organization (WTO), which became effective in January 2001. Although some sectors remain closed or subject to controls, and there are strict controls on capital-account convertibility, great progress has been made in the 25 years since the open-door policy began.

In the centrally planned economy, all large enterprises were controlled by the state and there were few, if any, private enterprises. The state-owned enterprises (SOEs) were required to produce in accordance with the plan rather than in response to market demand, and their internal management structures were thereby constrained. The enterprise accounting system, derived from that of the former Soviet Union, was not designed to identify individual company profitability but rather to account to the central authorities for the allocation of assets under the plan. Individual management and staff lacked incentives to improve the enterprises' performance. And the enterprises were often responsible not only for the production of goods for sale but also for the provision of welfare, pensions, schooling and hospitals for their local communities. One of the great challenges in the transition from a centrally planned to a free-market economy was, therefore, how to convert the SOEs into modern commercial enterprises.

Although China faced considerable challenges in its transition process, it did have one advantage – its proximity to the developed-market economy of Hong Kong. Hong Kong, which became a special administrative region of China in 1997, was well equipped to support the transition process. As an international financial center, Hong Kong was able from an early stage to intermediate between Chinese enterprises and global investors, enabling the former to raise capital and restructure themselves for the market.

The first section of this paper describes the development and current status of Hong Kong as a listing-and-trading venue for Chinese enterprises. The next section compares Hong Kong with other overseas stock markets, and with the domestic Chinese markets. The third section looks at China's internationalization strategy for its enterprises, and shows how listing in Hong Kong provided valuable support to this process. The fourth shows how listing in Hong Kong has helped Chinese companies to build some of the key elements of the international infrastructure that will act as a solid foundation for globalization in the future. The conclusion looks at possible future trends – how the role of the Hong Kong stock market in helping China enterprises to globalize is likely to develop in the future.

Hong Kong's role in listing China's enterprises

Historical development

From its establishment, Hong Kong has acted as an entrepot, an intermediary for trade, between China and the wider world. Hong Kong has been an enclave – a small region on the border that allowed China access to international goods and services while minimizing foreign contact and so maintaining the stability of its economy and society as a whole. The listing of China enterprises in Hong Kong in recent years is the latest manifestation of Hong Kong's historic role.

Shortly after the announcement of the Open Door policy, Hong Kong manufacturers began relocating their production facilities into mainland China, particularly in the Shenzhen and Pearl River Delta area adjacent to Hong Kong. By the mid 1980s, many of these manufacturers were listing on the Stock Exchange of Hong Kong (now HKEx). Thus, at an early stage, Hong Kong became a venue for raising capital for investment in the mainland. The community of market professionals in Hong Kong – investment bankers, lawyers, accountants and asset valuers – developed the skills to handle the mainland environment.

Mainland enterprises began investing in Hong Kong as well. Some of these enterprises grew and listed on the stock market, examples being the CITIC Pacific group in the 1980s and China Travel in 1992. These were early examples of China-related listings, later known as "red chips".

In December 1990, China launched its own stock market in Shanghai, with Shenzhen following in July 1991. However, these markets were small and could not support larger capital-raisings. Issuers' access was restricted by a quota system. At the same time, the rapid growth of the economy and progressive liberalization demanded more capital. It was natural for enterprises to look to Hong Kong. A number of enterprises restructured themselves under a foreign (Hong Kong)-incorporated company and applied to list on the SEHK as red chips. Some of these pioneers were well received by Hong Kong investors. The IPO of one, Denway, was 656 times oversubscribed.

From 1992, China-related enterprises also began to seek listings in overseas markets other than Hong Kong. The first known case was Brilliance China, which listed as a foreign-incorporated enterprise on the New York Stock Exchange (NYSE) in October 1992. To date, these listings on overseas market other than Hong Kong have been less numerous, and some of these enterprises cross-listed in Hong Kong at the same time.

Issuers tend to prefer the red-chip format because it enables them to undertake further capital-raising outside China. However, the Chinese authorities sought a more controlled channel for such listings, and also wished their enterprises to list directly in Hong Kong without the interpolation of a foreign holding company. Thus the H-share route was developed – "H" standing for "Hong Kong" – by which a China-incorporated enterprise listed in Hong Kong. The SEHK developed a specific set of additional rules for Chinese enterprises – to supplement the less-developed state of China corporate and securities law at that time – and entered into a five-party Memorandum of Regulatory Cooperation with the China Regulatory Securities Commission (CSRC), the Shanghai and Shenzhen stock exchanges and Hong Kong's Securities and Futures Commission (SFC). The objective of these arrangements was to place the investor in such enterprises on a par with investors in other companies listed on the SEHK.

H-share enterprises were required to comply with all the normal rules of the exchange. However, in addition, a new chapter of the SEHK's listing rules was written specifically to address their special circumstances. The enterprises were required to incorporate into their constitutive documents the contents of a new appendix to the listing rules – which essentially reproduced many of the provisions of the Hong Kong Companies Ordinance concerning shareholders' rights and directors' duties. The enterprises were required to prepare an accountant's report on listing, and financial statements thereafter, which complied with International Accounting Standards (IAS). In respect of differences between IAS and China accounting regulations, the enterprises were required to prepare a reconciliation. And in cases of dispute between management and shareholders, the company was bound to subject itself to arbitration in Hong Kong or Beijing.

Over the years since then, the mainland regulations have improved. For example, China now has a Companies Law and a Securities Law. The CSRC taps international experience in the operation and development of the market. It has signed some 20 memoranda of understanding with overseas regulatory institutions. To reflect these improving standards, some of the original Hong Kong rules have been modified. Originally, the

H-share enterprise was required to retain a financial adviser for three years after listing to maintain a channel of communication between the enterprise and the SEHK; that period has now been reduced to one year.

China enterprises have listed on other overseas markets as well. Two listed on the NYSE in 1994, such stocks becoming known as "N shares". One enterprise was listed in Singapore in 1997 "S shares". One B-share issue obtained a secondary listing in Singapore, and another was listed in GDR form on the London Stock Exchange. Several China-related enterprises obtained listings in Australia and Singapore. At one point, the strategy seemed to be to establish a beachhead for China enterprises on most of the world's major markets. However, the secondary-market turnover proved disappointing in most cases, and increasingly issuers focused their overseas efforts on Hong Kong.

The listing of China enterprises in Hong Kong progressed in accordance with changing global sentiment on China. However, in recent years, China's growth story has stood out as other countries in the region experienced recession in the wake of the Asian financial crisis, or were affected by the bursting of the technology bubble in the U.S. and elsewhere. Global investors have therefore kept returning to China and, in particular, to China enterprises listed in Hong Kong.

One major development of recent years has been the listing in Hong Kong of very large-scale state-owned/related enterprises as H shares or red chips. Examples include China Mobile, Petrochina, CNOOC and China Unicom. These enterprises were well received by global investors because they had dominant positions in their respective industries and, in most cases, had made a commitment to restructuring and adopting modern management methods, including investor relations. Some have also performed well. One of them, Petrochina, made profits of RMB46.9 billion (US$5.7 billion) in 2002.

Another trend has been for mainland private enterprises to seek a listing in Hong Kong. These enterprises did not enjoy as good access to the domestic capital market as the SOEs, and so were especially keen to tap the Hong Kong market. The first private enterprise H share listed in Hong Kong in December 2001, and more have listed as H shares since then. Hong Kong by this time had launched its Growth Enterprise Market (GEM), targeted at emerging companies with growth potential, and this proved an attractive venue for mainland private enterprises. At least four of these have listed as H shares on GEM. Many more have chosen to list in Hong Kong through a holding vehicle incorporated overseas, thereby circumventing some of the restrictions still imposed within China on the transaction of shares of China-incorporated companies.

Current status

Hong Kong is currently the leading overseas listing venue for mainland China-related enterprises. At February 2003, HKEx listed 148 China-related enterprises – 72 red chips and 76 H shares, which contributed 26% of its capitalization and 39% of its trading volume in the first two months of 2003. There are some 25 enterprises (13 of them China-incorporated) listed on the New York Stock Exchange, and a few listed in London, Singapore, Australia and other venues. Twelve of the NYSE-listed enterprises and some LSE-listed enterprises are also listed in Hong Kong and, in most cases, the bulk of the trading takes place in Hong Kong. In fact, some enterprises that initially sought only a U.S. listing, such as Brilliance China, have now applied for and obtained an additional listing on HKEx.

Why is Hong Kong successful in trading mainland China stocks? Hong Kong is seen by global investors on the one hand as the international "home market" for these stocks. On the other hand, mainland enterprises themselves, facing constraints on listing within the mainland, see Hong Kong as the most accessible international market. Hong Kong retail investors, as well as institutions, trade these stocks actively. Other merits of a Hong Kong listing include the analyst following; the experience and service quality of the intermediaries and professionals; the proximity to China, which facilitates information flow (and hence price formation); and the cultural proximity of investors. Statistics show only very limited participation in the market from mainland-based investors but, in time, as current restrictions are lifted, such participation will surely grow.

In one of its periodic surveys, HKEx asked its listed China-related enterprises what factors were most important to them in seeking an overseas listing. The results are shown in Figure 7.2 below. Mainland issuers are most concerned about the market's fund-raising capability and the market's international status and reputation for quality. The price-earnings (PE) ratio is also important to them.

Figure 7.2 Factors in selecting the venue for listing for mainland companies

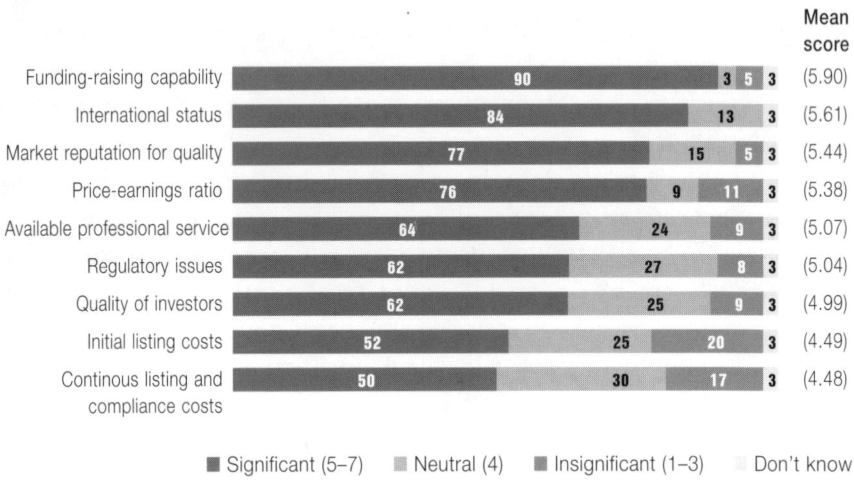

Note: Rating was on a scale of 1-7; the neutral score was 4.
Source: HKEx Primary Market Survey 2001/02

Stock-market developments in mainland China

Launched in 1990, the two mainland stock exchanges have grown in size and in their importance to the Chinese economy. Together, the two exchanges list more than 1,220 companies, with a total market capitalization of RMB3,833 billion (US$462 billion) at the end of 2002. Trading volume in 2002 was RMB2,799 billion (US$338 billion), the 16th-highest of world stock exchanges. However, to date, foreign portfolio investors are not allowed to participate in the A-share market. They are restricted to the narrow B-share segment, launched in 1992. At December 2002, the B-share market comprised 111 enterprises, with a capitalization of RMB80 billion (US$9.7 billion). B-share enterprises have not been very well received by foreign investors. In February 2001, the authorities permitted mainland citizens holding foreign currency to trade in the B-share market, and it is understood that the market is now more or less dominated by domestic investors.

In November 2002, the authorities announced the qualified foreign institutional investor (QFII) scheme, under which large foreign institutional investors will be permitted to invest in A shares subject to certain procedures on remittance and limits of 20% on aggregate investment and 10% on individual QFII investment. The restrictive nature of the scheme means that large-scale foreign participation is unlikely in the near term. However, the direction of gradual market opening has been set, and it can be expected that participation in the mainland stock market by foreign investors will increase.

Of course, the opening of the mainland market to direct foreign investment has implications for Hong Kong's role in listing mainland enterprises. Nonetheless, the mainland's need for international capital remains immense, and is unlikely to be satisfied by the limited foreign-investment money that will come in for the time being under the QFII scheme. Controls on the convertibility of the RMB set limits on the impact of the scheme. Even in the longer run, there should still be a large role for Hong Kong because of its higher quality standards and international dimension.

The internationalization strategy of China's enterprises

Since the adoption of the Open Door policy in 1978, there have been numerous attempts to reform the SOEs. However, these have had only limited success.

One strategy (*Zhua da, fang xiao* – "Seize the big, let go the small") was to merge the larger enterprises to create globally competitive giants, while leaving the smaller enterprises to make their way as best they could. The experience of Japan and Korea in developing large-scale globally competitive firms was cited as a model. The Asian financial crisis superseded this plan, and the problems experienced by both Japanese and Korean corporates also made their example less appealing. Nonetheless, merger within China's industrial base, which in many sectors is highly fragmented, remains an ongoing theme.

In the last few years, the recently retired premier Zhu Rongji launched a determined push to restructure the SOEs, with a view to completing the process within three years. This ambitious target has not been met, but the initiative did at least highlight the urgency of dealing with the SOE problem and resulted in the restructuring and subsequent listing overseas of some of the very large SOEs.

In the meantime, large numbers of SOEs were being listed on the mainland stock markets each year.[5] It was hoped that the injection of investors as new stakeholders in the enterprise would stimulate corporate governance and improve enterprise performance. However, the rather speculative retail investor base in China did not do much to stimulate corporate governance measures among issuers. And since these enterprises still continued to be controlled by the state as majority shareholder, it was difficult to break out of the existing mode. More recent attempts to strengthen governance by appointing independent directors – on the Western model – proved difficult for the same reason. Nor could the state divest in any significant way its shares on the stock market without causing serious market disruption. For example, the government's attempt to move in this direction during 2002 had to be aborted because of the negative effect on an already declining stock market. The authorities have begun exploring alternatives, such as direct sales of state shareholdings or assets to foreign or domestic investors. But these efforts are no more than marginal at present.

Listing SOEs on an overseas market such as Hong Kong offered a way out of the impasse. While the state remained the major shareholder even in such overseas listings, the greater weight of foreign institutional investors, as compared with the predominantly retail domestic investors, had an effect on enterprise governance. Enterprise management had to prepare themselves for overseas roadshows, to develop business plans and communicate them to investment bankers and analysts, and to report periodically on their progress. Of course, the process was not entirely smooth, particularly with the earlier listings. However, experience was built up on all sides. By the late 1990s, the authorities were starting to approve for overseas listing giant enterprises that were leaders in their respective industries, profitable and with good growth prospects. Many of these enterprises prepared carefully for listing by exposing their management to the international business environment, engaging consultants to develop a business-orientated internal structure, and even engaging in joint ventures or strategic partnerships with multinationals or overseas acquisitions.

The drive to upgrade enterprise performance became more urgent with China's accession to the WTO. In many sectors of the Chinese economy, because of rivalries between different localities, production is divided among numerous enterprises, none of which has sufficient economies of scale. The enterprises themselves lack technology, market know-how, strategic planning and modern management methods and systems. When barriers to foreign entrants are phased out under WTO commitments, these enterprises will find themselves facing foreign competition. The merger and overseas listing of such enterprises became an important means to improve enterprise competitiveness.

Benefits of overseas listing

The restructuring of large SOEs in preparation for listing typically follows a formula. Generally the SOE is a giant company, a sector leader, with more or less a monopoly. It has non-commercial activities such as the provision of education, welfare and health services to the community. These have to be taken out of the listed entity and non-essential staff laid off. The parent is left carrying the non-commercial element. As a result, the parent is anxious to be paid dividends by the listed entity. This has a good result: the dividend payout ratio is high, and the process is transparent. Also, the parent itself becomes freer to privatize or close down or sell the non-commercial elements: it no longer has to carry them indefinitely. So the restructuring process is not a zero-sum game. The core (listed) business becomes more profitable, and the non-core (non-listed parent) becomes more efficient. It is a win-win situation.

For private enterprises, the primary benefit of overseas listing is access to capital, which in the state-dominated domestic financial market is often difficult for them to obtain. Yet the discipline of listing also benefits the enterprise by forcing management to develop plans and professional organization structures. Private property rights in China are still imperfectly established, so overseas listing can reinforce the position of the enterprise and of the proprietor himself.

For more specialized enterprises, overseas listing is also beneficial. China's commercial banks will soon face direct foreign competition and urgently need to improve their competitiveness. For banks, the non-performing loan (NPL) problem is the major barrier to their commercial development, but there are political as well as economic difficulties in tackling NPLs. The process of overseas listing provides a rationale and a discipline to overcome these barriers and forge institutions that are competitive and attractive to investors. A start on this sector was made in 2002 with the listing in Hong Kong of the overseas operations of the Bank of China group. The insurance sector is currently under preparation for listing in Hong Kong, too.

Listing China enterprises overseas is beneficial to the enterprise, and ultimately to the country. Foreign investors and regulators are more choosy, scrutinizing the company carefully, and so stimulate good governance. This can create a virtuous circle of improving quality.

Listing as an important step toward globalization

The process of listing in Hong Kong has helped to upgrade the performance of the enterprises concerned, making them more internationally competitive. These enterprises in turn provide a model to others in the mainland, fostering a general climate of improvement.

The process of listing in Hong Kong exposes the enterprise to the international environment. The enterprise must communicate with, and sell itself to, global investment bankers and institutional investors and analysts. Nor is this a one-off process. In order to maintain investors' interest in their stock, after listing it is necessary for the enterprise to maintain contact continuously with international investors and the media. This is not just a matter of issuing press releases and financial reports, important though these are. As a listed company, the enterprise should ensure that its top management visit major institutional investors periodically, say twice a year, to brief them on the company's development. The experience of listing thus provides ongoing and intimate support for the enterprise's internationalization process. By listing in Hong Kong, the enterprise gains international recognition, which in turn is valuable in its dealings with business partners, customers and suppliers.

In addition to the direct internationalization benefits, there are also the indirect benefits of listing. In order to present itself as an attractive investment vehicle, the typical Chinese enterprise needs to restructure. Listing is the catalyst for such restructuring. Management also needs to be trained to deal with the international advisers and investors – again, listing is the catalyst for a change in mindset.

The benefits of listing in Hong Kong for the China enterprise seeking internationalization are summarized in Table 7.1 below.[6]

Some of the key elements of globalization include defining a clear strategy; building capabilities; deal-making and investment; forming an integrated international network; and managing knowledge internationally. As the Table shows, listing on an international exchange such as Hong Kong can help a company put some of the foundations of each of these elements firmly in place.

Table 7.1 The benefits of an international listing to globalization efforts

Element of Global Infrastructure	Contribution of International Listing
Clearly defined strategy	• Investment banker and investor scrutiny helps refine strategy • Consultants may help articulate strategy
Experience building	• Repeated shareholder communication reinforces "lessons" of global marketplace • Management regularly visit overseas investors
Deal-making and investment capabilities	• New emphasis on selection and training of management team • Build enterprise "self-knowledge" through internal restructuring • Listing makes new management incentives available (for example, options)
International integration	• Listing helps build global brand name • Listing facilitates further global capital-raising and expansion
International knowledge management	• Listing process and post-listing experience help enterprise absorb international knowledge • Exposure to investor scrutiny helps enterprise understand its international value

Conclusion

This paper has discussed how the process of listing in Hong Kong, and the experience of being a listed company, helps China's enterprises build the infrastructure foundation for globalization. Looking forward, in the context of the opening of China's market under WTO commitments and the QFII scheme, what are the prospects for the enterprises continuing to use the Hong Kong stock market in this manner? Will a listing in Hong Kong still be useful to them in acclimatizing to the international environment?

I believe that listing in Hong Kong will continue to be attractive to China's enterprises, even under WTO conditions. In fact, I suggest that there is scope for Hong Kong to contribute even more to this process than is currently the case.

Firstly, the opening of the mainland economy, although proceeding rapidly in some areas, still has a long way to go. Even when existing WTO commitments have been fully met in a few years time, China will not be a fully open economy comparable with, say, the Hong Kong economy. China's developing status, dispersed geography, cultural traditions and regional differences will continue to present hurdles to full interaction with the global environment; and some form of regulatory restrictions will remain for the long term. Convertibility of the currency is a major factor not subject to the WTO timetable.

Secondly, the mainland stock market is opening only gradually to foreign participants. The QFII scheme is quite restrictive. There are perhaps even more restrictions on foreign financial intermediaries operating in the securities and futures markets. Barriers to China's enterprises gaining access to international capital in the domestic stock market are likely to remain for the long term.

Thirdly, quality standards in the mainland market are unlikely to rise quickly to Hong Kong levels. Even when good regulations are in place, the experience of implementing them and building precedents and cases will take years. Hong Kong is likely to retain a quality edge over the mainland markets for a long time to come, and therefore it is likely to continue to attract international capital for the long term as well.

If, as suggested here, Hong Kong is likely to retain advantages over the mainland markets for the long term, consideration could be given to making greater use of these advantages to China's benefit. For example, there may be scope for mainland investors to invest in their own enterprises via the Hong Kong market. This would be the essence of the qualified domestic institutional investor (QDII) scheme currently being discussed by the mainland authorities. The QDII scheme would enable mainland investors to gain experience of international investment practice, while allowing the authorities to retain a degree of control over the process. The benefit to the mainland enterprises would be the opening of a further pool of interested investors. This would enable more of the better enterprises to obtain capital in Hong Kong, and climb more rapidly up the internationalization staircase. Given experience, and subject to proper regulatory oversight, the QDII scheme could even be extended to other investment instruments available in and through the Hong Kong financial markets.

Endnotes

1 This chapter draws substantially on research conducted by James Root and John Smith, first published in the *European Business Forum*.

2 For more information on this study, please refer to www.ebfonline.com issue 14, "Matching Global Growth to Industry Structure".

3 See "Your Best M&A Strategy", Sam Rovit and Catherine Lemire, *Harvard Business Review*, March 2003

4 *BusinessWeek*, February 26, 2001.

5 Under the central authorities' plan to merge the two markets, Shenzhen stopped accepting new listings in September 2000.

6 This table is based on elements of globalization drawn from A. De Meyer and P.J. Williamson, "Internationalization of Asian Companies – a new era?", INSEAD Working paper, 2002/68/ABA, 2002.

7 International accounting and consulting firms are permitted to conduct a wide scope of business in China. International law firms operate only in representative-office form but also enjoy quite wide business scope. Investment banks are restricted to representative offices and have to staff their assignments from overseas, mainly from Hong Kong.

CHAPTER

8 Evolving Capabilities

Creating networks to extend a company's reach and accessing financing to underwrite new stages of growth are two leading means to develop or extend tangible company assets. In each, the organization moves beyond its current outposts: in the first, by a single-step gain of an entire piece; and in the second, by gradual growth from within. It is hardly coincidental that the push for globalization, especially amongst companies from mainland China, has coincided with a wave of IPOs in domestic and overseas markets, as well as mergers, acquisitions or alliance building with foreign companies. This trend is very much in line with similar moves in Europe or the U.S., where alliance building especially has been used as a means to globalize. The advantage of these two means of company expansion is that neither necessitates surrendering or changing core competitive strengths. Rather, the company can grow without risking current growth.

However, companies that expand – whether through network acquisition or internally driven expansion funded by new investment – all face the task of maintaining organizational coherence. The risk is that expansion may produce growth in assets without a corresponding rise in value, which over time may translate into lost value (if only in opportunity cost). The skill of translating growth in tangible assets to growth in overall value is more commonly associated with system builders, or those who grow their network in a very gradual manner. Companies have to focus on the knowledge that is resident in all parts of their organization and, by doing so, acquire the necessary capabilities that would enable them to achieve efficiency, productivity and improved corporate processes. Two of the key building blocks in this process reflect inward and outward demands: branding and people. Companies that expand across borders encounter new cultures, societies and expectations, both internally with regard to their employees and externally with regard to customers and communities. In contronting these different constituencies, companies may have to adapt management systems or reshape branding and identity, which often demand the "unlearning" of resource-based advantages.

Many Asian companies in the past tended to employ relatives and friends – a practice clearly building on resource-based advantages. Some of Asia's biggest companies or subsidiaries are still run by the founding family – for example, the Charoen Pokphand (CP) Group and Bangkok Bank in Thailand, Chinatrust Commercial Bank in Taiwan, Ayala Group in the Philippines, Cheung Kong Group in Hong Kong, Matsushita in Japan and even Korea's Samsung Group. The belief was that people within the family – having grown up around the company and having had access to privileged information or connections – could add to the company's competitive advantages. In addition, there were also issues of trust: Asians have traditionally preferred to entrust the business to a very narrow circle of individuals, with whom they build long-term relationships. In only a few instances can professional managers overcome this barrier, to become as trusted as family members are from the start.

Different rules apply within the group of friends and relatives. This dichotomy has been articulated, for example, in Japan in *uchi* ("inside") and *soto* ("outside") and the dichotomy is an underlying principle in most Asian countries influenced by Confucianism. Relations within *uchi* are of a preferred nature, they are laid out for the long term, whereas everything *soto* is, by definition, chaos or is of a hostile nature. Lifetime employment within big Japanese companies has been clearly based on the mutual understanding of the corporate *uchi* as a community of fate. Similarly, when a Chinese entrepreneur seizes a business opportunity, he prefers to make a deal based on previously established *guanxi* ("connections") rather than seeking the anonymity of the market. To conclude the deal, the value of the handshake is regarded as being high and unassailable – it is based on trust. Trust-based relationships cannot be easily transferred to different loci within newly globalizing firms. Thus, while in the short term they are foremost amongst the resource-based advantages of a company, in the long term they risk becoming hindrances or obstacles to the company's growth because they are not easily transferred. Companies or founders that are able to expand the boundaries of *uchi* to the outside are more likely to succeed in globalizing because they are able to trust not only "insiders" but also outsiders, as both can be valuable as business partners.

Asian companies that intend to grow their organizations globally are increasingly adjusting their employment practices. It is now mainstream thinking that Asian-style lifetime employment may have hindered flexible adjustments necessary to absorb changes in demand. Sony and Samsung Electronics ended reliance on the lifetime employment practices in favor of merit-based systems. Companies in the second wave of globalization, such as Singapore Telecom, Olam and Li & Fung, invested heavily in state-of-the-art human-resource management systems, even when this meant hiring foreign professionals instead of home-grown managers. Some will say that these companies are stuck in old practices – since Li & Fung continues to be run by the sons of the founder, and Singapore Telecom is run by the son of Singapore's founding father. However, we would contend that, in both cases, the participation of a "family" member in the company's operations has had the effect of professionalizing and advancing the company's human-resources practices rather than the opposite. In both cases, professional managers have been hired to take key positions within the company and its subsidiaries. The roles of the founders, owners and managers are distinct, and it is hardly a coincidence that both companies have developed solid reputations amongst investors for their corporate governance, use of directors and transparency. Our message here is not to discredit wholesale the concept of "family" business but rather to assert that companies which are to globalize successfully must be astute in ascertaining which aspects of the practice to preserve and which to shed in their globalization process. The successful "family business" globalizer will develop the hybrid that fits the company's heritage and growth position.

A second "intangible" to be developed are global brands. Branding in Asia has often lagged behind the U.S. and Europe markets in variety and sophistication. Part of this can be attributed to the fact that markets are not as developed, with companies focused on survival and growth rather than on messaging and image. On the other hand, even Asian companies in developed markets have, until recently, largely emphasized price competition and market share rather than product innovation. Some of Asia's most successful regional companies are actually OEMs (Original Equipment Manufacturers). They make goods for other brands, while their own brands remain unknown. Today Samsung Electronics may have developed a relatively strong brand, but it began as a pure OEM in 1968. It built a manufacturing backbone for many years before making the difficult transition to innovating its own products and building its own image. Today China is called the "factory to the world" – but even though it manufactures for companies around the world, its own brands are relatively unknown. The Guangzhou-based company Galanz is the world market leader in microwaves, supplying the world's leading brands with the most advanced and cost-competitive products, with almost 30% global market share. However, the brand is almost unknown outside China. The situation is replicated in the global markets for televisions, refrigerators, semiconductors and other products.

What does this say about branding in Asia? A corporate brand is much more than the tangible composite of a product's style, function, features, price, models and ingredients. The brand is created in the hearts and minds of consumers – it's an intangible value. In fact, a brand is best thought of as the relationship between the product and its users. Nike is not a shoe or athletic gear – it is a mindset. A Coke is not just a drink, it is an experience, and nowhere in the world is the American Express Card just a piece of plastic. Customers will pay a premium for Nike, Coke and American Express products and services as they trust the reliability and the emotional value of these brands.

It has often been the case in Asia that the emotional content of a brand is somehow underdeveloped. In the 2003 *BusinessWeek* "Global Brand Scorecard", the top ten brands were all American or European. Of the 100 brands listed, only seven came from Asia: Toyota (11th), Honda (18th), Sony (20th), Samsung (25th), Nintendo (32nd), Canon (39th) and Nissan (89th). Of this list, only one, Samsung, is not Japanese. Companies from China and

Southeast Asia do not appear on the list at all. The hegemony of Western brands is easy to understand: they started much earlier than most of their Asian counterparts and so have had more time both to extend their reach and refine their offering to the customer. Asian companies are about to discover the power of strong branding. Samsung Electronics can surely be a role model for the successful creation of a global brand. In the late 1990s, the company launched its brand globally with bulging advertising budgets, including sponsorship of the Olympic Games. Samsung has finally been able to position itself as a premium brand. Sony pursued a similar strategy two decades earlier – the "It's a Sony" culture allowed the company to demand a premium on its products.

Some Asian challengers – particularly Chinese companies – have already established a presence using their own brand names in emerging markets, with products such as household appliances, consumer electronics and motorcycles. The next move is into developed markets, a strategy currently being employed by Haier, China's biggest appliance maker, which is selling refrigerators under its own name in the United States. Legend, China's biggest computer maker, has launched Lenovo as a global brand to position itself for overseas expansion. Some of China's leading companies have clearly discovered the power of global branding. TCL, the leading Chinese consumer-electronics maker, is using a slightly different strategy: it has acquired insolvent European and American makers such as Schneider Electronics and GoVideo and is retaining their brand names. Another coup which made the investment community prick up its ears was TCL's strategic alliance with Thomson, one of Europe's largest electronics companies, in late 2003. This move is undoubtedly catapulting TCL onto the forefront of globalization as it will market its products using the established brand name of Thomson.

Creating and sustaining brands is a complex and expensive endeavor and is a skill that can only be partially purchased (through consulting and public relations firms). It requires clear leadership and knowledge of the company's strengths vis-à-vis its competitors, as well as vision of where the company is going. It took years, and a great deal of money, before Sony and Samsung Electronics were able to establish themselves outside their home markets, and latecomers to globalization will find it no easier. Not only are their home markets becoming more competitive – in line with the opening up of industry and economic liberalization – but the demands of Western consumers are also becoming more complex. A global product cannot be too global, and a local product must appeal to even the consumer on the farthest shore.

This chapter, with contributions from two leading firms in these areas – the executive-search firm Heidrick & Struggles and the public-relations firm Ogilvy – discusses strategies for potential Asian globalizers to approach human resources and branding. Kevin Kelly and Miles Young both have years of experience in Asia which will be useful for latecomers trying to build these capabilities in complex markets. Both capabilities – if available and actively used – are systems-based advantages. They are a sine qua non for Asian companies wishing to become truly global players.

▲ MANAGING PEOPLE

L. Kevin Kelly
Managing Partner, Asia, Heidrick & Struggles International, Inc.

To most Westerners, it is almost an article of faith that business will continue to chart an increasingly international course. By investing directly in foreign markets, as well as by forging multinational networks of suppliers, customers and partners, many enterprises in the United States and Europe are approaching the day when every market is their home market. Yet until the late 1990s, one region of the world successfully resisted the globalization trend. Despite long traditions of trading, entrepreneurialism and commerce, most companies in East Asia and Southeast Asia[1] sat out the rush to internationalize. In this they were aided by capital controls and protectionist trade policies that allowed them to profit by exploiting their local resource- and relationship-based advantages. The home-field edge of East Asian companies was further reinforced by cultural norms and reporting conventions that allowed them to exploit information advantages over customers and competitors alike.

Today, though, the tide in East Asia appears to be turning decisively in favor of internationalization. One factor in this, certainly, is pressure from global capital markets and financial institutions. But East Asian firms and governments may well have withstood that pressure, at least in the medium term, were it not for the shock of the Asian financial crisis of 1997. The brutal economic conditions that followed the shock exposed managerial and strategic weaknesses that had gone unaddressed under the old ways of doing business. After the crisis of 1997, East Asia could no longer ignore the need for new managerial talent – and new managerial mindsets – to face the changed world of competition.

In this chapter, we will draw upon our own experience in the global market for talent, as well as high-level academic research, to present the key leadership and human resources strategies that Asian firms are executing in their efforts to globalize. We will briefly review how countries in the region are adapting to the new environment ushered in by increasing globalization, and we will examine specific local challenges to globalization. Also, we will profile the executive-recruiting environment, highlighting the specific needs and issues that animate the search for the region's next generation of corporate leadership.

Throughout Asia, corporate leaders will find economies and attitudes at different stages of development – from the fully Westernized worldview prevalent in Hong Kong to places like Thailand, where U.S.-style transparency and ethical standards have hardly penetrated. Business must tailor its compensation packages, recruiting pitches and mix of local and expatriate talent to each locale, balancing local considerations with the imperative to mesh the unit with the larger enterprise. As a leading executive-search firm – the first such firm to be licensed to operate in China – we are constantly reminded of organizations' need to maintain a diverse and effective talent pool. One measure of that need is that many of our searches involve finding an expatriate executive to replace a local manager, and just as many involve finding a local manager to replace an expatriate! Generally speaking, executive-recruiting consultants such as Heidrick & Struggles can help corporations develop their recruitment and development strategies, especially if the consultant effectively combines local knowledge with global reach.[2] But there is only one hard-and-fast rule that applies in all environments: Patience is a must. With their accumulation of thousands of years of history and cultural development, the various countries of East Asia cannot be expected to change overnight. But neither can they resist the tide of globalization forever. The organizations that succeed in this region will be those that best manage the tension between the traditional and the contemporary – in their recruiting as well as in their operations.

Geography and human resources in Asia

Any organization's recruiting strategy will be heavily conditioned by the different rates at which internationalization is taking hold throughout East Asia. In Singapore, Hong Kong and Malaysia, for example, internationalization is strongly influenced by local government policies and cultural constraints – findings that underscore the importance of recruiting both local and foreign-born executives who have the experience and communications skills needed to adapt to a wide range of political, cultural and commercial environments. It's safe to say there will never be a surplus of senior executives who can make the transition smoothly from Singapore, where internationalization is spearheaded by large, government-linked companies such as SingTel, DBS and Singapore Airlines, to Hong Kong, where smaller enterprises have recently taken the lead in the drive to internationalize, to Malaysia, where smaller enterprises are stepping up imports to gain much-needed foreign currency while larger enterprises wrestle with the managerial and strategic issues raised by privatization.

Elsewhere in Asia, Japan continues to wrestle with its long-running financial crisis. Its banks, in particular, have yet to come to grips fully with their bad-debt problems. Yet many prominent companies are showing other organizations in the region how to craft a winning globalization strategy. Sony has positioned itself to profit handsomely from the changing dynamics of the music business. And Nissan, under CEO Carlos Ghosn, a true superstar of internationalization, is a case study in the power of transformative leadership. Under Ghosn, Nissan has traded in its old, resource-based competitive advantages for the edge that comes from skillful knowledge management and technological aptitude. Both companies are leading a trend in Japanese business toward younger executives. Nearly every week brings fresh news of a venerable Japanese firm naming a 40-something executive to a senior spot, and we expect this movement to continue.

In Taiwan, corporations such as Acer and Taiwan Semiconductor have successfully leveraged their local advantages into prominent, respected places in the global information-technology supply chain. Skirting the cultural and language barriers posed by the American consumer market, Acer has grown into a go-to player in U.S. contract manufacturing and original-equipment manufacturing. "From our point of view," says Acer CEO Stan Shih, "the biggest upside is working through the well-established channels" in the U.S. Although the company has scaled back its U.S. efforts somewhat in the wake of the bursting of the technology bubble, the company is clearly in the U.S. to stay and is well positioned for its next round of growth. Companies like Acer are omnivorous in their recruiting, seeking talent from mainland China and Taiwan as well as the countries where their international operations are located.

Giant conglomerates such as Samsung Electronics have led the internationalization drive in Korea, often inducing their suppliers to "co-internationalize" with them. Through these efforts, many small and mid-sized companies have expanded into foreign markets, but many of those firms are still struggling to integrate their overseas operations into a fully functioning corporate network. The economies gained from networking – lower supply costs, consolidated back-office functions, and so on – should materialize in coming years, as Korean companies gain expertise in knowledge transfer and learn from the best practices of their more globally experienced rivals. For many Korean companies the key challenge is to hire executives with the communications skills to understand foreign markets as well as maintain a healthy information flow to and from the home office.

Given its vast size and enormous and diverse population, China is, not surprisingly, resistant to attempts at generalization. Most of the major development activity is still concentrated in China's coastal periphery, including the cities of Beijing and Guangzhou, as well as the Pearl River basin, near Hong Kong. But Shanghai is developing rapidly as a manufacturing center, and some companies are beginning to eye China's vast interior for its growth potential. Spurred by the country's acceptance into the World Trade Organization and Beijing's selection as the host city of the 2008 Olympic Games, China is rapidly improving its business environment. That is good news for overseas businesses as well as for local enterprises such as information technology company Lenovo Group, which has posted phenomenal growth by catering to China's vast domestic market. "Being in the WTO, as well as the upcoming 2008 Olympic Games in Beijing, are significant steps forward in China's progress as a strong presence in the international marketplace," says Lenovo Group CEO Yang Yuanqing. "It increases the pressure on Chinese companies to establish themselves in the international arena and simultaneously compete with foreign organizations on their own ground. It will test our skills at collaborating as well as competing, as we look for opportunities for developing the potentially vast consumer market both here and abroad." To meet those tests, both locally based and international enterprises are in the market for three categories of talent: foreign-born executives who are willing to commit to a full immersion in Chinese culture and business; local talent that has benefited from several years of overseas education, exposure and development; and home-grown managers who lack international experience but have the talent and potential to become global leaders.

The managerial mindset – and how it must change

Although many Asian companies have made impressive strides toward full globalization, many others have been reluctant to adapt, and have clung to business strategies that are becoming dangerously outmoded. If forced to single out one factor to account for the uneven pace of globalization among East Asian enterprises and their management, we would have to point to a generalized business mindset that has been slower to change than the business and economic environment. To speed the process of globalization, and to enable success once corporations expand outside their homeland boundaries, Asian leaders will have to reverse that mindset and craft sustainable strategies.

Emphasize reaping network economies over establishing a local presence

Foreign subsidiaries of East Asian firms frequently operate too independently of the home office. Rather than plug into company-wide networks, they tend to resemble small-scale replicas of headquarters. As they learn to share fixed costs across their foreign units, East Asian firms will better position themselves to operate at minimum efficient scale. Many companies will find themselves on a challenging learning curve as they adopt a new generation of human-resources technologies and tools already in wide use in the Western business world.

Rely on systems-based advantages rather than resource-based advantages

Organizations such as Malaysia's Petronas owe their local dominance to access to low-cost labor and materials, preferred access to capital, the protection of a high tariff wall, and licenses obtained through insider relationships. Such advantages are inherently non-transferable. Foreign operations such as BP (British Petroleum), by contrast, rely for their competitive advantage on quality-control systems, marketing expertise, and proprietary technology and know-how. Margie Yang, CEO of Hong Kong-based apparel maker Esquel, frames the imperative facing East Asian businesses this way: "Our company is in a very traditional industry, and in the past it has competed based on cheap labor. Today, it is necessary for us and many other companies in traditional industry sectors to incorporate much better management and foster more technology and creativity within the organization." Tapping system-wide marketing skills is part of this mandate. A growing number of leading East Asian companies have learned that lesson. Thailand's Charoen Pokphand, for example, has successfully transferred its agribusiness template across borders, in the process showing its regional counterparts how to maximize profit opportunities from foreign direct investment.

Depend on competitive advantages that can survive transplant from their local context

This is an especially pertinent issue for Singapore companies, whose home operations can take for granted a well-integrated, smoothly functioning local infrastructure. Attempts to transplant successful Singapore operations to other locales, even within Asia, have often foundered for lack of that local infrastructure advantage. Asian firms are beginning to recognize, though, that the successful transfer of know-how and systems outside their home market requires heavy investments in adaptation and new learning. This trend is likely to gain momentum in tandem with the growing awareness in the region that only people-oriented and knowledge-based strategies can produce a sustainable competitive advantage.

Close capability gaps in key areas

Put simply, the skills that allow companies to thrive at home are not always the same skills that they need to prosper in foreign markets, as Singapore's DBS bank discovered when it acquired Thailand's Thai Danu bank. A heavy reliance on specialization had served DBS well on its home turf, but when the bank needed an executive with a well-rounded skills portfolio to integrate the Thailand acquisition, it came up short. As regional firms gain experience in internationalization, they are learning the value of fitting the right executive to the task at hand. And they are learning the value of partnering with an executive-search firm to match capabilities with challenges.

Use technology, and not simply proximity, to transfer know-how, culture and information

Knowledge transfer is a relatively straightforward matter in organizations that operate with frequent face-to-face encounters among key personnel. But internationalization requires close coordination and communication among people who are widely separated by distance and frequently in different time zones. Although some companies deal with this problem by parachuting in managers from headquarters (at smaller firms, these managers are often members of the controlling family of shareholders), this is only a stopgap solution to a problem with its roots in Asian management systems. Of course, the earliest multinational companies faced the same challenge, and met it by developing a management culture that relies on explicit rules, procedures and memos to facilitate knowledge transfer. As Asian multinationals such as Samsung gain experience overseas, we are likely to see a similar emphasis on explicit knowledge management and transfer among Asian firms.

Operate through integration rather than specialization

Many Asian companies have thrived and prospered by linking vertically integrated units that develop a high degree of competence in a particular function, such as finance, marketing or sales. But such organizations tend to focus on tuning their competence to an ever-higher pitch. They place little emphasis on adapting their skills to the needs of a foreign marketplace, especially when that market is too small to enable the functional unit to realize economies of scale. This is a particular problem for firms based in Singapore and Korea. They appear to have special difficulty adapting their business model, with its emphasis on specialized competencies and strict operating routines, to markets and early-stage business environments that call for cross-functional coordination and improvization. But other Asian firms, such as Malaysia's Petronas, have used a small-team approach successfully, reinforced with intensive management development, to integrate foreign ventures into the larger enterprise. Petronas' successful integration of its ventures in South Africa and Turkmenistan is likely to serve as a model for other companies looking to break out of the limitations imposed by functional silos.

The necessary changes in managerial mindset detailed here have important ramifications for Asian firms seeking to recruit executive talent. The next generation of Asian corporate leaders has a historic opportunity to usher the region into the global era. The undertaking will require leaders who can communicate Western practices, ideas and values while respecting the bedrock strengths of local cultures. It will require executives who can act locally as they live, work and lead globally. "As our company continues to grow domestically and internationally," says the Lenovo Group's Yang Yuanqing, "new attributes of leadership will be called for and these will help to maintain cohesiveness of a larger and more complex organization."

Home-grown or hired gun? The recruiter's dilemma

The changing business environment in Asia demands new ways of thinking, managing and recruiting, both from indigenous corporations and from non-Asian businesses that seek to expand in the region. Let's now examine how progressive organizations are meeting the need for new people, new skills and new attitudes.

Talk to a senior executive operating anywhere in the Asian region, and you will hear a common refrain: Compared to Western countries, especially the U.S., managerial talent is scarce. Chang Sun, managing partner of Warburg Pincus Asia, frames the challenge this way: "The management talent pool is quite thin in Asia. Managers from local companies are typically good at basic functions such as selling and manufacturing, but lack a deep understanding of the concepts of shareholder value, transparency in information disclosure and management systems. Managers at multinational companies are often compartmentalized into one or two functional areas, but don't have the necessary training and experience in finance and general management to lead an entire organization. Then there is the hard choice of an expatriate or a local manager – a Westerner with rich industry experience but little country knowledge or language/cultural understanding, or a local executive who doesn't speak English but is extremely effective in the local environment."

In China, in particular, this shortage, combined with that country's high growth rate and rapid transition to a market economy, has produced a seller's market for talent that in more balanced conditions would be considered marginal. "To a certain extent," says Peter Wong, CEO of Standard Chartered Bank Hong Kong, "history is repeating itself. In Hong Kong 30 or 40 years ago, somebody who had a bachelor's degree was like a king or a queen. It's the same way in China today. People with university degrees from the States or from London suddenly command exorbitant, totally unreasonable salaries."

Even outside China's rapid-growth environment, there is a shortage of home-grown talent possessing the full range of skills necessary to be an effective leader at the highest levels of an organization. In seeking the next generation of leadership talent, some CEOs believe that there are three main priorities: Excellent interpersonal skills, the experience of handling an independent P&L, and management experience in a multinational corporation. At this stage in East Asia's economic development, there is a serious shortage of people who can fully satisfy all three criteria.

To some extent, the shortage is a function of the region's relatively brief experience with capitalism. Many companies, both domestic and international, that operate and recruit in the region face the challenge of developing well-educated, highly skilled managers who have little or no experience with capitalism. It adds an extra dimension to the task of measuring Chinese candidates against their American or European counterparts. Not long ago, a U.S. company was seeking candidates for a high-level post at its Chinese unit. We located a promising prospect; an up-and-coming Chinese executive, educated at the best schools in China and topped off with a degree from MIT. He was literally a rocket scientist. At his interview in the U.S., this candidate was asked to think of how he would try to crack a new market. "What," asked the interviewer, "would you do with a million [U.S.] dollars?" The candidate was unable to answer. Having been raised and educated in a communist state, he simply could not fathom having a million dollars.

Recognizing that they can't meet all their management needs with local hires, many firms look to optimize the limited talent pool by seeding it with what Morris Chang, CEO of Taiwan Semiconductor Manufacturing, calls "repatriates". By this he means Asian-born people who have studied and worked in the U.S., at times for periods as long as 20 years – "blond-haired, blue-eyed Asians", as they're sometimes known. They have absorbed U.S.-style management practices as well as U.S. attitudes towards markets, profits and capital. They have returned to their home country to stay, determined to implement all they have learned in the U.S. on native ground.

Another strategy used by chief executives, albeit with mixed results, is bringing in expatriates – often from the U.S. or Europe – for a limited-duration posting. However, without a commitment to live and work long-term in Asia, the cultural barriers are simply too high for expatriates to overcome during a typical three–five-year tour of duty. "A short-term stay for an expatriate is not useful," states Frank Ning, chairman of China Resources Enterprise, Ltd. "Unless a person plans to stay here five years or more, learns the language, and moves his family here, he or she is not likely to rise to the highest ranks." It is essential for companies recruiting expatriates to look for cultural sensitivity as well as an impressive package of business skills. "We blend our employee base with expatriates," says Peter Wong of Standard Chartered Bank Hong Kong. "This approach has failed many times in other companies when the expat doesn't have the cultural understanding and tries to do things within their own frame of reference without regard for the local culture."

Attaining the right blend of local and expatriate talent is as much an art as a science. Most global corporations find it difficult or impossible to replicate their culture in Asia without a healthy proportion of expatriates on the ground. In much of the region, especially in mainland China, Taiwan, Hong Kong and Japan, locals are often lacking particular technical skills, usually in the areas of operations, finance, human resources and general management. In addition, the local managers lack the high-level communications skills that business development demands. That's why

Western expatriates need to be willing to put in several years at each Asian posting. In addition to transferring skills and experience, one of their most important jobs is to instill their organization's culture in the senior local managers. Culture – the idiosyncratic way a company does business – can only be taught by those already steeped in that culture.

The task of balancing cultures also takes on particular urgency when choosing executives to run overseas outposts. Stan Shih of Acer recalls that when the company was making its first inroads into the U.S., "we used transplanted Asians more than U.S. executives because of the ease in communicating with headquarters". But that approach has the defects of its virtues, Shih admits. "Expatriates, while effective in communicating back to stakeholders, sometimes have a hard time understanding the locals." As the U.S. business has matured, Shih has come to rely on expatriate executives with years of experience outside their home cultures.

As Shih has discovered, the type of talent required for foreign operations changes as the business grows. The biggest challenge for many companies is matching talented people to the market conditions. Based on the different maturity levels of the various markets, companies need to tap different talent in different markets to capture market share efficiently and effectively. Chang Sun of Warburg Pincus Asia is also acutely aware of the need to allocate talent where it will add the most value. "For a small business," he says, "you need a scrappy but creative self-starter who can hustle to get the business off the ground and build a team around a concept or idea. But once the company grows to a more sustainable size in terms of revenue, you need a more seasoned executive who can build a complete management team as well as a management process."

Corporate leaders in Asia must also be wary of recruiting talent that is a prisoner of the local culture. This problem is especially prevalent in Japan, where the culture's deeply ingrained deference to authority impedes efforts to change business practices and strategies. More than one company has been frustrated when it has given a mandate for change to a Japanese executive with extensive Western training, only to see that executive falter, fearing to offend older colleagues. In fact, there is an entire generation of Japanese executives – those in their 30s and 40s, dubbed "the lost generation" – who seem paralyzed, torn between their recognition of the need for massive corporate change and a profound reluctance to violate cultural norms of respect for elders.

The most progressive Japanese companies have recognized this bind and have devised programs that give younger Japanese executives room for innovation and change without inflaming cultural sensitivities. "It is difficult [for executives in their 40s] because the seniority system still prevails in Japan," says Keiji Tachikawa, president and CEO of Tokyo's NTT DoCoMo. "DoCoMo is very aware of the need to nurture these younger people, and that is why we have established a new division for creating new ventures. Many of our younger executives are quite active in this division. It allows them to play an important role in the company while receiving the experience they need to advance. So far, i-Mode is the only success story from these many ventures, but it's early yet. We are still sowing the seeds."

Corporate leaders looking to succeed in Asia would do well to emulate Tachikawa's patient attitude. Only through a long-term commitment to employee education and development, say executives with experience in the region, can corporations overcome the cultural and attitudinal barriers that have prevented East Asian companies from fully exploiting the trend toward globalization. Koh Boon Hwee, chairman of Singapore Airlines, recalls the business environment in China in the early 1980s, when the country was taking its first tentative steps toward market liberalization. At the time, many Chinese managers, with no experience outside their home markets, simply did not recognize ethical conflicts that people with experience working for foreign companies found deeply troubling. Koh Boon Hwee dealt with this problem by, in effect, taking charge of the ethical education of its management cadre. "We sent about half a dozen people into Shanghai to recruit our management talent directly from the universities," recalls Koh Hwee, who at the time was working for Wuthelam, a large Singapore industrial group. "It was four or five years before some of the university recruits were ready to assume first-level management positions, but today, almost all of Wuthelam's second-level managers are from this batch of college graduates. The advantage is they didn't come with any baggage pertaining to the practices or values that the Chinese-company recruits had. We were able to instill in them the values we wanted them to have."

The next step in this process, not only in China but throughout Asia, is to develop and institutionalize professional-development programs such as executive coaching and mentoring, and professional education and training. Risk aversion and strict adherence to seniority will have to give way to a human-resources approach that puts promising executives in stretch roles to test and develop their leadership ability. What stands in the way of this next phase in Asia's business evolution? Habits of mind, ways of looking at the world. Many of Asia's senior executives have been slow to recognize that the prime source of wealth in today's economy is information, not hard assets; people, not factories and real estate; ideas, not natural resources or national monopolies. Their corporate counterparts in the U.S. and Europe have been more quick to act on this crucial economic shift. They are developing strategies to maximize their talent advantage – the only truly sustainable competitive advantage. Asian business still has time to catch up, but there is no time to waste. At stake is nothing less than the region's competitive position in the global economic race.

▲ BUILDING BRANDS

Miles Young
Chairman, Ogilvy & Mather Asia Pacific

The last 15 years have been the glory years of branding. Never before has so much been written or taught about brands; and never before have expectations been set higher for them. But in the long, global march of branding, Asia still remains something of a "Wild East"; a game played for high stakes, where the rules are not yet totally written, and where it remains unclear who the ultimate winners shall be. This is the time when the new frontiers for Asian brands are in the process of being defined.

Although the explosion of branding has been inextricably linked to the phenomenon of globalization, it would be a mistake to assume that it is a one-way process, where global brands simply penetrate Asian markets, and where the main competition is between themselves, global brand versus global brand. This may be a natural Western perspective, but it is very far from reality.

While it is a truism that the WTO is steadily bringing down trade barriers, and the global market is therefore becoming both bigger and more competitive, the real nature of that competitiveness is both richer and more complex. China's entry to the WTO, for example, opened the door for Western companies to tap the opportunities of a marketplace of over one billion consumers. By that same token, the door has opened for Chinese manufacturers to reach new markets among over four billion affluent consumers in the developed countries. Moreover, when it comes to the China market itself, Western business commentators (and indeed some Western businesses) have consistently undervalued and underestimated the significance and sophistication of domestic competitors.

But there remains withal a nagging question: how close to the true coda of branding are Asian brands? Do they have the same characteristics as the global brands which are household names today, and which have achieved their eminence over decades of brand-building effort? Even if they are adjudged true brands in character, are they capable of being brands on a genuinely global scale?

These questions apply as much to the first generation of Asian brands (for instance, the Japanese brands) as they do to the newcomers. Answering them is critical to assessing how attractive or (depending on one's perspective) how dangerous the new frontiers really are.

Why are brands so valuable? Essentially, it is because they add value to what an organization does. They add all the emotional values that help win and retain customers, supporters and fans. Brands can do this because they are ownable in an age of commodities. In today's marketplace, product differences based solely on technology, design, packaging or pricing are fleeting advantages. It is often the case in Asia that the "emotional" content of a brand is something which brand owners find it difficult, even embarrassing, to talk about, but this is the very essence of branding, and what ultimately distinguishes strong brands from weak ones.

Moreover, in an age of information overload, a brand is invaluable shorthand. Brands compress data better than anything else. Brands signal. They identify. They pull all the attributes together in a unique, easy-to-understand way.

Most important of all, strong brands are an essential profit strategy. They command greater loyalty, and so are less costly to sustain. Loyal customers make a dramatic difference in the bottom line. There is plenty of solid economic evidence to prove that a company that keeps just 5% more of its customers lifts profits by 50%. The key to loyalty is strong, well-supported, vital brands. Again, this is a verity which many brand owners in Asia's new frontier are less familiar with. In markets where market penetration and expansion have brought success, brand loyalty has not been a key priority. That, however, must also change as protectionist barriers erode.

Most recently in a perceptive report ("Getting Globalization Right"), Goldman Sachs projected a list of 27 global corporations most likely to succeed in this century. Of these, four came from Asia: Samsung, Hyundai, Sony and Petro-China, the choice reflecting in this case an analyst-led point of view.

Of course, it is human nature to want a "league table", but, to date no single table reflects the diversity or complexity of the Asian "brandscope". In particular, they do not reflect the state of brand development within the large and flourishing markets which make up Asia.

This begs the deeper question that "Asia" itself is a difficult concept when it comes to branding. Very few Japanese, for instance, would think of Japanese brands as "Asian" brands. A market such as Korea has little in common with a market like Thailand. Even close neighbors such as Singapore and Malaysia, or Hong Kong and Guangdong, have major cultural, lifestyle and consumer differences which challenge those of us who seek to create sub-regional synergies and efficiencies in cross-Straits or Pearl River Delta initiatives. It is the differences within Asia as much as the commonalities that make the new frontiers both challenging and, to communicators who have the patience to invest both money and time in consumer connection, rewarding.

Is Asia different?

It is a paradox that in searching for commonalities the best starting point is to understand differences. There are two quite fundamental differences in Asia which render it dangerous to generalize superficially about Asian brands. The first of these stems from fundamental differences in the business model; the second from a different philosophy of business.

"Japan is different – and Korea as well"

This is a common cry in Tokyo, and, however inconvenient it may be, it needs to be understood at more than face value.

For an outsider in Japan, it can be a shocking realization that what has been blithely assumed to be the same thing – branding in the West and branding in Japan – are in fact two totally different concepts. The very word "brand", stemming as it does from the branding iron and the cattle ranch, suggests the sense of "ownership" at the heart of Western branding. Behind this lies the whole apparatus of the branding theory, with its emphasis on individuality, uniqueness, differentiation. On the other hand, the Japanese word for branding is *noren*: originally connoting the entrance of a restaurant (or curtain), it means "trust". From this develops a whole view of branding which is much more corporate and abstract in feeling.

The difference is not just conceptual. It is also rooted in the market structure in which marketing operates. The highly tiered and fragmented distribution system, for instance, produces enormous demands on selling through the trade. Advertising becomes more a weapon for gaining distribution, and then demonstrating to the trade the worth of this. Historically, therefore, Westerners and Japanese have hardly been talking about the same thing when it comes to branding, and the supposed "defects" of Japanese branding when viewed ignorantly from the West are actually rooted in a deep conceptual and contextual difference – which is neither right nor wrong.

While Japanese companies have emulated their Western competitors in building their brands outside Japan, paradoxically at home most follow a very different model. Until recently, most have relied on the company name to provide an umbrella brand for *all* their product lines. The key to success was to keep the corporate name in front of consumers while ensuring that the products themselves incorporated the latest technology and delivered useful functional benefits.

Inheriting many of the values of feudal times, these companies offered not so much a job or a range of products as an all-encompassing way of life. Their paternal values brought peace of mind that many of life's big issues were being managed successfully and in safe hands.

Not only might you work for Mitsubishi, you could also bank there, take out their insurance policies, eat out in fast-food restaurants in which the company was a joint-venture partner, wear clothes they imported, and drive to work in a Mitsubishi Motors automobile. Your home might be built from timber Mitsubishi had logged, and furnished with smart appliances Mitsubishi Electric had devised.

In the bubble era, strong corporate brands showed that the Japanese miracle was a dream delivered. But in recent years a series of corporate scandals has added to the pain of Japan's 10-year economic decline and undermined trust in these umbrella properties.

For decades, Mitsubishi Motors employees had been hiding consumer complaints about their cars. Eventually, on August 22, 2001, Mitsubishi Motors admitted there had been a deliberate, systemic cover-up designed to avoid expensive recalls. With similar embarrassment, Mitsubishi Electric confessed that for years it had smothered complaints from customers whose television sets caught fire.

The Mitsubishi problems were but two of a series of incidents that not only challenged the Japanese reputation for quality control and manufacturing excellence but also dramatically evidenced the distance between Japanese "brands" and their consumers.

The big issue for the big corporate brands is that they have become empty. As consumers have become empowered and more discerning, their relationships with both products and brands have become more varied, and more complex.

It is the business model itself which dictates that the relationship with the consumer is not the foremost priority. Yes, consumers are very important, but so too are employees, the retail trade and many other constituencies whose needs must be satisfied. The compromises that please all these agendas are not necessarily the ones consumers are seeking. When the opinions of the manufacturer prevail over the needs of the consumer, strong brands simply cannot emerge; branding espoused as part of the CEO's credo is a very different thing from deep and systemic commitment throughout an organization. Fortunately, reality is rearing its head in two forms. Firstly, the intelligent part of the Japanese creative community has become more intelligently interested in branding than the traditional agencies. A magnum opus in this genre is the recent book by Yasumichi Oka, the founder of Tugboat, entitled *Brand*. While the book's approach is by no means Western, its author does absolutely understand the emotional underpinning of branding.

Meanwhile, changes in business ownership and the increasing success of foreign companies are demonstrating that there is more than one way to market. Significant advertisers such as Nissan, J-Phone and Nippon Lever have all in the past few years had significant success with advertising that escapes the traditional paradigm (awareness only) and shows that it is possible – even if difficult – to achieve both awareness dominance and image gain in a category.

As in Japan, there is no Korean word to express "brand". Moreover, the business model has been even more distinctive.

A group of large conglomerates, or *chaebol*, still dominates South Korea's economy. Ten years ago, the leading *chaebol* manufactured low-end products and sprawled across almost every sector of industry. Today the best have narrowed their focus, improved governance, and strategic planning, and set out to become not just makers of innovative products, but also to be global brands. Three potential global brands are already emerging from this transformation: Samsung Electronics, LG Electronics and Hyundai Motor Co. Domestically, though, as in Japan, the corporation has been the brand.

However, the last few years have seen a significant shift towards a more classic Western style of branding. One spur to this is the increase of foreign imports, over 50% of automobiles, and 25% of electronic goods, which are stimulating different patterns in a market that was previously near-hermetically protected. Studies of advertising show an increasing shift from product/factual messages to brand/image messages, particularly stimulated by the mobile-phone market where LG's "looks good" and Samsung's Anycall "battle series" campaigns both tap into different consumer segments and their distinct codes. Meantime research shows that intangibles are playing more of a role in consumer choice: the percentage believing that a product or brand with higher advertising content is more reliable, has increased from 36% in 1995 to 45% in 2002.

But perhaps the biggest change will be below the level of the top *chaebol*. Amore Pacific Corporation once dabbled in advertising, electronics and financial services. But when the premium cosmetic brands at the core of its business began to lose out to Chanel, L'Oreal and Estée Lauder in Korean department stores, management swiftly refocused the company on health and beauty and set out to build an international brand.

By 2002, their Lolita Lempicka perfume had taken 2.6% of the French fragrance market and became the fourth-biggest seller in the country. Amore Pacific's Laneige brand cosmetics are sold through 30 leading department stores in China and a range of skin-care products is planned for the U.S. The goal is simple – we will have become the world's fifth-largest cosmetics firm by the end of 2004.

Hankook Tire, another midsize company, has opened research and development centers in the U.S., Germany, and China, as well as six overseas sales offices, to increase quality and court foreign buyers who already include Ford, Volkswagen, Mitsubishi Motors and Volvo. Hankook has also become the largest tire supplier for passenger cars in China, with a 20% share of the market, a key step towards the goal of becoming the world's leading tire maker.

The Chinese mercantilist tradition

The second big Asian difference is the pervasive influence of mercantilism in the thinking and operations of Asian enterprises. Prevalent particularly in the Chinese diaspora, and now again in the Chinese motherland, this, at its best, takes the form of highly developed entrepreneurialism, an approach to business driven by "an eye for the right opportunity". There often remains a strong family component to businesses. While Western commentators have sometimes sniffed at the lack of strategic thought underpinning these enterprises, this disfavor has not impeded their success, or their ability to adapt, either to the lessons of the 1997 economic crisis or to government regulation encouraging focus. However, the family ownership or influences of many businesses has not been fertile territory for branding in the conventional sense. Manufacturer orientation, and the lack of a shareholder base to whom intangible assets form a critical compositor of health, have meant that branding is something to which, at best, lipservice is paid, and that classic brand management functions in the organization with real leverage have failed to develop.

In developing markets such as China, companies successful in many other ways sometimes adopt a "smash and grab" approach to branding: in the most extreme case, stealing the image of existing Western brands without understanding any of their underlying value systems. As an expression of "can do", this is admirable; as a premise for long-term success, it is doubtful. But it is precisely the long-term nature of brands which can be an uneasy fit with the mercantilist mindset.

No government has taken the issue more seriously than that of Singapore. Singapore is home to one of the first major Asian brands, Singapore Airlines. Since 1972 the airline's Singapore Girl imagery has helped to define both quality of service for the airline and the image of the island nation. The Singapore girl still flies the skies and although other airlines have imitated it, Singapore Airlines continues to set standards for ease and comfort for global travelers. Advertising alone did not create the brand. Singapore Airlines has been able to embed concepts of quality and service in every aspect of its interaction with travelers. It is a holistic experience.

More recently, Singapore's Creative Technologies has had global success with its Soundblaster card, found today in about 60% of the world's computers. However, the level of recognition and the scale are scarcely comparable.

Consequently, Singapore's government is now trying to encourage the development of strong local brands as a step in building global brands to secure the future of the economy. At the Singapore Brand Award 2002 ceremony, Senior Minister of State for Trade and Industry Tharman Shanmugaratnam said, "We need more SIAs, more Tiger Balms, more Hour Glasses, among companies big and small, in order to succeed in our next phase of growth." Fourteen companies received awards at the ceremony: SingTel, DBS, OCBC, UOB, Singapore Airlines, Asia Pacific Breweries, Brand's, F&N, Tiger Balm, Eu Yan Sang, Great Eastern, Informatics, Osim, and The Hour Glass. As the Minister pointed out, companies with strong brands consistently deliver higher than market-average returns to shareholders and carry a lower than market-average risk profile.

Indeed, Singaporean companies are investing more time and money in their brands. In 1999, a little over half of all respondents (52%) claimed that the brand strategy was not understood by most employees.[3] In contrast, today, that figure has fallen to 15%. However, half of the companies still think of brands simply in terms of the product. They believe that the "name" or "identity" of their *product* is the key factor and devote their efforts to activities that have an immediate impact on sales rather than on areas that generate more long-term impact such as brand strategy, brand building or research.

Other Southeast Asian countries share the same concern. In September 2003, the government of Malaysia budgeted a further RM100 million, on top of the RM100 million allocated the year before, to a fund for the development and promotion of Malaysian brands. By contrast, the Thai government tends to emphasize the importance of developing a marque denoting Thai origin to create international recognition (a strategy similar to the "Made in Taiwan" campaign which has been run sporadically in the last few years). While such campaigns can be helpful in raising general awareness of quality, they do not provide the same degree of support to the building of individual brands, which are sustained by specific consumer franchises rather than by generalized endorsements of national origin.

The big battleground

The branding battleground in Asia is rooted in the context of markets. At the risk of simplification, it is still quite illuminating to tease out the differences in the critical dimensions of cultural style and business focus.

Japan and Thailand, for instance, both come from creative cultures (as evidenced, for example, in advertising style), but their branding mindset tends to be corporate rather than consumer-led. South Korean approaches tend to be more pragmatic and are moving faster towards a classic consumer orientation than their Japanese counterparts. Taiwan, Malaysia, Indonesia and Singapore tend to group to a greater or lesser degree in the "classic Asian" corporate/pragmatic box; while China, with all the benefits of a new adopter, shows signs of classic consumer orientation, even if the creativity is still not there. India, by contrast, falls closest to the conventional Western model of branding; but, in India's case, years of government policy have until recently effectively restructured the playing field.

From these stereotypes, it is possible for individual brands to "escape" – just as Samsung has done, very much pushing towards the consumer/creative segment faster than its fellow Korean brands. Or, as we have seen, some Singaporean brands would be well established in the consumer/creative zone.

But the battleground has got another dimension to it – that of scale. Which Asian brands will be the global brands of tomorrow? There is a kind of journey, but the starting point must be to have a strong local brand, to graduate from the manufacturing role which characterized many Japanese or Korean brands 25 or 10 years ago, and which confines many potential Asian brands in OEM status today. Moving on, the journey can either lead to regional brand status or directly to global brand status. Many regional brands suffer a similar style of confinement, and find it difficult to move up to the next level. Some of the most promising new global brands have jumped straight to the most promising markets regardless of where they are; and some – most notably LG Electronics and Hyundai Motors Corporation – were focused on "BRIC"' well before Goldman Sachs gave it popularity. Whatever the pattern, the stronger the local franchise, the easier it is to gain international scale – which is why the immediate battleground revolves around the big four markets of Japan, Korea, China and India.

Of these, the first two now exhibit a very fair degree of maturity. The early stages of growth have been accomplished, and winning in the future depends on the degree of sophistication in finding competitive advantage. One of the anomalies of Asian branding is that Japanese companies abroad have often proved much more adept and flexible in pursuing a consumer orientation than they have at home. The success of Shiseido in China or Toyota in the U.S. are classic examples, reflecting the benefits of a devolved management style with the authority to use local consultants and methods. As a brand, Lexus could not have been invested in Japan; only now is it being introduced there. The corollary is also true: the core central drivers of global brand equity are sometimes stunted. It is critical to treat the consumers of the expert market with as much seriousness as the domestic – to practise "one brand indivisible". The battle of Japanese versus Korean brands in China is a good example. As a McKinsey analyst has put it: "Korean companies realized two or three years ago that they can't simply dump old products in China; the Japanese have only realized this in the last six to 12 months." The ability to touch consumers is also critical. For instance, research shows that the young Chinese consumer regards Sony more as a brand for mature businessmen than for them. By contrast, Samsung is seen as a "hip" and "cool" brand, something which Sony is now seeking to address.

The lesson is clear; once a company has achieved "brand power" (that is, a degree of scale and a basic consumer orientation), the key differentiator becomes brand energy – the extent to which it excites, motivates and achieves empathy with consumers. In the big categories of electronics and automotive, this is the battle Korean and Japanese brands must win as much against themselves as against in-market competitors.

Chinese brands – the short march

Meanwhile, what of Chinese brands? They have become a fashionable preoccupation amongst commentators, and rightly so. Both in the scale of the domestic market, for surpassing Japan and Korea, and in their vaulting ambition, they represent the most exciting part of the new frontier in Asian branding.

The underlying enabler is the extraordinarily fast pace of consumerization within China. Rising discretionary spending has fuelled surging penetration of durables – starting with televisions and now most manifest in the automotive market, as "Tier 1" cities rapidly become motorized societies with the retail and leisure structures that this spawns. As state-owned corporations have moved into the private sector to meet these needs, "branding" has been adopted by local clients, which in turn (contrary to the impressions often peddled outside China) dominate Chinese advertising expenditure. In turn, China has already overtaken the U.K. and Germany in size of advertising market and, by the end of the decade, is likely to surpass Japan to become the world's number-two market.

In the early days, Chinese brands scored over their Western competitors on price and on their ability to command and influence distribution channels. That scorecard is now no longer enough and behind the sheer quantity of advertising visible in China there is a revolution in quality.

This is particularly evident in brands with youth appeal but also in the fast-moving consumer-goods sector. Bright Dairy, for instance, China's largest dairy brand, now designs products from inception to the marketplace with the same kind of consumer vigor (maybe more so) as any of its foreign competitors. The fashion brand Semir, the Chinese GAP, has created a highly focused brand based around the theme of shouting "semir" which sounds like "what?" in Chinese. Li Ning, the sportswear brand that currently leads both Nike and Adidas, was created and branded by the Olympic gold medallist Li Ning, and started to motor when it invested in design and research and development that were consumer-based.

Within their domestic market, Chinese brands do have a killer advantage, *if they choose it*: they are potentially closer to their consumers than Western brands. This enables them to do things which in the Western context would seem wrong, but which work in China. A classic, if extreme, example is the TCL mobile handset which carried fake diamond ornamentation: what was initially derided by foreign manufacturers is now imitated by them. However, the proviso "if they choose" is an important one. It is easy to pick out examples of success; or indeed to paint a picture of overwhelming and unqualified optimism through the stated ambitions of CEOs. But real practice often falls short, and rooting strategy in the consumer is still the exception rather than the rule.

Looking outside China, the first generation of aspirant global brands are already jostling for position. Out in front is Haier. As its president, Zhang Haimin, has put it, "the objective of most Chinese enterprises is to export product and earn foreign currency. This is their only purpose. Our purpose in exporting is to create a brand reputation overseas." Zhang Haimin is an intuitive believer in the power of branding, from the famous sledgehammer framed in the reception lobby (used to destroy product defects) to the "international star service" program which creates customer loyalty. Haier has adopted a "difficulty first" strategy to enter the global market, first entering the U.S. and the E.U., and doing so with manufacturing capability, so that Haier appliances in the U.S. carry a "Made in America" label. At the same time, lead products are sought which have a real competitive advantage. In the U.S., it was the neglected category of small refrigerators, putting it on a path to achieve its objective of a 10% share of the U.S. market for full-size refrigerators by 2005.

The alternative strategy for Chinese brands is "easy first", looking at developing markets and using price as the primary advantage. For instance, Ningbo Bird, the cellphone brand, has now launched aggressively in India, where it is directly targeting the global manufacturers amongst the first-time buyers. At present the importance of branding is relatively low in such strategies; over time, positioning and image will come into play. This will be the moment of truth for many of the Chinese brands with global ambition: can they make the transition into real and longer-term consumer franchises?

India – Brahminical brands

Meanwhile, India's role within Asian branding is coming of age. One illustration of this is the "India versus China" debate. Global fixation on the China opportunity has tended to mask the arrival of India as an incubator of brands of high potential. Recently the corrective case has been expressed by sources as diverse as Peter Drucker and Arun Shourie, the former Indian

Minister for Disinvestment. This school of thought argues that China sold out to foreign multinationals; whereas, by contrast, the "new India" is developing its own industries and brands. Of course, even a cursory glance at the growth of Chinese brands reveals that this is a difficult argument to sustain, but nonetheless the end message is worth listening to: India has some distinct advantages when it comes to branding, and is considerably underestimated or even discounted when it comes to discussions about Asian branding.

The Indian advantage is in soft skills: knowledge and creativity. As Arun Shourie says, "an MBA costs about $5,000 in India. In the USA, an MBA costs around $120,000." India's Brahminical heritage, with its belief that "knowledge is wealth", seems well adapted to an economy where excessive regulation is being (slowly) removed.

India's knowledge advantage is well reflected in Wipro Technologies, which is well on track to being one of the world's top global technology-service providers based on the slogan "Applying Thought". In healthcare and biotechnology, brands like Nicholas Piramal and Bioon reflect the same knowledge-led approach.

But it would be a mistake to imagine that India's contribution to Asian branding is confined to this very added-value zone. In the FMCG category, Indian brands, often originating in regions and getting critical mass through national expansion, show vibrant growth and an ability to provide "close to the consumer" brand mixes which are breaking into the established dominance of the big Indianized multinationals. Examples are companies like Jyothi Labs and Cavinkare in the highly competitive segments of soaps, shampoos and perfumes. In the words of Cavinkare, "We can be more nimble-footed with our marketing strategies than the bigger players. By effectively managing finances, quality and distribution, we are offering more choices to the consumer."

The challenges on the new frontier

Like Asia itself, Asian brands exhibit as many different as common characteristics, and some are much closer to the classic Western brand model than others. But whether they are the corporate monoliths of Japan, early or partial adapters of branding, or the new arrivers of China, India and Southeast Asia, they all share the need to connect to the customer. So there are challenges that need to be overcome which *are* common to many of them, especially as they embark on similar journeys of building scale at the same time as creating added value.

These are not prescriptions; they are issues which probably require more introspection in Asian boardrooms:

- Who is the brand enforcer in the organization? This is not necessarily the same as the brand visionary but, rather, experience shows that strong brands need a champion in the organization who is almost pathologically obsessed with how the brand is articulated, and who seeks to minimize the risk of brand violation. Few Asian brands have such an enfranchised individual.
- What is the structural power of those who make brand decisions? Brand management as a function tends to be unempowered compared to sales or production functions. It does not attract the best and brightest in the organization and does not wield influence in internal debate. Yet it is the prerequisite of a truly brand-led company.
- Is the view of branding holistic? Brand is still far too often interpreted as being advertising; but in the language of Ogilvy & Mather, it is a "360° experience", in which every consumer touchpoint can add to (or detract from) the brand equity. Without this, a brand can easily become fractured or diluted.
- Is there a recognition that the essence of branding lies in emotion? Many Asian brands are constrained by over-rational approaches to their relationship with customers. Creating a culture in which "emotional capital" is respectable and can be openly and easily discussed is a critical success factor.
- Is there a willingness to accept that branding is for the long term? Some Asian brands have a very short-term horizon. Usually, brand strength correlates with the degree of consistency over time with which a brand strategy is employed. This in no way prevents or inhibits tactical behavior, but tactics need to speak with the voice of the brand.

These are not easy challenges to be tackled. Nor in the context of dynamic growth will it necessarily be evident that they are all urgent: after all, don't the sales keep on coming? Of course, they do: but the issue is about relative advantage. There is no doubt that the new Asian middle-class consumer, as he and she become more and more sophisticated and discriminating, will search for the nuances of best fit between them and their brands.

After all, a brand is a relationship between a product and a consumer, nothing else; and there is no reason why Asian brands should not create that relationship better and more sensitively than any others.

CHAPTER

9 Achieving Sustainability

The two parts presented in this chapter may seem to present contrasting visions but they are, in fact, highly complementary. Together they form a compelling picture of national and corporate competitiveness over the long term.

In the first, Professor Hirotaka Takeuchi argues that companies must be backed by strong global tendencies in their home markets in order to sustain initial successes at the global level. The author identifies three key markets – labor, financial and product – that have become deeply globalized. According to him, Japan's problem is that it has in fact disconnected from these markets, thereby ensuring its own economic stasis. This process – which he calls Japan's "unglobalization" from global markets, indicates a larger vision of long-term competitiveness built around robust local markets. Here Takeuchi's previous work on Japan is instructive. In the their recent book *Can Japan Compete?*,[1] Takeuchi and his co-authors present an anomaly; the co-existence of two Japans – one competitive, worldly, and world-class and the other inward-looking, uncompetitive (or anti-competitive) and mediocre. Japan's struggle is defined by the interplay between these two forces.

Porter, Takeuchi and Sakakibara may have been prescient in identifying Japan's malaise. Four years later, their case seems to have only become stronger; prolonging the conflict by refusing to reform seems only to extend Japan's stasis and move it closer to the edge of the global economy. In his contribution to this book, Takeuchi goes one step further to plot a path of recovery. In fact, if Japan can recognize the trends towards global markets in the three key areas of finance, labor and products, it can save itself and begin to chart its return to economic form. Notably, both arguments are as much about companies as about economies. Indeed, the World Economic Forum's own work on the subject shows that the competitiveness of companies is indeed integral to overall economic competitiveness.[2]

Professor Takeuchi's case for why Japan may risk another "lost decade" unless it rides the globalization wave leads to questions about the effect this would have on Japanese companies. Just as the robustness of the business sector helps to shape a country's competitiveness, it is also the case that the framework for the private sector is still very much determined by the government. The causality of competitiveness works both ways – from both business to the economy and vice versa. Takeuchi's argument calls today's Japanese economy "unglobal" with clear implications for Japan's companies. Long at the top of their respective industries world wide, Japanese companies may find the logic ominous.

This is disconcerting to us. When selecting companies to be included in this book, Japanese companies stood out for their long presence in the international market. Of the companies we call "the pioneers" in this book, two of three are Japanese, and we could have included many more from virtually every sector – Panasonic/Matsushita, Toshiba, Toyota, Honda, Shisedo, Dentsu, Itochu, Nomura, and the list could go on. Following the argument of Takeuchi's paper, one may conclude that more Japanese companies will encounter difficulties in the coming decade, hindered either by their home market or its habits. By the same reasoning, the other companies featured in the book will need a lot more than the aspects that we have just reviewed – finance, networks, branding and human resources – in order to sustain a global presence. They will also need their anchor markets, whether at home or elsewhere, to be sufficiently global in many of these areas.

There are parallels to be drawn between the "two Japans" mentioned above and other economies in Asia. Although Asia's global firms are as strong as any of their international counterparts, and come from throughout the region, it would be hard to name more than a handful from several Asian economies. Upon closer examination, there may be evidence that some countries are already characterized by the two competing forces – the worldly, competitive tendency as opposed to the insular, protective and ultimately uncompetitive one. Note that two of Asia's relatively "free" economies – Hong Kong and Singapore – have produced a disproportionate share of global competitors. The lessons for developing Asia are clear: competitive and open home markets are prerequisites for nurturing companies that can grow and compete at the global level.

We do not suggest that Asia's emerging markets should throw open their doors to global markets, but that they should, instead, strive towards open, competitive, home markets. Exceptions will necessarily exist to account for a country's specific circumstances, usually social or cultural, but these exceptions should be made after careful consideration.

If Takeuchi posits the globalization of three markets – labor, financial and product – the mastery of which helps to determine both economic and corporate competitiveness, the second paper in this chapter adds a fourth element to the picture: the social market. Bjorn Stigson and Margaret Flaherty of the World Business Council on Sustainable Development claim that corporate social responsibility (CSR) has now turned a critical corner and moved into the mainstream of global business today. Increasingly, companies are seeking out opportunities for themselves or their products to achieve social good, especially on the environmental front. In addition, global financial markets have begun to exhibit a keen regard for environmental sustainability and social regard in valuing companies.

Certainly these trends hold true in the West, where the rhythm of social responsibility is now well embedded in business dialogue and where consumers and financial markets are becoming more aware of companies' records on CSR. However, in Asia, as Stigson and Flaherty rightly point out, social responsibility remains on the fringes of the business community. While there are some practitioners of socially responsible investment and a few organizations advocating greater social responsibility from companies, it is still an uphill battle. More often, shareholders see their interests better served by pushing for better corporate governance or disclosure and do not see CSR as absolutely essential. Asian markets exemplify this mentality.

In the long term, markets and consumers may be changing. While the average citizen in many Asian countries may not yet consider CSR to be central to their investing or buying, this is not the case for those with more buying power, and international exposure. Because the "aware" class often serves as a signal or precursor to future trends in their respective societies, we predict that it is only a matter of time before CSR becomes common currency in Asia as well. In an era where the information and communications technologies enable industries to evolve virtually overnight, we can foresee it picking up faster in Asia than it did in Europe or the U.S.

Another trend that will stimulate the rise of CSR is Asia's tremendous demand for natural resources, which is particularly strident because of Asia's massive population. China, India and Indonesia will all have huge impacts and require huge amounts of natural resources, even if they grow at only moderate rates. Environmental issues have already entered national policy dialogue in China, where the government faces huge demands for energy and other resources. These strong resource needs and their related environmental concerns will make Asian governments and consumers more aware, and will demand serious consideration from the business community.

Asian companies may have less ground to cover to integrate CSR and sustainability issues into their everyday business considerations than did companies in the West. This is because Asian companies have long played substantial roles in their local communities. Lifetime employment, the iron rice-bowl, company-subsidized housing, the chairman as father figure, donations to the local temple – all attest to the fact that many Asian companies are already embedded into their communities. Corporate social responsibility is merely the next step, as companies extend concern for their communities to concern for society and the world at large.

In proposing that it is companies which need to respond to society, as opposed to being shaped by social forces, Stigson and Flaherty may seem to be opposing Professor Takeuchi's concern that a company's own home environment may push it in particular directions. Actually, the process of business growth and globalization is mutually reinforcing: companies will "push" society as much as vice versa. Thus, if Japan's leading companies want to grow because of their home market, and not in spite of it, we can foresee them helping to push for change. That way the three forces that Professor Takeuchi describes – the "unglobalizing" of Japan's labor, financial and product markets – do not lead to a permanent slide. Similar arguments could be made for Asia's other economies, which would do well to note that the uncoupling of Japan came in spite of many years of global leadership. In turn, economies still seeking to build global leadership will need to ensure that the trends towards "two economies" do not undermine the efforts of their companies to become competitive for the long term. The right environment will help them and also nurture other companies to deepen the local economy.

By the same token, for Asian companies to take up Stigson and Flaherty's CSR navigator in a more determined way, Asian societies also need to provide some impetus. Asia's companies are already receptive to the idea, and many of them are already making significant moves to promote social responsibility, viewing this as part of their ethical duties as members of society.[3] While these companies, as Asia's leaders, will provide some impetus for similar moves by their competitors, Asia's "lesser" companies may need to be pushed to change by consumers in product and financial markets. Asia has the beginnings of economic competitiveness and sustainable societies for the long term, but a great deal of work will still be needed from all sides – consumers, businesses, institutions and governments – to ensure that the progress does not stop.

▲ MAINTAINING COMPETITIVENESS

Hirotaka Takeuchi
Professor, Graduate School of International Corporate Strategy, Hitotsubashi University[4]

When Theodore Levitt of the Harvard Business School wrote "The Globalization of Markets" 20 years ago, the entire world stood in awe of Japan's postwar economic success. Japanese companies were seen as being amongst the most effective world competitors back then. In his provocative article, Levitt explained the surging success of Japanese companies in terms of their ability (a) to incorporate superior quality and reliability into their cost structure; (b) to sell in all national markets the same kind of products sold at home or in their largest export market; and (c) to compete on the basis of appropriate value – the best combinations of price, quality, reliability and delivery for products that are globally identical with respect to design, function and even fashion.[5]

Japan, 20 years ago, was depicted as a country that exemplified the globalization of markets. Levitt referred to "Japan" and "Japanese" 24 times in his article, far more than any other country. "The U.S./American" was second, at 14 references. "Japan/Japanese" was quoted almost three and a half times more than "Germany/German", four times more than "Britain/British/England", six times more than "Italy/Italian", eight times more than "France/French" and "Israel," and 12 times more than "Brazil/ Brazilian", "Korea" and Sweden". This suggests that Japan epitomized the pursuit of two ingredients Levitt considered essential in achieving the globalization of markets, namely the "unrelenting push for economy and value enhancement".

Now, 20 years after Levitt's article appeared, Japan is mired in a seemingly endless slump. Real-estate prices, after skyrocketing during the late 1980s, have plummeted by as much as 93.8% and are continuing to fall. The Nikkei stock price index, which peaked at 38,915 in December 1989, fell below 8,000 in March 2003. The unemployment rate surpassed the U.S. rate for the first time in 1999 and hit a record high, 5.4%, in 2002. The banking industry is showing few signs of recovery from its bad loans. Economic growth turned negative for the first time in postwar history in 1997 and Japan has been faced with a deflationary spiral since 2002.

Japan's competitiveness ranking has fallen as well. Once ranked No.1, Japan was ranked No.30 by IMD, the Swiss business school, in its 2002 World Competitiveness Ranking. It was the first year Japan had come in below Korea and Malaysia in the IMD ranking. Japan scored a little better in *The Global Competitiveness Report 2001–2002*, published by the World Economic Forum.[6] Its composite macro- and microeconomic rankings were No.20 and No.15, respectively, a far cry from its glory days in the late 1980s.

A myriad articles and books have been written on why Japan has fallen from its position as the world's preeminent economy. Revisiting Levitt's article offers yet another fresh insight. Japan's fall is linked to the extent to which Japan has been able or unable to participate in the globalization of markets. Although Levitt's article was primarily concerned about the globalization of the product market, this paper expands the domain to three areas – the labor market, the financial market and the product market – and investigates the assertion that Japan may have become "unglobal" in all three markets.

These three markets are integral parts of a nation's business environment. The business environment that Japan faces can be understood in terms of four interrelated influences: the context for firms' strategy and rivalry; the quality of factor (input) conditions; the presence of locally related and supporting industries; and the quality of demand conditions. These four influences are collectively called a "diamond" (as in baseball) by Michael Porter.[7] The labor market is included in factor (input) conditions and listed under "human resources". The financial market is also part of factor conditions, and is listed as "capital resources". Seen from a broader context, the financial market also constitutes an important supporting industry for Japanese companies to compete in the global market, and is therefore part of related and supporting industries. The product market is an integral part of demand conditions, since it is strongly influenced by how sophisticated and demanding the home market is.

Participating in the globalization of the labor market

To what extent are the Japanese participating in the emerging globalization of the labor market? Our interest with respect to this question is focused on whether or not they are participating in the more advanced, upscale, high value-added, knowledge-intensive, and white-collar segment of the labor market, rather than the low-end of the market often associated with blue-collar jobs. As used in this paper, the labor market connotes the high-end segment often associated with jobs in software, life sciences, chip design, engineering, finance, consulting, top management, and others. We examine several indicators below, starting with how eager Japanese students are to work for foreign-affiliated firms in Japan.

Among engineering students ready to go on the job market, only one foreign-affiliated firm, namely IBM Japan, has appeared consistently in the Top 20 List of Preferred Companies to Work For in Japan in selected years dating back to 1983, with DEC and Accenture each making one appearance.[8] A somewhat lower preference is exhibited by non-engineering students, with only IBM Japan appearing on the Top 20 Preferred Company list in two of the last six years for which data is available.[9] While today's graduates are not a fail-safe bell wether for Japan's labor market, they are perhaps the most "daring" of Japan's labor population and if they do not want to work for foreign companies in Japan, who does?

A second indicator of Japanese participation in the global labor market is the number of executives working as members of the corporate boards of global companies as well as members of the executive committees within leading investment banks and consulting firms in the world. Out of the top 20 companies on the Fortune 500 list, only two Japanese were listed on the boards, as of April 2003. These were Nobuyuki Idei, chairman and CEO of Sony, serving on the board of General Motors, and Yoshiaki Fujimori, president and CEO of GE Asia, serving on the board of General Electric. Only one Japanese (Masanori Mochida of Goldman Sachs) is currently a member of the executive committee of any of the top 10 investment banks in the world. Furthermore, there are no Japanese currently on the executive committee of any of the world's major consulting companies.

The third indicator of whether or not Japan is participating in the global labor market is the number of tenured faculty members working at leading universities outside of Japan. We examined the situation at the Harvard Business School as a case in point. Among the thousands of faculty members HBS has hired on the tenure track in its 95-year history, only a handful of Japanese have worked there as a full-time faculty member. What is even more striking is the fact that only Professor Michael Yoshino, who is now retired, received tenure as full professor at HBS. The situation is not all that different in other Harvard faculties.

The above indicators point to the conclusion that the Japanese are not advancing that much in either the corporate world or the academic world on a global basis. How could this be, given the heroic tales we often heard of modern-day samurai clad in business suits going out of their way to win the market-share battle in a number of important industries around the world? Or, given the images we have often seen of young Japanese students staying up until late at night to prepare for entrance exams, convinced that with "four hours of sleep at night we make it, five hours of sleep we don't" in order to get ahead in life? We turn to the next section for some explanations.

Obstacles to the globalization of the labor market

Why have Japanese companies not made significant advances in the global labor market? Simply put, they have not been able to do so because Japan's system for developing human resources, particularly its education system, has been out of sync with the rest of the world. The biggest obstacles here seem to be the idiosyncrasies of the education system and the lack of world-class business schools in Japan. These obstacles put Japan at a disadvantage with respect to developing specialized input (human resources), an important element of factor (input) conditions.

The roots of Japan's lack of competitiveness in the labor market can be traced back to its education system. We will explore its weaknesses in four major areas.

Outdated English-language program

To be able to compete effectively in the global market, English is essential. It was not such a critical input when Japan was producing tangible products such as steel, cars, motorcycles, hi-fi equipment, farm machinery, robots, microprocessors, carbon fibers and textiles. The ability to communicate in English, however, has become a critical input, especially in services, which explains why India has been successful in software and entertainment, and Israel in software and engineering.

The English-language program in Japan is out of sync with the rest of the world because of its heavy emphasis on reading and writing skills, rather than on verbal skills. Nobutaka Machimura, a former Minister of Education, explains the historical circumstances leading to this situation, as follows:

> *In Japan, the English curriculum was originally established during the Meiji period in order to translate materials written in English into Japanese. Thus, the English curriculum has come to focus more on reading and writing rather than speaking and listening since that time. The curriculum for communicating in English, on the other hand, has been largely ignored.*
>
> *Most of the English school teachers in Japan during the Meiji period were not required to have sufficient levels of speaking and listening abilities. This fact has been a big obstacle for Japanese policy-makers in reforming the English curriculum even though they realized the importance of communication in English. Policy-makers could not discharge those school teachers who*

> *couldn't speak and [understand]English sufficiently. Consequently, they could not realize the change towards a curriculum that focuses more on verbal skills in English.*[10]

Japan is paying a huge price internationally for this unfortunate heritage. Most Japanese trained in the traditional education system are disadvantaged when it comes to getting into world-class universities, graduate schools and companies because of their lack of proficiency in the English language. The Japanese have consistently scored low in the Test of English as a Foreign Language (TOEFL), which measures the ability of non-native English speakers to use and understand English as it is used in university settings. Since 1997, it has recorded a lower average score than most developed countries as well as most Asian countries, including Vietnam and Thailand.[11]

Deteriorating basic education system

In the past, Japan's basic education system was a subject for praise and envy from most countries around the world, as well as a source of strength for Japan. It was anchored in high standards and served to produce a large and uniform pool of well-trained personnel. More recently, however, its education system has begun to show signs of deterioration. For example, there is evidence that high school students are not working as hard as their counterparts in other OECD countries, as measured by the number of hours spent on homework for language, mathematics and science. Japan ranked last among the 27 OECD countries surveyed in 2000, the only country with less than three hours.[12]

In addition, many schools are suffering from a large and growing number of no-shows or "*toko-kyohi*"[13] in class. Partly in response to this problem, the Ministry of Education, Culture, Sports, Science and Technology (MEXT) instigated a "relaxation (*yutori*)" program at the elementary level in 2002, which in effect reduced the number of school hours by two hours per week. Some believe that this policy will further precipitate the deterioration.

Because of growing weaknesses in basic education, universities such as Tokyo University have to offer remedial courses in math, physics and chemistry for incoming students. In a recent large-scale survey of college freshmen, for example, more than 10% of students in liberal arts could not solve simple calculations involving fractions.[14]

Weak university system

Japan's university system is nowhere close to being competitive on a worldwide basis. According to the data compiled from the Gourman Report, Tokyo University, which is considered by far the best in Japan, is only ranked 99th among the top 100 universities in the world.[15] Part of the problem with the Japanese university system lies with the universities themselves. They have been content to exist in a highly regulated system and have exerted little pressure on students. Most classes are large lecture sessions, where students often engage in private conversation. Professors do not think twice about canceling class since there are almost no student evaluation systems in place.[16] In fact, when Hitotsubashi University recently decided to disclose the results of the five-point course/instructor evaluation at the undergraduate level, *Asahi Shimbun*, a daily newspaper with the second-largest circulation in Japan, featured the announcement in a lead article on its front page.[17]

Part of the problem also lies with students and the companies that hire them. Many students think of their college years as four years of vacation, or as a kind of moratorium, especially in the non-engineering programs. Because of tough entrance exams, getting into the best universities in Japan is difficult, but getting out is easy. Students have few incentives to study, since companies have relied on in-house training and have not been concerned with students' grades when hiring.[18]

In addition, Japanese universities have failed to produce enough students in important disciplines, such as computer software and biotechnology. For example, the number of Japanese college graduates who majored in biology-related subjects was 1,875 in 1996, as opposed to 62,081 in the U.S.[19] Furthermore, Japanese universities lack strong research programs in many important fields. Their focus is in applied work rather than original sciences. As a result, Japan has won just seven Nobel Prizes (actually nine if the two awards given in 2002 are included) in science in the last century.[20] This single-digit figure compares to 204 for the U.S., 71 for the U.K., and 64 for Germany. In economics, the record is even more depressing, with no Japanese having ever won the Nobel Prize, compared to 33 for the U.S. and seven for the U.K.[21]

Lack of world-class business schools

It is somewhat of a paradox that the second-largest economy in the world had only one business school 20 years ago. Today, there are some 30 business schools offering MBA programs in Japan, about a quarter of which are transplants of business schools from North America, Europe and Australia. Despite the surge in the number of Japanese business schools, they have a lot of catching up to do. Not only are they uneven in quality, but most Japanese business schools have failed to produce high-quality students prepared to work for professional firms around the world.[22] According to *The Global Competitiveness Report 2001–2002*, the quality of management schools in Japan was ranked 49th out of 75 countries/regions around the world.[23]

Part of the problem lies with how business schools are positioned in Japan. They are seen more as a continuing-education program rather than as an opportunity to switch and upgrade jobs. Thus, most of the so-called business schools offer courses on a part-time basis or at night. Part of the problem also lies with the faculty, most of whom do not have any experience teaching at leading business schools in the U.S. or Europe, nor have MBAs from those institutions. In addition, there are only two business schools in Japan offering a curriculum that is taught entirely in English. One of them is Hitotsubashi University's Graduate School of International Corporate Strategy, which was described as a "world-class" business school by both *BusinessWeek* and the *Financial Times*.[24]

Lack of world-class professional training extends beyond business schools. Up until now, Japan has not had law schools; these were established by MEXT in 2004. Although Japan is often cited as benefiting from a less litigious approach than the U.S., lawyers are still needed in any complex economy. The shortage of lawyers can delay business transactions in Japan and pose an acute problem, especially in technical fields.

The idiosyncrasies and weaknesses of the Japanese education system have worked against producing Japanese who are equipped with the proper specialized skills necessary to participate fully in the globalization of the labor market. They have been hampered by poor communication skills in English, inadequate problem-solving capabilities, a shortage of specialized training in software, biotechnology and other important disciplines, and a lack of professional business and legal training.

A world-class education system has become an increasingly important ingredient for competitiveness in an advanced industrial economy. Moving away from the tight control and micromanagement exercised by MEXT will go a long way toward rebuilding Japan's education system. Having said that, some of the recent moves on the part of the ministry are headed in the right direction. They include plans or actions to (a) convert national government universities into independent agencies; (b) foster competition within and across universities through the establishment of centers of excellence at graduate schools; (c) establish a new legal category of professional graduate schools and bring business schools, law schools and, eventually, medical schools under that umbrella; and (d) allow national university professors in the natural sciences to launch venture companies that use technology developed at universities or national research centers. These moves can serve as the first step toward upgrading the higher-education system in Japan.

Participation in the globalization of the financial market

To what extent is Japan participating in the globalization of the financial market? To examine this question, we will take a close look at the securities market, which is the most sophisticated, high-value-added, knowledge-intensive and lucrative segment of the financial markets. We will use two indicators to examine whether or not Japan has been able to participate in the emerging globalization of the capital market – the worldwide market share for global M&A deals, and the worldwide share for underwriting services.

There has been a sudden surge in the pace of M&A activities involving Japanese securities firms in recent years. Major M&A deals included Renault's investment in Nissan; GE Capital's acquisition of Japan Lease; JT's (Japan Tobacco) acquisition of RJR Nabisco's overseas cigarette business; NTT DoCoMo's investments in AT&T Wireless and KPN Mobile; NTT's acquisition of Verio; Vodafone's investment in Japan Telecom; and DaimlerChrysler's investment in Mitsubishi Motors, all of which took place after 1999. Given these activities, we would expect Japanese securities firms to be gaining significant market share for M&A deals. However, they have not been able to take advantage of this favorable environment and come out as top contenders in global M&A deals. On the list of the top

10 market-share holders for global M&A deals from 1999 to 2002, there are no Japanese securities firms, a telling indication of their uncompetitiveness.[25]

The second indicator is a similar listing of the top 10 market-share holders of global equity underwriting services. Here again, with the exception of Nomura in 2001, none of the Japanese securities firms are included as the leading underwriters of new issues.[26] As with M&A deals, they have not been able to penetrate the global underwriting-services market at all. These two sets of data paint a very bleak picture of where Japanese securities firms stand with respect to one of the most lucrative segments of the global financial market.

As well as not participating as top contenders in the global securities market, Japanese securities firms seem to be retrenching from their international operations as well, judging from the number of employees working in the overseas offices of the three leading Japanese securities firms.[27] In the case of Daiwa Securities, the total number of employees (including local hires) in their overseas offices peaked in 1997. The retrenchment of Japanese employees dispatched to foreign offices began much earlier. Both Nomura Securities and Nikko Securities (Nikko Solomon Smith Barney since 2000) started to reduce the number of Japanese employees working in overseas offices in 1992.

Obstacles to the globalization of the financial markets[28]

The above analysis points unequivocally to one conclusion: Japanese securities firms have not been able to participate in the globalization of capital markets. This section of the paper will explore the reasons why Japan has not been able to do so.

The biggest obstacle here seems to be the government. For years, Japan operated largely outside the international capital markets. Up until 1996, when the Japanese government introduced an unprecedented financial reform policy, often referred to as the "Japanese Big Bang", the government discouraged foreign companies from taking stakes in Japanese companies. In addition, foreign financial-services firms were not allowed to compete effectively for funds. In the securities industry, foreign direct investment was not liberalized until 1967, branch-office licenses were not granted until 1971, and membership in the Tokyo Stock Exchange was extended to only six foreign firms in 1986.

The dominant owners of Japanese companies have been Japanese banks, insurance companies and other domestic companies that sought stable business relationships through cross-shareholdings. The government imposed stringent regulations on where they could invest. During the immediate postwar period, a series of laws was introduced to regulate the financial market, including the separation of banks and securities firms and the establishment of specialized financial institutions (such as banks for long-term loans and banks concentrating on loans to small- and medium-sized companies). These regulations were intended to allocate scarce financial resources to necessary sectors while the capital market was still undeveloped and bank loans represented the dominant form of corporate financing.

Extensive government regulations ranged from official approval requirements to so-called administrative guidance. For example, securities firms not only needed a license to operate but also Ministry of Finance (MOF) approval for decisions such as setting up new branches, pursuing mergers and entering businesses outside of traditional securities services. In addition to the formal laws and rules, MOF officials promulgated numerous guidelines, many given verbally. Thus, executives from securities firms would visit the MOF desk once or twice a day, and sometimes lobby MOF bureaucrats at expensive restaurants at night.

The capital-market regulations were designed to "protect" shareholders by ensuring that securities firms stayed in business. The approach has been referred to as the "convoy system", in which all ships are slowed down so the slow ships (that is, the weakest firms) can keep up. This was accomplished by guaranteeing profitability to the securities firms through fixed commissions. The government – through approval requirements, guidance, subsidies and other means – inserted itself in corporate decisions instead of trusting the process of market competition to sort them out.

Inward-looking rivalry also exacerbated the problem. In the Ministry of Finance, for example, there was a strong rivalry between the Banking Bureau and the Securities Bureau. Because each bureau tried to protect the territory of the firms it traditionally supervised, new products such as floating-rate notes and medium-term notes that might blur the demarcation between banks and securities firms were never introduced. As a result, Japan became globally uncompetitive in financial services, and Japanese companies were hindered from gaining access to sophisticated financial products.

Japan's lack of competitiveness in financial services influenced the behavior of Japanese citizens, who did not seem interested in pursuing sophisticated financial instruments. Savings comprised nearly 60% of household assets held in Japan, with a high proportion of savings held in low-risk assets such as bank deposits and postal savings. In contrast, savings account for only 11% of household assets held in the U.S., with securities leading all financial instruments at 43%. Securities accounted for only 9.7% of total assets held in Japan in 1999.[29]

All of this points to the government as being the biggest obstacle in the way of the globalization of the capital market. Government policies in the past effectively worked to raise entry barriers, suppress competition, allow the weakest player to survive, discourage innovation, concentrate on the underdeveloped home market and discourage overseas investors.

Starting in the late 1990s, the Japanese government started introducing a series of measures aimed at increasing the free flow of funds across borders and making Japan a more integral member of the international community. They cover a wide range of revisions involving accounting and auditing standards, corporate governance standards, legal standards and tax standards. These revisions provide a glimmer of hope that Japan will actively participate in the globalization of the financial markets in the not-too-distant future.

Participating in the globalization of the product market

Unlike in the labor and financial markets, Japanese companies have participated actively in the globalization of the product market thus far. Japan is a world leader in a number of important industries, ranging from industrial sewing machines to video games. Levitt saw this coming 20 years ago. He singled out Japanese companies as a role model for fulfilling the three criteria required of an effective world competitor back then.

He also pointed out that the Japanese embodied the theory that, "If a company forces costs and prices down and pushes quality and reliability up – while maintaining reasonable concern for suitability – customers will prefer its world-standardized products." He recognized that Japan's distinction rests in "its unrelenting push for economy and value enhancement…[which] translates into a drive for standardization at high quality levels."

To be sure, Japanese companies are still effective world competitors. They still adhere to Levitt's theory. Why, then, is Japan mired in an endless slump? Why is it trailing Korea and Malaysia in the IMD World Competitiveness Ranking? We will try to answer such questions by examining three assertions linked to globalization.

"Unglobal" consumers?

The first assertion is that Japanese consumers have become "unglobal". In other words, only a limited number or percentage of Japanese consumers are buying Western brands, and that these numbers have not increased much in the last 20 years. Just as the Japanese government restricted the entry of foreign securities companies into Japan, there may be restrictions on foreign brands coming into Japan. Or, just as Japanese college graduates are showing little interest in working for foreign-affiliated companies, Japanese consumers may not be buying Western brands any more.

To examine this assertion, we first took the top 50 brands in the world (excluding Japanese brands)[30] and investigated whether they were excluded from the Japanese market. We discovered that this is not the case, as all of the world's top 50 brands are in one way or another present in the Japanese market. They are either being sold here or being offered as a service here.

We then investigated whether the Japanese consumers are no longer buying the brands that used to be very popular 20 years ago. This sample included Louis Vuitton, Mercedes Benz, McDonald's and Disney. The data depicting annual sales for Louis Vuitton,[31] Mercedes Benz,[32] and McDonald's[33] and the number of visitors to Tokyo Disneyland[34] tell us otherwise. As data show Japanese consumers are still in love with these brands, even 20 years after the brands' first appearance.

Two Japans

The second assertion is that there have always been two Japans – the competitive Japan and the uncompetitive Japan – but what is new is the situation where the uncompetitive Japan is beginning to drag down the entire economy. The uncompetitive Japan has two segments. One is the group of internationally traded industries in which Japan has never achieved a significant world export position. Included under this heading are huge sectors such as agriculture, chemicals, consumer packaged goods, medical products, software and virtually all services. The other segment consists of "unglobal" industries such as retailing, wholesaling, transportation and logistics, construction, energy, and healthcare services, all of which are in the service sector.[35]

We found strong evidence of this assertion, especially as it relates to services. Japan has an extremely weak international position in services. In comparing the manufacturing sector with the service sector, average international sales per company of the service sector is extremely small (only 3.7% to be exact) relative to that of the manufacturing sector.

In fact, we can find only one service industry in which Japan has been a clear-cut world leader, namely the video-game software industry. Nintendo, Sony and Sega dominate this industry, with Microsoft playing catch-up. To be sure, there are other pockets of international success in the service industry. Animated movies immediately come to mind, as *Spirited Away* won the Academy Award in 2003. In the music business, karaoke may be another example of international success. In educational services, an after-school supplemental education program known as *Kumon* has received international acclaim. It boasts of 6,700 franchised centers that teach the *Kumon* method of learning outside of Japan. These examples, however, constitute isolated segments within a much larger industry cluster – that is, animated movies within the entire movie business, *karaoke* within music, and the after-school supplemental programs within education.

The Japanese weakness in services stems from a number of factors, some of which we have already discussed. First, the Japanese weakness in the English language is a major impediment, since international services tend to involve extensive personal communication. Second, there is a shortage of specialized talent that can deliver high-quality service in securities, engineering or software, largely as a result of the weak education system. Third, a range of significant service industries (for example, securities, education, health care, and so on) are regulated by the government, making them uncompetitive in the international arena. Finally, since the standard of personal service is exceptionally high, involving large numbers of people, it does not lend itself to the "standardization at high quality levels" that Levitt refers to, and is too costly to replicate abroad.[36]

Anticipatory demand vs. idiosyncratic demand

The third assertion relates to the nature of demand in the home market. Japan has been successful in product categories where sophisticated and demanding home customers have anticipated the needs of other nations (we will call this "anticipatory" demand). Conversely, Japan has not done well in product categories where there has been a misalignment between the idiosyncratic needs of the home customers and the needs of the global market (we will call this "idiosyncratic" demand). In the latter, Japanese customers may be sophisticated and demanding, but their needs do not necessarily anticipate those of other nations.

Examples of Japanese anticipatory demand abound. In fax machines, the unavailability of the Japanese-language typewriters and telex machines coupled with tight office space constraints, large time differences with foreign markets, and expensive telephone charges created a very sophisticated and demanding local market. In robotics, the highly efficient operational practices of Japanese manufacturers, shortages of skilled workers, and tight plant configurations led to sophisticated home demand. In electronic keyboards, limited living space and crowded conditions created the need for products that are much smaller than pianos, can be put away after use, and can also be used with headphones to limit the noise to which others are exposed. In trucks and forklifts, a strong tendency in Japan towards overloading, poor road conditions, high energy costs, and tight space constraints created very demanding home market needs. In air conditioners, small and multiple-use rooms, closely packed houses, hot and muggy summers, and high electricity charges led to stringent local needs.[37]

But more importantly, in all of these cases, the needs of sophisticated and demanding customers in Japan became a leading indicator of broader trends in world demand. In other words, Japanese home demand provided an early warning indicator of buyer needs that became widespread. Japanese demand for compact, light, portable, quiet, multifunctional, energy-efficient products that are affordable and reliable led to these being sought after in other countries as well. Japanese companies that fulfilled these demand conditions, gained undefended routes for entry into foreign markets, not only in the product categories mentioned above, but also in radios, audio equipment, cameras, TV sets, motorcycles, cars, copiers, machine tools, and other consumer electronics and appliances.

Not all sophisticated and demanding needs at home, however, turn into anticipatory demand. In detergents, for example, Japanese consumers have a unique demand for light, compact detergents because they typically go shopping on foot or by bicycle almost every day and carry their own groceries, in addition to living in small homes. However, Kao's premium-priced, concentrated detergent "Attack", which became instantaneously popular in Japan, has had virtually no impact in overseas markets. In plastics, Japanese consumers are very sensitive to appearance and packaging, so manufacturers prepare literally thousands of grades, and supermarkets and other buyers demand shopping bags made of almost flawless high-density polyethylene and reject bags with even tiny spots. No other country is willing to pay higher prices for flawless shopping bags, making Japanese plastics uncompetitive overseas. In apparel, Japanese customers are extremely sensitive to attributes such as fabric, texture and stitching, have a strong attachment to designer brands, are very conscious about the latest trends, and are willing to pay some of the highest prices in the world. These demand conditions, however, are idiosyncratic to Japan and do not anticipate needs elsewhere. As a result, no Japanese manufacturer has become a dominant global player in apparel, nor in detergents and plastics.[38]

The conclusion to be drawn from past examples seems apparent. Sophisticated and stringent home needs benefit national competitiveness only if they anticipate needs elsewhere in the world. If they are idiosyncratic to the nation, they will undermine the competitiveness of local companies. The "unglobalization" of the product market takes place when there is a misalignment between Japanese home needs and the needs of the global market.

Recent examples also seem to suggest the pervasiveness of idiosyncratic demand in Japan. To lend support to this contention, we examine four recent Japanese mega-hit products. Two of them – a mobile phone with a camera/video function, and a plasma-display panel TV, a high-quality TV only one-seventh the thickness of a normal TV – are very new to the Japanese market. The other two – car-navigation systems, and "Washlet", a warm-water bidet toilet introduced by Toto – are long-running best-sellers in Japan. Unit sales of car-navigation systems have increased six-fold since 1997,[39] and the increasing penetration of Washlets within Japanese households reached 47% in 2002.[40]

The question that needed to be evaluated by the Japanese producers was whether these products would take off in other countries as well. In 2003, it was too early to tell with respect to the first two products. Would American and European consumers be prepared to spend $250 to send and receive photos ($350 for video images) and emails over a mobile phone when a regular mobile phone costs less than $50? Similarly, would they be willing to spend $4,000 or so for a 32-inch TV with a flat, thin and high-quality plasma display when a normal 32-inch TV costs around $600? Today, in 2005, we know the answer, but in 2003 it was far from clear whether they would be examples of anticipatory or idiosyncratic demand.

As for the car-navigation systems and Washlet, the verdict is already in. They have not yet taken off in other countries, probably for a very simple reason. Consumers in other countries are not willing to pay a premium price since they do not see the value of the added features. For $2,000 or more, a car-navigation system enables Japanese drivers to automatically search for the best route and avoid traffic jams. Since Japanese roads are complex, crowded and often under repair or construction, a navigation system enhances value, even at that price. American drivers, on the other hand, seem content to use the Thomas Guide for $30. Washlet gives Japanese consumers a lot of comfort for $700 (the latest version costs over $2,000), such as a warm seat with adjustable temperature, a warm-water shower cleaning capability with a movable nozzle (water temperature and shower strength are adjustable), a dryer, a deodorizing feature, a water-saving function, and even automatic flushing. Most Westerners, however, have stuck with the standardized, low-cost toilet that has been around for ages.

These examples should serve as yet another reminder that the needs of Japanese consumers may be out of sync with the needs of the global market. To get back on track, Japanese companies need to go back to the basic "theory" postulated by Levitt 20 years ago, which is to make and sell "goods [and services] of the best quality and reliability at the lowest price".

Conclusion

Twenty years ago, the formula for success for Japan was to offer globally standardized products that were advanced, functional, reliable and low-priced. To regain its competitiveness, Japan needs to rebuild its business environment (that is, the diamond) with a relentless focus on globalization. It needs to change the context for firms' strategy and rivalry ("second base" of the diamond) by eliminating government practices that limit domestic rivalry and distort the nature of competition away from forms that are valued in foreign markets. It must also upgrade the underlying inputs that firms draw on in competing (factor conditions) through the globalization of its labor and capital markets. In addition, it has to elevate the sophistication of home demand (demand conditions) by focusing on the anticipatory needs of its product market. Finally, Japan needs a strong, global financial market as its supporting industry and the formation of clusters around related industries within the financial market.

Will Japan become globally competitive again? Japan is a nation that has demonstrated an extraordinary capacity to transform itself when it is confronted with a seemingly insurmountable challenge – for example, the devastation after World War II, the Oil Shock of the 1970s, and the Yen Shock of 1985. The bigger the challenge and adversity, the more mobilized it becomes to undertake change. This paper suggests that Japan has become "unglobal" in the labor and financial markets and could possibly be heading in that direction with the product market. This kind of a message may be just the challenge Japan needs.

Looking towards the next 20 years, there is an increasing number of believers who say that Japan's future lies in its role as a global trendsetter in cutting-edge music, film-making, design, fashion, architecture and other creative categories of every stripe. According to these believers, Japan will dominate the "Gross National Cool" index in the future, just as it tried to do with Gross National Product in the past.[41] In fact, *Time* magazine carried a 21-page article in which it pointed out that the future of Japan could be salvaged by creative and cultural enterprises. Here's what it had to say about Japan as a global trendsetter:

> *Pokémon has supplanted Astroboy in the hearts of schoolkids in more than 65 countries, and 60% of the world's animated-cartoon series are made in Japan. Games running on PlayStation 2 and (to a lesser degree) Nintendo's Game Cube rule the videogame universe just as tightly as before, despite a frontal attack from none other than Microsoft and its sinister-looking black Xbox. And high-end Japanese fashion designers such as Hanae Mori, Yohji*

> *Yamamoto and Issey Miyake are not only as vital as they once were; they have also been joined by a generation of young turks such as A Bathing Ape, Jun Takahashi and Naoki Takizawa who set the style for hipsters from Berlin to Bangkok and beyond. Japanese films, TV series, music acts and lifestyle magazines, meanwhile, routinely spark fads all over Asia. (Turn on MTV in Singapore or Hong Kong and you are just as likely to see Ayumi Hamasaki as J. Lo.) According to Tsutomu Sugiura, director of the Marubeni Research Institute, an economic think tank, Japanese cultural exports – such as from the media, licensing, entertainment and other related industries – have tripled over the past 10 years to \$12.5 billion, while manufacturing exports have increased by only 20%. Granted, \$12.5 billion seems like a rounding error in Japan's \$4 trillion economy (Toyota alone hauls in nearly \$11 billion in sales every month), but it's still the result of a growth rate almost unheard of anywhere else.*[42]

Judging from the above, 20 years from now, Japan may be better known as an exporter of culture/content than as an exporter of high-quality/low-cost products. The next-generation, globally minded leaders who are coming to power in Japan, however, believe that Japan can become both an exporter of culture/content and an exporter of high-quality/low-cost products. They believe that Japan can become the world's foremost creator of "cool". There is still a sliver of hope for Japan on the globalization front.

▲ GROWING WITH SOCIETY

Bjorn Stigson
President, World Business Council for Sustainable Development
Margaret Flaherty
Director, World Business Council for Sustainable Development[43]

As companies grow from national into global businesses, they will naturally confront new situations, societies and circumstances. Indeed, the challenge for a growing company is not only to manage the "business" side of the growth equation but also to astutely navigate the *social* sides of their expansion. If the *business* side comprises the familiar elements of human resources, finance, branding and the like, the *social* side of expansion has come to imply such issues as community responsibility, environmental sustainability, workplace health and labor matters, among others. It is true that this latter set of issues are not new, in that they have always existed in the field of sustainable development, but their importance to companies has increased almost exponentially since they were first defined. What is remarkable is that what used to be defined as "development" issues, today are integral aspects of agendas of virtually all global companies. In a sense, the corporate mandate has shifted from a concern with monetary or shareholder value, to a much larger concern that the company grow with society. This means that the company actually takes sustainable development as its own primary aim. This means looking beyond "shareholder" value to a larger concept of societal value in all its aspects – the environment, culture, workers and community.

We propose that the prioritization of societal value will yield benefits not only for society but also, and importantly, for the company itself. That is because the global tasks of sustainable development and business development are intimately linked and complementary. As the world has acknowledged that expanding businesses should take on global and social responsibilities, the corporate community has also realized that the business case for sustainable development is a strong one, backed not only by a business agenda but also by strong public-policy and environmental considerations.

Unfortunately, this is easier said than done. Although there are a number of initiatives of Asian companies, or companies operating in Asia, that highlight innovative, profitable ways toward a sustainable future, the field is also littered with companies that have adopted the language without the practice. We should not automatically assume disingenuousness on the part of the companies; frequently, it may be simply a lack of tools or information. There is still much work to be done to develop consistent and recognized standards, especially in Asia, where the CSR movement is still taking shape around a very loose set of issues. The World Business Council for Sustainable Development (WBCSD), which we represent, is part of a larger global effort to gather knowledge, share best practices and track implementation of the profits of sustainable development.

To aid companies that wish to take action in this area, the WBCSD has developed a "CSR navigator" which incorporates a number of strategic issues that companies should take into account when attempting to integrate sustainability thinking into their core business practice. Every company's situation is different, and the guidance we provide should be tailored to the company's stage of development, its regional or global footprint, and its specific capabilities. A significant part of the WBCSD's mission is to raise awareness of the business case for sustainable development. Most agree that it is a good thing, but we hope to show that it can be a profitable choice as well.

Setting the stage

The evolution of sustainable development

The history of sustainable development is a relatively modern one. The 30-year journey started in 1972, when the U.N. Stockholm Summit took place, focusing on global environmental challenges. At a U.N. conference in Bergen, Norway, 18 years later, business representatives were present, for the first time at such a meeting, to discuss how they could contribute to the making of a sustainable society. The participants realized that the protection of the environment and business interests could be mutually beneficial. At the Rio Earth Summit in 1992, the focus was broadened to include both the environment and economic development, recognizing the close links. And finally, the World Summit for Sustainable Development (WSSD) in 2000 marked the first time the three pillars of sustainable development – social responsibility, environmental progress and economic viability – were seen in an integrated way. The business community was particularly active in this meeting and, indeed, there were more CEOs than heads of governments present. The meeting symbolized a new shift to focus on implementation rather than norms and principles of sustainable development.

Two sustainable development agendas

Today there are as many agendas on sustainable development as there are interest groups, but the business community needs to address two issues in particular: a public-policy agenda and a business agenda.

The public-policy agenda is based on a mix of plans or agreements recently committed to, such as the Millennium Development Goals, Agenda 21, the Doha Declaration, the Monterrey Consensus and the different Multilateral Environmental Agreements, which have been concluded in the past 10 years. This public-policy agenda consists of environmental and social challenges identified as being common to all societies. Although it is not driven from inside the business community, the agenda includes issues that all companies will face, such as:

- globalization and global governance
- the alleviation of poverty
- sustainable production and consumption
- the health of the ecosystems
- energy and climate change
- the role of innovation and technology
- accountability and reporting
- risk.

On the global level, this past decade has witnessed a number of international agreements setting goals for the international community. The difficulty with these goals is that they are political compromises. They are more or less binding and more or less supported by individual countries. There are also often challenged because of scientific uncertainty or because the analysis that underpins them is unclear.

Further, different parts of the world have very different priorities for sustainable development. In the European Union, the focus is on climate, sustainable production and consumption, public health and natural resources. The G77 countries want more Official Development Assistance (ODA), debt relief, and access to technology, health services, water and energy. The priorities of the United States are on the war on terror and improved local governance in developing countries. In Africa, the focus is on the New Partnership for Africa's Development (NEPAD).

Given this background, it is not strange that governments find it difficult to come to concrete agreements at international summits. The multiple interests shaping the public-policy agenda also present a challenge to business: how can a company operating internationally manage the different social demands?

The business agenda, by contrast, focuses on why addressing sustainable development makes good business sense while, at the same time, improving the environmental and social performance of a company. The business agenda also provides guidance for companies in how to manage the transition to sustainable practices. The business agenda is continuing to evolve along with the ways in which issues are being considered. For instance, we see companies broadening their considerations to include both the environment and wider social and sustainability challenges. At the same time, what was once discussed just in boardrooms is now actively being integrated into business models and company branding.

As they begin to manage sustainability issues, companies are reaching out to form working groups and partnerships with governments and other organizations. On an industry level, for instance, there is a growing interest from business looking at performance and sustainability challenges for the entire value chain of an industry. They want to understand future challenges better in order to create more stable platforms for long-term investments, and to strengthen their "license to operate". Companies can also influence the performance of their peers via voluntary, industry-specific standards, such as the Responsible Care program in the chemical industry.

Because sustainable development is a relatively new field that is not yet fully regulated by governments, companies are seeing themselves as active players in designing policies. A number of working groups facilitate this process, such as the China Council for Sustainable Development described below.

Companies may involve civil society (NGOs or other interest groups) in their efforts towards sustainable development in order to gain expertise, new ideas, credibility or trust. The WBCSD is just one example; various U.N. or independent organizations, such as the IUCN–World Conservation Union and the International Institute for Sustainable Development (IISD), may address other issues.

The business case for sustainable development

Regardless of the larger social or environmental reasons backing the case for sustainable development, the best way to secure the active involvement of the business community is to build a strong business case for it. Our book *Walking the Talk*, released at the 2002 WSSD, outlines the sustainable-development case from a societal perspective. Here, we define the business perspective. We are convinced that there *is* a compelling case, but that it needs to be made in a way that is easily understood and applied by business leaders. The key elements of the case are described below.

- **Market valuation**
  Historically, the value of a company was defined mainly by physical assets such as land and access to raw material. Today, however, it appears that an increasing amount of a company's market capitalization can come from intangible assets. These intangibles include reputation, brand, ability to adapt and change, public perceptions and the ability to engage in dialogue and partnerships with stakeholders. It is hardly coincidental that the value of these assets is highly influenced by the company's management of the public-policy agenda discussed above. In addition, a growing field of evaluations indicates a positive correlation between leadership on sustainable development and superior performance of a company's stock price.
- **Efficiency**
  A number of "normal" business practices increase efficiency and profitability while improving the environmental and social performance of a company, including eco-efficiency, safety and local community interaction. Eco-efficiency refers to a company's ability to reach "zero pollution" in its operations; that is, through optimized processes that prevent pollution in the first place. With waste recycling, the by-products and wastes of one industry are used as raw materials and resources for another. Eco-innovation refers to the use of new knowledge to make old products more resource-efficient to produce or use. New services, such as leasing products rather than selling them, change companies' perceptions, spurring a shift to product durability and recycling. Shared resources, such as arise in networked offices, can also increase the effective use of physical assets. All of these actions are good for the company and create more resource-efficient societies in general. In order to enable both the public and business community

to understand and implement these, the WBCSD started a collection of case studies that contains many examples of companies that have taken action.

Another area that has proven to bring value to a company is safety. If machinery is well maintained, staff are adequately trained and accidents are reduced to a minimum, companies will reap rich benefits in efficiency savings, as well as eliminating the danger of costly repairs, delays and reputation-damaging law suits. In the same way, "being a good neighbor" will create a more stable and efficient environment for plant operations and will facilitate approvals for new investments and government regulations.

Taiheiyo Cement Corporation: Using urban waste for "Eco-cement"

Japan generates 450 million metric tons of waste per annum, but the construction of new landfill sites is virtually impossible because of the "not in my backyard" (NIMBY) syndrome. Previously, the Japanese cement industry has used up to 24 million metric tons of industrial waste per year to make mixed and ordinary Portland cement. However, urban waste and incinerated ash was not being utilized for cement production.

To address the waste problems in Japan and to explore the opportunities for using urban waste, Eco-cement was developed by Taiheiyo. The objective of this research, and the project that emerged, was to develop technologies that utilized urban wastes, such an incinerator ash and sewage sludge, to ultimately prolong the life of landfill sites in areas suffering waste-disposal problems. A further objective of this research was to design processes that removed toxic and harmful elements from the waste products being used for the cement production.

As a result of the research, the basic idea of "Eco-cement" was developed by Taiheiyo. There was extensive dialogue with various stakeholders during 1991–1992, when work on developing the pilot plant started as a national project funded by the Ministry of International Trade and Industry (MITI). The pilot plant test was conducted by a consortium made up of Taiheiyo, Aso Cement Co., Ltd., Ebara Corporation and

Dowa Mining Co., Ltd., while the operating and remodeling costs were shared by the first three of these companies.

As a part of the Eco-town Plan of Chiba Prefecture in Japan, the first Eco-cement plant was designed in 1998 to address serious waste-disposal problems in the Prefecture, where, annually, disposal of incineration ash in landfills had reached around 240,000 metric tons.

The Eco-cement process has successfully converted urban wastes to a product whose quality has been recognized as safe by research scientists and engineers. The recently constructed Eco-cement plant in Ichihara will use incinerator ash from 26 cities and municipalities, with a production capacity of about 350 metric tons per day.

Eco-cement is a breakthrough because, up until now, the waste-management market has been dominated by brokers, the transport industry, the owners of landfill sites and some machinery makers. Eco-cement is one of the first examples of a manufacturer of basic materials becoming involved in the use of urban wastes as alternative fuels and raw materials.

- **License to operate**

  A company's response to the public-policy agenda will affect its reputation or how it is perceived by society. This can, in turn, affect a company in various ways. For instance, investment approvals in developing countries today often include considerations of a company's environmental and social track record, which can determine where a company can and cannot grow. In addition, in an age in which a company's employees are becoming key assets, the best and brightest are increasingly considering a company's values, principles and reputation in deciding where to work. Lastly, government, trade unions, NGOs and other organizations are more likely to give a company with a good sustainable-development performance the benefit of the doubt. To a growing degree, therefore, companies will have to verify their credentials via sustainable-development reporting.

- **Risk reduction**
  A coherent and thorough sustainable-development policy and procedures can reduce the risk of environmental issues becoming a problem for a company, thereby reducing its overall risk profile. Asbestos litigation, pollution spills and clean-up costs are all examples of how companies can be plagued by environmental issues long after the problem occurs. As its risk profile is reduced, the company will be rewarded through reduced costs of capital and insurance.
- **Market opportunities**
  The focus on sustainable development will lead to both the development of new markets and increased returns from products and brands with positive environmental and social properties. Although there are still questions about how much more customers are willing to pay to purchase more environmentally friendly products, there is little doubt that people are becoming more sensitive to these matters. The increased use of terms and images linked with sustainability in advertising should bolster the case that the process of educating customers and companies about environmental issues can be mutually reinforcing. Another new market opportunity lies in the developing world, where the majority of growth in consumer markets and labor will occur. To stimulate these huge markets, which are dominated by young populations, it is in the interest of business to support a supply of products and services that are affordable and will increase people's quality of life. The social and economic well-being of these new markets is necessary if we want to maintain open and stable global markets. Finally, another type of new market is seen in the growing marketization of environmental protection. Sulfur-emissions trading has existed for a long time in the U.S., and we now see CO_2-emissions trading in the E.U. and in the U.S. via the Chicago Climate Exchange (CCX).
- **Protecting the resource base of raw materials**
  We are currently consuming many natural resources at a faster rate than they can be replenished, and yet major industries depend on sustaining our natural resource base for their existence and success. For companies relying on the food or pharmaceutical

industries, the proper functioning of ecosystems such as climate, rainfall and waterways, fisheries, top-soil or forests is a prerequisite to their continued existence. For industries based on non-renewable resources , such as mining and the fossil-fuel-based energy sector, the conditions under which we extract and use the natural resources will determine their viability – both short- and long-term.

Innovation and technology can help us to address the dilemmas presented by a growing population, increasing living standards and the physical limitations of the planet. However, there is no guarantee that they will be sufficient for the task. Clearly, business needs to improve its efficiency in order to use fewer resources of which we have only a limited supply. Eco-efficiency principles have proven profitable in the short term and will also determine a company's longer-term viability.

Generating greener electricity in China

Rapid economic growth has increased China's demand for electricity. Although the country has huge coal reserves, burning coal is one of the most environmentally damaging ways to generate electricity.

In 1999, ABB, together with the Alliance for Global Sustainability, launched its biggest-ever study of sustainable development. Called the China Energy Technology Program (CETP), its aim was to analyze the true, cradle-to-grave impact of a range of power-generation options, focusing on the needs of Shandong, a rapidly developing coastal province between Beijing and Shanghai. The CETP involved some 70 scientists, engineers and academics from three continents, as well as representatives of local stakeholders, in a study that took nearly three years.

The results showed that it is both feasible and economically and socially justifiable to generate more electricity with less air pollution and associated damage to health and the environment. In addition, the program showed that there are cost-efficient ways to cut air pollutants and stabilize greenhouse-gas emissions. A more sustainable electricity-supply industry requires the use of improved technologies, fuel treatment and diversification, and demand-side management.

The CETP provided a platform to explore various options and trade-offs for sustainability, based on the preferences of stakeholders. Though the project dealt with just one province, the methodology developed should be applicable to other locations. Hence, the CETP could bring significant environmental benefits, not just in China, but globally.[44]

- **The meaning of life**
  In all religions there is a strong sense of responsibility toward nature, neighbors and future generations. Business is an integrated part of society and needs to share the responsibility for handing over to future generations a world that will make it possible for them to meet their needs. As the Nobel Prize winner Murray Gell-Mann expressed it: "Sustainability means living on nature's income rather than its capital."

The WBCSD response

To deal with these agendas, the WBCSD has developed two work streams. The first is Council Projects funded by the entire membership which cover many of the public-policy agenda items such as climate change, poverty eradication, corporate social responsibility and corporate accountability. We currently have three Council Projects: Energy and Climate, Sustainable Livelihoods, and Accountability and Reporting.

The second type of programs are focused sector projects, which address what sustainable development really means for a particular industry and help companies convert this knowledge into action. These projects are a unique feature of our work, and are unique in the global effort to achieve sustainable development. They are practical initiatives, which complement government activities. They are rooted in independent research, to work out how critical industries can meet sustainability challenges. Each of our projects adopts a participatory approach to develop solutions broadly supported by stakeholders. Acceptance by stakeholders is necessary for industry to maintain its license to operate and to achieve a stable environment for long-term investment.

The outcome of these projects is not simply a series of recommendations. Rather, projects develop targets and indicators to measure the sectors' progress toward sustainability, which then makes it easier for companies to engage in change. We know from our work that companies are prepared to take action to make that change happen.

Many may ask whether CSR is different for companies from developing and developed countries. This question is especially potent in Asia, where Western sensitivities over labor standards, human rights, religious and political freedom and the environment seem to be luxuries that many Asian businesses cannot yet afford. Asians ask how the industrialized West could impose their visions of these issues when they have pursued capitalist expansion unfettered for more than a century. Asian businesses engaged in the day-to-day struggle to be competitive may see the scrutiny of their practices as unwarranted. Moreover, in many Asian countries, companies have served social objectives for a long time, particularly under state communism. Also, bonds of family and friendship have traditionally played a more important role in the East than in the West, where the separation of ownership and control and the impact of mobility have weakened such ties.

Today, however, concerns can no longer be localized. Not only do companies increasingly operate across multiple borders, but socially responsible investment has also reached a stage in Europe and the U.S. where it is affecting the way companies work all over the world. Smart business leaders, whether in Asia or elsewhere, will see the competitive advantage in anticipating the demands for greater accountability and socially responsible practices. In the WBCSD's dialogues with stakeholders worldwide, we discovered that while CSR may mean different things from place to place, the constant theme was that companies should engage with and listen to communities to strengthen their license to operate.

Piloting CSR in emerging markets: The China Business Council for Sustainable Development

A key vehicle for promoting business involvement in sustainable development worldwide are country-specific groups linked to the WBCSD global network. One such group is the China Business Council for Sustainable Development, which was started in 2003 and which is one of the first organizations of this kind in China. Bringing together a cross-section of national and foreign companies such as Sinopec, Novozymes, BASF, Shell, BP and Lafarge, the China BCSD – a joint initiative of the WBCSD and the China Enterprise Confederation (CEC) – aims to implement more sustainable practices in the country.

Despite the high growth levels of China's economy, Chinese companies face major challenges in implementing more sustainable practices, such as improving resource and energy efficiency. Another challenge is the need to restructure industry sectors to achieve economies of scale that will enable these sectors to afford environmentally friendly modern technology. We hope that the China BCSD can provide its members and companies in the wider community with the experience and knowledge to achieve the best solutions for the specific conditions in China. Specific priorities for 2004 include:

- Raise awareness and build capacity on sustainable development in management schools and public administration institutions
- Promote higher environmental standards and eco-efficiency within Chinese industry
- Cooperate actively with Chinese authorities on policy development.

A CSR navigator

Perhaps our most relevant work for companies seeking to globalize involves corporate social responsibility (CSR), or strategies by which companies work toward social change. The WBCSD's CSR navigator provides guidance for companies on managing the implementation of CSR and thus is both a tool and a conceptual approach that can be adapted to suit a company's individual situation. It indicates direction and demands vision, but does not dictate the speed of progress. It is flexible enough to respond to individual challenges and dilemmas. The navigator emphasizes that the vigor with which a particular company pursues its vision on CSR is specific to that company's individual location – its geography, industrial sector, and so on – and should be tailored to what works best for the company. The WBCSD navigator consists of distinct reference points, which can be used along a company's CSR journey.

Determine your "magnetic north"

Companies should determine and articulate their CSR direction – their "magnetic north" – at the start of their journey. Repeatedly, our global consultations have reinforced this simple message. Though the terminology might be different – people variously refer to values, ethics, religion, tribal custom or codes of conduct – the overriding message is clear: determine and articulate your company's vision and values, your corporate "magnetic north". Tell people what you stand for and what you are prepared to be judged on. If you fail to do this, other people will tell you what you should do. Determining a company's "magnetic north" is neither easy nor straightforward. However, it is essential if the company is to address the complex and expanding business/social agenda emerging in the new millennium. So the message is: start now. Involve your best people throughout your organization. Demonstrate top-level involvement and commitment. If you don't, your company will fall behind, and any attempt to embark on the CSR journey will be longer and harder.

Build-in the strategic business case

Integrating social responsibility into an overall company strategy demonstrates a company's readiness to ensure that social concerns are an integral part of business strategy. A holistic approach to the challenges we face in our companies is usually the most productive. Our advice is to approach CSR as you would any investment: look for positive returns or reduction of risk; seek buy-in from managers, supervisors and employees; work with them, provide support and encourage them to recognize the good business sense of a CSR strategy. The intrinsically pragmatic approach to business in Asia means that companies that embrace globalization will generally accept the discipline imposed by exposure to international capitalism and the need to conform to global best practice.

Focus on individuals

Overall, CSR reaches out to the collective entity of stakeholders – shareholders, employees, communities, NGOs, consumers, partners and others. But to be truly effective, CSR needs to take account of the implications for individuals. Determine ways for the individual – whether citizen, consumer, employee, or manager – to contribute to CSR as well as the means for determining individual accountability.

The primary direction of globalization is toward liberalism, which is built partly around individualism. Indeed, the increasing wealth of Asians may itself lead to a shift in cultural values away from collectivism and toward individualism. As we shall see, companies that recognize the power of the individual are already capitalizing upon this trend. Micro-credit programs such as that built by Deutsche Bank are also boosting this vital level of business activity.

Deutsche Bank: Micro-credit Development Fund

From the rural villages of Asia to the urban centers of the United States, small loans to emerging entrepreneurs create opportunities for self-employment and dignified lifestyles for millions. With micro-credit, loans are given to those who need it most – the poor at the grassroots level. Without micro-credit, such loans would not be possible as these people are unable to meet the requirements of traditional banking practices, which call for collateral or previous credit experience.

Micro-credit institutions are proving to be a revolutionary force in enabling families to rise from poverty through the creation of opportunities for self-employment. Also, in the context of group-borrowing structures, recipients of micro-credit are proving to be good credit risks. Micro-credit institutions lending to the poor typically achieve repayment rates exceeding 97%, with such loans currently reaching nearly 23 million borrowers. The industry continues to grow rapidly.

In recent years, micro-finance has established itself as being particularly effective in fighting poverty. By providing unsecured micro-loans of, typically, US$100 to the world's poorest, institutions such as the Grameen Bank in Bangladesh have enabled millions to rise above the poverty line. Moreover, such institutions operate profitably and often have repayment rates higher than commercial banks. For the past few years, the Deutsche Bank Micro-credit Development Fund has been working to assist such institutions by providing capital and technical support.

A loan from the Deutsche Bank Micro-credit Fund of US$75,000 was made to the Society for Helping and Awakening Rural Poor through Education (SHARE), which serves very poor skilled and unskilled rural female entrepreneurs in India. This loan, at 10:1 leverage, realizes a US$750,000 increase in lending capacity over the average 11.5-month term (equivalent to US$780,000 per annum), for a total impact of US$3,900,000 over the five-year Deutsche Bank Micro-credit Fund loan term.

With loans from SHARE, Hafiza Bee, her husband and their six children are experiencing newfound hope. Hafiza's relationship with SHARE began in 1988 when she organized four other women to become the first group in their village to participate in the SHARE loan program. With her first loan of US$80 (Rs4,000), Hafiza purchased a buffalo. Sales of three liters of milk a day gave her a sense of achievement as she repaid the loan and also had funds to cover household expenditures. With the additional income, the family could begin to save a portion of the earnings from her father's tailoring business. Additional loan proceeds have resulted in expanded family enterprises, including new sewing machines for her sons, who are now tailors in the family business. Hafiza began to expand her own hand-stitching and embroidery business, which resulted in her appointment as a teacher of a government stitching center in her village and provided her with a regular monthly salary.

Determine your legacy: Foster competence and capacity

To ensure a focus on long-term sustainability, companies should instill an ethic of education and learning, and institute processes to foster it. Strive to leave as small an industrial footprint as can reasonably be expected but as large a local contribution and sustainable livelihood legacy as you can. It is no longer enough to provide a salary and pay taxes. People want to learn how to build a better future. With Asia's burgeoning populations, this attention to fostering sustainable livelihoods will be a long-term business imperative.

Unilever: Entrepreneurs in Indonesia

In Indonesia, 90% of all businesses are small or medium-sized and are responsible for generating over half the country's income. They are a major engine for growth in the local economy, so the Indonesian government is keen to find new ways of encouraging more entrepreneurs to start businesses.

Unilever Indonesia works with over 2,000 small and medium-sized suppliers and distributors, and is therefore an appropriate partner to work with the country's Department of Trade and Industry and others to create more first-generation small business start-ups.

A series of pilot projects started in 2000 has been highly successful, not only for the economy but also for Unilever Indonesia. One scheme has involved training unemployed youths to become entrepreneurs selling Unilever products, while another has created a new distribution channel for the company to reach small shops and kiosks in rural areas. Unilever Indonesia is now establishing a business incubator to provide training and business advice for entrepreneurs.

Source: Global challenges local actions (Unilever ESR overview)

Put employees first: Assets, agents and ambassadors

In the quest to enhance shareholder value, be prepared to say that your employees are the number-one consideration among a range of other stakeholders. This does not negate the importance of other stakeholders but CSR includes decisions about setting priorities, facing dilemmas and making trade-offs. Community groups, regulators, NGOs and employees are all vital when addressing CSR. But, based on our global consultations, we believe that employees and employee relations can carry more weight in addressing CSR. Transform your workforce into active agents for change. Convince them that socially responsible business practices are central to a company's continued success. Encourage diversity, initiative and an open exchange of ideas. Provide the skills training to make jobs more portable. Survival in Asia's growing knowledge-based economies depends upon this and, collectively, your employees can be the greatest driver for promoting good CSR practice.

Know your neighbor: Community and culture

Understand and define who and what your community is and assess its implications for your operations. Invest in identifying what makes communities different or similar. Explore how local culture, language and religions complement or conflict with management approaches. Show respect for differences as well as similarities.

This is as important for Asia-based corporations as it is for outsiders seeking to expand their operations into Asian markets.

Debate and dialogue: Establish a system and process

Focus on the process for systematic and transparent dialogue. Use this to understand the impact of your company on people's lives. This is best done early, with an attitude of constructive engagement. Inaction means losing contact and becoming out of touch with those that matter. A constant theme in our stakeholder dialogues was the call for greater interaction and consideration of stakeholders' views.

Pursue smart partnerships

Strategic collaborations with clear objectives are an essential component for any company looking to address corporate social issues and we encourage companies to foster such relationships. However, companies should recognize that partnerships that result only from the desire for publicity often dilute the truly positive effects of valuable collaboration. Partnerships that provide cover for inaction or have dubious objectives will sap people's energy and waste time and money. Involve your employees, consult stakeholders and look for win-win situations.

Asian government intervention in business through industrial and trade policies will remain important in strategic sectors. This has shaped the characteristic enterprises that have developed and foreign investors must work within that context. In China, in particular, the state is involved in attracting firms and guiding their activities, and is also a major business operator and therefore a potential collaborator, partner or, even, competitor.

China Council Task Force on Business and Sustainable Development

The China Council[45] is a long-standing advisory group to the Chinese government consisting of foreign experts and senior Chinese government representatives. It has been operating for the last 10 years, making a variety of policy recommendations directly to senior Chinese leadership to improve government functions, transparency, financial markets and business practices. Task forces on specific topics run for two to three years and are the Council's primary work. They cover topics such as energy policy, financial markets, environmental markets, the WTO and the environment, and so on. In 2002, a new Task Force on Business and Sustainable Development was established with a mandate to report policy recommendations back to the Council. The Task Force will make recommendations on new government policies to encourage more sustainable business practices in China's rapidly growing economy, by comparing best international and Chinese practices in four sectors: pulp and paper, cement, petroleum refining, and sugar.

Remember, reputation matters

Reputation is a key business asset and should be carefully protected. That is part of the business case for investing in CSR, which provides the framework in which a company does, and is seen to be doing, the right thing for reasons other than immediate financial returns. Transparency and credibility will build a strong reputation over time and generate loyalty that can be relied upon in times of crisis.

Be a good guest, but let your story be heard

Your company is a guest in various communities and should behave accordingly. Show respect and consideration for your hosts. At the same time, find the appropriate way to communicate openly with them about your contributions to society. That open relationship will also be an asset if problems arise.

Measure and account for what you do

Take a positive and proactive attitude to measuring and reporting progress. Whatever method your company selects, the important thing is to be prepared to meet demands for measurement and accountability. Indications are that these demands will increase in the years ahead. If you are not properly equipped to manage this challenge, your credibility and reputation will suffer. One of the ways to approach this challenge is to align your company's principles with a code of practice, examples of which are mentioned in our last section, "Going forward". Internal accountability will make the transition to better practice easier, however. See the adidas-Salomon case below, for an example of the way in which one of the realities of modern business – the outsourcing of operations to cheaper labor markets – can be monitored to protect against reputation-damaging revelations.

adidas-Salomon: Supply-chain management

Using an external supply chain has allowed adidas-Salomon to keep its costs down and remain competitive. However, the company's supply chain is long and complex, relying on about 570 factories around the world. In Asia alone, its suppliers operate in 18 different countries. Moreover, its cost-saving use of external suppliers is not without risks: in particular, the company has less control over workplace conditions at its suppliers' factories than it would have at company-owned sites.

Outsourcing supply should not mean abdicating moral responsibility. Therefore, adidas-Salomon has designed and implemented a comprehensive global supply-chain management strategy, which allows the company to source from the cheapest *acceptable* sources rather than from the cheapest *possible*. The company has its own "standards of engagement" (SOE) and the level of acceptability is based on the values of the company itself. Contractors, subcontractors, suppliers and others are therefore expected to conduct themselves in line with adidas-Salomon's SOE.

Before a relationship is formed with any new supplier, an internal audit is carried out to ensure that working conditions in that supplier meet the company's SOE criteria. All business partners sign an agreement committing them to comply with the SOE and to take responsibility for their subcontractors' performance on workplace conditions. The monitoring process is continuous, as suppliers are audited at least once a year, and more often if serious problems are detected.

Handle information, knowledge and technology with care

The results of the technology revolution and the implications of our knowledge-based economy are only just beginning to be apparent but they are bringing profound change on a global scale. Communications technology offers great potential for inclusion and education and new ways for companies to communicate their philosophies and accomplishments. But the frontiers of new technology also pose challenges: they can exclude and are open to exploitation, and careful thought is needed to safeguard against this. The Internet is opening Asian businesses to the world, and companies need to be ready for the ramifications of this: greater scrutiny, unpredictable competition and security risks. Coherent communications and cyber-ethics strategies, with effective training, are the way forward here.

Going forward

In conclusion, there are a number of key developments that companies will need to watch closely as they move in to a more sustainable, socially responsible business era.

First, they will need to pay more attention to, and have more sensitivity for, the concerns of suppliers and customers, especially as the latter become more informed. The questions of human rights and the tolerance of religion in the workplace will continue to gain momentum and visibility as issues of fundamental importance.

Public antipathy to corporations which, for example, use child labor or attempt to foist genetically modified produce on unsuspecting consumers, will lead to a rise in the use of product labels that guarantee the absence of such practices. We will see ever-closer scrutiny by stakeholders and the media of business practices, accountability, transparency, treatment of employees, treatment of customers, ingredients, marketing, advertising and sourcing. The levels of board/CEO compensation will also be watched carefully and, to avoid reputation-damaging criticism, should be kept commensurate with a company's performance. Companies that can survive such scrutiny with relatively unblemished reputations will benefit from positive media coverage and publicity. One route to this goal is adherence to codes of practice and external standards such as those provided by the U.N.'s Global Compact, the Global Reporting Initiative, the Global Sullivan Principles of social responsibility, or the Social Accountability 8000 standard (SA8000).

The key challenge for business in contributing to a sustainable future will not be how corporations are managed. It will, rather, be how we address the expectation that business should play a larger role in building well-functioning societies. A successful future awaits companies that can link existing decision processes with input from society in a meaningful way. Business cannot and should not replace governments. But it is also impossible to provide goods and services in a sustainable way in non-functioning societies.

Business cannot succeed in societies that fail.

Endnotes

1 Michael Porter, Hirotaka Takeuchi and Mariko Sakakibara, *Can Japan Compete?* UK: Macmillan, 2000.

2 The Index of microeconomic competitiveness comprises two variables, one of which refers directly to "company operations and strategy". Michael Porter and Klaus Schwab, *The Global Competitiveness Report 2002-2003*, Oxford University Press, 2003.

3 See, for instance, the strong statements for CSR in *Asia's New Crisis: Renewal through Total Ethical Management* (Richter and Mar, ed., , Singapore: John Wiley and Sons, 2004) in which companies such as Ayala Corp, Mitsubishi Motors and Woori Bank, among others, present their visions of CSR as deeply integrated within the company's overall ethical approach.

4 This article has been adapted from Hirotaka Takeuchi, "The Globalization of Markets Revisited: Japan After 20 Years" in Rohit Despandé and John Quelch, *eds., The Globalization of Markets*, San Francisco: Jossey-Bass, forthcoming.

5 Theodore Levitt, "The Globalization of Markets", *Harvard Business Review*, May-June, 1983.

6 Peter K. Cornelius, Klaus Schwab, Michael E. Porter, *Global Competitiveness Report 2002–2003*, Oxford University Press, New York and Oxford, 2003.

7 For a full description of the diamond framework, see Michael E. Porter (1990), *Competitive Advantage of Nations*, Chapter 3.

8 Works Institute of Recruit Co., Ltd.

9 Ibid.

10 Interview with Nobutaka Machimura, Director-General, Election Bureau, Liberal Democratic Party on March 18, 2003.

11 TOEFL, Official Website for The Test of English as a Foreign Language.

12 OECD, "First Results from the OECD Program for International Student Assessment (PISA) 2000".

13 *Toko-kyohi*: Students who refuse to attend school and are absent more than 30 days in one year.

14 Okabe, K., Kose, N. and Nishimura, K. (1999), *College Students Who Cannot Calculate Fractions* (*Bunsu ga Dekinai Daigakusei*). Tokyo: Toyo Keizai Shinpousha.

15 The Gourman Report, 1997

16 Porter et al (2000), pp.143–147.

17 *Asahi Shimbun*, January 5, 2003.

18 Porter et al, (2000), p.145.

19 Ibid, p.144.

20 Ministry of Education, Culture, Sports, Science and Technology, "White Paper, Science and Technology, 2002".

21 *Asahi Shimbun*, November 30, 2002.

22 One exception is Hitotsubashi University's Graduate School of International Corporate Strategy, which placed all of its first-time graduates with professional firms and global companies last year.

23 *The Global Competitiveness Report 2001–2002*, p.429.

24 As quoted in October 2, 2000, issue of *BusinessWeek* and *Financial Times* of October 30, 2000.

25 Thomson Financial, based on announced or completed value excluding split-offs and open market repurchases.

26 *Investor Dealer Digest (IDD),* based on international or global initial public offering values.

27 Based on interview with Daiwa Securities, Nomura Securities and Nikko Solomon Smith Barney.

28 This section draws on Porter et al (2000), pp.23–27, 33–35 and 62–63.

29 Federal Reserve Board, "Flow of Funds Accounts of the United States 2001".

30 *BusinessWeek*, "The 100 Top Brands", August 6, 2001.

31 "Import Market & Brand Year 2002", Yano Research Institute.

32 Based on interview with Daimler Chrysler Group Japan.

33 McDonald's, Corporate Website.

34 Oriental Land, Corporate Website.

35 Porter et al (2000), pp.5–6.

36 Porter (1990), p.406.

37 Porter et al (2000), p.108–109, and Porter (1990), pp.402–403 for further discussion of these examples.

38 Porter et al, (2000), pp. 34–35 and 108–110, and Porter (1990), pp. 402–404 for further discussion of these examples.

39 Ministry of Land Infrastructure and Transport.

40 Economic and Social Research Institute, Cabinet Office, Consumer Trends.

41 "Gross National Cool", *Foreign Policy*, May-June 2002, p.24.

42 "What's Right with Japan", *Time*, August 11, 2003, p.24.

43 The World Business Council for Sustainable Development (WBCSD) is a coalition of 175 leading international companies that share a commitment to sustainable development. The WBCSD's mission is to provide business leadership as a catalyst for change toward sustainable development and to promote eco-efficiency, innovation and corporate social responsibility.

Member companies are drawn from 35 countries and more than 20 major industrial sectors and are represented in the council by their CEOs or equivalent. The WBCSD also benefits from a regional network of 40 national and regional Business Councils for Sustainable Development (BCSDs) and partner organizations, representing over 1,000 local members mainly in developing countries. The network's presence in Asia includes BCSDs in Korea, Thailand, the Philippines, India, Indonesia and Malaysia, Hong Kong and Taiwan. The China BCSD was formed recently, and the WBCSD has strengthened links with the business community in Japan through the newly formed Japan Business Federation.

44 Source: ABB Sustainability Report , June 2002.

45 The Council is co-chaired by Bjorn Stigson and Zhang Yanning, the Vice-Chairman of the China Enterprise Confederation.

CHAPTER

10 Reflection: The European Experience

■ Sir Geoffrey Owen

Senior Fellow, Institute of Interdisciplinary Management,

London School of Economics, U.K.

For some large European companies, internationalization is nothing new. Firms such as Siemens in Germany, Ericsson in Sweden, or the two great Anglo-Dutch groups, Royal Dutch Shell and Unilever, have been engaged for many years in creating and managing production and sales subsidiaries all over the world. Within Europe itself, the creation of the European Economic Community at the end of the 1950s forced firms in the original six member countries, and then in the countries such as the U.K. which joined later, to develop Europe-wide strategies, often involving cross-border investment as well as exports from their home base.

This historical experience might be thought to have given European firms an advantage, vis-à-vis their Asian counterparts, in coping with the increase in international competition which began in the 1970s and became even more marked in the 1980s and 1990s. Yet this latest phase of what has come to be called "globalization" differs from the past in two important respects, and poses new challenges even for the most experienced multinationals.

First, there are more players in the game. The rise of Japan and the so-called Asian tigers has profoundly altered the dynamics of competition in a variety of industries, ranging from textiles to electronics. The success of these late-industrializing nations has encouraged other countries, notably China and India, to abandon autarky and protectionism in favor of more outward-looking policies. For European firms, this policy shift has created new market opportunities, but it has also opened the way for new competitors. Indian software firms are already making an impact on the world market, and it may not be long before Chinese manufacturers of personal computers and other electronic products graduate from their role as subcontractors and compete under their own names against the established suppliers.

Second, there has been a sea-change in the world's capital markets. The era of managerial capitalism, in which managers of large, publicly quoted companies enjoyed a high degree of discretion in deciding what businesses to enter and how to allocate resources between them, has given way to what has been called investor capitalism. Shareholders, mostly in the form of large investing institutions such as pension funds, mutual funds and insurance companies, are demanding a greater say in the affairs of the companies in which they invest.

While this phenomenon is most marked in the U.S. and the U.K., where the stock market is large and active, it is also affecting countries in Continental Europe where the stock market has traditionally played a smaller role. Thus German and French companies, many of which now have a sizeable proportion of their shares owned by Anglo-American institutions, are obliged to pay more attention to shareholder value – or face the possibility of a hostile takeover. This means, among other things, dealing more promptly with under-performing businesses. Investors are not happy when a company cross-subsidizes the bad parts of its portfolio with profits from the good. They are also skeptical about the ability of corporate managers to run disparate businesses successfully.

These two pressures, from global competition and from capital markets, have set in train a restructuring of European industry, and a reappraisal of strategy within European companies. The central thrust has been specialization and internationalization. Managers of multi-product companies have had to decide which of their businesses, if any, are capable of holding their own in international competition and earning an adequate return for their shareholders. Once that decision has been made, the next step is to look for ways of adding to their international strength in their chosen field, perhaps by means of acquisitions, alliances or joint ventures.

Take the chemical industry, which has undergone an extraordinary structural transformation over the past 20 years. In the early postwar decades, the industry was dominated by a group of research-intensive companies – including Imperial Chemical Industries (ICI) in Britain, Rhone-Poulenc in France, Bayer, Hoechst and BASF in Germany – which were pursuing broadly similar strategies and were organized in similar ways. They were operating in a wide range of businesses, and these businesses were linked to each other by shared technologies and by a high degree of interdependence in the supply of feedstock and intermediate chemicals.

Vertical integration and horizontal diversification made sense as long as their laboratories were turning out a stream of innovative products and processes, supporting rates of growth for the industry which were well in excess of GDP growth. But the golden age came to an end in the 1970s. For a mixture of reasons, including the slowdown in the world economy after the first oil shock, the emergence of new petrochemical producers in the Middle East and elsewhere, and an apparent decline in the productivity of research, the industry entered a period of maturity. Products that had powered its earlier growth, such as plastics and synthetic fibers, acquired the status of commodities; what mattered now was high volume and low cost, rather than innovation. In addition, synergies on which the industry had relied in the past were becoming less important; one example was the spectacular series of advances in molecular biology, weakening the traditional link (through synthetic organic chemistry) between chemicals and pharmaceuticals.

The outcome of all this was that the big chemical companies found themselves unable to compete profitably across such a wide front. To succeed in what were increasingly becoming international markets (not least because their larger customers, such as the car manufacturers, were operating on a global scale), they needed to be at or near the leading edge in cost, or technology, or both. Resources had to be concentrated on businesses which had a realistic chance of becoming internationally competitive, and withdrawn from those which did not. The response has been a shift towards de-integration and de-diversification throughout the European chemical industry.[1]

Two examples are ICI in Britain, which spun off its pharmaceutical subsidiary in 1993 and transformed what was left into a specialty chemicals company, and Hoechst in Germany, which converted itself, through acquisitions and divestments, into a pure pharmaceutical business, now known as Aventis. In both cases a major strategic objective was to establish a substantial presence in the U.S. ICI now derives about a third of its sales from the U.S., a fifth each from Continental Europe and the Asia Pacific region, and less than 15% from the U.K.

The influence of investors on these decisions can be seen most clearly in the case of ICI. Two years before the de-merger, ICI was the subject of a raid on its shares by Hanson, one of several "predators" which were active in the U.K. at that time; their raison d'etre was to take over poorly managed companies and break them up. Hanson had seen that the value of ICI's profitable pharmaceutical division was submerged within the rest of the group. If it could be separated and floated as an independent company, it would be rated more highly by the stock market than ICI itself; a break-up was an obvious way of increasing shareholder value. Although Hanson did not in the end make a bid, the episode underlined for the directors of ICI the urgent need to satisfy shareholder expectations, and this was part of the rationale for the subsequent de-merger.[2]

Unlike ICI, Hoechst never faced the threat of a hostile takeover, but stock market considerations almost certainly influenced its choice of strategy. If it was to compete for capital on the same terms as its American competitors, it needed to make itself attractive to American investors. Hoechst also wanted to be able to use its shares as a means of acquiring other companies, especially in the U.S., and it could not do so if its shares remained at the depressed level at which they had stood for most of the 1980s. Thus there was a financial as well as an industrial argument for the restructuring that took place in the second half of the 1990s.

What Hoechst did was revolutionary by German standards. It was an early example of the new focus within German business on shareholder value, and not everyone agreed with Hoechst's stance. One of its German competitors, Bayer, has so far declined to go along with the fashion for specialization. While it has narrowed its portfolio to some extent in recent years, this company still believes that it derives strength from diversity and, in particular, that the combination of pharmaceuticals and chemicals within the same organization yields genuine synergies. Investors remain skeptical, and there are periodic demands for Bayer to hive off its pharmaceutical division, as ICI did; one possibility would be to merge the pharmaceutical side with one of Bayer's larger American competitors, giving the business the international dimension that it lacks.

Although some of the pressures affecting these companies are specific to the chemical industry, the same trend towards specialization and internationalization has been evident in other sectors. The electrical-engineering industry was dominated in the 1950s and 1960s by broadly based companies, most of which manufactured "everything electrical", from steam turbines and telephone switching equipment to refrigerators and TV sets. As electronics-based products came to the fore, several of them moved into computers, semiconductors and related products.

An extreme example of such diversification was Siemens in Germany. Operating in a national environment in which the stock market was relatively undemanding, this company was able to maintain a conglomerate structure until well into the 1990s, even though some of its businesses, such as semiconductors, were making heavy losses in some years. In the second half of the decade, after a long period in which investors had become increasingly dissatisfied with the company's poor return on investment and declining share price, Siemens changed course. It announced a restructuring plan which involved the divestment of businesses amounting to one-seventh of its total turnover. This included the semiconductor operation, which was later floated on the stock exchange as Infineon; Siemens also put its computer business into a joint venture with Fujitsu.

Although Siemens remains a broadly based group (some investors would like to see the portfolio narrowed further), these and other decisions represented a partial retreat from the conglomerate, vertically integrated business model on which Siemens had relied for most of its earlier history.

In France the electrical industry has gone through structural changes which are in some respects more radical than those that took place in Germany. In the 1960s and 1970s the two leading players were Compagnie Generale d'Electricite (CGE) and Thomson, both of which manufactured a wide range of electrical and electronic goods. After a complicated series of acquisitions and divestments – orchestrated in some cases by the French government – the industry has been reorganized in a way which allows each of the surviving firms to specialize in a narrower range of businesses. Thus CGE has been split two ways – into Alcatel, which, along with Siemens and Ericsson, is now one of the leading European manufacturers of telecommunications equipment, and Alstom, which is part of the world oligopoly of power-systems manufacturers, other members being General Electric of the U.S., and Siemens and ABB in Europe. Similarly Thomson, now re-named Thales, specializes mainly in defence electronics, while its consumer-electronics operation has been hived off as an independent company. Thomson has also sold its remaining stake in semiconductors, which had been organized as a joint venture with an Italian company, SGS. Thomson no longer has any direct interest in this business, now known as STMicroelectronics, which has evolved over the past few years to become one of Europe's most successful semiconductor manufacturers. All these companies – Alcatel, Alstom, Thales, Thomson Multimedia and ST Microelectronics – are competing on a global scale; several of them have made large acquisitions in the U.S.

This, then, is the general picture – a shift from diversity to focus, and from a national or regional dimension to globalization. But implementing this redirection of strategy has proved difficult, and there have been as many failures as successes. Faced with the challenge of globalization, European companies have had to face up to two crucial questions. First, how specialized do they want to be – is there a danger that, by putting all their eggs in one basket, they may expose themselves to unexpected setbacks in their chosen industry? Second, how global do they want to be – is it essential for them, because of the nature of the industry they are in, to be represented in all the world's major markets? In North America and Asia as well as in Europe? If the answer is "Yes", do they have the resources and capabilities to support a global strategy?

On the issue of specialization versus diversity, many European executives have gazed with envy and admiration at General Electric of the U.S., which has shown a remarkable ability to run disparate businesses with great success. Some of these businesses, such as aero engines and power equipment, are clearly global in character. The target set by Jack Welch, the recently retired chief executive, was that GE should be the world's No 1 or No 2 in all its businesses, and, although some mistakes have been made along the way (for example, an ill-judged foray into investment banking), that goal has been largely achieved.

How did Welch do it? A partial explanation lies in GE's choice of industries, which are generally capital-intensive oligopolies with high barriers to entry and relatively stable technologies. GE has tended to avoid businesses "where market leadership provides few advantages, or where rapid swings in market tastes, or in product and process technologies, can undermine the advantages of an established leader".[3] Three examples are computers, semiconductors and consumer electronics; GE withdrew from all of them, having tried and failed to build world-leading businesses. To some extent, then, there was a degree of relatedness among GE's businesses, and this made it more feasible for the head office to manage them effectively and to share resources and skills across the organization.

The GE case shows that diversification, if skillfully managed, can still be a viable strategy. A success story on a smaller scale is the British engineering company GKN. Since the 1980s this company has built a position of world leadership in vehicle components, but until recently it has combined this with an entirely unrelated operation – a pallet-pooling business known as CHEP, run as a joint venture with Brambles of Australia. There were financial advantages in this combination – one side of the group was cash-hungry, while the other generated cash – but no industrial or managerial synergies. Eventually, however, the pallet business reached such a size – and became such a big contributor to Brambles' profits – that a parting of the ways became necessary. In 2001 it was de-merged from GKN and became wholly owned by Brambles, leaving GKN to focus on what had become its core activities, vehicle and aerospace components.

Policies towards diversification have to be pragmatic, and investors can sometimes be persuaded that a balanced portfolio of businesses has some advantages. Nevertheless, European experience over the past two decades suggests that to become a world leader in two or more unrelated businesses is difficult. One thinks, for example, of Pilkington, the British company which sought to offset the cyclical nature of its main business – flat glass – by diversifying into the apparently related field of eye care. A large acquisition was made in the U.S. in 1987 to provide the critical mass that it needed in this field. The hope was that Pilkington could be an international leader in both sectors, and that by the mid 1990s eye-care would account for at least 30% of group sales. However, within a few years the company discovered that the skills necessary for success in eye-care were a long way from Pilkington's existing capabilities. The eye-care business was subsequently sold, and Pilkington has returned to its heartland, concentrating on making itself the world's most innovative and most productive producer of flat glass.

Pilkington's mistake was to think that eye-care was more linked to its existing business than it was, and to fail to identify the different competences that would be needed in this new field. This underlines the most critical issue which companies must take into account before they embark on a globalization strategy. Have they assessed with the necessary rigor the strengths and weaknesses of the business in which they have decided to specialize? If they are lagging behind their principal international rivals in technology or market presence, how realistic is it to suppose that the gaps can be filled?

The consequences of failing to address these questions fully can be seen in the sad story of Marconi, the British electronics group which was created out of what had been the country's largest and most diverse electrical/electronics group, General Electric Company (GEC). The new management team which took over after the retirement of GEC's long-serving managing director, Lord Weinstock, in 1996, took the view that the conglomerate model was no longer appropriate to the new era of global competition. Specialization was deemed to be essential, but in what sectors? GEC's strongest business at the time was defense electronics, but the new team believed – as, indeed, had Lord Weinstock some years earlier – that this business would benefit from being linked to a builder of the "platforms", principally aircraft, on which GEC's electronic systems were installed. This meant, in the British context, some form of association with British Aerospace. After various alternative schemes had been considered, the GEC directors concluded that the best way of maximizing shareholder value would be for GEC to de-merge its defense-electronics business into British Aerospace, with GEC shareholders acquiring a substantial stake in the enlarged group. British Aerospace, which changed its name to BAE Systems following this transaction, would thereby become one of the world's largest and most integrated defense contractors.

The next step was to decide what to do with the rest of GEC. One of its largest constituents was a telecommunications equipment company, in which Siemens held a minority interest. In what proved to be a disastrous misjudgment, the board of directors took the view that, despite the company's weak position in the world market for telecommunications equipment, this was the sector it should concentrate on. There was widespread euphoria among investors at that time about what seemed to be the unlimited growth prospects for the telecommunications industry, driven by deregulation and new technology.

GEC's senior managers thought that, with the help of some judicious acquisitions, the company could lift itself into the world telecommunications league, alongside such players as Alcatel in Europe and Lucent in the U.S. The first step was to buy out Siemens' minority stake in the telecommunications company, and this was followed by two large acquisitions in the U.S. The subsequent change of name from GEC to Marconi, the inventor of wireless communications, was meant to symbolize the company's new vocation.

As it turned out, the American acquisitions – for which Marconi paid a very high price, reflecting the over-heated stock market at the time – were made shortly before the collapse in the stock market and the end of the telecommunications boom. By 2001 Marconi found itself in a dire financial state, heavily indebted because of the acquisitions and facing a sharp downturn in its markets. A refinancing scheme was subsequently negotiated with its bankers and bondholders, but shareholders lost most of their investment.

What are the lessons from Marconi's collapse? The judgment by the post-Weinstock management that GEC was competing in too many businesses was probably correct, but the choice of telecommunications equipment as the main focus of investment was based an over-optimistic view of the prospects for that sector and of Marconi's ability to catch up with the world leaders. The necessary realism was missing.

A second lesson is the need for caution when companies are contemplating a major push into the U.S. Marconi had bad luck in the timing of its U.S. acquisitions; no-one at that time was predicting the collapse of the telecommunications boom, and Marconi's deals were applauded by most City analysts. But there is a long history of European companies coming unstuck in the U.S. through failing to assess accurately the quality of the business they are acquiring, and the steps that will be needed to absorb and integrate it. A classic case is Renault's unhappy experience with American Motors; after buying a controlling stake in the late 1970s, the French company struggled for several years to make the business profitable, before selling it to Chrysler in 1987. Whether the Daimler-Benz/Chrysler merger will have a happier outcome remains to be seen.

Realism, then, is essential, as is a willingness to learn from other companies' mistakes. But there is also a deeper question which would-be globalizers must answer. What makes an industry global? In what circumstances will a global player have an advantage over national or regional players?

The American academic Michael Porter has drawn a useful distinction between global and multi-domestic industries. In the former, a firm's competitive position in one country is significantly affected by its position in other countries; it has no choice but to go global if it wishes to stay in the game. In a multi-domestic industry, according to Porter, competing internationally is discretionary. "A firm can choose to remain domestic or can expand internationally if it has some advantage that allows it to overcome the extra costs of entering and competing in foreign markets".[4]

The principle seems straightforward, but applying it in practice is not easy. Take the case of telecommunications services. British Telecom (BT), the dominant network operator in the U.K., was privatized in the early 1980s, and quickly set its sights on becoming a global operator. The U.S. was one of its prime targets. In 1987 it tried to merge with MCI, the second-largest American long-distance carrier, but was outbid by WorldCom. BT then formed an alliance with AT&T, known as Concert, to provide telecommunications services to international business customers. But the joint venture never fulfilled BT's expectations, partly because there were too many conflicts of interest between the partners. By 2001 BT was in severe financial straits, having over-paid for third-generation mobile-telephone licenses both in the U.K. and elsewhere, and was forced to scale back its ambitions. The Concert alliance was terminated, and BT revised its strategy; henceforth its goal was to be a European rather than an international player.

Will BT be at a competitive disadvantage as a result of these decisions? Should telecommunications services be regarded as a global industry, or will regional players survive? The answer is far from clear. BT's German counterpart, Deutsche Telekom, also embarked on a global strategy in the second half of the 1990s, and has stuck to it. It made a number of acquisitions, of which by far the largest was that of Voicestream, an American mobile-telephone operator. These transactions saddled Deutsche Telekom with huge debts, and there has been some speculation that it might be forced to withdraw from the U.S. So far, however, it is adhering doggedly to its chosen course; it is the only one of the former European monopolists to be pursuing a genuinely global strategy.[5] France Telecom, by contrast, is concentrating mainly on building a strong European organization, both in fixed-line operations and in mobile networks.

As for the new entrants to the telecommunications business, one firm which set out from the start to establish itself as a global player is Vodafone, the British mobile-telephone operator. Making full use of its highly valued shares, Vodafone made a series of acquisitions in the late 1990s. The two biggest were Airtouch in the U.S. and Mannesmann in Germany. But Airtouch was subsequently merged with another U.S. mobile-network operator to form Verizon, in which Vodafone now has a 45% share. This arrangement leaves Vodafone with something of a dilemma. Verizon does not use the Vodafone brand name, and its network is based on a technology which is not compatible with that of Vodafone. The issue for the British company is whether to increase its stake in Verizon, which would be expensive, or devise an alternative strategy for promoting its brand in the US.[6]

The structure of the telecommunications industry is still evolving, and it would be rash to assume that consolidation in the hands of a small number of global operators is the inevitable outcome; there may well be scope for regional as well as global strategies. Interestingly, the same is true of a more mature sector, the motor industry, which is usually regarded as a paradigm case of globalization.

The French company Peugeot derives some 80% of its business from Europe; it sells virtually nothing in the U.S. Yet over the past decade the company has achieved an impressive record in sales growth and return on investment. While Peugeot does not exclude the possibility of establishing itself in the U.S. at some point in the future, it is in no hurry to do so, and its main aim over the last few years has been to strengthen its position in Europe, East as well as West. A recent decision was to form a joint venture with Toyota to assemble cars in the Czech Republic. While other European companies have made ambitious moves outside Europe (Daimler-Benz in the U.S., Renault in Japan), the head of Peugeot, Jean-Martin Folz, is taking a more prudent line. "The chances are", one commentator wrote, "that Mr Folz will stick to his principle that being a European middleweight champion is good enough."[7]

Even that limited objective has taken a good deal of pain and effort. Peugeot's rise into the "premier league" of European car manufacturers involved, first, the merger with Citroen in 1974, and then, four years later, the acquisition of Chrysler's European operations, which included Simca in France and Rootes in the U.K. The latter transaction was almost a step too far, involving as it did several years of heavy losses before the acquired companies were fully integrated into the Peugeot empire. It is not surprising, after that experience, that Peugeot takes a cautious view of cross-border acquisitions. The record of some of its peers – notably BMW's mismanaged takeover of Rover in the U.K. – only reinforces this caution.

Peugeot's ability to pursue a European rather than a global strategy reflects the fact that, in this industry and some others, the European region constitutes a large, homogeneous market which provides opportunities for economies of scale as great as those available in the U.S. In these industries globalization means, in the first instance, Europeanization, and, as Peugeot's success indicates, it may not be necessary to go further than that.

This is not to say that Europeanization is easy. On the contrary, the history of trans-national mergers in Europe is littered with examples of problems caused by cultural and other incompatibilities. There are also institutional differences within Europe – for instance, the presence or absence of employee representatives on the board of directors – which can complicate matters still further. These difficulties are highlighted by recent events at Corus, the Anglo-Dutch steel-making group, where the Dutch supervisory board, apparently responding to the concerns of Dutch employees and shareholders, overruled a decision by the managing board to sell the group's aluminum subsidiary. This was, perhaps, an exceptional case, caused in part by financial weakness in the British arm of Corus (it has been hard hit in recent years by the strength of sterling against the euro), and there are other cases – such as the merger between Hoechst and Rhone-Poulenc to form Aventis – which suggest that cultural problems, if properly managed, can be handled effectively. But the Corus affair shows that shifting from a national to a European dimension, through mergers and acquisitions, takes a great deal of careful planning as well as firm but tactful implementation.

Is there a natural progression from national to regional to global? That depends in part on the economics of the industry concerned. The predecessor company to Corus, British Steel Corporation, was almost certainly right to conclude, in the late 1980s, that it had to break out of its national base, and that a merger with a Continental steel-maker was the best available option. By that time a genuinely European steel market was emerging (governments no longer regarded steel as a strategic asset that must be kept under national control), and this led to extensive rationalization in the industry, of which the Corus merger was one example. So far this rationalization has taken place on a European rather than a global scale, and there is not much evidence that the European leaders – Arcelor (formed by a three-way merger between France's Usinor, Luxembourg's Arbed and Spain's Aceralia) and Thyssen Krupp in Germany – are looking for acquisitions in the U.S.

Other European markets remain obstinately national. In retailing, for example, differences in national regulations and buying habits have so far precluded the emergence of European giants comparable to those which dominate the motor industry or the steel industry. This has not stopped some retailers from entertaining global aspirations, but their motives are somewhat different from those that apply to manufacturing sectors.

For companies which have already achieved a dominant position in their domestic market, globalization often appears to be the only available means of providing shareholders with the growth in sales and profits they have come to expect. This was the consideration which led Marks & Spencer, the British clothing retailer, to expand into North America, and later into Continental Europe, during the 1970s and 1980s. But Marks & Spencer underestimated how hard it would be to transfer to foreign markets a retailing formula which had worked well in the U.K. One of its worst mistakes was to buy Brooks Brothers, an up-market American men's-wear chain which had little in common with Marks & Spencer's business in the U.K. But even the Marks & Spencer stores which were built in Continental Europe yielded meager returns. They were all sold, along with Brooks Brothers, in 2001, as part of a wide-ranging restructuring of the business.[8]

Marks & Spencer misjudged what was needed to compete in unfamiliar territory. Does this mean that global strategies in retailing do not work?

The recent troubles at Ahold, the Dutch company which set out to become one of the world's largest food retailers but is now enmeshed in a financial crisis, suggest the need for caution. But there are other examples which point in a different direction.

Take the case of Tesco, the British supermarket group. In the mid 1990s this company was in a similar situation to Marks & Spencer. Its share of the U.K. market had risen to the point where further expansion was difficult, not least because of likely opposition from the competition authorities. A logical step was to build or acquire stores in Continental Europe, and then to use that enlarged European operation as the basis for attacking other markets. This was the route which Tesco appeared to be following in 1997 when it made its first overseas foray, buying a medium-sized chain of French supermarkets. But the acquisition was not a success. The company it had bought was operating in a market dominated by large and well-established hypermarket groups, such as Carrefour, and Tesco found itself unable to make the further acquisitions that were necessary to close the gap. Tesco then shifted tack, redirecting its efforts towards less-developed markets, principally in Eastern Europe and the East Asia, where it believed its expertise in operating large supermarkets and hypermarkets could be put to good use in countries where this type of shopping was just beginning to take off. So far, the strategy appears to be working well; Tesco currently operates over 2,300 stores across 13 countries, and is the number one operator of hypermarkets in Hungary, Poland, Slovakia and Thailand.[9]

The Tesco experience indicates that retailers can succeed internationally if they have some distinctive capabilities which give them the edge over local competitors. This industry seems more accurately described as multi-domestic, to use Michael Porter's phrase, than as global; whether or not to go global is, as Porter suggests, a discretionary decision, and the economics of the industry are not such as to lead inevitably to the kind of global consolidation that has occurred, say, in the motor industry. Some commentators have predicted that the world food-retailing industry will within the next decade or so become dominated by a handful of giant companies – Wal-Mart of the U.S., Carrefour of France and perhaps Tesco are seen as likely members of the "big league" – but this is almost certainly wrong. Since most food products are sourced locally, there are no compelling economies of scale in purchasing that might give the big international retailers a decisive advantage.

What general lessons can Asian firms draw from European experience? The first lesson – and this applies to both global and multi-domestic industries – is that the would-be global player must be rigorous in assessing what its distinctive strengths are, and whether they are sufficient to support a global strategy. The greatest Japanese triumphs in the 1970s and 1980s were in automobiles and consumer electronics. In both sectors – though this was easier to see with hindsight than at the start of the Japanese assault on world markets – firms such as Toyota and Sony had developed a competitive advantage, based principally on manufacturing efficiency and product quality, which gave them an edge over Western manufacturers. An obvious contrast is with Daewoo, the Korean car-maker, whose grandiose global ambitions far outran its capabilities.

A second lesson is the need for caution in using mergers and acquisitions as the principal avenue for global expansion. Acquisitions can make sense if the target firm is reasonably well managed and can be fitted easily into the acquiring company's organization. A good example was the takeover by NSK, the Japanese ball-bearings manufacturer, of the largest British ball-bearings firm, Ransome Hoffman Pollard, in 1990; there were obvious synergies between the two firms, and implementation of the merger posed no insuperable problems. Mega-mergers involving a shift into a different line of business – such as Matsushita's ill-judged move into Hollywood in the mid 1990s – are a different matter.

Most Asian firms in any case prefer partnerships to acquisitions, but even here careful judgment is needed, especially on whether the motives of the Asian and non-Asian partner, and their longer-term hopes for the collaboration, are compatible. It is arguable that Honda's relatively weak position in the European car market, compared to its strength in the U.S., is at least partly due to its reliance, during the 1980s and into the early 1990s, on its alliance with Rover in the U.K. (The alliance came to a sudden end in 1994 when Rover's owner, British Aerospace, sold the company to BMW.) Although this cooperation had been a useful learning experience for Honda, it may have lasted for too long, distracting the Japanese company from its primary task of building up its own European organization.

A third lesson is not to compete on too many fronts. This is a tricky issue for those large Asian firms, especially in such countries as India and Korea, which straddle a number of industries. Some of them operate a network of associated enterprises, either wholly owned or linked together by interlocking shareholdings, and their financial and political strength derives in large measure from these arrangements. Moreover, because most of them are family-owned, they do not face the same shareholder pressure to "de-diversify" as European and American conglomerates. But the managerial arguments for specialization are compelling, as is clear from the partial break-up of the *keiretsu* structure in Japan, and the unwinding of the Korean *chaebols*. It makes sense to start the process early, rather than waiting for a crisis to precipitate it.

It would, of course, be the height of arrogance to suggest that Asian globalizers must follow exactly what Western firms have done. It may be that, just as novel manufacturing techniques have come out of Asia in recent years, so Asian firms may work out their own route to globalization, developing a managerial style which suits their particular culture and history. But that is not an argument against learning from other people's mistakes.

Endnotes

1 Ashish Arora and Alfonso Gambardella, "Evolution of industry structure in the chemical industry", in Ashish Arora, Ralph Landau and Nathan Rosenberg, eds., *Chemicals and Long-term Economic Growth*, John Wiley, 1998.

2 Geoffrey Owen and Trevor Harrison, "Why ICI chose to de-merger", *Harvard Business Review*, March-April 1995.

3 Michael Goold, Andrew Campbell, and Marcus Alexander, *Corporate-level Strategy: Creating Value in the Multibusiness Company*, John Wiley, 1994, p.252.

4 Michael Porter, "Changing patterns of international competition", in David J. Teece, eds., *The Competitive Challenge*, Ballinger, 1987.

5 Martin Fransman, *Telecoms in the Internet Age*, Oxford, 2002.

6 *Fortune*, March 17, 2003.

7 *The Economist*, April 6, 2002.

8 Judi Bevan, *The Rise and Fall of Marks & Spencer*, Profile, 2001.

9 For an account of Tesco's global strategy, see Peter Child, "Taking Tesco global", *McKinsey Quarterly*, 2002, No 3.

PART III

Future Directions

CHAPTER 11 Conclusion

A key theme of this book is that the globalization of Asian firms that has occurred in recent years, and is now accelerating, is a process of corporate transformation that involves building layer upon layer of new capabilities needed to succeed in global competition. As such, the expansion of Asian companies does *not* stem primarily from bold, headline deals or establishing footholds ("planting flags") in foreign markets. The deliberate process we describe in this book is what we have likened to "climbing a globalization staircase".

The nine case studies in this book provide rich insights into what is involved in climbing that staircase and important lessons concerning the opportunities and pitfalls along the way. But there remains one other critical question to address: even if a company adopts a systematic and controlled approach to globalizing its business, how does it know that it has succeeded? At what point along the journey?

We would venture that this "success" here is largely a question of sustainability. A company that has successfully globalized its business will have built its expansion into its future business model – and, vice versa, built its future business model around its global nature – and thus be able to sustain it over the long term. More broadly we can say that companies will need to know and be able to answer the following questions:

- What will be the characteristics of a sustainable global company in the future?
- How do we avoid building yesterday's global corporation?

These questions are the topic of this last chapter. They do not have a single, easy answer. But we believe that at least some of the characteristics of tomorrow's successful Asian global firm are starting to become clear, along with some of the future issues that such a company must be able to address.

Sustainability and future demands on the Asian global firm

"Too big and important to fail" used to represent a convenient excuse throughout much of Asia for the state to prop up many an inefficient or loss-making company. That was before the painful fall and eventual dismembering of Daewoo and the rebuilding of Samsung around Samsung Electronics. However, there are still signs that Asian governments waver when faced with a failing giant. Just recently, the takeover of D'Long's assets by the Huarong Asset Management, a government distressed assets firm, is yet another sign that some governments are locked in by social or other difficulties that would arise in a corporate failure. Nevertheless, looking to the future, there can be no doubt that sustainability is a critical issue that cannot be taken for granted, even by a global giant.

This fact is not unique to Asia. Geoffrey Owen's recounting of the falls of Marconi and ICI reminds us of the many seemingly impregnable global organizations in Europe and the U.S. that have crumbled almost overnight. More recently the debacles of Enron, Worldcom and Arthur Andersen, not to mention the dozens of businesses hollowed out by their collapses, should serve to remind us all that failure is a real, ever-present possibility. The risks are only accentuated by a highly globalized, interconnected marketplace.

In retrospect we would contend that the competitive waters of global markets are far more treacherous today than even just one or two decades ago. George Yip and Ruimin Lin have argued persuasively that this diminishes the chances of Asian globalizers being able to enter fields which have already been well plowed by European and American multinationals. We do not mean, in any way, to diminish the accomplishments of Asian pioneers such as Sony, Samsung and Kikkoman. However, the changes in the global environment – and most recently around security and geopolitics – mean that the successful global company today will probably need more than an adroit sense of strategy and competitive advantage. Today, companies contend not only with each other, but with a multitude of stakeholders who may, at any time, thwart the company's global ambitions. In the past, customers and suppliers held the same sort of veto power over a company. Today stakeholder groups are not just those with whom a company has direct relations – thus, customers, suppliers, employees, the government and the surrounding community – but a broader circle pushed outwards by developments in international markets, information and technology.

Looking to the future, the Asian global firm is likely to have to respond to a slew of potential threats to its sustainability, including:

- An increasingly efficient "global knowledge economy" where information that is readily codified and transmitted is readily available to all, so that global companies will need the ability to develop and move tacit, complex knowledge around the world if they are to add value to the market.
- A more open market for technology and specialist skills where new competitors can more easily catch up with established firms by buying what they lack from suppliers of specialist technologies, consultants and freelance designers,[1] thus diminishing the value of an assets-based competitive edge.
- A shift from competition between individual firms to rivalry between competing networks and complex alliances of companies. These are already seen in the standards battle in third-generation telecommunications, and new pan-global alliances such as TCL-Thomson or Huawei-3 Com[2] which could create airline-style alignments in multiple global sectors.
- The anti-globalization movement, which has become an increasingly vociferous, educated and skilled lobby group,

adopting in some cases "corporate"-style tactics to reinforce their demands.

- Pressures for global firms to contribute to finding solutions to global problems that were formerly regarded as outside the corporate sector's core responsibilities, such as environmental degradation, global warming, poverty, the digital divide, HIV/AIDS and other diseases, and international security.

These challenges will call for renewed emphasis on the question of sustainability. They also demand that Asian companies in the process of globalizing develop strategies that not only respond to but, more importantly, anticipate and intercept the changing realities. The challenge for companies today is not to match up to today's global champions but to know what is needed to ensure their place among tomorrow's.

Towards sustainability

As this book has demonstrated, approaching the globalization challenge in the same way as climbing a staircase is an important first step towards building a sustainable global company. This process includes:

- carefully defining a globalization strategy that matches with organizational resources and competitive strengths
- experimentation and organizational learning that takes place consistently and is reinforced through operational processes
- extension of knowledge flows "end to end", that is, ensuring that knowledge gained in one area (geographical, functional) is transmitted to the rest of the organization
- consistency in adhering to a single strategic vision, yet knowing when to pull back in order to reassess and make another approach
- ensuring that your customers are continually able to improve their own operations by doing business with you.

These and other "takeaways" highlighted in Part I may be only moderately discernible in today's globalizing Asian companies, but they will become more important in the next decade. Thus, companies with advantages in these areas are likely to see their leadership become more pronounced and distinctive.

A second step involved broadening the definition of what drives sustainability to consider both the degree to which your company is rooted in truly globalized labor, financial and product markets (as forcefully argued by Hirotaka Takeuchi) and the quality of its relationships with a broader set of stakeholders – some of whom may not even have direct relationships with your firm (as shown by Stigson and Flaherty).

This expansion of the stakeholder circle poses a new conundrum. The fact that the circle is at any point in time indefinable and seemingly infinite invalidates the company's external relations strategies. In other words, what may have been conceived as external affairs, corporate communications, or community or public relations is no longer sufficient if the external parties with whom the company must deal are not always present or obvious. It is not only a question of preventing your company being surprised or "backsided" by an unexpected occurrence in one of your markets. Crisis management is too late, in a sense. The company must be proactive in enabling its stakeholders to support, or at least acquiesce to, the company's global vision.

Companies have traditionally focused their community or stakeholder relations primarily in corporate social responsibility or corporate citizenship ("CSR" for short). Stigson and Flaherty have presented broad thinking and specific examples of how companies may orient their CSR programs. Their message of being proactive cannot be emphasized strongly enough. But our message is also that CSR per se is not enough. Global and regional companies, and those that aspire to be so, must rethink corporate social responsibility in the framework of sustainability – for company and for society. In fact, a company that views CSR only as a means of pacifying potential opponents will eventually find its own sustainability threatened. Instead, it must conceive of influencing its social ecosystem, which has embedded in it the elements of both its own prosperity and its own destruction.

This is particularly the case in Asia, where companies play roles that go beyond the roles that they traditionally have played in the West. Ironically, while companies in Europe and the U.S. are shrinking their social elements – by outsourcing or paring back healthcare, pension management, or employee benefits – we believe that companies based in Asia will need to maintain a broader social role in order to achieve corporate sustainability, albeit in new ways. The "iron rice-bowl" may have been discarded long ago, but if Asian companies are to further succeed in globalizing in today's environment, they will need to create the ability to contribute to (and influence) their broader social ecosystems.

This is easier said than done. Hard as it is to imagine, we believe that companies can take their cues from basic principles of marketing (though in using marketing to illustrate, we do *not* mean to say that all is as shiny, or superficial, as marketing is sometimes made out to be). Today, the successful market-entry approach is seen as one that fits product with environment first and then, almost by stealth, is able to influence its environment according to its product. As they adapt to the local environment, "foreign" companies adopt a domestic persona.

Some of the most common examples of this are found in the consumer industries such as foods and beverages, where companies such as Nestlé, McDonald's, Yum (Kentucky Fried Chicken and Pizza Hut), and Starbucks have entered Asian markets successfully only by adapting their products to suit local tastes. They altered their image, product mix, and even core revenue streams, while preserving just enough of the original to attract customers who otherwise would have shied away from the unfamiliar (coffee in a tea drinkers' land? Cheese for a lactose-intolerant people?) Companies enter markets by looking at their own product line and adapting it to create a local image that meets local tastes and sensitivities.

In these cases, the great sign of success is a survey-finding that a majority of Japanese thought McDonald's was a Japanese invention. Of course, once they have a foot in the door, companies can become bolder in introducing totally new products or trends that would not have worked at the outset. By this time, customers trust the brand and are willing to try something new, which may, of course, be the old or original product of the company.

Companies looking to build into their social ecosystem need to start from the same premise – that they must adapt first and only then, after they have won trust, hope to influence. It is surprising how many companies with brilliant marketing or market-entry strategies fail to grasp a similar principle when dealing with communities and society. Whereas they would adapt to markets, they will assume they can delude or "pull a fast one" on a community. Why they would believe that a community is less savvy or demanding than a consumer remains a mystery, considering that communities often have more at stake than the few dollars wasted on an uneaten bun.

Adaptation requires understanding of the needs, motives and aspirations of the community in which the company operates. This "second" layer of knowledge – in the same way that such information about a consumer group will enable a company to predict buying habits – is the key to engaging communities in a constant dialogue about the company's growth. Involving the community in the company's operational decisions can involve "town halls" or publicity in the mass media. But these communication tools should not be mistaken for actual consideration. We are not claiming that companies should allow communities or social groups to make decisions for them. However, companies will earn the trust of communities only by engaging them as equal partners in development over the long term.

Here we should deal with the question of "offshoring" – or "outsourcing" – given the current prevalence of the trend. Certainly, offshoring can have immense effects on both communities – both the one left behind and the one accepting the new business.

Outsourcing is only the most recent attention given to what has long been a source of developing competitive advantage, as companies pare off divisions in an attempt to focus on their core competency. We believe that this process can be a healthy one and can incite new development along the way. Offshoring on the other hand – moving divisions abroad for cost (rather than functional) reasons – is more contentious. We advocate simply that a company contemplating offshoring should do so only with a full picture of its costs and benefits; and then, once it makes the decision, to be totally honest and humane in its approach. This means alerting the "losing" community early on and enabling as much transition as possible. In the new community, despite its rather advantageous position, the company should enter, again, as partner rather than "claimant" on future workers. The process of partnership should exist even when a company is seen as a "savior" for a community in need of investment or jobs.

The third step towards creating a new type of Asian global firm with more resilience and sustainability against the changing future environment requires the development of a sophisticated network for managing knowledge around the globe. Just as success in decades past was built first on having the best or most resources, to the best or best application of technology, the company which prospers tomorrow will be the one with the best knowledge and ability to use it.

Such knowledge networks and capabilities, therefore, will be essential for reaching the top of our globalization staircase in the future. Our "pioneers" (discussed in Chapter 2) generally have the best processes for capturing and using organizational knowledge. Their sustainability challenge will be knowledge renewal. The newcomers, at the relative foot of the globalization staircase, may just be realizing what their organizational knowledge is, how it is generated, and how to disseminate it internally. Moving up the staircase will require not only the requisite infrastructure, networks, financing, and human resources management, but also the ability to continually upgrade the way they acquire and use knowledge across the organization.

Building the future Asian global firm

As we have stressed above, in strategizing and approaching global markets, companies should seek to build tomorrow's global company. The challenge is not to mimic the successful habits or competencies of today's giants but, rather, to be able to fashion the firm with tomorrow's markets and challenges firmly in mind. This requires not only an understanding of how future global markets will operate but also how risks and uncertainties may shape their evolution.

What we know about today's markets and global champions suggests three core areas of focus and challenge for the future Asian global firm:

1. The need to build a more "networked" type of firm, not thinking of itself as a linear value chain, but part of a global ecosystem
2. The need to remain entrepreneurial while globalizing rather than seeing the process as cloning a successful formula in multiple markets
3. The need to see globalization as a process of learning from and leveraging knowledge from around the world – thereby creating a mutually reinforcing synthesis for the company's capabilities and knowledge, which are vetted and transformed by reality.

More "networked" firms

When executives talk about needing to build a networked company, they are almost always talking about internal networks. Certainly, internal networks – the thruways for knowledge, information, skill, and best practice transfer within the organization – are necessary and building them is not a simple task. It will involve restructuring of the typical functional organization found in many Asian firms today, in which each department independently pursues excellence in activities such as production, finance, sales or marketing, to create modern "front-end/back-end" structures. Restructuring of the type used to create a new type of networked organization at San Miguel, the Philippines' largest beer maker, is a good example of this. San Miguel created a modern "front-end/back-end" structure where the "back-end" dealt with the core brewing operations, while the new front-end units focused on improving the distribution system. The two were linked with new IT infrastructure, transfer pricing and knowledge management processes.

Companies will also need to make their supply chains more transparent, creating a clear "line of sight" from suppliers through the manufacturing process to the end-customer. This goes beyond the use of customer management and supply-chain management software. As a manager at Swire Beverages, a Coca-Cola bottler that supplies 215,000 retailers, observes: "We have introduced systems to track sales by product from each outlet daily and to integrate sales and inventory data with information on distribution and production capacity. But to use these tools to maximum advantage the company will need to improve its ties with its retail partners, understanding their customer base and needs more fully."

These types of restructuring to create improved internal networks and then extend these to suppliers and distributors will be important. But perhaps an even greater challenge for tomorrow's global company is to think beyond internal networks, and even beyond its suppliers and distributors, to the company's broader external network.

This process involves conceiving of the company as a part of a global ecosystem and reflects our message that sustainability should not only reflect a company's ability to build and renew itself in new markets, but also its interactions with its social community and global environment. Spatially conceived, this might be seen as a contrast between a linear or two dimensional organization, with its own product and value chain with suppliers at one end and customers at the other end. If community and the world are present, they would be at the very end. The linear model makes operational decisions simple because reactions can only be bidirectional. Inputs and outputs are clear. The challenge, we propose, is to fashion the company in a multi-dimensional manner that incorporates the global ecosystem in each part of the organization's structure. Community thus moves from indirect to direct, from merely reactive to integral.

The principle argument for a company to be networked in the global ecosystem is not driven primarily from "social" concerns but, rather, reflects the reality of globalized, interconnected markets in which information, risks and threats reverberate between and across markets without regard for traditional boundaries – whether state/national boundaries or those which segregate consumer groups, cultural trends, industry divisions, or other such groupings along which markets have traditionally been based. The image of the ecosystem accurately reflects this interconnected nature and thus is fitting for a company that seeks an existence within a synthesized whole.

Maintaining an entrepreneurial spirit as the organization globalizes

The second key capability for tomorrow's global company is to remain entrepreneurial while globalizing, rather than seeing the process as replicating a successful process. This principle draws from the fact that the most recognized global giants today are successful innovators in multiple ways in different industry spaces and markets. Kikkoman's initial entry into the American market was intended to build a market presence based on a successful pattern established in Japan. But instead of merely replicating the model it had already developed, the company remained innovative enough to imbue its approach with a sensitivity of the local market, which then enabled the company to pounce on and create new market spaces. Indeed, the remarkable fact is that Kikkoman in America has created products which even ran counter to its creations at home.

The growth of the private sector in China – first in unique industries from automobiles and agriculture to technology and travel – has created a new breed of entrepreneur. Observers often worry when, after a period of initial success and wealth, the company starts to expand, often in an illogical manner. Thus, New Hope group spins new arms in venture capital, property, technology and services. D'Long started in the basic industries but quickly grabbed other opportunities in finance and real estate. Fosun Hi-tech also invests in real estate and heavy industries. What watchers may miss is that the entrepreneurial pursuit has enabled these companies to be *imaginative* about their potential market presence and quick enough to build a stake. The downside is that great ideas or ventures require deep business capabilities which may be underestimated by the deal-making company, and as a result become white-elephant investments. This tendency is especially prevalent in a market as vast and under-developed as China. Thus, the continued development of "Chinese capitalism" will necessarily begin to absorb the lessons of prudence, and temper any irrational exuberance.

Nevertheless, it remains clear that the best investments are often born of imagination – the ability to picture and execute success in a market space that seems to require vastly different capabilities from those which a company has apparently honed. The ability to retain entrepreneurship even as industries and markets tend towards segmentation will be a key element underpinning a company's ability to surprise and surpass its competitors.

Globalization as a process of learning from the world

As the company develops a presence in multiple markets its survival as a whole will depend in large part on its ability to enhance and transfer its knowledge throughout the entire organization. This means identifying insights gleaned from one business line or market and being able to disseminate these insights internally in a way that is useful for other businesses. The use of "intelligence" about market practices and company strengths can be both motivational and actionable by different people. The challenge for Asian companies that may have grown up in a fragmented or hierarchical pattern will be to overcome compartmentalization to feed knowledge not only horizontally but also vertically, in *both directions*. Stories of car-factory workers who have suggested line improvements which are then adopted across the organization are just one side of the story. The real sign of success, for Asian companies with strict vertical hierarchies, will be to let knowledge flow upwards as commonly as orders flow downwards in today's companies.

Equally important will be for Asian global challengers to globalize their innovation processes as well as their supply chains. This will help them to outflank incumbent global competitors that innovate based on taking knowledge in a single geographic cluster (usually their home base) and spreading it around their network of subsidiaries. The potential advantages of globalizing innovation are huge: harnessing localized pockets of technology, market intelligence and capabilities scattered around the world opens up the opportunity to create a powerful new source of competitive advantage through more, higher-value innovation at lower cost.[3]

Aspects of Asian culture may seem antithetical to this two-way synthesis, and that is perhaps the great test for Asian globalizers: to know what to keep and what to discard. Certainly cultural transformation need not mean merely adapting "wholesale" principles of "Western management". Rather, successful models will not only filter and adapt but also reinforce through human resources, systems management, and other key organizational structures.

The tiger's leap

The demise of national fiefdoms in the face of falling barriers to cross-border trade and investment, the need to match the advantages of Western multinationals, and the end of growth through opportunistic diversification mean that as we enter the next round of competition it is becoming imperative for Asian companies to globalize. With some notable exceptions, such as the pioneers described in this book, too few Asian corporates have built full-fledged global companies where virtually every aspect of the business spans national borders to form an integrated international network. In Asia's changing environment, many more will have to grasp this challenge.

But as latecomers to the internationalization game, Asian companies are unlikely to win by mimicking the strategies followed by the Western companies that went before them on the path to globalization. They need to play to the strengths of their Asian heritage to create a new breed of Asian multinational whose competitive advantage is drawn, in part, from its distinctiveness from today's global giants from the Americas and Europe. Key to these new Asian global firms will be a strong emphasis on creating networks that achieve a full and sustainable integration with the future global ecosystem, an ability to maintain an entrepreneurial spirit as they expand their size and international reach, and the capability to globalize both innovation and the supply chain. The challenges are formidable. For those with the determination, focus and resources necessary to climb the globalization "staircase", however, the rewards will be commensurately great.

Endnotes

1 See P. J. Williamson and Ming Zeng, "Strategies for Competing in a Changed China", *MIT-Sloan Management Review*, Summer 2004.

2 See Ming Zeng and Peter Williamson, "China's Hidden Dragons", *Harvard Business Review*, October 2003.

3 See J. Santos, Y. Doz and P. Williamson, "Is Your Innovation Process Global?", *MIT-Sloan Management Review*, Vol 45, No. 4, Summer 2004, pp.31-37.

INDEX